Locating the English Diaspora, 1500–2010

T0385468

MIGRATIONS AND IDENTITIES

Series Editors
Kirsty Hooper, Eve Rosenhaft, Michael Sommer

This series offers a forum and aims to provide a stimulus for new research into experiences, discourses and representations of migration from across the arts and humanities. A core theme of the series will be the variety of relationships between movement in space – the 'migration' of people, communities, ideas and objects – and mentalities ('identities' in the broadest sense). The series aims to address a broad scholarly audience, with critical and informed interventions into wider debates in contemporary culture as well as in the relevant disciplines. It will publish theoretical, empirical and practice-based studies by authors working within, across and between disciplines, geographical areas and time periods, in volumes that make the results of specialist research accessible to an informed but not discipline-specific audience. The series is open to proposals for both monographs and edited volumes.

Locating the English Diaspora, 1500–2010

Edited by

*Tanja Bueltmann, David T. Gleeson
and Donald M. MacRaild*

Liverpool University Press

First published 2012 by
Liverpool University Press
4 Cambridge Street
Liverpool
L69 7ZU

This paperback version published 2014.

British Library Cataloguing-in-Publication data
A British Library CIP record is available

ISBN 978-1-84631-819-1 cased
     978-1-78138-112-0 paperback

Typeset in Minion by R. J. Footring Ltd, Derby
Printed and bound by CPI Group (UK) Ltd, Croydon CR0 4YY

Contents

Notes on Contributors

Dean Allen is currently a Senior Research Associate at Stellenbosch University in South Africa. Having lectured at universities in the United Kingdom, Ireland and Australia, he has published widely on the history and politics of sport and society throughout the British Empire, most notably South Africa. His particular interests are colonialism, imperialism and the identity of sporting groups and nations. His monograph, *Logan of Matjiesfontein: Cricket, War and Empire in South Africa*, will be published shortly.

Tanja Bueltmann is Lecturer in History at Northumbria University. Her research interests are in wider British World history, especially ethnic associationalism. Tanja Bueltmann's first monograph, *Scottish Ethnicity and the Making of New Zealand Society, 1850 to 1930*, was published in 2011 (Edinburgh University Press, SHR Monograph Series). She is co-investigator of the AHRC-funded English Diaspora project, which explores the English in North America in transatlantic perspective between the mid-eighteenth century and 1950. Moreover, she continues to examine the Scots abroad. Having recently been awarded funding from the British Academy for her project 'Ethnicity, Associationalism and Civility: The Scots in Singapore and Hong Kong in Comparative Perspective', she is currently writing her second monograph on ethnic associational culture and formal sociability in the Scottish diaspora to 1930.

David T. Gleeson is Reader in History at Northumbria University where he teaches American history. He has just completed a manuscript on Irish immigrants in the Confederate States of America to be published in the Civil War America Series by the University of North Carolina Press. David is also a co-investigator on the AHRC-funded 'Locating the Hidden Diaspora: The English in North America in Transatlantic Perspective, 1760–1950'.

Joe Hardwick is Lecturer in British History at Northumbria University. He has published articles on aspects of the Church of England and the British Empire in the *Journal of Imperial and Commonwealth History* and *Historical Research*. He is currently writing a monograph for Manchester University Press's 'Studies in Imperialism' series on the Church of England's engagement with the settler empire in the period between the loss of the North American colonies and the coming of colonial self-government in the 1850s.

Gillian I. Leitch is a Senior Researcher at CDCI Research Inc. in Ottawa. Her PhD thesis at the Université de Montréal, 'The Importance of Being English? Identity and Social Organisation in British Montreal, 1800–1850', was a study of British identities in nineteenth-century Montreal, of which the English were a vital part. Her post-doctoral work at the University of Edinburgh focused on the familial and transnational identities and networks of three British immigrant families in Canada.

Amy J. Lloyd is a Leverhulme Trust Early Career Fellow in the School of History, Classics and Archaeology at the University of Edinburgh. She completed her PhD in history at the University of Cambridge in 2010. Her dissertation – which she is currently revising for publication – examines popular perceptions of emigration in Britain between 1870 and 1914. She has recently started a new research project on English emigration to Canada between 1900 and 1914.

Donald M. MacRaild is Professor of History and Associate Dean for Research at Northumbria University. He has published numerous articles and chapters in books, and has authored, edited or co-edited eleven books. His most recent book is *The Irish Diaspora in Britain, 1750–1939* (Macmillan, 2010), which is a revised, expanded and extended edition of his 1999 study of the Irish in Britain. He was visiting fellow at the Australian National University in 2010–11 and is principal investigator on an AHRC-funded project, 'Locating the Hidden Diaspora: The English in North America in Transatlantic Perspective, 1760–1950', for which this volume is in many ways a preliminary investigation. He is also completing a book on Ribbonism in Ireland and Britain with Kyle Hughes.

Glyn Parry is Senior Lecturer in History at Victoria University of Wellington, New Zealand. He has published on early modern history in the *Historical Journal*, the *English Historical Review*, the *Journal of Ecclesiastical History*, *Historical Research*, the *Huntington Library Quarterly* and many other leading journals, as well as publishing a monograph with Cambridge University Press on the Tudor intellectual William Harrison. His contribution to this volume develops some ideas discussed in his biography of an important early modern imperial advocate: *The Arch Conjuror of England: John Dee* (Yale University Press, 2011).

Brad Patterson is an Honorary Research Associate at the Stout Research Centre for New Zealand Studies, Victoria University of Wellington, New Zealand. He was formerly founding director of the university's Irish-Scottish Studies Programme, and, in 2010, held the W.F. Massey Fellowship at Massey University. The author or editor of nine books and numerous articles, he is co-author of a major study of New Zealand's Scots, to be published by McGill-Queen's University Press in 2012. His research interests, beyond New Zealand history, include Irish and Scottish migration and the political economy of nineteenth-century settler capitalism.

Doreen Skala earned her MA in history from Rutgers University, Camden. Her research is focused on eighteenth-century transatlantic social history with an emphasis on England and the Middle Atlantic region. She is currently engaged in transcribing and annotating Benjamin Chew's London journal, 1743–1744.

Monika Smialkowska is Senior Lecturer in English Literature at Northumbria University. Her research interests fall into two categories: the early modern genre of court masque, and post-renaissance adaptations and appropriations of early modern authors and genres. Currently, she is exploring the ways in which the 300th anniversary of Shakespeare's death in 1916 was celebrated across the world. As part of this project, she was awarded a short-term Folger Shakespeare Library fellowship. She has published a number of articles and is working towards a monograph on this topic.

William E. Van Vugt is Professor of History at Calvin College, Grand Rapids, Michigan, where he teaches courses in English and American history. He earned his MA in American history at Kent State University and his doctorate in economic history at the London School of Economics and Political Science under the mentorship of Charlotte Erickson. His books include *Britain to America: the mid-Nineteenth Century Immigrants to the United States* (1999); *Race and Reconciliation in South Africa: A Multicultural Dialogue in Comparative Perspective* (as co-author and editor, 2000); *British Buckeyes: the English, Scots, and Welsh in Ohio, 1700–1900* (2006); and *British Immigration to the United States, 1776–1914* (4 volumes, Pickering and Chatto, 2009). He has also written numerous scholarly articles and chapters in books on migration and the economic history of the North Atlantic.

David Walker is Associate Dean and Head of the Humanities Department at Northumbria University. He is the author, with Stuart Sim, of *Discourses of*

Sovereignty (Ashgate, 2003), as well as articles and book chapters on Bunyan and other nonconformist writers. He is currently editing a volume of primary sources on religion and depression in the long eighteenth century to be published by Pickering and Chatto, and an article on Bunyan in the 1650s for the forthcoming *Oxford Handbook of John Bunyan*.

James Watson is Associate Professor in History at Massey University in New Zealand. Having lived in Ilkley between the ages of two and nine, and having had a Yorkshire-born father, he has an interest in the county and in the whole relationship between the United Kingdom and New Zealand. In addition to numerous articles and chapters in books, he has authored or co-edited four books, the two most recent dealing with the Ulster-born Prime Minister of New Zealand, William Ferguson Massey.

Robert J.C. Young is Julius Silver Professor of English and Comparative Literature at New York University. His *White Mythologies: Writing History and the West* (1990), *Colonial Desire: Hybridity in Culture, Theory and Race* (Routledge, 1995), and *Postcolonialism: An Historical Introduction* (Blackwell, 2001) have been among the most influential books in the field of postcolonial studies. He has also written *Postcolonialism: A Very Short Introduction* (Oxford University Press, 2003), *The Idea of English Ethnicity* (Blackwell, 2008), and he is currently writing a book on translation. Prior to moving to New York, Robert Young was Professor of English and Critical Theory and a fellow of Wadham College, Oxford University. He is General Editor of the quarterly *Interventions: International Journal of Postcolonial Studies*. His work has been translated into twenty languages.

Introduction

Locating the English Diaspora: Problems, Perspectives and Approaches

Tanja Bueltmann, David T. Gleeson and Donald M. MacRaild

From the early seventeenth century, when sustained migrations began a process of re-peopling in the emerging colonies of settlement, emigrants from the British and Irish Isles outnumbered those from any other European nation. Methods of counting frustrate the historian of the English: over the four centuries from the earliest migrations until the outbreak of the Second World War, those living in the colonies or the United States who had been born in England or were of English extraction exceeded those from Scotland and Ireland, but it is impossible to disentangle the English from the British. This remained a problem in the second half of the nineteenth century, and was compounded by the fact that many who left from English ports were not English themselves. But indicative emigration rates point to the continued importance of English people as a source for New World populations. While in the period from 1881 to 1910 Scotland was losing between seven and ten people per thousand of population, and Ireland between seven and fourteen, the much larger population of England was producing more emigrants, albeit at the lower rate of between five and six per thousand.[1] Yet while the significance of the English has been noticed by historians of emigration, it is not acknowledged by historians of ethnicity: scholars recognize the English as a key population source in the Anglophone world but say relatively little about their contribution as immigrant communities.

In the United States, Charlotte Erickson studied the English but ultimately labelled them 'invisible'. Bernard Bailyn consciously overlooked them since they did not qualify as marginal in the first British Empire. Carl Wittke also

---

1   See Marjory Harper and Stephen Constantine, *Migration and Empire* (Oxford: Oxford University Press, 2010), pp. 1–3, for a useful discussion of the statistical picture.

chose to leave them out. Oscar Handlin, who saw migration as a disturbing 'uprooting' process, simply ignored them.[2] The idea that the English might, like every other settler group, be an ethnic community is ignored or refuted.

Since America holds sway in Anglo-world traditions of studying ethnic communities, it perhaps stands to reason that the neglect of the English in the US would have had an effect on historians elsewhere. And so it has. Studies of English settlers in Australia or New Zealand focus upon the group simply as one component of a series of demographic shifts, or else drift loosely between 'English' and 'British' when describing the identities of those who came from England. So notable is the contrast between the volume of scholarship on Irish or Scottish ethnicity and that on the English that it becomes not only reasonable, but also important, to ask: why was there no English Diaspora? Constantine and Harper, writing of Canada, consider the oversight to be a result of the English being regarded as a 'founding people' rather than an ethnic group.[3] In this respect, Young's chapter, which concludes this volume, describes a new way of looking at the English – not as a traditional minority Diaspora, but as a 'sovereign state Diaspora' akin to those of Portugal or Spain, the other greater territorial imperialists.

Of course, the English did not help themselves to be noticed in a world of competitive ethnicity. Imperial propagandists, such as J.R. Seeley, spoke of the empire as 'English' (including its pre-revolutionary American components).[4] If the empire was English, perhaps only others could be ethnic within it. To complicate matters further, Englishness, though it intimated a separate, discrete and much narrower identity that was necessarily crowded out or lost in a world dominated by Britain and, later, 'Greater Britain', nonetheless provided the core values of Britishness. Indeed, in the later nineteenth century a deliberate imperial nationalism began to emerge, which drew upon older symbols of national identity and promoted them through the agency of clubs, societies and the church. By this point, on the eve of the Boer War (1899–1902), the English were certainly promulgating an identity distinct from, but entwined with, Britishness.[5]

---

2   Charlotte Erickson, *Invisible Immigrants: The Adaptation of English and Scottish Immigrants in Nineteenth-century America* (Ithaca, NY: Cornell University Press, 1990); Bernard Bailyn (ed.), *Strangers in the Realm: Cultural Margins of the First British Empire* (Chapel Hill, NC: North Carolina University Press, 1991), pp. 10–11; Carl Wittke, *We Who Built America* (New York: Prentice Hall, 1939); Oscar Handlin, *The Uprooted: The Epic Story of the Great Migrants that Made the American People* (New York: Little Brown, 1951).

3   Harper and Constantine, *Migration and Empire*, p. 14.

4   J.R. Seeley, *The Expansion of England: Two Courses of Lectures* (London: Macmillan, 1883).

5   See Krishan Kumar, *The Making of English Identity* (Cambridge: Cambridge University Press, 2003) for 'imperial nationalism'. For an emphasis upon a much older Englishness, see Adrian Hastings, *The Construction of Nationhood: Ethnicity, Religion and Nationalism* (Cambridge: Cambridge University Press, 1997). English nationalism was a particularly important self-defence mechanism in South Africa, where the

Many middle-class English migrants did not advance their own cause by maintaining only a transient, partial and sometimes conditional relationship with empire and the colonies. While the Scots, Irish and Germans built ethnic pillars within the British World, many Englishmen saw themselves as sojourners not emigrants. Such people did not put down roots: they created 'mini-Britains' rather than 'neo-Britains'.[6] Yet while Young trenchantly considers the English as a 'disappeared' ethnicity in his account (Chapter 13), other contributors to this volume, for instance Watson in his study of English associationalism in New Zealand (Chapter 10), present sustained evidence of English activity that reveals the degree to which they behaved 'ethnically' as a group in much the same way as other migrant groups. In short: several of the authors deal with and accept the invisibility of the English, while others take the opposite view.

The present collection took shape from a conference held in the summer of 2010 at Northumbria University.[7] Attracting scholars from across the English-speaking world, the papers presented there, a selection of which are published here, gave recognition to the English as an identifiable emigrant group, exploring the nature and character of English identity during the creation of the cultures of the Anglo-world. At all points since the Elizabethan period, which Parry investigates in Chapter 1, empire helped to explain and shape what it meant to be English. Institutions such as the Anglican Church; Anglo-cultures in literature, pastimes and folk practices; sporting traditions, including cricket; the St George's Society and English county societies; hostility towards the English; ideologies such as Anglo-Saxonism – each of these helped underpin a shared Englishness that spanned the globe, and our contributors look at each of them in turn. Overall, the volume concurs with Robert Young's suggestion that the identity of Englishness was largely invented in the colonies for Englishmen abroad or else for those of English extraction who wished to express their ancestral identity.[8] The result is a set of discussions that we hope will provide a starting point for further discussions and discovery within the realms of what we term the 'hidden Diaspora'. In order to support this claim, a brief discussion of Diaspora is necessary.

British and Irish were increasingly outnumbered by the Dutch. See, in particular, John Lambert, 'Maintaining a British Way of Life: English Speaking South Africa's Patriotic, Cultural and Charitable Associations', *Historia*, 54.2 (2009), pp. 55–76.

6 Robert Bickers (ed.), *Settlers and Expatriates* (Oxford: Oxford University Press, 2010).

7 The conference was established as a foreground for our AHRC-funded project (2011–14) 'Locating the Hidden Diaspora: The English in North America in Transatlantic Perspective, 1760–1950' (project grant: AH/I001042/1).

8 Robert J.C. Young, *The Idea of English Ethnicity* (New York: Blackwell, 2008).

The Problem of Diaspora and
the Invisibility of English Ethnicity

Standard accounts of the development of Diaspora studies ignore the English, except as progenitors of an empire against which outsiders were defined. In part this is a result of the politicization of Diaspora, drawing elementally upon the original Jewish experience of systematic victimization and the denial of a homeland.[9] To a large extent, the most powerful traditions of writing within a Diasporic framework – those associated with Jews, Armenians, South Asians, the Africans of the Atlantic slave trade and the Irish – share victimhood, oppression, forced exile and reluctant migration as driving meta-narratives. Amnesia about English ethnic culture is, in fact, hardened by the tendency to focus on groups that suffered from imperial oppression. In a world of 'competitive victimhood', colonists and imperialists are the benchmark against which the coherence of Diasporas is measured.[10] As a result, Diaspora appears weaker for nationalities or ethnicities not suffering from the radical disjuncture caused by war, colonization and oppression. If these experiences are key elements in the evocation of a diasporic consciousness, the English – oppressors rather than the oppressed, colonists not the colonized – do not fit the typology. In the modern period England colonized more than any other nation; consequently, the English escape observation as progenitors of their own ethnic Diaspora.

An assumed absence of a sense of Diaspora among the English derives partly from the weak and bitty nature of Englishness at home. Contemporary English identity, under pressure in a dissolving United Kingdom, drifts, almost self-consciously, between tub-thumping populism and teary-eyed public spectacle. Englishness loses out in the recent vogue for what we term identity politics as English people experience 'cultural cringe' against anything that separates Englishness from Britishness. In 2001 the ethnic category, 'Irish', was added to the UK census, but 'English' was not; in Scotland, 'Scottish' and 'Irish' were identified as ethnic categories alongside 'British'. With each act of 'sub-categorization' the identity of being 'British' is fractured, divided and weakened, with Englishness emerging as something of a leftover category.[11] Both diffidence and hostility, however, figure strongly in a liberal

---

9   For an introductory typology, see Robin Cohen, *Global Diasporas* (London: Routledge, 2008); also Kevin Kenny, 'Diaspora and Comparison: The Irish as a Case Study', *Journal of American History*, 90.1 (2003), pp. 134–62.

10   Masi Noor, Rupert Brown and Gary Prentice, 'Prospects for Intergroup Conciliation: Social Psychological Indicators of Intergroup Forgiveness and Reparation in Northern Ireland and Chile', in Arie Nadler, Thomas E. Malloy and Jeffrey D. Fisher (eds), *The Social Psychology of Intergroup Reconciliation: From Violent Conflict to Peaceful Co-existence* (New York: Oxford University Press, 2008), pp. 97–115, draws specifically on Irish examples.

11   See also David McCrone, 'Who do you say you are? Making Sense of National Identities in Modern Britain', *Ethnicities*, 2 (September 2002), pp. 301–20.

rejection of the bellicose history of English state-building. On a popular level, Englishness is associated with the final flickering of empire and with soccer fans draped in the cross of St George or nationalist politicians. In comparison to Scottish nationalism, or the Orange and Green traditions of Northern Ireland, Englishness appears inchoate.[12] Small wonder that the English, who cannot together articulate a common, relevant Englishness in England, have played no part in capturing the hidden English Diaspora in America and pay little heed to the strong expressions of English ethnicity and cultural identity in the former colonies.

Historians perpetuate our ignorance of English ethnicity. The immigrants' Anglo-culture also explains the oversight of English ethnicity abroad and an apparently absent or weak diasporic identity. Since English ethnicity is largely perceived as a passive or invisible entity, and because England provided the civic and political institutions that societies abroad modified and that every other immigrant ethnicity was defined against, Englishness itself has been virtually forced from view. If, for example, American culture sprang from English culture, how could the English be ethnic like everyone else? As with other ethnic groups, the English had to prove their compatibility with their new home. English associational life in the United States, for instance, was partly about demonstrating their acceptability to the host populace. To some extent this process was aided by the rising tide of Anglo-Saxonism and the acclamation of a shared racial heritage, which in turn marked out southern Europeans and Hispanics as inferior and pointed to the possibility of con-cordance between Yankee Americans and the English/British.[13] In the early twentieth century – in the face of mass immigration by non-WASP peoples and in an international context that presented new challenges to the hege-mony of the English-speaking world – Anglo-Saxonists resolutely presented race as a binding connection between British and American worlds and as a bridge between America, England and Canada.[14]

Crucially, in America, where they settled most numerously, the English passed from interest as interpretative fashions changed. English immigrants and their culture had a strong role to play when the 'germ theory' of American society held fast, which saw a democratic American culture inherited from the forests of ancient Germany via Britain. America was cast as a sub-category

---

12 Robert Colls, *Identity of England* (Oxford and New York: Oxford University Press, 2004).

13 See Paul A. Kramer's trenchant analysis of the coming together of British and American ideologies within a framework of Anglo-Saxonism: 'Empires, Exceptions, and Anglo-Saxons: Race and Rule between the British and United States Empires, 1880–1910', *Journal of American History*, 88.4 (2002), pp. 1315–53. Also see Bueltmann, Chapter 7 below.

14 For early Anglo-Saxonism, see Reginald Horsman, *Race and Manifest Destiny: The Origins of American Racial Anglo-Saxonism* (Cambridge, MA: Harvard University Press, 1981); Edward P. Kohn, *This Kindred People: Canadian–American Relations and the Anglo-Saxon Idea, 1895–1903* (Montreal: McGill-Queen's University Press, 2005).

of England. When the 'germ theory' was superseded by Frederick Jackson Turner's thesis of environmental exceptionalism, the emphasis moved from inheritance of culture to its re-making and transformation. In this new model, which was popular in the early twentieth century, English roots were dispersed in unique American soil. Moreover, the influence of American exceptionalism ranged beyond historical studies. Richard M. Dorson, the distinguished father of American folklore studies, argued against the simple transfer of English popular cultural traditions – by which he expressly meant folk traditions – to the United States.[15] His words echo developments in ethnic history: 'calendar custom and domestic usage, the heart of England's folklore, have made little impress on the mobile civilization of the United States, and folk-narrative, a weak point in merry England, has for the most part had to make its own way under the Stars and Stripes'.[16] Dorson's folklore, like the nation's history, was underpinned by that exceptionalism.[17] The English fared even less well when, in US ethnic history, the migration thesis replaced Turner's idea. Propagated by pioneering non-Anglo-Saxon historians from Oscar Handlin through to John Bodnar, the migration school emphasized how non-British immigrants created a hyphenated, plural America, which relied neither on 'Albion's seed' thesis nor on Turner's 'melting pot'.[18] Either way, for much of the twentieth century, there was no room for the English.

In prosaic terms, then, little credit is given to the notion of distinctive English roots.[19] While scholars such as David Hackett Fischer (on the colonial period) recognize the sheer weight of English immigrants, ethnicity is not considered important. Only Rowland Berthoff, who examined English societies alongside those of the Scots and Welsh, has touched on the notion of the English as a distinct ethnic faction in industrial America.[20] In spite of the large number of English arrivals in the US and their importance to the growing American industrial economy, scholars of immigration to America have done relatively little to recognize English ethnicity. Charlotte Erickson saw the English as a group that either blended in rapidly or else forged an Anglo-American culture that removed the need for ethnic self-expression.[21]

---

15 Richard M. Dorson, Buying the Wind: Regional Folklore in the United States (Chicago: University of Chicago Press, 1964).
16 Richard M. Dorson, 'The Shaping of Folklore Traditions in the United States', *Folklore*, 78.3 (1967), pp. 161–62.
17 Such is the argument of William A. Wilson, 'Richard M. Dorson's Theory for American Folklore: A Finnish Analogue', *Western Folklore*, 41.1 (1982), pp. 36–42.
18 David Hackett Fischer, *Albion's Seed: Four British Folkways in America* (New York: Oxford University Press, 1989), pp. 4–5.
19 Charlotte Erickson, 'English', in S. Thernstrom, A. Orlov and O. Handlin (eds), *Harvard Encyclopaedia of American Ethnic Groups* (Cambridge, MA: Belknap Press of Harvard University Press, 2nd edn, 1980), p. 320.
20 Rowland Berthoff, *British Immigrants in Industrial America, 1750–1922* (Cambridge, MA: Harvard University Press, 1953).
21 Erickson, *Invisible Immigrants*.

Ultimately, in the nineteenth century, the 'English had no ethnicity in American eyes'.[22]

The situation is hardly better in the traditional settler dominions of Canada, Australia and New Zealand. The English may have been the largest national group to settle in these countries, but English ethnicity is under-played next to the identities of their Scottish or Irish cousins. Even the major surveys of mass migration emphasize the British and the Celtic components of United Kingdom migration, and say little about the distinct English ethnic forms.[23] While Harper and Constantine have written the English into their study of colonial migrations in the nineteenth and twentieth centuries, they say little of their culture,[24] a trend also notable in Australian studies of English settlement.[25] Hence, Hammerton and Thomson's study of post-war mass emigration from Britain to Australia stresses their invisibility, often using the terms 'English' and 'British' interchangeably to label people born in England.[26] Among the few works that specifically examine the Australasian English, Jupp's general account offers an interesting but superficial explora-tion, and in any case does not investigate English ethnicity.[27] In New Zealand there is no specific study of English ethnic cultures, though the migrations from England are discussed in all general accounts and in Arnold's classic three-volume micro-history.[28] Phillips and Hearn's recent study of British Isle migration to New Zealand gives recognition to the English as a distinct migrant group; however, the authors' focus has largely been on establishing a migration profile of the English rather than their ethnic culture – though some suggestions as to English legacies are made.[29] Patterson's wide-ranging overview of English culture in New Zealand for this volume (Chapter 9) is the first such study.

---

22 Kathleen Neils Conzen et al., 'The Invention of Ethnicity: A View from the U.S.A.', *Journal of American Ethnic History*, 12 (1992), pp. 5–7.

23 Eric Richards, *Britannia's Children: Emigration from England, Scotland, Wales and Ireland since 1600* (London: Hambledon & London, 2004).

24 Harper and Constantine, *Migration and Empire*.

25 For example, Janet Doust, 'Two English Immigrant Families in Australia in the Nineteenth Century', *History of the Family*, 13 (2008), pp. 2–25.

26 James Hammerton and Alistair Thomson, *Ten Pound Poms: Australia's Invisible Migrants* (Manchester: Manchester University Press, 2005), pp. 11–15.

27 James Jupp, *The English in Australia* (Cambridge: Cambridge University Press, 2004).

28 James Belich, *Making Peoples: A History of the New Zealanders, from Polynesian Settlement to the End of the Nineteenth Century* (Auckland: Penguin, 1996); *Paradise Reforged: A History of the New Zealanders, 1880 to the Year 2000* (Honolulu: University of Hawaii Press, 2001); Rollo Arnold, *The Farthest Promised Land: English Villagers, New Zealand Immigrants of the 1870s* (Wellington: Victoria University Press, 1981); *New Zealand's Burning: The Settler's World in the Mid-1880s* (Wellington: Victoria University Press, 1994); *Settler Kaponga, 1881–1914: A Frontier Fragment of the Western World* (Wellington: Victoria University Press, 1997).

29 Jock Phillips and Terry Hearn, *Settlers: New Zealand Immigrants from England, Ireland and Scotland* (Auckland: Auckland University Press, 2008), esp. pp. 68ff. and 158ff.

Towards an English Diaspora.
The Genesis and Development of Englishness

By transcending the traditional meaning of Diaspora (the dispersion of people across space), as well as the narrative of exile and victimhood, several of the contributors to this volume present an alternative conceptualization of Diaspora: that of an international community of people with shared ethnic-national roots and a heightened, potentially politicized sense of common identity, whose adherence to that community is measurable in empirical rather than conceptual terms.[30] This conception recognizes Diaspora as actively maintained by its own members – in associations, through the Anglican Church, or through sports. By studying these structures, contributors unravel the values that underpin the cultures of English migrants, the pastimes and customs they introduced, utilizing them as indicators of degrees of conscious Englishness. In portraying these alternative images, this collection combines reaffirmations of existing ideas with fresh empirical research, and ground-breaking new conceptualizations, documenting the ways in which the English can be located as a Diaspora.

There is little doubt that, in the early modern period, the empire, which in-cluded the future United States, was England's empire. The economic interests being served by early forays into the Americas were those of southern English companies and traders. Most of the seventeenth-century traffic in migrants also came from England, and England was well represented among the im-migrants even when the Scots and Irish became heavily involved. Indeed, Parry, in his highly original reinterpretation of the sixteenth-century origins of the first English empire, shows just how important North America was for England's emerging international prestige and sense of national destiny. However, Parry reveals more than just another piece in a story of emigration; instead, he strikes at the heart of that identity. In a wide-ranging and deeply researched account, he reinterprets the 'mythologies' of the first English Diaspora and the early empire. Elizabethan England's early imperial ventures were wrapped up with old myths about Englishness, including readings of the Arthurian legend as partly a narrative of English imperial expansion. Central to the latter was the promise that the golden age of an oceanic empire would rise again. Expansion into the Americas fitted this mythology and English people were seduced by it.

Walker follows this with a consideration of one of the most important English cultural transfers in the seventeenth- and eighteenth-century Atlantic world: English Republican ideas. However, as he shows, the English radical

---

30 For a discussion of this type of Diaspora, focusing on the Irish, see Donald M. MacRaild, '"Diaspora" and Transnationalism: Theory and Evidence in Explanation of the Irish World-wide', Symposium: Perspectives on the Irish Diaspora, *Irish Economic and Social History*, XXXIII (2006), pp. 51–58.

traditions of the Civil War period, which influenced the American revolutionaries a century-and-a-half later, were not mere sidestreams to English currents
of thought, but were adapted and blended with other Protestant ideologies
to create the body of beliefs associated with the American struggle against
Britain. Moreover, as Walker argues, there was not a single republicanism
in America, but instead several republicanisms, for Dutch and German, as
well as English/British, Protestant traditions also influenced politics there.
Similarly, English traditions, from architecture and literature to fox hunting
and Morris dancing, were transported with the settlers and then were remade
to fit American society. Thus, as Skala argues in Chapter 3, the appearance of
fox hunting in Philadelphia was not a simple cultural transfer, for many of
the men who brought fox hunting to Pennsylvania would later fight against
the British.[31] Yet, through their activities in the Gloucester Fox Hunting Club,
members were effectively making America more English, turning it from a
colonial society into a provincial one – and one that would be an equal partner
in the British Empire. Picking up the English immigrants' role in the life of
the United States in the nineteenth and early twentieth centuries, Van Vugt
draws upon his recent scholarly collection of immigrant letters,[32] concentrating upon the main waves of English settlement in the American colonies, and,
later, the United States. It was the English migrants' common language and
relative ease of assimilation, writes Van Vugt in Chapter 4, that facilitated
their migration and contributed to the fact that the English Diaspora in
America remained relatively hidden, though an essential foundation of the
culture and economy of the United States.

The hold of English culture in America is never better demonstrated than
in its approval for one of the world's great playwrights, William Shakespeare.
In Chapter 12, Smialkowska offers a fascinating exploration of this particular
cultural legacy, and an examination of the continuities and discontinuities of
English culture in the American republic, by exploring American celebrations
of the 300th anniversary, in 1916, of Shakespeare's death. Many Shakespeare
tercentenary tributes reconstructed the 'merry old England' of the Elizabethan
period, throwing light on the issues of 'Englishness' repeatedly broached in
America: what was 'Englishness'; to what extent was Shakespeare seen as
'English'; what purposes did the chosen version of 'Englishness' serve in 1916;
and how was it adapted to fit the American context? Smialkowska explores
the idea of Elizabethan England promoted by the tercentenary entertainments
in conjunction with their representations of Shakespeare and Elizabeth I.
The chapter highlights that the adoption of Shakespeare into the American
literary canon has not been unproblematic: he was associated with the 'old

---

31 See also T.H. Breen, 'An Empire of Goods: The Anglicization of Colonial America,
    1690–1776', *Journal of British Studies*, 25.4 (1986), pp. 467–99.
32 W.E. Van Vugt, *British Immigration to the United States, 1776–1914*, 4 vols (London:
    Pickering and Chatto, 2009).

world' and its aristocratic and monarchical structures of authority, inimical to American democratic principles.

The endurance of cultural traditions, as well as their flexibility in new world contexts as traced by Smialkowska, is also evident in another distinct transfer: that of cricket. Allen's exposition in Chapter 11 on cricket demonstrates how the association of this sport with Englishness grew within the empire. He provides important historical context for the way in which, today, cricket continues to echo the old allegiances of empire, being a sport played overwhelmingly in what was the British imperial domain. At a more localized level, the emergence of cricket clubs and the playing of English team games represented a telling example of another transferred culture, with interesting effects upon national and colonial allegiances being noticed acutely in times of war.

One of the most enduring symbols of English culture overseas was the Anglican Church. In Chapter 5, Hardwick corrects previous oversights and demonstrates firmly that Anglicanism has an important role in any discussion of a putative English 'world'. Not only does Hardwick question whether historians are correct to argue that the Church became less English as it migrated overseas, he also explores whether colonial churchmen simply assumed that the colonial branch of the Church was as much the Church of the English people as that at home. By sampling a range of sermons, charges, clerical correspondence and periodical literature, focusing on North America and Australia in particular, Hardwick traces the emergence, in the early nineteenth century, of the idea that the Church would play an integral role in the creation of colonies. However, the hopes of establishing replicas of the English Church overseas were eventually dashed, as colonial churches never were facsimiles of the mother church. But while the vision of an Anglo-world that had the Church at its heart was never likely to be realized because the settler colonies were too diverse in terms of the settlers' ethnicity and religion, the crucial idea that the Church should be the necessary component of colonial Englishness (and Britishness) persisted nonetheless.

Secular organizations were also important in shaping Englishness overseas.[33] Like the Scots and Irish, the English placed a high premium on conviviality and sociability, which they laced with toasts to their shared nationality and race, fully recognizing the global scattering of English people. While ethnic associations are a common feature of migrant life, English associationalism has received little attention, although it too sprouted a lively scene of clubs and societies all over the world. The St George's societies of New York, Charleston and Philadelphia were formed during the colonial period, and the nineteenth century saw many more such developments, both in Canada and the US. St George's societies formed in Toronto, Quebec and Ottawa in the

---

33   Tanja Bueltmann and Donald M. MacRaild, 'Globalising St. George: English Associations in the Anglo-World to the 1930s', *Journal of Global History*, 7.1 (2012), pp. 79–105.

1830s and 1840; Baltimore's branch appeared in 1866.[34] More generally in the 1850s and 1860s societies spread to the Midwest – Ohio, Illinois, Wisconsin and elsewhere.[35] At the same time, they spread southwards to New Orleans and Knoxville, Tennessee.[36] As immigrants went westwards, the St George's tradition accompanied them. By 1910 there were branches in Los Angeles, Boulder, Pasadena, San Francisco and Oakland.[37] North of the border, across Calgary, Alberta and Winnipeg, Manitoba, another, more militant working-class organization, the Sons of England, was particularly popular.

The ethnic associationalism of the English was not, however, uniform: it was shaped by the local contexts in which it emerged. Leitch's discussion (Chapter 6), which explores the evolution of public expressions of English ethnic culture in Montreal – a city in which the English were a minority in the face of the Irish and French-Canadians – provides important new insights in this respect. In Montreal, the English proclaimed their Englishness to foster a sense of collective community spirit, celebrating ethnic festivals and playing cricket. It was only in the 1830s, however, when the French-speaking community was increasingly radicalized in opposition to British rule in Canada, that distinct ethnic associations first emerged in Montreal's British immigrant community, with Irish, Scots and English setting up associations.

Half a world away in Australia, English ethnic societies also began to spread from the middle of the nineteenth century. The earliest occurrence was registered in Adelaide and Melbourne in the late 1840s and early 1850s.[38] By the turn of the twentieth century, there were St George's societies all across Australia.[39] However, much less activity was registered in another Australasian colony, New Zealand, where the number of St George's societies, as Patterson shows in his study of the English in New Zealand, pales compared to that elsewhere (Chapter 9). What New Zealanders did do, however, was to form county associations, which Watson explores in Chapter 10 through the prism of the Yorkshire societies. These were among the most successful county societies,

---

34 *Charters and bye-laws of the St George's Society of Toronto… 1862* (Toronto: no publisher, 1863), p. 4; *Quebec St George's Society, Officers and Members, with the reports for 1846* (Quebec: J.C. Fisher, 1846), front cover; for Ottawa: Anson A. Gard, *The Hub and the Spokes: or the Capital and its Environs* (Ottawa: Emerson Press, 1904), p. 47.

35 *Wisconsin Patriot* (Madison), 23 August 1856; *Milwaukee Daily Sentinel*, 12 March, 3 and 25 April 1858; *Daily Cleveland Herald*, 25 and 26 April 1861; *Chicago Tribune*, 2 May 1861, 16, 22, 27, 28 and 31 March 1864, 5, 12 and 26 April 1864.

36 E.g. *Daily Picayune* (New Orleans), 11 May 1891; *Knoxville Journal*, 18 February 1891.

37 *Los Angeles Times*, 24 April 1885, 6 April 1887; *Rocky Mountains News* (Boulder), 2 January 1887; *Los Angeles Times*, 1 January 1891, 25 April 1895, 25 April 1904; *Evening Bulletin* (San Francisco), 14 November 1885; *Los Angeles Times*, 25 April 1904; *Oakland (CA) Tribune*, 1 February 1924.

38 *South Australian Register* (Adelaide), 18 January 1845; *Melbourne Argus*, 19 March 1847.

39 *Sydney Morning Herald*, 9 December 1893; *West Australian*, 24 June 1898, 28 April 1900; *Brisbane Courier*, 25 October 1904, 1 February 1913; *Camperdown Chronicle*, 1 May 1913.

surviving separately or in combination with Lancashire societies for many years. In tracing the evolution of these societies, the chapter documents how organizations celebrating a national sense of 'Englishness' had little success in New Zealand before the First World War. Watson argues that, in the first place, there seems to have been only a weak sense of a collective 'English' identity, since the assertion of a separate Englishness by the majority potentially threatened to divide a community that placed a strong premium on social cohesion, working towards a 'British' and imperial destiny. What the New Zealand chapters highlight is that the timing of migration, as well as the type of English migrants arriving, is crucial to explain divergent developments, in this case of English associational culture, throughout the Anglo-world.

In more ideological terms, a vital element in the shaping of Englishness abroad was Anglo-Saxonism, which, based on common heritage, served as a point of reference for English migrants. From the latter half of the nineteenth century, however, the idea of common heritage was increasingly framed through race: ideas of the superiority of the bloodstock of the British Isles, with the English at a racial apex, were, as Bueltmann shows in Chapter 7, increasingly interwoven with the English culture transferred. These ideas influenced populist notions in the late nineteenth century when the British Empire faced challenges from the emerging Anglophone power-house of the United States, as well as from alien powers such as Russia and Germany. Anglo-Saxonism, encapsulated here in Bueltmann's discussion of Goldwyn Smith, saw Victorians writing about the idea of emphasizing English and British power by cementing the colonies into a vast union against rising threats – a movement brilliantly captured by Duncan Bell[40] – or, as in Smith's case, by campaigning for an Anglo-Saxon union between the US and Canada. Bueltmann's chapter, then, documents how geopolitics were framed by divergent appropriations of Anglo-Saxonism, which also provided a key trope of English ethnicity, for instance for English associations.

Men such as Smith, and the activities of English associations, show that the most important expressions of a common English, British and imperial identity can be found outside Britain. We see this very clearly in terms of expressions of Englishness. While the English at home hedge around the nature of their national identity, the English in the colonies did not. Importantly, institutional manifestations of Englishness were formed, not by the English in England, but by English people or their offspring in the colonies and the US. When the Royal St George's Society came into being in 1894, this was a conscious reflection of global and imperial Englishness rather than a society constructed for people at home. The society was little known at home and spent more time in communication with the empire than with the home

---

40 Duncan Bell, *The Idea of Greater Britain: Empire and the Future of World Order, 1860–1900* (Princeton, NJ: Princeton University Press, 2007).

country. Hence while not all contributors to this volume concur with the conceptualization of the English as a distinct ethnic group, the collection nonetheless supports Young's assertion that Englishness was invented in the Anglo-world beyond England's shores, aligning with the notions of Irishness as invented overseas described by Declan Kiberd.[41]

While the English, in general, clearly were not a victim group in the way that the Jews or the Irish were, we suggest that being English in the colonies or America nevertheless led to some critical commentary – even in loyal Canada. Lloyd's chapter, which explores the hostility towards English migrants in Toronto that resulted in a sustained transatlantic dialogue and debate about what it meant to be English, thus provides important new insights into a little-understood issue. While British immigrants were usually described in terms of their preferred migrant status, Lloyd documents that being English did not necessarily serve as an advantage in Canada in the early twentieth century, and that numbers alone did not account for easy integration and reception. Englishness, then, was at a considerably greater risk in some places than in others. Conflict between the English and the increasingly powerful Irish in cities such as Boston, for instance, emphasizes the need for us to be more circumspect in ascribing to the English a position of dominance – and might also bring into question once more the extent to which, by the 1880s, the Irish were a victim group at all.[42]

Conclusions

Despite their numerical significance, and the fact that they played a found-ing role in forging colonial societies around the globe – indeed perhaps in some ways because of that role – the English have never been seen as a Diaspora. Instead, other migrant groups throughout the Anglophone world – emphasizing the disruption and victimhood of Diaspora-formation – have defined themselves against the English. Yet much of the work of this collection of scholars suggests that, far from being invisible immigrants, the English created distinctive religious, social and cultural traditions and organizations in the new worlds in which they settled whose imprint has not been noticed by historians. The ways in which the English shaped the development of new settlements and contributed to their making was, however, important. This collection examines a range of these ways, aiding the location of the hidden English Diaspora. It does not do so uncritically. The authors have differing approaches, and not all of them see Diaspora as a useful tool. Indeed, the

---

41 Declan Kiberd, *Inventing Ireland: The Literature of the Modern Nation* (London: Jonathan Cape, 1995), pp. 1–2, 21.
42 Berthoff, *British Immigrants*.

collection deliberately ends with Young's explanation of the many and varied reasons why the English have not been counted among the world's many Diasporas. Whatever the complexities of these issues – indeed because of those very complexities – we hope this will be the beginning, not the end, of discussions of the neglected English.

Chapter 1

Mythologies of Empire and the Earliest English Diasporas

Glyn Parry

Our modern mythologies of empire and migration need to take into account the mythologies through which the sixteenth- and seventeenth-century English perceived themselves and the world, myths that in succeeding centuries germinated in different forms throughout the English Diaspora. To understand early modern thinking we must surrender some of our modern preconceptions. We have abandoned charismatic prophecy as a method of political explanation. Sharing the Enlightenment belief in applying a scientific approach even to the mysteries of human emotion, we prefer opinion polls.

However, this chapter engages with a pre-Enlightenment society and political culture in which only the opinions of the powerful few mattered, a culture that possessed few political mechanisms for peacefully transforming the body politic. To the powerful, expectations of a different future could be defined in one word – treason. In such a society one of the few semi-legitimate pressure valves for expressing the hopes and desires of the mass of English people was a belief in prophecies of abrupt political change, either to recover a lost golden age or to perfect human society in preparation for the apocalypse. This chapter discusses some ways in which a prophetic sense of the future informed early ideas of empire and migration, because they were inextricably linked to the question of what it meant to be English in the sixteenth century.

The Earliest Meanings of English

There were different answers to the question of what it meant to be English. Eight hundred years previously the Northumbrian, the Venerable Bede, had given an historically accurate answer. The English were originally a Germanic people, distinct from the native Britons, and from each other as the Angles, Saxons and Jutes. The glory of their conversion to Christianity and the formation of the *gens anglorum* belonged to Rome alone, and from 596 in his *Ecclesiastical History* Bede talked of the English race, reflecting the papacy's conscious policy of suppressing incessant tribal warfare by constructing broader identities.[1]

However, in the twelfth century Geoffrey of Monmouth set out to remedy what he considered to be Bede's deficiencies, and in doing so thoroughly muddied the waters. Where Bede focused on ecclesiastical history, Geoffrey exalted the chivalric history of British kings. He wove them into pseudo-classical Trojan origins and the Brut myth, in the process grafting English identity on to sensationalized British history before the Anglo-Saxons. That glamorous story depicted successive British dynasties wielding imperial power within the British Isles. This partially fulfilled the prophecy with which Geoffrey began his *History of the Kings of Britain*, when the goddess Diana promises Brutus that 'From your descendants will arise kings, who will be masters of the world.' Geoffrey centred his story on this imperial destiny. In the process he created one of the compelling heroes of western culture, that great imperial figure Arthur, who first mastered Britain, then Ireland, Iceland, Gothland, the Orkneys, Norway, Denmark and finally Gaul. He was about to fulfil the Sybilline prophecies and annex the Roman Empire when he was frustrated by Mordred's treason.[2] We should not underestimate how compelling in the right circumstances early modern politicians found this imperial vision, modelled ironically not just on Alexander, Charlemagne and other emperors, but on the claims of tenth-century English kings, the Danish Cnut and the Norman kings of England.[3]

Geoffrey inserted into his *History* the prophecies of Merlin, enigmatic animal imagery that would be rewritten and reinterpreted in every political crisis over succeeding centuries. Merlin's prophecies began by reinforcing Britain's global imperial destiny: 'The islands of the ocean will fall under his sway and he will occupy the glades of France. The house of Rome will tremble before his rage, and his end will be unknown'.[4] Arthur and Merlin would be important in Elizabethan imperial ideology, both at elite and popular levels. According to Edward Topsell's criticism in 1599, 'the simple and vulgar sort imagine that there is no Scripture like to Merlins prophesie'.[5]

1 *Bede's Ecclesiastical History of the English People*, ed. Bertram Colgrave and R.A.B. Mynors (Oxford and New York: Clarendon Press, 1969), Bk I, chs. 15, 23–26.
2 *Geoffrey of Monmouth: The History of the Kings of Britain*, ed. Michael D. Reeve, trans. Neil Wright (Woodbridge and Rochester, NY: Boydell Press, 2007), Bk I, ch. 17, p. 20.
3 John S.P. Tatlock, *The Legendary History of Britain: Geoffrey of Monmouth's Historia Regum Britanniae and Its Early Vernacular Versions* (Berkeley, CA: University of California Press, 1950), pp. 307–12.
4 *The History of the Kings of Britain*, ed. Reeve, p. 144.
5 Edward Topsell, *Times Lamentation: Or an Exposition on the Prophet Joel, in Sundry Sermons or Meditations* (London, 1599), p. 63.

The Reformation further confused the hybrid origins of the English. Protestants now sought to tie myths of national origins to biblical history, to Japhet, the son of Noah, who peopled Europe and whose successors, Samothes and his descendants before Brutus, provided a religious blood-line back to the Old Testament. This history made Joseph of Arimathea the apostolic bringer of Christianity to England, and gave the obscure King Lucius new prominence as the first Christian king in Europe. Published in prestigious sixteenth-century histories such as *Holinshed's Chronicles* (1577, 1587), this story appeared in standardized and encapsulated form in cheap histories and popular print into the eighteenth century, thus connecting Protestant England to the biblical story, but especially denying the papacy a role in propagating the faith in England.[6]

Recent historiography has added to these Protestant assumptions a focus on political theory, particularly the ideologies of *imperium* embodied in Roman law, so that David Armitage has summarized English imperial ideology as Protestant, maritime, commercial and free.[7] This mythology is particularly difficult to criticize because intervening history has made it part of our own.

The Origins of the First English Empire

The recognizable characteristics of the empire encapsulated by Armitage took centuries to develop. None of them appertained under Henry VIII, for example. Previously the default setting of English foreign policy had been to maintain good relations with whoever controlled the Netherlands, and especially Antwerp, the major outlet for the wool that constituted the bulk of England's under-developed and narrow tradeable economy. In the early sixteenth century that required good relations with the Habsburgs, hence Henry's Spanish marriage. It also meant that Henry could not offend the Habsburgs by following up Henry VII's claims to parts of America through the discoveries of the Cabots. Nor could he exploit Robert Thorne's discoveries in 1527.[8] Henry's marital policies in the 1530s therefore revolutionized England's foreign policy – England became largely isolated, retaining its Netherlands outlets only through mutual economic interest and Charles V's financial dependence on the Netherlands provinces.

---

6   Margaret Spufford, *Small Books and Pleasant Histories: Popular Fiction and its Readership in Seventeenth-Century England* (London: Methuen, 1981); Christy Desmet, 'Afterlives of the Prose Brut in Early Modern Chronicle and Literature', in William Marx and Raluca Radulescu (eds), *Readers and Writers of the Prose Brut* (Lampeter: Trivium Publications, 2006); Adam Fox, *Oral and Literate Culture in England, 1500–1700* (Oxford: Clarendon Press, 2000), pp. 226–28, 238–39, 248–57.

7   David Armitage, *The Ideological Origins of the British Empire* (Cambridge: Cambridge University Press, 2000).

8   Richard Hakluyt, *Divers Voyages Touching the Discovery of America and the Islands Adjacent* (1580), ed. John W. Jones (London: Hakluyt Society, 1850), pp. 27–52.

Thus the first organized, large-scale English diaspora began when English Catholics exiled themselves from Henry VIII's religious policies to Habsburg lands, especially the nearest Catholic intellectual centre, the university of Louvain, which was by the late 1540s a bastion of ultra-orthodoxy. This was redoubled by a further wave of emigration under Edward VI's more radically Protestant regime. After a temporary hiatus under Mary the exodus resumed under Elizabeth, when numerous Catholic clergy and substantial Catholic families went into exile, remaining in Europe for generations, and supplemented by waves of migration following anti-Catholic pogroms.[9]

Even more, but for the back-door influence of the Spanish Habsburgs, the first organized English American colony would have welcomed a Catholic diaspora. Sir Humphrey Gilbert led the first expedition to locate a suitable site for an English colonial venture in the early 1580s. The results were unspectacular. Following long-established sea-routes to the fabulous cod fishery off Newfoundland, Gilbert annexed the territory in 1583 to become the first and last American colony, one that Britain could not give away to Canada in 1947. However, few appreciate that Gilbert's financial backer was Sir George Peckham, a leading Catholic who provided a safe house for Jesuit and secular Catholic missionaries at Denham in Surrey, the site of a spectacular series of demonic exorcisms in 1586, intended to demonstrate the sole legitimacy of Holy Mother Church.[10]

While Gilbert was preparing his expedition, Peckham consulted the polymath intellectual John Dee (of whom more later) about 'the title to Hochelaga', the area of the St Lawrence around what is now Montreal, since the papacy had divided the world between Portugal and Spain – could English Catholics legitimately settle there when the pope had given the Americas to Spain?[11] Though secretly an ordained Catholic priest for nearly thirty years, Dee normally denied the papacy power to assign America, except when his belief that Elizabeth I was the rightful Queen of Castile made it useful to accept the pope's donation of America to that Crown.[12] Undoubtedly on this occasion the pope had erred once again. Peckham had substantial political backing for his plan – Sir Francis Walsingham saw great advantage in solving England's Catholic recusancy problem by shipping the offending gentry off to the St Lawrence. Only less than subtle pressure from Spain through the

---

9 Peter Marshall, *Religious Identities in Henry VIII's England* (Aldershot: Palgrave, 2006), pp. 230–58, 263–76.
10 David Beers Quinn, *The Voyages and Colonizing Enterprises of Sir Humphrey Gilbert* (London: Hakluyt Society, 1940), pp. 243–50, 255; Samuel Harsnett, *A Declaration of Egregious Popish Impostures* (London, 1603)
11 Bodleian Library Oxford MS Ashmole 487, under 16 July 1582.
12 Glyn Parry, *The Arch Conjuror of England: John Dee* (New Haven, CT, and London: Yale University Press, 2011), pp. 144, 130.

confessors to Elizabeth's remaining Catholic courtiers prevented Montreal becoming the capital of English Catholic North America.[13]

By the late sixteenth century there were organized English seminaries at Douai, Rheims, Rome and Valladolid, later joined by closed religious orders for pious Catholic women, which continued until the French Revolution. A head-count of the English Diaspora before the 1620s would have forced one to conclude that it was not Protestant, maritime, commercial and free, but Catholic, terrestrial, religious and persecuted.[14]

The Catholic Definition of English

That diaspora soon created a Catholic definition of what it meant to be English, self-consciously reviving Bede's conception, downplaying Arthur and Lucius and emphasizing English Germanic origins and dependence upon the papacy. In 1565 the Catholic exile Thomas Stapleton published (at Antwerp, we should note) the first English translation of Bede's *Ecclesiastical History*, whose title could equally be translated as 'The History of things done in the Church of the English Nation'. Stapleton's dedication to Queen Elizabeth and her 'Imperial Crowne' condemned the 'mis-information of a few for displacing the ancient and right Christian faith', begging that she would end her schism and restore the ancient condition of Englishness. Elizabeth's realm, he insisted from Bede, was christened in the apostolic faith of Rome by Augustine, who christened 'Ethelbert the first Christian king of Englishmen', and had continued under 'our dear forefathers' for almost a thousand years. He contrasted the newly invented, foreign, Protestant religion with 'the primitive faith of the English church'. The Catholic faith was the same 'which was first grafted in the hearts of Englishmen', Protestantism was 'a bastard slippe proceding of an other stocke [...] And therefore not to be rooted in your graces dominions.' To the general reader he stressed that 'our forefathers, the first Christian Englishmen', obeyed 'one supreme head in Christ's Church the Apostolic Pope', and he bolstered his argument with an historical narration of the 'coming in of us Englishmen'.[15]

---

13 Quinn, *Gilbert*, pp. 278–79.
14 W. Kelly (ed.), *Liber Ruber Venerabilis Collegii Anglorum de Urbe, 1579–1783* (London: Catholic Record Society, 1940, 1943); E. Kenson (ed.), *Registers of the English College at Valladolid* (London: Catholic Record Society, 1935); E.H. Burton and T.L. Williams (eds), *The Douay college Diaries* (London: Catholic Record Society, 1911); Geoffrey Holt, *St Omers and Bruges College, 1593–1773* (London: Catholic Record Society, 1979); P.R. Harris (ed.), *Douai college documents 1639-1794* (London: Catholic Record Society, 1972); A. Kenny (ed.), *The Responsa Scholarum of the English College, Rome, 1598-1685* (London: Catholic Record Society, 1962–63).
15 Thomas Stapleton (trans.), *The history of the Church of Englande. Compiled by Venerable Bede, Englishman* (Antwerp, 1565), sigs. *2v, delta 3v, *3r, delta 2v, delta 3r, A3r, B2r–v.

Stapleton elaborated his case in a companion book, *A Fortresse of the faith, first planted among us Englishmen, and continued hitherto in the universall church of Christ* (1565). This provoked a major controversy by stressing the continuity of the English since that time of conversion, as part of the universal, true Catholic religion of 'all Christendom', a national identity far different from that being actively constructed by Protestants in the 1560s, in which they redefined Catholicism as an alien superstition that frequently resorted to magical means for its treasons.[16]

Stapleton's considerable historical scholarship failed to shake Protestant conceptions of 'British' Englishness. A generation later another Catholic exile, Richard Verstegan, published *Restitution of decayed intelligence in antiquities, concerning the most noble and renowmed English Nation* (1605). Verstegan complained that 'divers of our English wryters have bin as laborious and serious in their discourses of the antiquities of the Britans as yf they properly appertained unto Englishmen, which in no wise they can or can do, for that their offsprings and descents are wholly different', citing abundant linguistic evidence.[17]

Only the historically ignorant, Verstegan pointed out, relied on the Brut myth and the Britons, which encouraged writers to confuse the English with the British. Verstegan traced the English from Noah through Japhet's great-grandchild Tuisco, who named Tuitshland (Deutschland). In contrast to Elizabethan Protestants who criticized the Saxons as uncouth foreigners, the English lacked no honour 'in descending from so honourable a race'. Therefore Verstegan reduced the 26-year reign of Arthur 'the famous king' to a single line, in contrast spending many detailed pages on the hagiographic story of the papal desire to convert the Anglo-Saxons, the *angli*, because they resembled *angeli*, still part of modern English mythology. Verstegan's definition of Englishness also required him to downplay Danish influences and make the Norman invasion a transient event. Henry I restored the 'English both in name and nation'.[18]

The confusion that Stapleton and Verstegan deplored in Protestant conceptions of Englishness is amply demonstrated in our major source for Tudor society, the often-quoted *Description of England* published by the Protestant clergyman William Harrison in *Holinshed's Chronicles* in 1577 and 1587. The first of Harrison's three volumes was confusingly called the *Description of Britain*, in which, for example, his chapter 'Of the General Constitution of the Bodies of the Britons' actually contrasts the bluff, uncomplicated English with the Machiavellian cunning utilized by lesser breeds such as the Italians, the Spanish and the French.[19]

---

16   Stapleton, *A Fortresse of the Faith* (Antwerp, 1565), sig. b2v, pp. 1–4.
17   Richard Verstegan, *A Restitution of Decayed Intelligence: In Antiquities. Concerning the Most Noble and Renowmed English Nation* (Antwerp, 1565), sig. +3v.
18   Ibid., sigs. +4r, B1r, B3r, R2v, X2r, Z2r-Z3r-v, Aa1r.
19   William Harrison, *The Description of Britain*, in Raphael Holinshed, *The First and Second Volumes of Chronicles* (London, 1587), Bk I, ch. 20.

It is debatable how far we can stretch Harrison's colloquial English patriotism to a national community, given that limited technology kept community identity intensely local, let alone allowing any connection with an overseas 'imagined community'.[20] Harrison's personal knowledge of his society was confined to London (where he was born), Oxford (where he was educated) and Essex (where he was a rector). He borrowed or stole the rest, largely from John Leland who *had* travelled the length and breadth of the country but whose attempts to summarize that experience in a national chorographical picture famously drove him mad.[21]

Such contradictions are often written out of our mythology of the Diaspora, but our understanding of what might loosely be called the Protestant mythology of empire needs significant revision. Recent historians of political thought have argued the importance of civil law in early modern thinking about sovereignty and empire. However, this marginalizes what contemporaries obviously considered a more popular and profoundly influential set of medieval mythologies, galvanized by the Reformation period's susceptibility to apocalyptic prophecy.[22]

Arthurian Origins and the Protestant Mythologies of Empire

The sixteenth century constructed its expectations of empire not from later justifications of imperial growth and migration but from inherited medieval ideas of apocalyptic destiny. For eight centuries Europeans had cherished prophecies of a heroic Last World Emperor. This apocalyptic prophecy originated in eighth-century Mesopotamia, where Christians struggling to come to terms with the shattering effects of the Arab invasions drew upon ancient Jewish ideas of an earthly period of prosperity under a messianic leader to construct a dazzlingly seductive prophecy, variously attributed to an obscure Bishop Methodius or to the Sibylline prophets, especially Sibylla Tiburtina.[23]

---

20 Benedict Anderson, *Imagined Communities: Reflections on the Origins and Spread of Nationalism* (London: Verso, 1983).

21 James P. Carley, 'Leland, John (*c*.1503–1552)', *Oxford Dictionary of National Biography* (Oxford: Oxford University Press, 2004); online edn, http://www.oxforddnb.com/view/article/16416 (accessed 12 January 2011).

22 Richard Tuck, *Philosophy and Government, 1572–1651* (Cambridge: Cambridge University Press, 1993); Armitage, *Ideological Origins*; Anthony Pagden, *Lords of all the World: Ideologies of Empire in Spain, Britain and France c1500–c1800* (New Haven, CT: Yale University Press, 1995).

23 Robert J. Wilkinson, *Orientalism, Aramaic, and Kabbalah in the Catholic Reformation: The First Printing of the Syriac New Testament* (Leiden and Boston, MA: Brill, 2007), pp. 102–14, 125–29; Wilkinson, *The Kabbalistic Scholars of the Antwerp Polyglot Bible* (Leiden and Boston, MA: Brill, 2007), pp. 57 n. 24, 85.

Contrary to older Christian expectations of a climactic battle between Christ and Antichrist at Armageddon, this prophecy promised a period of peace and prosperity *within* history, when the Last World Emperor would establish his throne at Jerusalem, from where he would create global harmony by propagating true religion, a prospect summed up in the phrase 'one flock, one pastor'. Rapidly taken up by the Byzantine Empire, this prophecy soon became a motif of the Holy Roman Empire, adopted by propagandists in the emperors' long struggle with the papacy. By the sixteenth century the Habsburgs increasingly monopolized this messianic role. Around 1500 the emperor Maximilian I seriously considered seeking the papacy to fulfil these family expectations, while the election of Charles V as emperor in 1519 encouraged an outpouring of treatises by European intellectuals describing his apocalyptic duty as Last World Emperor. Many expected his descendant Maximilian II to prove an imperial 'cosmopolite', a citizen of no country but the universal kingdom of Christ, a designation self-consciously adopted by numerous European intellectuals in the mid-sixteenth century 'Republic of Letters', many of them alchemists. They expected Maximilian to heal broken Christendom before ushering in lasting global peace and prosperity.[24] When Philip II appeared close to achieving global presence if not dominance for his imperial authority after 1580, the textual and iconographical outpourings drawing upon this ancient concept reached a peak.

What has this to do with the English? Rather more than has previously been acknowledged. Arthur, far from being an exclusively Tudor ancestral claim, was one of the nine worthies of Christendom adopted by the Habsburgs as part of their mythical ancestry. When Henry VIII and Charles V met in the 1520s, Arthur provided one of the central themes of the iconography around their celebrations – but as a compliment to Charles more than Henry.[25] Gerard Mercator, who might be described as geographer to the house of Habsburg, included stories of Arthur's extensive empire on his great world map of 1565. This included an account, from a text attributed to one Jacobus Cnoyen, of

---

24 Marjorie Reeves, *The Influence of Prophecy in the Later Middle Ages: A Study in Joachimism* (Oxford: Clarendon Press, 1969), ch. VI; Marie Tanner, *The Last Descendant of Aeneas: The Hapsburgs and the Mythic Image of the Emperor* (New Haven, CT: Yale University Press, 1993), pp. 119–45; John L. Phelan, *The Millennial Kingdom of the Franciscans in the New World* (Berkeley and Los Angeles: University of California Press, rev. edn, 1970), pp. 5–16; John S. Mebane, *Renaissance Magic and the Return of the Golden Age: The Occult Tradition and Marlowe, Jonson, and Shakespeare* (Lincoln, NE: University of Nebraska Press, 1989); Alexandre Y. Haran, *Le Lys et la Globe: Messianisme Dynastique et Rêve Imperial en France au XVIe et XVII Siècles* (Paris: Seyssel, Champ Vallon, 2000); Margaret C. Jacob, *Strangers Nowhere in the World: The Rise of Cosmopolitanism in Early Modern Europe* (Philadelphia, PA: University of Pennsylvania Press, 2006), ch. 1.

25 S. Anglo, *Images of Tudor Kingship* (London: Seaby, 1992), pp. 45–55; Anglo, *Spectacle, Pageantry and Early Tudor Policy* (Oxford: Oxford University Press, 1969).

Arthur's colonists penetrating as far as the North Pole. Medieval travellers' tales seemed to confirm their continuity there.[26]

Henry's willingness to concede Arthur as a Habsburg icon reflects the default setting in English foreign policy. By the 1560s, however, that was less easy to maintain, partly because Philip II's fixation on his messianic destiny encouraged him to enforce religious orthodoxy and centralized political control over the 17 diverse Netherlands provinces.[27] The disastrous result that we call the Dutch Revolt had a profound effect on English history, not only transforming English foreign policy but also English conceptions of empire. When Henry VIII claimed that 'this realm of England' is an empire, he meant at most the British Isles, if his claims to Scotland are included. Elizabeth I and some of her influential politicians, such as Lord Burghley, agreed, but others, notably those gathered around the Earl of Leicester, argued equally hard for an Elizabethan empire that had wider European and even American claims.

The first half of Elizabeth's reign was therefore a lynchpin in English history, when, having abandoned its traditional Habsburg alliance, the Elizabethan regime cast around for an alternative directing vision. Leicester and his followers tried to provide it by adopting (or, if you prefer, stealing) important elements of Habsburg imperial mythology, and then using them to construct an alternative but surprisingly similar prospect, which came to be called the 'Protestant cause', usually defined as solidarity with international Protestantism, opposition to antichristian papal tyranny and global advancement of evangelical religion.

John Dee and the English Diaspora

These elements were widely known among European and English politicians and intellectuals, but one important link between the Leicester group and the Habsburgs was the cosmopolitan intellectual John Dee. One can easily misunderstand Dee's importance, and his role has too often been restricted to that of a propagandist for an Elizabethan Atlantic 'British Empire', in a series of treatises allegedly relying on civil law theories.[28] However, he does provide a useful window into some elements of that borrowed imperial vision. They might bemuse, even baffle the modern mind, but I would contend that

---

26　E.G.R. Taylor, 'A Letter dated 1577 from Mercator to John Dee', *Imago Mundi*, 13 (1956), pp. 56–68.

27　Geoffrey Parker, *The Grand Strategy of Philip II* (New Haven, CT: Yale University Press, 1998), pp. 102–07.

28　Ken MacMillan with Jennifer Abeles (eds), *John Dee: The Limits of the British Empire* (Westport, CT, and London: Praeger, 2004); MacMillan, 'John Dee's "Brytanici imperii limites"', *Huntington Library Quarterly*, 64 (2001), pp. 151–59; MacMillan, 'Discourse on History, Geography and Law: John Dee and the Limits of the British Empire, 1576–1580', *Canadian Journal of History*, 36 (April 2001), pp. 1–25.

they connect elite intellectual imperial visions with popular expectations of a future of peace and prosperity, which for centuries to come would help to generate those English conceptions of Utopian improvement that underlay the earliest English diaspora.

Like many contemporary European intellectuals, Dee confidently expected an imminent 'restoration of all things' to their first perfection, including geographical knowledge and global empire. After witnessing Maximilian of Habsburg's coronation as King of Hungary at Bratislava in early September 1563, Dee began describing himself as a 'cosmopolite', a citizen of no country but Christ's imminent global kingdom.[29] The following January in Antwerp, that key city to both Habsburgs and Tudors, he wrote *Monas Hieroglyphica*, or the Hieroglyphic Monad, dedicated to Maximilian. Even Renaissance readers, accustomed to works of the most luxuriant eccentricity, struggled with Dee's kabbalistic inventiveness in constructing his Monad, a talisman incorporating all the planetary symbols and therefore concentrating the beneficent astrological rays of the planets. Dee believed that 'our IEOVA' had chosen him alone to receive 'this sacred art of writing', the Monad, knowledge lost since God revealed it to Adam.

Dee's *Monas* offered Maximilian 'cosmopolitical theories' to usher in this 'fourth, great, and truly metaphysical revolution' of universal empire, an idea, we might say, going the rounds at the time.[30] Dee's blatant play for patronage also employed political flattery. The Monad combined symbols representing the sun, the moon, the Cross and the astrological sign Aries, ascendant at the Creation, all monopolized by the Habsburgs and displayed at Maximilian's coronation to symbolize his inheritance of universal empire.

How Dee's ideas emerged from previous centuries of European mystical scholarship lies beyond the scope of this chapter, but here we need to understand that Dee deeply admired the twelfth-century mystic Joachim of Fiore, whom he called 'Joachim the Prophesier', and that he collected books by Joachim's many disciples. Those texts became the *locus classicus* for prophecies of spiritual triumph under a Last World Emperor.[31] Many of Joachim's medieval followers studied alchemy, which explains why Dee hid in the centre of his occult *Monas* an offer to help Maximilian achieve universal empire by creating what 'cosmopolitan' alchemists had been seeking for centuries – the philosopher's stone. Not simply the means to transmute base metals into gold, the stone to these men had miraculous powers to restore human health, perfect society, even clean up politics, and therefore with divine help usher in that final age of peace and prosperity under the Last World Emperor.

---

29 John Dee, *Monas Hieroglyphica* (Antwerp, 1564), dedication, following Guillaume Postel, *De La République des Turcs* (Paris, 1561), title page.
30 Wilkinson, *Orientalism, Aramaic and Kabbalah*, p. 97 n. 11; Wilkinson, *Kabbalistic Scholars*, p. 87.
31 Marjorie Reeves, *Joachim of Fiore and the Prophetic Future* (Stroud: Sutton, 1999); Reeves, *Influence of Prophecy*, pp. 293–392.

Mystical nonsense, we might say, as did some critics at the Elizabethan Court, who muttered that Dee's book contained dangerous conjuring in its kabbalistic figures and designs. But Dee had his defenders, including, we should note, the queen herself. Elizabeth had been brilliantly educated by leading Cambridge intellectuals. Many of them pursued the philosopher's stone, notably Sir Thomas Smith, who became her secretary. No wonder she grew up to practise alchemy herself, constructing and staffing distilling houses and collecting a library of alchemical manuscripts. She patronized men who offered riches through transmutation. Elizabeth's knowledge of 'all parts of Philosophy', including alchemy, became known throughout Europe. Alchemists dedicated books to her. Elizabeth revelled in her reputation for philosophical enquiry. She told her 1585 Parliament that 'I am supposed to have many studies, but most philosophical. I must yield this to be true that I suppose few (that be no professors) have read more.' She quickly emphasized that she observed scriptural limits to her enquiries, which suggests their occult direction.[32]

In this context Elizabeth's carefully controlled iconography suggests previously unnoticed alchemical significance in her 'Pelican' and 'Phoenix' portraits, both painted by Nicholas Hilliard about 1575.[33] Hilliard's portraits began a fashion for connecting these symbols with Elizabeth. Henceforth they featured in New Year's jewels gifted to her.[34] This sudden innovation in her iconography has never been explained, but it coincided with the period from which much evidence survives about Elizabeth's alchemical interests. The pelican symbolized the penultimate stage of making the philosopher's stone, when the potency of the red elixir was multiplied a thousandfold by reiterated dissolution and coagulation, using a vessel resembling a pelican piercing its own breast.[35] The red phoenix, a Renaissance emblem of the uniqueness and self-renewal of hereditary monarchy, also represented the red powder or elixir, the last of the four colour changes during the Great Work to create the philosopher's stone. It thus represented the stone itself.[36] In 1574 several courtiers presented Elizabeth with rich jewels featuring a

---

32 Parry, *The Arch Conjuror*, pp. 71–80; T.E. Hartley, *Proceedings in the Parliaments of Elizabeth I*, 3 vols (Leicester: Leicester University Press, 1981), II, p. 32.

33 Roy Strong, *Gloriana, the Portraits of Queen Elizabeth I* (London: Thames and Hudson, 1987), pp. 79–81.

34 John Nichols, *The Progresses and Public Processions of Queen Elizabeth*, 3 vols (London: Nichols, 1823), I, p. 324.

35 Lyndy Abraham, *A Dictionary of Alchemical Imagery* (Cambridge: Cambridge University Press, 2001), pp. 133–34, 143–44.

36 Strong, *Gloriana*, p. 82; Ernst Kantorowicz, *The King's Two Bodies: A Study in Mediaeval Political Theology* (Princeton, NJ: Princeton University Press, 1997), pp. 385–401, 413–15, 510; BLO MS Ashmole 1394, p. 75: 'De Lapide Philosophico seu de Phenice'.

phoenix.[37] By 1577 alchemists closely associated with Dee believed Elizabeth would shortly possess the stone.[38] William Cecil, Lord Burghley, believed even more fervently in the philosopher's stone. The beliefs of these leading figures set the tone for a Court that in the 1570s, that decisive decade for Elizabethan imperial ambitions, became obsessed with the prospects of alchemical transformation on both the mundane and cosmic levels.

This context makes Dee's *imperial writings* shed new light on his advisory role in the sometimes furious struggles between Elizabeth and her councillors over policy towards the domestic and international crisis caused by the Dutch Revolt, which would determine English history for centuries to come.

Dee and the Empire in America

Historians usually connect Dee with American discovery and colonization, describing his writings as the first statement of English Protestant imperialism. However, there was nothing very 'Protestant' about Dee or his 'British Empire'. Influential contemporaries such as Leicester and his group were less interested in whether Dee made a coherent case for Elizabeth's rights in America than whether he could persuade her to pursue Arthur's lost British Empire in Europe as part of a Protestant foreign policy towards the Netherlands. Putting Dee's writings into their proper historical context also reconnects them with the occult philosophy central to Dee's thinking. That context also removes erroneous attempts to connect Dee's 'imperial' writings with his role in the planning and direction of Martin Frobisher's voyages in 1576–78.[39] Dee certainly understood civil law theories of empire, but neither the queen nor her councillors respected theoretical limits when events suddenly required flexibility in making actual policy.

We can observe Dee's mind working through these issues in his copy of Ferdinand Columbus's *History of the Life and Deeds of the Admiral Christopher Columbus* (1571). Dee interacted with the text, busily jotting notes

---

37 Nichols, *Progresses*, I, p. 379; T.H. White, *The Bestiary: A Book of Beasts* (New York: Jonathan Cape, 1960), pp. 182–84; Edward Topsell, *The Elizabethan Zoo* (Boston: Nonpareil, 1979), pp. 108–11.

38 See below, pp. 30–31, and Abraham, *Alchemical Imagery*, p. 152.

39 Robert C.D. Baldwin, 'The Testing of a New Academic Trinity for the Northern Passages: The Rationale and Experience behind English Investment in the Voyages of Frobisher, Jackman, Davis and Waymouth 1576–1605', in Anna Agnarsdottir (ed.), *Voyages and Exploration in the North Atlantic from the Middle Ages to the XVIIth Century: Papers Presented at the 19ᵗʰ International Congress of Historical Sciences Oslo 2000* (Reykjavik: Institute of History, University of Iceland, 2000), pp. 61–98; W. Sherman, 'John Dee's Role in Martin Frobisher's Northwest Enterprise', in Thomas H.B. Symons (ed.), *Meta Incognita: A Discourse of Discovery. Martin Frobisher's Arctic Expeditions*, 2 vols (Hull, Quebec: Canadian Museum of Civilization, 1999), I, pp. 283–98.

and comments in the margin,[40] as he read it alongside Giovanni Battista Ramusio's great collection of *Navigations and Voyages*, during Martin Frobisher's second and third voyages to the North-West Passage in 1577–78.[41] Dee's marginalia reveal that he sought in Ramusio 'the customs of acquiring dominion'.[42] Dee summarized these as the stages of '1. Discovery 2. Conquest 3. Quiet possession'.[43] This supported his other marginalia in Ramusio about the North-West Passage.[44] He heavily marked reports that the Indians near the North-West Passage cultivated fertile soils and had a European level of civilization. Dee found most exciting reports of 'White men arrayed with cloth as in France'. These confirmed his belief, probably acquired from his studies with Mercator in the 1540s, that remnant Arthurian colonies still controlled the North-West Passage, confirming Elizabeth's inherited rights over that gateway to the fabulous East. The picture may be irresistibly risible to the modern mind: every morning the colonists would go down to the dock to await the arrival of ships from Camelot. But in early 1578 Dee used these pages in a work on the 'Limits of the British Empire' commissioned by Elizabeth at Leicester's prompting.[45]

Tudor concepts of 'empire' did not depend solely on Dee's writings. Elizabeth believed her Atlantic sovereignty rested on her Crown's inherent prerogative. Philip and Mary had asserted as much in Letters Patent of 1555, granting the Muscovy Company the power to 'subdue, possess and occupy' and 'get the Dominion' over all lands 'of infidelity'. Parliament confirmed these privileges in a 1566 Act. Richard Hakluyt printed both texts in his *Principal Navigations* (1589). Contemporaries believed long before Dee wrote that the Crown's imperial power and the authority of statute law controlled overseas trade and new-found lands. Dee knew this through his close connections with the Muscovy Company. When he petitioned in 1583 to monopolize the

---

40   *Historie Del S.D. Fernando Colombo; Nelle quali s'ha particolare, et vera relatione della vita, et de' fatti dell'Ammiraglio D. CHRISTOPHORO COLOMBO, suo padre* (Venetia, 1571), now British Library shelf-mark 615.d.7; W. Sherman, 'John Dee's Columbian Encounter', in Stephen Clucas (ed.), *John Dee, Interdisciplinary Studies* (Dordrecht: Springer, 2006), pp. 131–40.

41   Giovanni Battista Ramusio, *Navigationi et Viaggi* (Venice, 1563–65), Trinity College Dublin shelf-mark DD.dd.40, 41, vol. 2, sig. D8v, and vol. 3, fo. 323v; references to the BL 615.d.7 copy of *Historie Del S.D. Fernando Colombo* in vol. 3, fos. 2r, 6r–v, 80r, 82v, 83r; on Ramusio, see W. Sherman, 'Bringing the World to England; The Politics of Translation in the Age of Hakluyt', *Transactions of the Royal Historical Society*, 6th series, 14 (2004), pp. 199–207.

42   *Historie Del S.D. Fernando Colombo*, vol. 3, fo. 7r.

43   Ibid., fo. 3, fos. 169v–170v 82r, 183r–v, 280v, 338r, 341r, 357r, 359r, 426v; on Madoc, fos. 7r–v, 78r, 82r–83v, 398v; 39v, 169r–v, 204v; 41v, 114v; Montezuma's 'legend' of Madoc 235r, 238v.

44   Ibid., vol. 1, fos. 374r–375r.

45   Ibid., vol. 3, fos. 417r–v, 441v, 445v, 448v, 449v–450r, 451v; MacMillan and Abeles, *Limits of the British Empire*, p. 38.

North-West Passage, under the Muscovy Company's patent, he expected to make laws in that region that observed 'the religion and laws of this realm'.[46]

Nor was Dee's advice limited by modern conceptions of political theory. When a supernova appeared in the constellation Cassiopeia in 1572, Dee told Edward Dyer that it might 'signify the finding of some great Treasure or the philosophers stone', a prediction he felt to be confirmed by Frobisher's apparent discovery of gold in 1576.[47] We need to remember such occult connections when assessing Dee's, and indeed Elizabethan, ideas about empire.

Historians believe that Dee wrote exclusively about American empire because of his involvement in planning the Frobisher voyages. Yet this is another myth, an optical illusion in the confused historical record. The financial backer of Frobisher's first voyage, the Muscovy merchant Michael Lok, rebuffed Dee's brazen attempt to take over the project when Dee heard of it sixteen days before Frobisher first sailed in early June 1576. Lok had spent twenty-five years and enormous sums of money collecting everything that Christendom knew about the North-West Passage. He was not about to let Dee share the glory. Like Dee, Lok expected Frobisher to encounter an advanced civilization in the North-West Passage. He used the same travellers' tales to prove that 'the new found lands' were 'full of people and full of such commodities and merchandize' as the Scandinavian countries.[48] Lok's credit ran out during preparations for Frobisher's second voyage, which only went ahead after the Customs official and money-lender Richard Young began counter-signing Lok's bills of exchange. As part of the deal Lok had to pay for Dee's share in the 'Company of Cathay' in November 1576, a share that has misled historians, but which Dee only received because he was Young's brother-in-law. Only after that did Dee become a prominent figure in running the Frobisher voyages.

After Frobisher returned from his first voyage in October 1576 boasting about his route to China, Burghley's draft charter gave the 'Company of Cathay' monopoly over that trade route, but notably failed to mention occupying territories. At that stage Dee's belief in an Arthurian America was irrelevant to Burghley's policy.[49] However, in early 1577 claims by alchemists to have found gold in a stone brought back by Frobisher transformed the government's agenda. Burghley's March 1577 instructions for Frobisher's second voyage now required him to fortify places for 'possessing of the Country' and its presumed

46   R. Hakluyt, *The Principall Navigation Voiages and Discoveries of the English Nation* (London, 1589), pp. 304–09, 394–97; The National Archives, SP 15/28 PartI/54.

47   J. Firmicus, *Ad Mavortium Lollianum Astronomicon lib.VIII per N. Prucknerum ... ab innumeris mendis vindicati* (Basle, 1533), University College London shelf-mark Ogden A.9, in Manilius, *Astronomica 5* (Julian Roberts and A.G. Watson, *John Dee's Library Catalogue* [London: The Bibliographical Society, 1990] #251).

48   BL MS Cotton Otho E VIII, fo. 47v.

49   TNA, SP 12/110/21; BL MS Add. 59681, p. 16, printed in MacMillan and Abeles, *Limits of the British Empire*, p. 45.

gold mines.[50] The Council claimed a territorial empire in America without Dee's imperial writings. They dealt only tangentially with Arthur's American empire. Rather ominously for later enforced migration, the Privy Council sent with the third Frobisher voyage of 1578 a hundred condemned criminals to over-winter on Baffin Island, so as to establish English possession. This first, involuntary English American diaspora was to shelter in prefabricated houses, which fortunately for them went down with one of the ships.

The fact that Dee's increasing importance in the Frobisher enterprise reflected Young's financial clout underlines that Dee's 'imperial' writings were not simply concerned with American exploration. The real purpose of Dee's imperial writings – applying his magic to advance the 'Protestant cause' during the central crisis of Elizabeth's reign, the Netherlands Revolt – opens new vistas into Elizabethan ideas of empire.

Broadly speaking, Dee's writings show increasing interest in Arthur's European conquests. Their apparent concern with American empire conceals Dee's deeper interest in recovering Britain's empire in mainland Europe, in the unusual circumstances of the late 1570s. Rather than his 'magus' reputation marginalizing Dee from the Elizabethan Court, his 'philosophical' knowledge and practices helped to shape his imperial vision. In the right circumstances they made him more useful to politicians seeking to advance the 'Protestant cause'.[51]

Dee and the Empire in Europe

In return for his occult advice Dee required free access throughout Elizabeth's dominions under her 'protection absolute' to perform mysterious future services for the 'British Empire'. These would not apply human policy but 'the Almighty his will and direction'. Dee's advice directed by God would recover Elizabeth's northern and western British Empire and, more intriguingly, the 'homage and arrearages' of 'your Easterly and Southerly disdainful Vassals and Tributaries', because Dee's advice also pertained to areas '*besides* that portion of the world', by which he meant America.[52]

These mysterious allusions point to the hidden meanings of Dee's imperial writings, because, among the writers verifying Arthur's empire, Dee placed first Johannes Trithemius's book *On the Seven Planetary Intelligences*,[53] central

---

50 TNA, SP 12/113/12 items 10 and 11.
51 W.H. Sherman, *John Dee; The Politics of Reading and Writing in the English Renaissance* (Amherst, MA: University of Massachusetts Press, 1995), pp. 12–19, 148–200, attacks 'The myth of the magus' and minimizes the impact of Dee's occult beliefs on his imperial writings.
52 BL MS Add. 59681, pp. 72–74, in MacMillan and Abeles, *Limits of the British Empire*, pp. 97–100 (my emphasis).
53 BL MS Add. 59681, p. 41, in MacMillan and Abeles, *Limits of the British Empire*, p. 67.

to proving Arthur's empire over 30 kingdoms.[54] Dee's respect for Trithemius suggests why he felt 'strangely stirred up' by the Trinity to write about the magical restoration of the British Empire. Trithemius's book did not discuss Arthurian historical narrative or address questions of empire. It described how the angelic spirits governing the seven planets controlled history. Each angel ruled successive periods of 354 years and four months, giving each epoch distinctive characteristics, including Arthur's empire. The cataclysmic political and religious changes that marked each new period formed steps towards the Second Coming of Christ, the Eschaton.

Dee believed that the 1572 supernova, which he measured within the sphere of Venus, increased that planetary angel's influence. God was signalling through the new star, he told Edward Dyer, his frequent knowledge-broker to Court, that a decaying world would be restored by angelic magic and the discovery of the philosopher's stone.[55] Therefore he dated *Memorials* to the year of the world 5540, 'The Fifth Year, of the Star Sent from Heaven and Returning Directly There'.[56]

Like his dedication of his *Monas* to Maximilian II, Dee's belief in Arthur's empire shows that, like his ecumenical generation of European intellectuals, he believed in the centuries-old vision of a reformed world, unified politically and religiously under a Last Reforming Emperor. Dee saw Arthur as part of his search 'for the pure verity, understanding, and recovering of divers secret, ancient, and weighty matters' of universal knowledge. His first Arthurian studies at Louvain with Gerard Mercator and Gemma Frisius, sometime cosmographer to Charles V, introduced him to Habsburg court culture, which celebrated Arthur as the model for a Habsburg *Endzeitskaiser*.[57]

Elizabeth as Last World Empress

The watershed change in Elizabethan policy towards an anti-Habsburg position by the 1570s persuaded devotees of the 'Protestant cause' that Elizabeth should become a Protestant Last World Emperor. According to Edward Topsell, the 'learneder sort' applied these ancient prophecies of Methodius and the Sibyls to her, while as we have seen 'the simple and vulgar sort imagine that there is no Scripture like to Merlins prophesie'. We should note how the latter encouraged popular expectation of a golden future, but

54 BL MS Cotton Vitellius C.VII, fo. 262r.
55 Dee's notes in J. Trithemius, *De septem secundeis* (Frankfurt, 1545), Cambridge University Library, shelf-mark Dd*.4.5.11 (E); Roberts and Watson, *Catalogue*, # 678, at p. 92.
56 BLO MS Ashmole 1789, fo. 58v; John Dee, *General and rare Memorials pertaining unto the arte of navigation* (London, 1577), sig. e*4v.
57 BL MS Add. 59681, pp. 57–58, in MacMillan and Abeles, *Limits of the British Empire*, pp. 81–83; Anglo, *Images of Tudor Kingship*, pp. 45–55.

the former had more immediate impact on conceptions of empire. After the collapse of Spanish control in the Netherlands in late 1575, Leicester and his followers encouraged Elizabeth to accept the proffered sovereignty of Holland and Zealand.[58] One enthusiast believed she would thus become 'sovereign of the sea', able to resolve religious differences 'in all Christendom'.[59]

Leicester's followers argued in the House of Commons in early 1576 to petition Elizabeth to accept Dutch sovereignty.[60] That year even Elizabeth imagined herself bringing peace to the whole of Christendom.[61] Dee's associate in magical learning, James Sandford, another Leicester client, months later gave Elizabeth the cosmic apocalyptic role previously reserved for the Habsburgs. Plagiarizing a Habsburg astrologer's predictions that a conjunction of Jupiter and Saturn in 1583 would bring abrupt imperial changes, Sandford added for good measure the widespread expectation that either the world would end in 1588, or 'at least governments of kingdoms shall be turned upside down'. Elizabeth, in whom 'there must needs be some diviner thing [...] than in the Kings and Queens of other countries', would lead humanity in the End Times.[62]

Sandford dedicated his translation of Giacopo Brocardo's *The Revelation of St John Reveled* to Leicester. Following Joachim of Fiore, this foresaw Christ's religion dominating 'the whole world. No other religion, no other law, and rule to hear then that of the Gospel.'[63] Soon the belief that Elizabeth would usher in world peace permeated the excitable underworld of popular prophecy. Manuscripts circulated declaring that 'Elizabeth now Queen of England is ordained of God to be Queen of Jerusalem'.[64] Dee and others predicted the restoration of the Kingdom of Israel.

In this expectant atmosphere Dee printed his *General and Rare Memorials* in September 1577, urging Elizabeth to recover Arthur's vast European empire, to the 'south, and east', at a time when, Dee later recalled, 'great hope was conceived (of some no simple politicians) [meaning Leicester and his followers], that her Majesty might, then, have become the Chief Commander,

---

58 Topsell, *Times Lamentation*, p. 63; Topsell, *Certein Letters wherin is set forth a Discourse of the Peace that was attempted and sought to have bin put in effecte by the Lords and States of Holland and Zelande in the year of oure Lorde 1574* (London, 1576).

59 BL MS Harley 285, fos. 32r–36v, at fo. 36r, John Hastings to Burghley, Brussels, 2 December 1575.

60 Joseph M. Kervyn De Lettenhove, *Relations Politiques des Pays-Bas et de L'Angleterre sous la Regne de Philippe II*, 11 vols (Brussels: s.n., 1882–1900), VIII, p. 249; *Calendar of State Papers Spanish*, II, pp. 522–24.

61 Kervyn De Lettenhove, *Relations Politiques*, VIII, pp. 213, 222–23.

62 James Sandford, 'Epistle Dedicatorie', in *Houres of Recreation, or Afterdinners, Which may aptly be called, The Garden of Pleasure* (London, 1576), sigs. A5v–A6r.

63 Jacopo Brocardo, *The Reuelation of S. Ihon reueled* (London, 1582), fo. 32v.

64 Richard Bancroft, *A Sermon Preached at Paules Crosse the 9 of Februarie, being the first Sunday in the Parleament, Anno 1588 [i.e. 1589]* (London, 1589), sigs. B2r, B3r–v, B4v.

and in manner Imperial Governor of all Christian kings, princes, and states'.[65] Dee's assertion of Elizabeth's Arthurian claims hence contributed to the Elizabethans stealing an ancient imperial mythology from the Habsburgs.[66]

There were other parallels to the Habsburgs that Dee could only reveal secretly 'in convenient Time and Place' to Privy Councillors or Elizabeth.[67] Little time remained, felt Dee, self-consciously writing as 'Cosmopolites', citizen of the 'Mystical City Universal'. For while echoing the apocalyptic tone of *Monas Hieroglyphica*, *Memorials* also offered Elizabeth the philosopher's stone that Dee had offered to Maximilian. This would enable Elizabeth to become the Reforming Empress of the Last Days. Therefore he proposed that revenue raised for a navy to control the North Sea should also support an alchemical research institute. This proposal fuelled public expectations that Elizabeth would acquire the philosopher's stone in 1577.[68]

Conclusion

Why should the mythology of the second English Diaspora, allowing the Catholics the privilege of creating the first, matter to historians of the later Diaspora? What on earth is the connection between apocalyptic fantasies of the Last World Empire, the 'one flock, under one pastor', the philosopher's stone and the later English mass-migrations? Well, perhaps historians interested in previous motivations for empire should pay attention to the apocalyptic prophetic tradition, because it contributes to a fuller understanding of the history of empire and migration.

The nineteenth-century British Empire was famously said to be the empire on which the sun never set. However, the first of these was the empire of Philip II, after he took the Portuguese throne and its enormous eastern possessions in 1580. Philip's propagandists seized upon the idea of their sovereign as the Last World Emperor, the one pastor who would rule the global flock. Philip, an alchemist and patron of alchemists, shared this messianic vision, as Geoffrey Parker has ably demonstrated.[69] It explains why he ruined Spain

---

65 BL MS Harley 249, fo.95v; Glyn Parry, 'John Dee and the Elizabethan "British Empire" in its European Context', *Historical Journal*, 49.3 (2006), pp. 643–75.

66 John Dee, 'Compendious Rehearsal', Appendix in Thomas Hearne (ed.), *Johannis, confratris & monachi Glastoniensis, chronica sive historia de rebus Glastoniensibus*, 2 vols (Oxford: Sheldonian Theatre, 1726), p. 527; BL MS Add. 59681, pp. 72–74, in MacMillan and Abeles, *Limits of the British Empire*, pp. 97–100; Bart van Es, *Spenser's Forms of History* (Oxford: Oxford University Press, 2002), pp. 141–42, 147; Pagden, *Lords of all the World*, pp. 29–40.

67 BLO MS Ashmole 1789, fo. 102v; Dee, *Memorials*, p. 60.

68 See BLO MS Ashmole 57, Dee's 1577 transcription of Thomas Norton's 'Ordinall of Alchemy'; C. Nicholl, *The Chemical Theatre* (London: Routledge, 1980), pp. 18, 245 n. 88.

69 Parker, *The Grand Strategy of Philip II*, pp. 102–07; Parker, *Philip II* (Boston and Toronto: Little, Brown, 1978), p. 47

in his Netherlands disaster. It therefore helps to explain the profound shift in English foreign policy towards an anti-Habsburg setting from the 1560s, both tactically in the Netherlands and strategically across the globe. At a very fundamental level the shift in English focus towards a global perspective responded to Philip's belief in his messianic destiny. At yet another level the pursuit of future happiness in idealized overseas territories by English migrants looks like a secularized version of the apocalyptic expectation of a time of peace and plenty under the Last World Emperor.

Those expectations, which flourished in the Civil War and Interregnum, died hard during the seventeenth century. It took a concerted conservative cultural counter-revolution, whose roots can be traced to the 1580s, to marginalize these beliefs from elite political society after the restoration of Charles II, when they were perceived as a political threat.[70] The extent to which we discount the influence of prophetic ideas among the English people in later centuries reflects the success of the restored establishment in marginalizing the prophetic impulse and the magical view of the world that supported it. Yet it was never entirely suppressed. Despite the ruthless use of censorship, legal persecution and social deprecation against belief in astrology, alchemy and a prophetic future of prosperity and contentment, those ideas survived in popular Protestantism as the vision of the New Jerusalem, an expected cathartic change from old ways of living and ruling. Its most obvious manifestation is in the most successful of the English diasporas. Twenty-first-century intellectuals might find American evangelical apocalyptic thought alien, but it has real effects on American foreign policy, especially in its apocalyptic expectations about the future of Israel, which John Dee would have recognized. Perhaps we should reconsider the role of the English Diaspora in smuggling apocalyptic thought from the seventeenth century into the modern world.

---

70 Patrick Curry, *Prophecy and Power: Astrology in Early Modern England* (Princeton, NJ: Princeton University Press, 1989).

Chapter 2

The English Seventeenth Century in Colonial America: The Cultural Diaspora of English Republican Ideas

David Walker

Eighteenth-century American republicanism was borne across the Atlantic from more than one European political culture. The Dutch emigrant population in New York and Pennsylvania and the French Huguenot population in South Carolina contributed significantly to the rich array of beliefs that comprised American republican thought. Indeed, the influence of such traditions makes it more appropriate to talk of plural republicanisms than of a singular political discourse. Given our concern in this volume with the English Diaspora, however, the argument that follows has two foci. In the first instance, a historiographical survey is presented demonstrating the influence of English republican writing on the political thought of colonial America from the later seventeenth century. In the second we analyse the extent to which the original settlers in New England took with them a nascent republicanism derived from their religious beliefs. The English Puritanism exported to America was shaped by a distinctively English politics, a politics that provided a fertile field from which English republicanism of the later colonial period would grow. From 1629 in particular, cultural and political discourse in colonial New England, where English settlers predominated, was shaped decisively by its presence.[1] From the early 1600s, New England, as we shall see, provided a rich and sympathetic context in which republican ideas were received in the eighteenth century. The discussion demonstrates the extent to which the cultural diaspora of English republican ideas was embedded in the writing and actions of English immigrants to Massachusetts from the outset. Before engaging with the force of English Puritanism

---

1 See David Hackett Fischer, *Albion's Seed: Four British Folkways in America* (Oxford: Oxford University Press, 1989), pp. 13–205.

directly through the selected works of, among others, John Winthrop and John Cotton, the chapter examines discursively the arguments and debates surrounding the impact on, and extent to which, the 'classics' of English republican literature were accepted and embraced during the colonial and revolutionary periods.

Colonial America and the Historiography of English Republican Ideas

English republican writings from the seventeenth century have played a dynamic role in the historiography of colonial America. James Harrington's *Oceana* (1656), Algernon Sidney's *Discourses Concerning Government* (1698), John Milton's prose composed in 1649–60 and *Cato's Letters* (1720–24) – to name the most significant works – and the transformation of these political ideas into a Whig canon in the eighteenth century, have had a strong presence in traditional readings of this subject. Sidney, for one, was much admired by Thomas Jefferson and John Adams, two of the American Republic's founding fathers, and Massachusetts owes its state motto to an inscription written by Sidney in the visitors' book at the University of Copenhagen: *Manus, haec inimical tyrannis / Einse petit placidam libertate quitem* (This hand, enemy to tyrants, / By the sword seeks calm peacefulness with liberty).[2] In both Europe and America Sidney's works enjoyed an immense reputation. In accounting for the literature of protest generated in America by the Stamp Act of 1765, Benjamin Franklin believed that the motivation for denial of the Act by the people originated in 'a strong sense of liberty, a public spirit that despises all selfish private considerations, and thence a determination to risque everything rather than submit voluntarily to what they deem an unconstitutional exertion of power'. To support his assertions Franklin drew on what he saw as a great tradition of English political thinkers on liberty. In his '"F. B". Second Reply to Tom Hint', Franklin's remarks on liberty referred for precedent to 'your *Seldens*, your *Lockes*, and your *Sidneys*'. As Alan Craig Houston has informed us, in the 'decades of political and intellectual turmoil surrounding the Revolution' these authors 'were repeatedly turned to for example, inspiration, and instruction'.[3]

While a chapter such as this, in a volume such as the present one, seeks to promulgate the notion of cultural continuums between England and her colonies, we must beware of imagining that English republicanism was a

---

2   Algernon Sidney, *Discourses Concerning Government*, ed. Thomas G. West (Indianapolis, IA: Liberty Fund, 1996), p. xvi. For a broader consideration of Sidney's impact on America and its politics, see Alan Craig Houston, *Algernon Sidney and the Republican Heritage in England and America* (Princeton, NJ: Princeton University Press, 1991), ch. 2.
3   Citation and quote in Houston, *Algernon Sidney*, p. 224.

singular discourse. Although the aristocratic and anticlerical republicanism of writers and thinkers such as Algernon Sidney and Robert Molesworth, for instance, appealed to the American Whigs, and party elites, of the later eighteenth century, they would find a less ready and receptive audience in the men of the Revolution that were inspired by Thomas Paine's *Common Sense* (1776). Thus, while we seek for diasporic connections, we should not be surprised to learn that Americans were almost as varied in class, creed and politics as were their fellow and former countrymen in England. Equally, we can also argue that such political or intellectual differences did not prevent them all coming under one umbrella as a single people who were, together but in different ways, shaped by English texts of a variety of hues and periods.

It follows from this that there was rather more to republican political thought on either side of the Atlantic than the concern to preserve and further empower an agrarian oligarchy. In the 'Black Times' of 1776, when Washington's army was retreating through New Jersey en route to Pennsylvania, we get an intriguing snapshot of diverse republican thought and the uses to which it could be put. Captain Alexander Graydon revealed in his *Memoirs* that a friendship existed between General Washington and Thomas Paine. The great English radical and author of *Common Sense* was a member of the revolutionary army as it made its retreat. Although they were fighting in a common cause, says Graydon, Paine was incorrect in his belief that Washington shared his politics. Paine believed in 'reforming, republicanizing and democratizing the world, than which nothing was more foreign to the views of the General, or those of the others who took a lead'.[4] As the biological product of Virginia landowning stock, and as an intellectual product of the Enlightenment, Washington held to 'a philosophy of moral striving though virtuous action and right conduct, by powerful men who believed that their duty was to lead others in a changing world'.[5] In this respect, and in many others, Washington was closer to the classical republicanism mediated through the early modern Atlantic republic of letters than he was to the democratic equivalent espoused by radicals such as the future author of *The Rights of Man* (1790).

For some time now scholars have noted persistent transatlantic interconnections with communities of Americans sharing intellectual roots with communities of Englishmen on the other side of the Atlantic. The works of Zera Fink, Gordon S. Wood, Bernard Bailyn, John Pocock and Caroline Robbins – in themselves classics in their field – have drawn our attention to the powerful connection between the political literature of the English seventeenth century and America's own republican moment a century later.[6] Bailyn

---

4   Alexander Graydon, *Memoirs of His Own Time, with Reminiscences of the Men and Events of the Revolution*, cited in David Hackett Fischer, *Washington's Crossing* (Oxford: Oxford University Press, 2004), p. 139.

5   Hackett Fischer, *Washington's Crossing*, p. 13.

6   See Zera Fink, *The Classical Republicans* (Evanston, IL: Northwestern University Press, 1945); Caroline Robbins, *The Eighteenth-Century Commonwealth Man: Studies in the*

and Wood drew substantially on the literature of English republican thought from the mid-to-later seventeenth century and its adaptation in England from the Glorious Revolution in 1688. Significant editions by John Toland of Harrington, Milton and Sidney in the late 1690s did much to revive interest in the great republican writers of the 1650s and 1680s. Toland's recovery of mid-century political writing found a ready audience in the Whig political establishment and acted as a stimulus to republican writing in England in the early eighteenth century. Scholarly editions of the works of Harrington, Sidney and Milton were readily available to Americans and added considerably to the dissemination of English republican ideas in colonial America. Toland, says Justin Champion, was a colossus of the English intelligentsia in his day: 'his pen had been at the command of government ministers and European princes', and 'he had written for German queens, Savoyard princes and, Irish peers and English earls'.[7] Toland provided an invaluable service to the development of political ideas in his time, making available to a European and American audience works that would have been more difficult to obtain. He was at his most active in the years between the Glorious Revolution in 1688–89 and the ascendancy of Walpole in 1720, years analogous with the return of the puritan ascendancy in New England led by Cotton Mather.[8]

The work of Bailyn and Wood was further developed in the mid-1970s by J.G.A. Pocock, who connected the civic humanism of the great sixteenth-century Italian humanists – Francesco Guicciardini, and more notably Niccolo Machiavelli – to the English republican writings of Harrington, Neville and Sidney. Pocock developed the argument and influence of civic humanism in early modern Europe and applied it to the Atlantic world in the century following the British Civil Wars and Glorious Revolution. For Pocock, the American Revolution and Constitution were the culmination of a range of ideas originating in the old countries. Accordingly, the Declaration of Independence and the Constitution of 1783 'in some sense form the last act of the civic Renaissance and the ideas of the civic humanist tradition – the blend of Aristotelian and Machiavellian [...] provide an important key to the paradoxes of modern tensions between individual self-awareness on the

---

Transmission, Development, and Circumstance of Liberal Thought from the Restoration of Charles II until the War with the Thirteen Colonies (Indianapolis, IA: Liberty Fund, 2004 [1959]); Bernard Bailyn, *The Ideological Origins of the American Revolution* (Cambridge, MA: Harvard University Press, 2nd edn, 1992 [1967]); Gordon S. Wood, *The Creation of the American Republic, 1776–1787* (Chapel Hill, NC: University of North Carolina Press, 2nd edn, 1998 [1969]).

7 Justin Champion, *Republican Learning: John Toland and the Crisis in Christian Culture, 1696–1722* (Manchester: Manchester University Press, 2003), pp. 1–4.

8 Richard Middleton, *Colonial America: A History, 1585–1776* (Oxford: Blackwell, 1996), p. 177; Philip S. Haffenden, *New England in the English Nation, 1689–1713* (Oxford: Oxford University Press, 1974), pp. 1–38; David S. Lovejoy, *The Glorious Revolution in America* (Hanover, NH: University Press of New England, 1972; Wesleyan Edition, 1987), pp. 122–59.

one hand and consciousness of society, property, and history on the other'.[9]
More recent work by Paul Rahe, Eric Foner, Jonathan Israel and Joyce O.
Appleby has further complicated our view of colonial American republicanism by mapping its relationship with liberalism and the political thought of
John Locke.[10] Although they are considered separately now, as Eric Foner
has argued, 'in the eighteenth century [...] these languages overlapped and
often reinforced one another'. Foner goes on to state that it was the 'pervasive
influence of Protestant morality [...] [that] tempered what later would come to
be seen as liberalism'. Jonathan Clark, on the other hand, sees religion as being
the central factor in explaining the Revolution. Insofar as the word 'liberty'
was understood in colonial America, it rested between the personal liberty,
associated with liberalism, and the 'public liberty of the republican tradition'.[11]
Such a sentiment was recognized by Thomas Jefferson in the foundation
documents for the University of Virginia. Jefferson believed that Locke and
Sidney should be read alongside one another. In the minutes for the Board of
Visitors for the University of Virginia, 4 March 1825, writes Vickie B. Sullivan,
the 'Board enjoined its scholars to imbibe the prescribed dose of American
liberty directly from its sources in the thought of these two Englishmen'.[12]

The origins of, and connections between, English and American republicanism have thus rightly become a significant field. At the opening of his
chapter on sources and traditions in *The Ideological Origins*, Bailyn has as
his epigraph a citation from the last will and testament of Josiah Quincy, Jr,
1774, bequeathing to his son, 'when he shall arrive to the age of fifteen years,
Algernon Sidney's works, – John Locke's works, – Gordon's *Tacitus*, – and

---

9 J.G.A. Pocock, *The Machiavellian Moment: Florentine Political Thought and the Atlantic Republican Tradition* (Princeton, NJ: Princeton University Press, 1975), p. 462.

10 Eric Foner, *The Story of American Freedom* (New York: Norton, 1998), pp. 8–9; Paul A. Rahe (ed.), *Machiavelli's Liberal Republican Legacy* (Cambridge: Cambridge University Press, 2006); Jonathan Israel, *Radical Enlightenment: Philosophy and the Making of Modernity, 1650–1750* (Oxford: Oxford University Press, 2001); Israel, *Enlightenment Contested: Philosophy, Modernity, and the Emancipation of Man 1670–1752* (Oxford: Oxford University Press, 2006); Joyce O. Appleby, *Liberalism and Republicanism in the Historical Imagination* (Cambridge, MA: Harvard University Press, 1992).

11 Foner, *The Story of American Freedom*, pp. 8–9; J.C.D. Clark, *The Language of Liberty, 1660–1832: Political Discourse and Social Dynamics in the Anglo-American World* (Cambridge: Cambridge University Press, 1994). For a recent essay asserting the strength of the successes enjoyed by the Church of England in New England in the seventeenth and eighteenth centuries, see Jeremy Gregory, 'Refashioning Puritan New England: The Church of England in British North America, c. 1680–1770', *Transactions of the Royal Historical Society*, 6th series, 20 (2010), pp. 85–112.

12 Vickie B. Sullivan, 'Muted and Manifest English Machiavellianism: The Reconciliation of Machiavellian Republicanism with Liberalism in Sidney's *Discourses Concerning Government* and Trenchard and Gordon's *Cato's Letters*', in Rahe (ed.), *Machiavelli's Liberal Republican Legacy*, pp. 58–86 (p. 58). See also, in the same volume, Margaret Michelle Barnes Smith, 'The Philosophy of Liberty: Locke's Machiavellian Teaching', pp. 36–57.

Cato's Letters. May the spirit of liberty rest upon him!'[13] Thomas Gordon's
Tacitus is an important eighteenth-century edition of the classical world's most
trenchantly critical historian of tyranny by one of the century's most acute
analysts of contemporary politics.[14] Written by John Trenchard and Thomas
Gordon, *Cato's Letters* (1720–24) were published in the *London Journal* under
the name of the Roman stoic famous for his stern and virtuous demeanour
and his refusal to bend the knee to tyranny. Initiated as a response to the
financial scandal of the South Sea Bubble, the *Letters* proceed to criticize the
venality of public life in politics, trade and commerce in the early eighteenth
century. Along with the same authors' *The Independent Whig*, a more intem-
perate publication with a distinctly anticlerical content published in two parts
from December 1719 and January 1720, these works were widely distributed
and read in colonial America. Indeed, *Cato's Letters* and Locke's *Two Treatises
on Government* were found with great 'frequency in colonial libraries'. They
also appeared from 1722 in the Philadelphia publication, the *American Weekly
Mercury*, and 'in newspapers in New York, Boston, and South Carolina'.[15]
Cato's Letters were unashamedly republican: they developed an unmistak-
ably 'Machiavellian and neo-Harringtonian critique of corruption and of the
republic which is its opposite'.[16] Sullivan, on the other hand, sees 'Cato as an
important Machiavellian', not because of his neo-Harringtonianism, but for
his compatibility 'with the peaceful pursuits of a Lockean'.[17] The sentiments
espoused by Trenchard and Gordon in *Cato's Letters* – 'that nothing can fill
the mind [of man] but the love of God, of virtue, and of his country'[18] – as we
shall see below, were themes present in the political discourse of seventeenth-
century New England.

In his elaboration of sources and traditions in *The Ideological Origins*,
Bailyn uncovers a rich tradition of classical learning and knowledge of
English republican and liberal philosophy in the formation of American
political thought in the eighteenth century. The epigraph captures succinctly
the manner in which English political ideas rested on classical precedent and
history.[19] An American reading Sidney, Harrington, Locke, Trenchard and
Gordon in the eighteenth century would encounter systems of political thought

---

13 Bailyn, *The Ideological Origins*, p. 22.
14 On the influence of Tacitus on early modern political thought generally, see Peter
    Burke, 'Tacitism, Scepticism and Reason of State', in J.H. Burns and Mark Goldie
    (eds), *The Cambridge History of Political Thought, 1450–1700* (Cambridge: Cambridge
    University Press, 1991), pp. 479–99, esp. pp. 484–90.
15 See Gordon's entry in *ODNB*. Gordon was a Scot and a mentee and amanuensis
    of the Radical Whig writer, Trenchard; see also Houston, *Algernon Sidney*, p. 231;
    John Trenchard and Thomas Gordon, *Cato's Letters: Or, Essays on Liberty, Civil and
    Religious, and Other Important Subjects*, ed. Ronald Hamowy, 2 volumes (Indianapolis,
    IA: Liberty Fund, 1995), I, p. xxxvi
16 Pocock, *The Machiavellian Moment*, p. 468.
17 Sullivan, 'Muted and Manifest English Republicanism', p. 76.
18 Trenchard and Gordon, *Cato's Letters*, II, p. 727.
19 Bailyn, *The Ideological Origins*, p. 22 and ch. 2, *passim*.

that were often read through the prism of Roman history and mediated by the republican and Whig intellectuals and writers of early modern England. To advocate the reading of these works is to school the recipient in texts that dispute the status of monarchy as the only acceptable system of governance. This is achieved through the systematic criticism of venality and the threat of tyranny in contemporary society and governance. All of these authors champion the accountability of the powerful to a representative assembly and advocate the imposition of checks and balances to prevent any individual from achieving absolute ascendancy.

The ubiquity of classical, particularly Roman, knowledge among the educated in the early modern world has been much remarked upon in studies of the history of ideas in the period.[20] For Carl Richard, knowledge of the classics, read raw and also as mediated through Whig and American writing, had a profound impact on the formation of the American Republic. The classics engendered in the Founders, says Richard, 'a sense of identity and purpose' and also 'a thrill of excitement at the opportunity to match their classical heroes' struggles against tyranny and their sage construction of durable republics'. As well as classical influence on practical politics there were other more abstract concepts to consider such as the importance of virtue in public life and the defence of individual liberty. Liberty for the Anglo-American mindset in the eighteenth century was a precious commodity. Any encroachment upon it had to be resisted at all costs. Negligence in this regard could readily be observed in the tyranny practised in France. Precedents could easily be discerned in the past. Early modern Americans enjoyed higher rates of literacy *per capita* than in Europe, and took their knowledge of ancient historians such as Tacitus seriously. From the benchmark historian of ancient Rome and critic of venality and corruption, Americans learned that 'Tyranny was the worst fate' to become a free-born people, because it deprived one of not just 'liberty', but also virtue.[21] Such knowledge was adapted by contemporaries in both Europe and America. 'Enlightenment rationalism', says Bailyn, in both its liberal and conservative form 'was more directly influential in shaping the thought of the revolutionary generation'.[22]

---

20 See Carl J. Richard, *The Founders and the Classics: Greece, Rome, and the American Enlightenment* (Cambridge, MA: Harvard University Press, 1994). Richard takes issue in his Introduction with Bailyn's assertion that the classics 'were "illustrative, not determinative"' of political thought in eighteenth-century America, on the grounds that Whig thought in the period had been read through the classical historians by 'nostalgic aristocrats disgruntled by monarchical and democratic encroachments upon the power of their class' (p. 2). See also Richard, *The Golden Age of the Classics in America: Greece, Rome, and the Antebellum United States* (Cambridge, MA: Harvard University Press, 2009). In Richard's vein, see also David Armitage, 'Literature and Empire', in Nicholas Canny (ed.), *The Oxford History of the British Empire: The Origins of Empire* (Oxford: Oxford University Press, 1998), pp. 99–123.
21 Richard, *The Founders and the Classics*, p. 8. See also Wood, *The Creation of the American Republic*, p. 51.
22 Bailyn, *The Ideological Origins*, p. 26.

This proto-republican and Whiggish view of the future United States, with its teleological model of historical inevitability, invests considerable intellectual capital in the foundational texts of seventeenth-century English political literature, and has in turn met with some resistance from practitioners of the so-called 'new American (sometimes Atlantic) history' that has come to enjoy prominence.[23] One criticism from this quarter is that the texts that are referred to above by Harrington, Milton and Sidney – forged as they were in the furnace of civil war and revolution – are a seemingly *natural* intellectual and cultural extension of the English Diaspora in the early modern period. Accordingly, they provided precedents, legitimacy and credibility to the revolutionary action of the 1770s and '80s. Such thinking has come under pressure most recently from the publication in 2006 of Brendan McConville's controversial revisionist work, *The King's Three Faces: The Rise and Fall of Royal America, 1688–1776*. McConville posits an un-revolutionary, un-radicalized America happy for much of the eighteenth century to flourish under the protective and prosperous aegis of the monarchical British state. This reading of the sources in the colonial period suggests that, far from endorsing and developing the memory of the English seventeenth century with its civil wars, sectarian violence, republican government and revolution, the overwhelming majority of Americans in the eighteenth century were trying to forget it. McConville is struck by the extent to which Americans in the years between 1688 and 1774 identified with 'devotion to the monarchy, the imperialization of political life, patriarchy as political and social expectation, [and] a British historical understanding and perception of time'. Other factors include fierce antagonism towards Catholics and a 'socially mobile yeoman population' that saw the king in personal as well as institutional terms. Republicanism, though the period's great writers are associated with this tradition, was not popular on either side of the Atlantic. 'Representative government, republicanism, democracy, and the redistribution of property – horrified the common as well as the great.' The medieval theory of the king's two bodies jumped 'the Atlantic with the monarch's subjects'.[24]

All of this presents a picture of a royalist America in step with, and in no way opposed politically to, later Stuart and Hanoverian England until the later eighteenth century. This was particularly the case in the southern colonies where the religious practices of the Church of England prevailed. McConville goes on to concede that the New England colonies by the later seventeenth century had developed distinctive differences from the mother country that became a constant feature of comment from visitors. This distinctiveness was fundamental: 'Dress, religion, food, architecture, race

---

23 For a recent summing up of the historiography, see Jack P. Greene and Philip D. Morgan (eds), *Atlantic History: A Critical Appraisal* (Oxford: Oxford University Press, 2009).

24 Brendan McConville, *The King's Three Faces: The Rise and Fall of Royal America, 1688–1776* (Chapel Hill, NC: University of North Carolina Press, 2006), pp. 7 and 21.

relations, economies, and governmental institutions all seemed different from London and England's southern counties.' In a letter to the Bishop of Landaff written in 1768 William Livingstone remarked that 'his New England contemporaries' still cleaved to the manners and mores of 'seventeenth-century English puritans'.[25] He does not, however, concede that the political theology imported by the puritan settlers of the seventeenth century had a significant impact on the development of the colony. The argument elaborated below takes issue with this perspective, asserting instead that insufficient attention has been paid to the puritan origins of republican practice in the settlement of the New England colonies by orthodox and revisionist accounts.

Clearly, the historiography of colonial America as it relates to the dissemination of republican ideas is vexed. The older orthodoxy associated with Bailyn, Wood, Pocock et al. is being challenged by the revisionist theories of a new generation of Americanists. Both parties, however, see the eighteenth century as being formative, with neither party paying particular attention to religion. As recent work by John Coffey and Alister Chapman has suggested, Classical republicanism and its adaptation by English and American Whigs is placed misleadingly within a dominant Enlightenment narrative of progress, with 'modernization and secularization [marching] hand in hand'. Jonathan Scott has also argued strenuously for the central importance of religion in any understanding of political thought in the period. For Scott, there is no true understanding of English republicanism without a corresponding awareness of the role played by the application of Christian humanist moral philosophy.[26] The political experience of the puritan settlers has gone largely unnoticed in Whig and emergent revisionist historiography, where the emphasis has been placed firmly on the century following the Glorious Revolution of 1688. It is to this aspect of the English experience in America that we now turn.

Winthrop, Cotton and the Christian Commonwealth

In the most recent one-volume treatment of America from the sixteenth century to the present, David Reynolds states that empire, liberty and faith are 'central to American debate'.[27] All three were present from the earliest English settlements, particularly in New England. Republican ideas, along

---

25 Ibid., pp. 23–24 and 26.
26 John Coffey and Alister Chapman, 'Introduction: Intellectual History and the Return of Religion', in John Coffey, Alister Chapman and Brad S. Gregory (eds), *Seeing Things Their Way: Intellectual History and the Return of Religion* (Notre Dame, IN: University of Notre Dame Press, 2009), pp. 1–23 (p. 3). In the same volume, see John Coffey, 'Quentin Skinner and the Religious Dimension of Early Modern Political Thought', pp. 47–74. See also Jonathan Scott, *Commonwealth Principles: Republican Writing in the English Revolution* (Cambridge: Cambridge University Press, 2004), p. x and chs. 2–3.
27 David Reynolds, *America: Empire of Liberty* (Harmondsworth: Penguin, 2009), p. xix.

with puritan religion, were imported to America from British shores from the early seventeenth century and are implicit in the works of New England's most prominent settlers. An early example of this is evident in John Winthrop's *A Model of Christian Charity* (1630). Like the rest of the early modern world, politics and religion in colonial America are impossible to meaningfully separate. It is therefore no accident that 'the major contributors to the literary record in the first three decades of colonization were those in public positions who grappled with the thorny issues of church and state'.[28] They often did so from a perspective implicitly critical of England and in a language that is rich in metaphor and imagery derived from their reading in Scripture and a humanist training in rhetoric. John Winthrop's opening statement in *A Model of Christian Charity* seems to advocate in uncontroversial terms the natural order of early modern hierarchy: 'God almighty in his most holy and wise providence, hath so disposed of the condition of mankind, as in all times some must be rich, some poor, some high and eminent in power and dignity, others mean and in subjection.' Crucially here Winthrop places the power to dispose firmly in the hands of God. Very quickly, however, we become aware of a state of nature underpinned by implicit belief in a contract between rulers and ruled, 'so that the rich and mighty should not eat up the poor, nor the poor and despised rise up against their superiors and shake off their yoke'.[29] Winthrop saw emigration to the American colonies as an expression of God's will. In *Reasons to be Considered* (1629), an exhortation to the godly to forsake their mother country for pastures new, Winthrop explicitly sets out his stall:

> All other churches of Europe are brought to desolation, and our sins, for which the Lord already begins to frown upon us, do threaten us fearfully, and who knows but that God hath provided this place to be a refuge for many whom he means to save out of the general calamity; and seeing the church hath no place left to fly into but the wilderness, what better work can there be than to go before and provide tabernacles and food for her, against she come thither?[30]

The language here is suitably apocalyptic in its tone and content. Europe is described as a place of spiritual devastation and Winthrop's is a voice in the wilderness pronouncing the will of God to the elect. These fortunate people are singled out under the terms of Calvinist predestination for special treatment and can be spared the fate of the 'general calamity' reserved for

---

28　Emory Elliott, 'The Dream of a Christian Utopia', in Sacvan Bercovitch (ed.), *The Cambridge History of American Literature: Volume 1, 1590–1820* (Cambridge: Cambridge University Press, 1997), pp. 183–204 (p. 189).

29　John Winthrop, *A Model of Christian Charity* (1630), in Alan Heimert and Andrew Delbanco (eds), *The Puritans in America: A Narrative Anthology* (Cambridge, MA: Harvard University Press, 1985), pp. 82–92 (pp. 82 and 83).

30　John Winthrop, *Reasons to be Considered for Justifying the Undertakers of the Intended Plantation in New England and for Encouraging Such Whose Hearts God Shall Move to Join with Them in It* (1629), in Heimert and Delbanco (eds), *The Puritans in America*, pp. 71–74 (p. 71).

the unregenerate. The godly are pathfinders, a vanguard especially selected 'to go before' and prepare a place for the faithful. As the editors of an influential edition of puritan writing in America have described it, *Reasons to be Considered* can be read 'as a record of the dialogue between those who promoted and those who resisted the idea of Puritan migration', and in the best tradition of Renaissance rhetoric, Winthrop is persuasive. The text also works to clear the conscience of those wishing to leave a nation that had been seemingly forsaken by God.[31] As Francis Bremer has written, Winthrop was driven to migrate as much by his 'concern for religious reform' as by other factors such as the undertaking of a mission, or embarking on an 'errand into the American wilderness'. Stephen Foster has similarly drawn attention to Winthrop's fears for the godly in Caroline England.[32]

Winthrop's critical reading of contemporary religion in Caroline England would find support in many quarters, not the least of which came from the most influential and well-respected puritan divine of the 1630s, John Cotton. When the *Arbella* was waiting to sail from Southampton in 1630 John Cotton appeared at the dock to wish them well and gave a sermon blessing the venture. As Delbanco and Heimart have noted, the text of Cotton's sermon is warm in its encouragement of the pilgrims while simultaneously warning them not to lose touch with their mother church in England and to be not unmindful of our 'Jerusalem at home'. He also urges them to 'forget not the womb that bare you and the breast that gave you suck'.[33] To balance the equation Cotton is keen to stress the advantages that lie ahead in their venture. Prominent among these are trade – 'our Saviour approveth travail for merchants'; colonization – 'when the hive of the commonwealth is so full that tradesmen cannot live by one another, in this case it is lawful to remove [to another country]'; and 'for liberty of conscience' – the right to practise one's religion in peace.[34] Cotton, of course, did not board the *Arbella* and leave England with Winthrop in 1630, but we can see from his text that the pursuits of liberty, commerce and faith are at the heart of Cotton's text. Like Winthrop, Cotton is mindful of the need to provide for the common good and to put the welfare of the community above the immediate needs of the individual. As *God's Promise to His Plantations* (1630) draws to a close Cotton urges the emigrants to 'go forth, every man that goeth, with a public spirit, looking not on your own things only, but also on the things of others, Philippians 2:4. This

---

31   Heimert and Delbanco, 'Headnote', in *The Puritans in America*, pp. 70–71.
32   Francis J. Bremer, *John Winthrop: America's Forgotten Founding Father* (New York: Oxford University Press, 2003), p. 148; Stephen Foster, *The Long Argument: English Puritanism and the Shaping of New England Culture, 1570–1700* (Chapel Hill, NC: University of North Carolina Press, 1991), pp. 108–09.
33   John Cotton, *God's Promise to His Plantations* (London: William Jones, 1630), in Heimert and Delbanco (eds), *The Puritans in America*, p. 79.
34   Ibid.

care of universal helpfulness was the prosperity of the first plantation of the primitive church, Acts 4:32.'[35]

Writing and preaching at the beginning of Charles I's Personal Rule (1629–40) Cotton had yet to feel the full antipathy of the religious and political establishment. The 1630s in England witnessed a considerable increase in the power of Archbishop Laud and the acceleration of radical Arminianism.[36] At the heart of puritan anger regarding ecclesiastical reform was the widespread return of ceremonialism in the Church and the prominence and celebration of the communion table, 'raised and railed-off' and 'placed like an altar at the east end of the chancel'.[37] Further bones of contention included the belief espoused by the Arminian Church hierarchy in the doctrines of free will and free grace, the denial of double predestination and the dilution of Calvin's authority. Cotton viewed the observation of ceremonies as idolatrous, and said so in the conformity debate in the early 1630s. He was joined in this position by Thomas Hooker, another influential puritan who similarly fled the mother country for New England.[38] These factors, and others, would by the beginning of the 1640s result in Civil War in all three kingdoms. In June of 1633, by now disillusioned, Cotton sailed for New England. Two weeks after his arrival he was appointed as 'teacher' in the First Church of Boston. In 1634 he wrote to a former colleague in England explaining why he left: 'If we may and ought to follow God's calling three hundred miles, why not three thousand. Our Saviour's warrant is in our case, that when we are distressed in our course in one country (*nequid dicam gravius*) we should flee to another.' Indeed, Cotton takes time to inform us that, far from deserting his flock, he was actively encouraged to do so on the grounds that it was 'better for themselves, and for me, and for the church of God, to withdraw from the present storm [in England] and to minister in this country'.[39] In this Cotton was part and parcel of the diaspora of puritan ministers that took place between 1631 and 1643.[40] By 1649 Cotton's disillusionment with the situation in the Old Country leaves him confident enough to preach a fast-day sermon in defence of the regicide. The sentiments expressed in this sermon were shared by many

---

35 Ibid, p. 80.
36 The classic treatment of this is Nicholas Tyacke, *Anti-Calvinism: The Rise of English Arminianism, 1590–1640* (Oxford: Oxford University Press, 1987). But see also Richard Cust, *Charles I* (Harlow: Longman, 2005), pp. 133–47, and Austin Woolrych, *Britain in Revolution, 1625-1660* (Oxford: Oxford University Press, 2002), pp. 73–84, for an elegant summing up and re-statement of what is still a contentious topic.
37 Woolrych, *Britain in Revolution*, p. 77.
38 On the conformity debate, see Tom Webster, *Godly Clergy in Early Stuart England: The Caroline Puritan Movement, c. 1620–1643* (Cambridge: Cambridge University Press, 1997), pp. 151–66 (p. 163).
39 John Cotton, *Mr Cotton's Letter Giving the Reasons for His and Mr Hooker's Removal to New England* (1634), in Heimert and Delbanco (eds), *The Puritans in America*, pp. 95–96 and Headnote. The Latin translation by the editors reads 'Lest I should do anything more serious'.
40 See Webster, *Godly Clergy in Early Stuart England*, pp. 253–338.

of his fellow New Englanders. After the Restoration in 1660 New England proved to be a safe haven in exile for three of the regicides: 'In particular the Bay Colony's leaders welcomed two regicide judges [and] New Haven housed a third regicide incognito for thirty years.'[41]

Cotton claims to be motivated by the highest principles of liberty, empire and faith. His justification for leaving England is also a document of exhortation for others of the godly to do the same. Winthrop's *A Model of Christian Charity* demonstrates a similar sentiment of godly discipline married to a politics of virtue and probity in pursuit of the common good:

> It is by a mutual consent, through a special overvaluing providence and a more than ordinary approbation of the churches of Christ, to seek out a place of cohabitation and consortship under a due form of Government both civil and ecclesiastical. In such cases as this, the care of the public must oversway all private respects, by which not only conscience, but mere civil policy doth bind us; for it is a true rule that particular estates cannot subsist in the ruin of the public.[42]

Winthrop puts his faith in providence before the rule of earthly princes, and as has been well documented by historians of religious and political thought in the early modern period, this consideration is of primary importance to followers of Calvinist Protestantism.[43] As the historian Mark Valeri goes on to demonstrate, Calvin's works were reinterpreted throughout the colonial period to fit the prevailing socio-economic and political context. Despite his seemingly straightforward acceptance of the doctrine of passive obedience, for instance, Calvin, in his *Institutes of Christian Religion*, in this regard was 'at all times the master of equivocation'. Exceptions to this rule are justified by the obligation to obey God above all others, and 'by raising up "open avengers from among his servants", arming them "with his command to punish the wicked government and deliver his people, oppressed in unjust ways, from miserable calamity"'. Further justifications for rebellion include the presence of a godly magistrate 'resisting in the name of the people'. In the Latin edition of the *Institutes* (1559), 'Calvin begins to change his mind'. Although this in itself is not realized 'in a clear and unequivocal theory of revolution', it opens the door to a more liberal interpretation of resistance theory.[44]

---

41 See Francis Bremer, editor and introduction, 'In Defense of Regicide: John Cotton on the Execution of Charles I', *William and Mary Quarterly*, 3rd series, 37.1 (1980), pp. 103–24; McConville, *The King's Three Faces*, p. 30.

42 Winthrop, *A Model of Christian Charity*, in Delbanco and Heimert (eds), *The Puritans in America*, p. 91.

43 See Mark Valeri, 'Calvinism and the Social Order in Early America: Moral Ideas and Transatlantic Empire', in Thomas J. Davis (ed.), *John Calvin's American Legacy* (Oxford: Oxford University Press, 2010), pp. 19–41.

44 Quentin Skinner, *The Foundations of Modern Political Thought; Volume 2 The Reformation* (Cambridge; Cambridge University Press, 1978), p. 192.

As Patrick Collinson has demonstrated, in the early modern world there was a vocabulary of resistance available to the godly and a willingness on their part to deploy it. This included 'the conviction that monarchy is a ministry exercised under God and on his behalf; that it is no more and no less than a public office'. As a public office, its holder can be held accountable, and not necessarily to God alone, 'and [...] there is a difference between monarchy and tyranny'.[45] Winthrop's *A Model of Christian Charity* with its oft-quoted metaphor of a 'City on a Hill' stipulates a Bible commonwealth, a Christian utopia, with a unique political organization. With its nod to the 'care of the public' and concern for its ruin, alongside a constitution formed by an implicit debt to mutual consent and therefore contract, it anticipates a relationship between the rulers and the ruled that seemingly takes no account of *jure divino*. In Winthrop's Christian utopia, 'no man is made more honourable than another'. Instead he exists 'for the glory of his creator and the common good of the creature, man'.[46] He confines his strong sense of community values, as any good Calvinist would, to the elect in the eyes of God, comforted by the certainty of God's grace. 'This is the cause why the Lord loves the creature, so far as it hath any of his Image in it; he loves his elect because they are like himself, he beholds them in his beloved son.'[47] Winthrop shares much here with Milton, who would assert twenty years later in the heat of defending polemically the newly minted English republic that personal probity, virtue, the common good and consent and contract are essential to the physical and spiritual well-being of new as well as established states. In *A Defence of the People of England* (1651), Milton would state bluntly: 'By that Law of nature, and of God, that whatever is for the safety of the state is right and just.'[48] Winthrop's care for the public good would also find favour with Locke and with Jefferson, both of whom were firmly of the opinion that the people have a right to political self-determination.

Winthrop was a working politician in a new colony and an integral member of his community. His concerns were more pragmatic than abstract. In this respect he shared something with the revolutionaries of the eighteenth century in colonial America. The 'pamphleteers, essayists and miscellaneous commentators' who were 'spokesmen' for the Revolution were not part of a 'detached intelligentsia' divorced from their context. They resembled Winthrop in that they too prized virtue and 'the basic value of

---

45 Patrick Collinson, 'The Monarchical Republicanism of Elizabeth I', in Collinson, *Elizabethans* (London: Hambledon, 1993), pp. 31–57 (p. 44).

46 Winthrop, *A Model of Christian Charity*, in Delbanco and Heimert (eds), *The Puritans in America*, p. 83.

47 Ibid, pp. 87–88.

48 John Milton, *A Defence of the People of England* (1651), in Don M. Wolfe (ed.), *The Complete Works of John Milton*, 8 volumes (New Haven, CT, and London: Yale University Press, 1953–82), IV.i, pp. 317–18.

personal property, its preservation and the fostering of economic growth'.[49]
Indeed, 'the word "commerce" in the eighteenth century', as Colin Jones
has recently remarked, 'denoted intellectual communication as well as commercial trading'.[50] The relationship between liberty and faith celebrated in
America throughout its history is here articulated by Winthrop as a natural
extension of English puritan thought, transformed, in Reynolds's formu-
lation, into evangelicalism.[51] Educated according to a humanist syllabus
that privileged classical learning, Winthrop was raised in the tradition of
European Calvinism and its 'hotter' English variant. With its inherent theory
of resistance to the ungodly monarch, Calvinism enabled a politics that did
not naturally recognize the monarch as a deity. For people of Winthrop's
persuasion, the only true king was Christ.

Although no republican, Winthrop's sentiments are nevertheless implicitly
republican of the late sixteenth-century gentry variety identified by Patrick
Collinson. Winthrop and his brethren lived through the French wars of
religion and the Dutch revolt against absolutist Spain. When it came to the
political organization of the colony Winthrop demonstrated a republican
sensibility. And with his adherence to commonwealth principles, he arrived
on American shores with the Pilgrims. Massachusetts puritans, as Edmund
S. Morgan has written, 'carried out a revolution, rendered bloodless only by
three thousand miles of ocean that separated them from the government
they would have to overthrow to do what they did. In Massachusetts they
created what amounted to a republic.'[52] They did so by inaugurating 'annually
elected rulers' in substitution 'for an hereditary monarchy and independent
self-starting churches for the whole hierarchical structure of the Church
of England'. As a consequence New England found itself despised and dis-
trusted by royalists in the southern colonies and described as a 'hotbed of
republicanism'. In 1675 'Virginia agents in London' met resistance 'against
incorporating their own colony' on the grounds that a bad precedent had
been set in Massachusetts. Such incorporation, in the view of London, 'led
only to independence and antimonarchical and republican ideas'. Loyalty
to the crown only stretched as far in Massachusetts as the covenant would
allow.[53] The reputation of New Englanders for enthusiasm for independence
was picked up critically in the early eighteenth century by the economist and
governor of the East India Company, Sir Josiah Child, who was unequivocal
in his statement that New England 'was more prejudicial, and in prospect
more dangerous' to the mother country. The colony enjoyed 'virtual autonomy

---

49 Bailyn, *The Ideological Origins*, p. vi.
50 Colin Jones, *The Great Nation: France from Louis XV to Napoleon* (Harmondsworth:
    Penguin, 2003).
51 Reynolds, *Empire of Liberty*, p. 24.
52 Edmund S. Morgan, 'America's First Great Man', in Morgan, *The Genuine Article* (New
    York: Norton, 2004), p. 9.
53 Lovejoy, *The Glorious Revolution in America*, p. 125.

within the empire'.[54] The absence of church courts, church weddings and ales, tithes, bishops, Sunday sports and maypoles meant the New England way of life was founded on principles that were markedly different culturally to early seventeenth-century England.[55] The absence of an Episcopal Church hierarchy meant also a radically altered relationship between Church and state.

The first Great Migration to New England began in earnest in 1630 and continued until 1642, years that coincide almost exactly with the Personal Rule of Charles I. Alan Taylor has suggested that approximately 14,000 people migrated from the mother country to New England during these years, taking with them their faith, their piety and their property. Another scholar suggests the figure may have been higher still.[56] Taylor's figure represents 30 per cent of the total number of English people who migrated to the Atlantic world. Thereafter emigration tailed off dramatically. Although not all emigrants left for New England because of their religion, for those of a puritan disposition the 1630s was a dark decade, one that saw the godly fleeing a land filled with a 'multitude of irreligious lascivious and popish affected persons'. Edward Johnson's remarks, as Virginia DeJohn Anderson goes on to elaborate, were commonplace in the literature of seventeenth-century New England, where popery, debauchery and arbitrary government were seen by Protestants of every degree to be common bedfellows.[57] America, for the puritans, was truly the Promised Land, the place where the godly might find a home away from persecution and tyranny. Settlements by English puritans in Plymouth (1620) and Massachusetts Bay (1630) 'succeeded handsomely' – not because they were founded purely for economic gain but because they created 'refuges for English people beset by religious, economic, and political woes at home'.[58] Or, as Cotton Mather rather more eloquently puts it in the justly famous opening words of his monumental *Magnalia Christi Americana* (1702): 'I write the wonders of the Christian religion, flying the depravations of Europe to the American strand.'[59]

---

54 Alan Taylor, *American Colonies: The Settling of North America* (Harmondsworth: Penguin, 2001), pp. 172, 178. Taylor has framed it thus: 'in effect they converted their commercial charter into a self-governing colony three thousand miles away from bishops and king [...] [and] established the most radical government in the European world: a republic', p. 165.
55 Taylor, *American Colonies*, p. 179.
56 Taylor, *American Colonies*, pp. 164–70; Elliott, 'The Dream of a Christian Utopia', p. 190.
57 Edward Johnson, *The Wonder Working Providence of Sion's Saviour in New England*, cited in Virginia DeJohn Anderson, 'Religion, the Common Thread of Motivation', in Karen Ordahl Kupperman (ed.), *Major Problems in American Colonial History* (Boston, MA: Houghton Mifflin, 2000), pp. 98–109 (p. 99).
58 Virginia DeJohn Anderson, 'New England in the Seventeenth Century', in Canny (ed.), *The Origins of Empire*, p. 49.
59 Cited by Sacvan Bercovitch, 'The Puritan Vision of the New World', in Emory Elliott (ed.), *The Columbia Literary History of the United States* (New York: Columbia University Press, 1988), pp. 33–44 (p. 42).

Conclusion

Political self-determination in New England between the first settlements and the foundation of the United States was anything but inevitable. The foundations for making it possible, however, were laid very early. The political theology of the puritans created a Christian commonwealth that was from the outset independent in its structure and democratic within severely prescribed limits. Well before the revolutions in seventeenth-century England, this was recognized by the authorities. Accordingly there was basic distrust of the settlements on the part of the Crown. This can be seen in the actions of Charles I in 1634. When he recognized that the 'sub-patenting of Massachusetts [...] to John Winthrop's puritans' was suspicious, Charles 'issued a writ of *quo warranto* requiring the Massachusetts Bay Company to justify its jurisdiction'.[60] Despite attempts by the Crown in the 1630s, and also by Cromwell in the 1650s, to shorten the reins of control in New England, the determination of colonists to exercise self-determination and government remained a problem for the mother country. There is more, therefore, to the diaspora of English republican thought and literature in the American colonial period than the dissemination of an English republican canon within an Enlightenment narrative of rational and progressive politics. The Founding Fathers, intimate as they were with the language of Harrington, Sidney, Milton and Locke, were building on theories of independent political organization that derived first inspiration from the Bible.

Politics and its expression in the seventeenth century was an extension of theology. Winthrop and the other Bay colonists created a Bible commonwealth that prioritized the common good. From the early seventeenth century 'the occupational spectrum of future New Englanders placed them at the more prosperous end of English society [...] New England attracted very few members of the upper class.' The attraction instead was for skilled tradesmen. Artisans dominated the population in the later seventeenth century by 'a ratio of nearly two to one'. Despite, says Anderson, Winthrop's assertion aboard the *Arbella* that order and degree should be respected and maintained, 'New Englanders would discover that the process of migration' had levelling tendencies from the outset.[61] Unlike the colonies to the south – Chesapeake and Virginia – the 'wealth structure' of New England communities was 'far more equitable'.[62] By the end of the seventeenth century an economically self-sufficient, self-confident and highly commercialized society 'that was both

---

60   Steven Sarson (ed.), *The American Colonies and the British Empire*, 4 volumes (London: Pickering and Chatto, 2010), I, p. xxiv.

61   Anderson, 'Religion, the Common Thread of Motivation', pp. 103–04. See also Taylor, *American Colonies*, p. 159.

62   Jack P. Greene, *Pursuits of Happiness: The Social Development of Early Modern British Colonies and the Formation of British Culture* (Chapel Hill, NC: University of North Carolina Press, 1988), p. 25.

the most entrepreneurial and most vociferously pious in Anglo-America' had established itself in New England.[63] This is hardly surprising. The puritan immigrants were from the most commercially successful areas of England: 'the southeast, particularly London, East Anglia, and Sussex'.[64]

An English diaspora of political ideas came into existence in New England at the initial point of settlement. It developed tremendous energy in the seventeenth century and provided a receptive context for the dissemination of the English republican canon in the century following. By the early eighteenth century the sense that New England had a divinely constituted role separating it from the rest of the American colonies was coming to an end and society generally was becoming more secular. 'Wealth and not property', we are informed, 'rather than piety, became the basis for political leadership and participation.'[65] Emphasis on social class and economic determinism, by Anderson and others, has contributed to and been supported by the shift in recent years in the historiography of the Revolution and the colonial period more generally. Historians such as Gary Nash and Ray Reynolds have written histories of popular radical republicanism that are firmly committed to a history written from the bottom up.[66] Thomas Paine is a case in point. As one of his modern editors has informed us, Paine made much of never having read Locke. 'His political philosophy is less the product of a system and more a response to the polemical cut and thrust of contemporary political philosophy [...] Paine's political theory was forged in political conflict and hammered out in the midst of war and revolution.'[67] One could say as much about Milton, Harrington, Sidney and indeed Locke himself.[68] Moreover, Paine's boast that he had not read Locke does not prove that the influence of Locke is not present in his writing and his thought. Throughout the century following the Glorious Revolution the reputation of the great seventeenth-century English writers of political thought flourished in America. It did so, however, from a base built by the great puritan settlers of the seventeenth century in New England who took their version of biblical republicanism and Christian humanism and applied it to the practice of government in the New World.

---

63   Taylor, *American Colonies*, p. 159.
64   Ibid., p. 161; see also Nick Bunker, *Making Haste from Babylon: The Mayflower Pilgrims and their World: A New History* (London: Bodley Head, 2010).
65   Greene, *Pursuits of Happiness*, p. 64.
66   Gary B. Nash, *The Unknown American Revolution: the Unruly Birth of Democracy and the Struggle to Create America* (London: Pimlico, 2007); Ray Reynolds, *A People's History of the American Revolution: How Common People Shaped the Fight for Independence* (New York: Harper Perennial, 2001).
67   Mark Philp (ed.), *Thomas Paine: Rights of Man, Common Sense and Other Political Writings* (Oxford: Oxford University Press, 1998), p. x.
68   Richard Ashcraft, *Revolutionary Politics and Locke's Two Treatises of Government* (Princeton, NJ: Princeton University Press, 1986); John Marshall, *John Locke: Resistance, Religion and Responsibility* (Cambridge: Cambridge University Press, 1994).

Chapter 3

Fox Hunting and Anglicization in Eighteenth-Century Philadelphia

Doreen Skala

Among the men who met each day at the London Coffee House in Philadelphia, the precursor of the merchant exchange, to drink punch, eat biscuits and discuss business were 27 who, on 29 October 1766, penned an agreement to create the Gloucester Fox Hunting Club (GFHC), the first fox-hunting club in America.[1] Mere months after the repeal of the Stamp Act, an act that had provoked the worst crisis in the American colonies' relations with England to that point in history, these men agreed to spend at least two days each week taking part in a uniquely English sport.

These newly successful merchants and lawyers of Philadelphia, whom this essay will call the 'professionals', could gain only limited access to Philadelphia's Quaker-dominated elite society. They would have been familiar with the steps fellow professionals in England took to establish themselves as gentlemen and raise themselves above their near rivals. Following in their footsteps, the Philadelphia professionals intended to elevate themselves by becoming English gentlemen; though born in America at a time when the colonies were becoming more consciously American, they intended to Anglicize.

The founders of British colonial America were predominantly English, bringing their English culture to the North American shores. Though some of them had hoped to alter aspects of their culture to create better societies – the puritans' City upon a Hill or Penn's Holy Experiment – the settlers never

---

1 William Gregory, 'William Gregory's Journal, from Fredericksburg, Va., to Philadelphia, 30th of September, 1765, to 16th of October, 1765', *William and Mary College Quarterly Historical Magazine*, 13.4 (April 1905), p. 227; clubs differed from private fox-hunting parties in that the clubs held regular meetings at a designated site, and all the club's hounds were kenneled together and maintained by the huntsman who was paid through the club's subscription fees.

totally 'abandoned' their cultural heritage.[2] The cultural continuity and regional identities of David Hackett Fischer's *Albion's Seed* were under constant pressure from time, distance, environment and deliberate design, all of which combined to transform Englishmen into Americans in colonies quite different from one another and from the mother country.[3] By the early to mid-1700s the colonists were less English than their great-grandfathers had been, and it was they who needed to refresh their Englishness, to re-Anglicize.

There has been much historiographical discussion and debate about Anglicization – 'the importation of English institutions and English ideas' – in colonial America, and it has been approached through various disciplines.[4] John Murrin examined political, religious, military and legal Anglicization in colonial Massachusetts, tracing its evolution from puritan religious utopia to moderate, secular English province. He maintained that during the course of the eighteenth century colonists were moving closer to union with one another by 'revitalizing a common inheritance', and by virtue of their rediscovered Englishness, especially their English rights, the colonists were ultimately forced to claim their independence.[5] Unlike Murrin, who stressed the role of English politics, T.H. Breen focused on economics. In his 'Empire of Goods', Breen argued that colonists were Anglicized through their participation in the English marketplace.[6] Relying more on material culture, Richard Bushman used his *Refinement of America* to show how colonial Americans used Anglicization to gain respectability and gentility, and how Anglicization brought about a cultural transformation of colonial America.[7] This essay presents yet another approach, using leisure activities to determine if and how the colonists Anglicized.

'Pretty good sport'

The fox hunt was originally a function of pest control performed by farmers and gamekeepers, but it gradually became an elite sport, practised by the nobility. For the nobleman, his country estate was a retreat where he could indulge his love of country in a sport that affirmed his 'finer inherited qualities'.[8] It was

---

2   John M. Murrin, 'Anglicizing an American Colony: The Transformation of Provincial Massachusetts', unpublished PhD thesis, Yale University, 1966, p. 14.
3   David Hackett Fischer, *Albion's Seed: Four British Folkways in America* (Oxford: Oxford University Press, 1989).
4   Murrin, 'Anglicizing an American Colony', p. 20.
5   Ibid.
6   T.H. Breen, 'An Empire of Goods: The Anglicization of Colonial America, 1690–1776', *Journal of British Studies*, 25.4 (1986), pp. 467–99.
7   Richard Bushman, *The Refinement of America: Persons, Houses, Cities* (New York: Vintage Books, 1993).
8   Stanley J. Reeve, *Radnor Reminiscences: A Foxhunting Journal* (Boston: Houghton Mifflin, 1921), p. xv; An example is George Villiers, the second Duke of Buckingham,

during the late seventeenth century that the fox hunters' emphasis changed from killing the fox to chasing it. The hounds gave chase, and the hunters were along to be spectators of the sport, to ride and to socialize. The fox hunt was also an occasion for non-participants, drawing crowds along hunting borders to watch. The sounds of the horses, hounds and horns would have made it an exciting event for all.[9]

As the sport of fox hunting evolved, it was not only the nobility who enjoyed participating – it became emblematic of all high society in the late seventeenth and early eighteenth centuries. Even the fox-hunting term 'tally-ho' was a way of articulating high status. It derives from Norman French and became a shibboleth used to differentiate between the hunting gentleman and others, between the French-speaking Norman aristocrats and the Saxon peasants.[10] Fox hunting had social cachet for several reasons. It was a costly sport to indulge in. One had to be able to afford to maintain horses and hounds and to purchase the tack and accoutrements that were de rigueur for the sport. Fox hunting was a sport for those with immense amounts of leisure time to devote to recreation and the often long journey to the country. A French visitor, François de la Rochefoucauld, after riding to hounds in England, described fox hunting as 'one of the Englishman's greatest joys', and wrote that fox hunters 'think nothing' of riding 'fifty or sixty miles' during a hunt.[11]

The perceived high status of fox hunting made it an appealing recreation for the aspiring middle class of England – merchants, bankers and men of trade – who hoped to use it as an entrée into the world of the gentry. For them, still living and working in the metropolis in the early eighteenth century, fox hunting on a country estate was not feasible. They therefore began to hunt on the outskirts of London in the hope of advertising that they had both the wealth and leisure not to care if 'the entire day was wasted' on sport.[12] They would surely have been quite noticeable in their hunting costumes on the streets of London.

---

who delighted in fox hunting at Cliveden, his northern England estate, and became quite well known for his fox-hunting skills between 1660 and 1678. Roger Longrigg, *The History of Foxhunting* (New York: Clarkson N. Potter, 1975), p. 58.

9 Andrea McDowell, 'Legal Fictions in Pierson v. Post', *Michigan Law Review*, 105 (February 2007), p. 749.

10 James Howe, 'Fox Hunting as Ritual', *American Ethnologist*, 8.2 (May 1981), p. 284. According to the Oxford English Dictionary, 'tally-ho' derives from a meaningless French exclamation used in deer hunting as early as 1662. *Oxford English Dictionary Online*, s.v. 'tally-ho', http://www.oed.com (accessed 28 August 2010).

11 François de la Rochefoucauld, *A Frenchman in England, 1784: Being the Mélanges sur l'Angleterre of François de la Rochefoucauld*, ed. Jean Marchand, trans. Sydney Castle Robert (Ann Arbor, MI: University of Michigan Press, 1933), p. 52.

12 David C. Itzkowitz, *Peculiar Privilege: A Social History of English Foxhunting, 1753–1885* (Hassocks, Sussex: Harvester Press, 1977), p. 40; the metropolitan fox hunters may well have enjoyed the hunt, but they chose to hunt because it was fashionable, as the 'sport gives the vogue a dash of color'. Caspar Whitney, *A Sporting Pilgrimage* (New York: Harper & Brothers, 1895), p. 45.

These men may not have been able to reap the full benefits of fox hunting, but their sons could. By the time the younger men reached adulthood they had been educated at university, owned all the accoutrements of gentility and could spend weekends at the family's country estate, indulging in a noble recreation. These young Englishmen would have had the opportunity to acquaint young colonials, also attending university or apprenticing, with English culture, including the love of fox hunting.[13]

Though fox hunting had been brought to the American colonies by some of the earliest English settlers, the Pennsylvania Quakers found it to be too much of a blood sport for their liking, and it was outlawed in Quaker Philadelphia.[14] In fact, no fox-hunting club existed anywhere in America before the GFHC was established in 1766, though in the 1730s and '40s the Eastern Chesapeake and Tidewater tobacco elite, all England-born, were taking part in unregulated fox hunts.[15] By the end of the eighteenth century fox hunting had become quite popular in America outside New England, where puritan bias against leisure activities precluded it.[16]

The 27 Philadelphia professionals who established the GFHC had followed the path to gentility blazed by the English merchant. They had attempted to refine themselves by emulating the English lifestyle, but as working men they were unable to live a leisured existence and consequently had been unable to participate in Philadelphia's Quaker elite society. It would seem that for this reason they undertook to create a rival genteel society, one that was less Quaker and more English, and the GFHC was one element of their Anglicization.

In the opening paragraph of the *Memoirs of the Gloucester Fox Hunting Club*, published in 1830, William Milnor Jr stated that, when the club began, 'elegant society was then comparatively limited, the occasional intercourse of congenial minds, gave a zest to the relaxing hours, devoted to active recreation and cheerful conviviality'.[17] The GFHC founders created a club in which refined gentlemen associated with other refined gentlemen in a refined setting and refined association. In his introduction to Milnor's *Memoirs*, Robert

---

13   T.H. Breen, 'Ideology and Nationalism on the Eve of the American Revolution: Revisions Once More in Need of Revising', *Journal of American History*, 84.1 (June 1997), p. 19.

14   Pennsylvania Statutes at Large, 'An Act Against Riotous Sports, Plays, and Games', 12 January 1705–06 (2 St.L. 186, Ch. 127), http://www.palrb.us/stlarge/index.php (accessed 27 March 2011).

15   Longrigg, *Foxhunting*, p. 169; it was not until 1781 that a second club, the St George's Hunt Club in Long Island, New York, was established.

16   Italo Pardo and Giuliana B. Prato, 'The Fox-Hunting Debate in the United Kingdom: A Puritan Legacy?', *Human Ecology Review*, 12.1 (2005), p. 149.

17   William Milnor, *Memoirs of the Gloucester Fox Hunting Club near Philadelphia* (New York: Ernest R. Gee, 1927), introduction. Milnor's *Memoirs* does not specifically name the GFHC founders. He does describe the creation of the club, the original uniform and other similar, general information about the club. The *Memoirs* consist of stories told to Milnor by members who joined the club some time after the original 27, some sixty years after the club's creation.

Wharton, a later four-term mayor of Philadelphia, stated that the members themselves 'excited the emulation and elicited the applause of numerous younger friends [by whom they] were admired'.[18]

In full uniform, the GFHC members would make their way through the streets of Philadelphia on Tuesday and Friday mornings from October to April, crossing the Delaware River by ferry and arriving at William Hugg's tavern at Gloucester Point, West Jersey, present-day Gloucester City, New Jersey, where they would enjoy a sumptuous breakfast before beginning the hunt. Although the hunt usually took place in the woods and fields of what are today Camden and Gloucester counties, it was not unusual for the hunters to ride further in the course of a hunt, once riding from Haddonfield to Salem, forty miles south.[19] In the early days of the GFHC, the hunt occasionally took place in Pennsylvania. In December 1767 the GFHC met at the Blue Anchor Tavern on the Darby Creek and went to Lower Tinicum, Bucks County, 'a fox hunting' and 'rid about the wood till 2 oClock [sic] and No Sign of a fox', returning to the Anchor for supper.[20]

Early eighteenth-century fox hunting, as practised by the Gloucester club, differed from the version that became standard towards the end of the century and thereafter. The hunters met in the pre-dawn hours for a hearty breakfast before setting off for a day of hard riding. The hunters joined their huntsman, who was waiting with the hounds, having already blocked potential places for foxes to hide. The assembly then proceeded to a covert, a brushpile or area of heavy undergrowth, where they expected to find a fox. The earliness of the start allowed the eighteenth-century hunters to chase the fox while it still had a full stomach from its nocturnal feasting, making it slower. This factor allowed the hounds, which had been bred to hunt the shifty rabbit, to catch more readily the fleet fox. After 1753, when Hugo Meynell had transformed his harriers into 'foxhounds', breeding them for speed and endurance, the fox hunt generally began at a more respectable hour, ten or eleven.[21] After having been drawn from a covert the fox would run, and the hunters and hounds would give chase until the fox was caught or escaped. The assembly would then enjoy a post-hunt feast and display the day's trophies – the brushes or fox tails.[22]

Though the Gloucester club was composed predominantly of native Philadelphians, its rules were clearly patterned after those of English fox-hunting clubs. The president of the club, like the English master of the hunt, was to ride at the front of the hunting train, and he had sole responsibility for conducting the hunt and making sure all rules were followed. The Gloucester

---

18 Ibid.
19 Ibid., p. 17.
20 Jacob Hiltzheimer Diaries, American Philosophical Society, Philadelphia, Vol. 2. Entry for 26 December 1767.
21 Itzkowitz, *Peculiar Privilege*, p. 8.
22 Milnor, *Memoirs*, p. 7.

club had a formal uniform, similar to that of English clubs, of a 'dark brown cloth coatee, with lappelled dragoon pockets, white buttons and frock sleeves, buff waistcoat and breeches'.[23] Although English fox hunters are popularly known for their red jackets, red was not the traditional uniform, which was more often green, grey or yellow – earth tones like the GFHC brown.[24] The GFHC, like the English fox hunters, also wore a black velvet cap. As in clubs in England maintained by gentlemen, membership in the GFHC was by subscription only, and all aspiring members had to receive the vote of two-thirds of the current membership to join.[25] Also, as with English clubs, members could be expelled for behaviour unbecoming a gentleman, and this too required a two-thirds majority.[26] The GFHC was quite English in form and appearance.

The charter, the rules and the *Memoirs* do not reveal any connection between English fox hunting and the GFHC, but in examining some of the activities of the club it becomes apparent that it was very English in tone and action. In the *Memoirs*, the GFHC is described almost as if it were a public service association rather than a hunting club, helping suffering farmers to rid their lands of the evil fox, claiming that the farmer 'hailed the hounds and the huntsman'.[27] The indigenous grey fox was not, however, the hunters' preferred prey. The Gloucester club imported and bred the red fox, which was 'peculiar to European climates'.[28] The grey fox could not be hunted in the English fashion as it tends to take refuge in a tree rather than run.[29] If the GFHC was not indulging in English fox hunting, why would they unleash these creatures, described as the 'more mischievous red-skin stock [...] imported rogues of bad habits and dispositions', in the New Jersey farmlands?[30] In addition, there were plenty of dogs in the colonies, but the Gloucester club had a pack of 'imported English fox hounds', another example of its attempt to be more English.[31]

Several of the founding GFHC members were apparently avid fox hunters and rode to hounds frequently in the winters between 1765 and 1767. On one occasion, a fox was set loose and was chased by a pack of hounds and horsemen until dark. The wily fox ran up a tree to escape, but one hunter climbed

---

23 Itzkowitz, *Peculiar Privilege*, p. 7.
24 Longrigg, *Foxhunting*, p. 119.
25 Two early English 'subscription packs' were the Cheshire pack in 1746 and the Colchester town pack in 1754. G.E. Mingay, *A Social History of the English Countryside* (London: Routledge, 1990), p. 145.
26 Milnor, *Memoirs*, p. 45.
27 Ibid., p. 17.
28 Ibid., p. 32. The first red foxes are believed to have been imported into Maryland in 1730. Allen Potts, *Fox Hunting in America* (Washington DC: Carnahan Press, 1912), p. 7.
29 Longrigg, *Foxhunting*, p. 172.
30 Milnor, *Memoirs*, p. 29.
31 Ibid., p. 16. The GFHC was not alone in importing English hounds. Robert Brooke imported English hounds to Maryland in the 1650s, Thomas Walker to Virginia in the 1740s, James Delancey, governor of the Province of New York, in the 1760s, and George Washington in the 1770s.

up after it. When he had 'got up said tree then the fox jumped Down & Killed him Self'.[32]

The GFHC founders may have ridden to hounds as a form of exciting and adventurous recreation, but this cannot solely explain their importation of English hounds and foxes, nor can it explain why they chose to create a social club based on a distinctly English sport. A brief reconstruction of colonial Philadelphia and a closer examination of the founders of the GFHC will illuminate the motivations of these men – to use fox hunting as an element of their plan to recreate themselves as gentlemen.

'Those worthy of imitation'

Among the first settlers to arrive in what was to become Philadelphia were English Quakers seeking religious freedom in William Penn's 'Holy Experiment'. The Quakers who emigrated to Penn's community in 1681 were predominantly poor immigrants from north and west England who came with little but their dreams of a better life, taking refuge in caves along the Schuylkill River when they arrived.[33] In the late 1690s Penn's disagreement with his chiefs over quitrents was followed by the Quaker merchants demanding greater participation in the leadership of the city and eventually becoming the ruling class. This new elite wanted to maintain their newly established political and economic power, and families such as the Allens, Norrises and Carpenters closed ranks. By the 1720s the Quakers had created a thriving town. But it was not only the economic situation of the Quakers that had changed; some of their earlier ideals and ethics had changed as well. As time passed, these successful Quakers moved away from the Quaker ideal of plainness and began to accumulate material comforts and to be rather ostentatious. They built great estates outside the city limits, they owned grand coaches with liveried servants and they dressed in fashionable clothes. They spent their days reading, gardening, attending tea parties and socializing with other Quakers. These were people of leisure.[34]

The Quaker elite had become the Philadelphia aristocracy that William Penn had envisioned for Pennsylvania. Penn and his fellow Quakers may have wanted a society free from religious persecution, but in no way did

32 Hiltzheimer Diaries, 12 December 1767.
33 Mary Maples Dunn and Richard S. Dunn, 'The Founding, 1681–1701', in Russell Weigley, Nicholas B. Wainwright and Edwin Wolf (eds), *Philadelphia: A 300-Year History* (New York: Norton, 1982), p. 11.
34 Frederick B. Tolles, *Meeting House and Counting House: The Quaker Merchants of Colonial Philadelphia, 1682–1763* (Chapel Hill, NC: University Press of North Carolina, 1948), p. 113; H.V. Bowen, *Elites, Enterprise, and the Making of the British Overseas Empire, 1688–1775* (New York: St Martin's Press, 1996), p. 135.

they envision social equality.[35] It was well known that some men were meant to lead, while all the others were meant to follow. In fact, Penn's belief in a stratified society is evident in the fact that he 'made no provisions' for a civic government but rather expected that chief landholders would govern society.[36] By 1730 the Quaker aristocracy dominated the economic, social and political landscape of Philadelphia.

Philadelphia grew both demographically and economically during the first half of the eighteenth century. One of the greatest economic changes that took place in the city was the birth of a new sub-class: men of wealth but not property. By the 1720s the fathers of the founders of the GFHC, mostly 'seaport merchants', were becoming increasingly wealthy, but they still had to work hard and were unable to live a leisured existence.[37] They found themselves therefore unqualified for the very genteel Quaker Philadelphia society.

A similar situation had existed in England in the 1660s. Prior to this period, a hierarchical system had worked to keep England separated into two distinct social classes, the aristocracy and the commoners. But London had become a great commercial metropolis, and many men who had accumulated immense wealth there were nonetheless barred from polite society. The division in society was not strictly economic, however; it was also based on cultural superiority. By the mid-seventeenth century, the English middle class had grown in size, and it began to separate into sub-classes.[38] Although they would never be true aristocracy, which was based on birth and land, those in the middle yearned to separate themselves from those below. The more successful of the middle class, generally merchants and bankers, wanted to be seen to be gentlemen, and they believed that by emulating the aristocracy, refining themselves, they would gain respect and status.[39]

Philadelphia's aspiring elite, the professionals, employed the same process of refinement. However, rather than emulate their local social superiors, Philadelphia professionals Anglicized themselves by emulating the English merchant elite culture instead of their rich neighbours. They turned to distinguished London merchants, 'citizens of the world', as models.[40] In the colonies

---

35 Tolles, *Meeting House*, p. 110.
36 Dunn and Dunn, 'Founding', p. 25.
37 Gary B. Nash, *The Urban Crucible: The Northern Seaports and the Origins of the American Revolution* (Cambridge, MA: Harvard University Press, 1979), p. 9. Nash defines seaport merchants as 'importers and exporters, wholesalers and retailers, builders of ships, wharves, and warehouses'; Gordon S. Wood, *The Americanization of Benjamin Franklin* (New York: Penguin, 2004), p. 55.
38 Richard Bushman, 'American High-Style and Vernacular Cultures', in Jack P. Greene and Jack R. Pole (eds), *Colonial British America: Essays in the New History of The Early Modern Era* (Baltimore, MD: Johns Hopkins University Press, 1984), p. 363.
39 François-Joseph Ruggiu, 'The Urban Gentry in England, 1660–1780: A French Approach', *Historical Research*, 74.185 (August 2001), pp. 250–70.
40 David Hancock, *Citizens of the World: London Merchants and the Integration of the British Atlantic Community, 1735–1785* (Cambridge: Cambridge University Press, 1995), p. 25.

as in England, there were several components necessary to the refinement process. To begin with, for a man to become a gentleman he had to be seen to be a man of leisure. Owning a home distinct from his workplace indicated a man's sound financial situation, the leisure time he had available to devote to planning, erecting and running an estate, and his ability to provide a legacy for his offspring. If he was unable to purchase land and erect an estate, he could visually divorce himself from his work by living in a separate location. Having the time and wealth to be involved in social clubs and other recreational, civic or cultural activities was a sign that a man had become a gentleman. Additionally, social gatherings were prime opportunities to display one's refinement. Among the activities favoured by these nouveaux English gentlemen were book clubs, debating societies, 'plays, picture galleries, libraries, museums, pleasure gardens', and sports, such as cricket, boxing and fox hunting.[41] An education, or at least literacy, was a sign of refinement. A man might not be able to attend university himself, but by providing an education for his sons he was showing the importance he placed on education. Maintaining a library, or at least being familiar with books on varied subjects such as literature, science and philosophy, was another mark of a man's refinement. The attainment of refinement was evidenced, too, by a man's manners and speech. Courtesy and civility were signs that he had become refined.[42] Consumption was another hallmark of refinement. The interior decor of a man's house could speak volumes about him – whether he had good taste or bad, or whether he preferred domestic or foreign styles. By dressing himself and his family in the latest fashions, a man could flaunt his taste and prosperity. If a man was seeking to exhibit his refinement, he might also purchase carpets, jewellery, chinaware or furniture. Ultimately, a gentleman, a man who had attained refinement, possessed many things, but most importantly he possessed freedom – freedom from want, from others and from ignorance.[43]

'Mingle the dulce with the utile'

Though it was entirely possible to attain refinement in the colonies, many of the young professionals of the GFHC were sent by their merchant fathers to Europe for their academic and social education, especially to England. Young colonials hoping to practise law were sent to the Middle Temple in London; three founders of the GFHC, Thomas Willing, John Dickinson and Benjamin

41 John Brewer, *The Pleasures of the Imagination: English Culture in the Eighteenth Century* (New York: Farrar, Straus and Giroux, 1997), p. 59.
42 Bushman, 'American High-Style', p. 358.
43 Wood, *Americanization*, p. 38.

Chew, attended the Middle Temple.[44] England was the spring from which culture flowed, so it was also imperative that young professionals should travel there to be steeped in its culture. The young men were expected to return home having learned to imitate the styles, manners and customs of the English elite. Like their English counterparts, they toured England, staying with friends or acquaintances at country estates, experiencing the life of the English country gentleman, a life the young colonials would attempt to replicate when they returned home to America.[45] Those who did not travel were able to learn about English culture by reading imported English books and newspapers or hearing the stories of those who had travelled abroad or who had recently emigrated.

A few brief biographies will illustrate more specifically how some GFHC members became familiar with English culture through travel and business connections. David Potts left the family iron business at Valley Forge after the death of his father and became an iron merchant in Philadelphia. James Wharton Jr, the son of a successful merchant, and his partner Enoch Story were rope manufacturers and merchants with many customers in English ports. Thomas Lawrence Jr was a Philadelphia merchant who exported deer and beaver skins and furs through a London agent.[46] Andrew Hamilton III, who himself travelled to England in 1765, inherited his father's warehouses along with his mercantile business. These men, all charter members of the GHFC, had direct contact with English merchants and traders and were regulars at Philadelphia's London Coffee House.[47]

Through these connections, these colonial men learned the significance of fox hunting in becoming a true Englishman. Richard Bache, for example, had lived in both the Yorkshire Dales, which were teeming with fox hunts, and London. He would have been familiar with the sport and may well have seen the metropolitan merchants heading out of London for a day of fox hunting. Bache was born in 1737, the son of an excise collector in the village of Settle in Yorkshire. Bache emigrated to New York City in 1760 to

---

44 H.A.C. Sturgess (ed.), *Register to the Admissions of the Honourable Society of the Middle Temple, From the Fifteenth Century to the Year 1944*, Vol. I (London: Butterworth, 1949); the number of young colonial professionals attending Middle Temple 'reached its height in the mid-eighteenth century'. C.E.A. Bedwell, 'American Middle Templars', *American Historical Review*, 25.4 (1920), p. 680. Young men would enter a clerkship or apprenticeship in a lawyer's office to become familiar with legal procedures and practice. To learn the history and the system of laws, the young men were sent to Middle Temple, where they were expected to read the law books in the extensive Temple libraries, to attend court hearings and to be influenced by Inn-trained lawyers.

45 William L. Sachse, *The Colonial American in Britain* (Madison, WI: University of Wisconsin Press, 1956), p. 43.

46 William I. Roberts III, 'Samuel Storke: An Eighteenth-Century London Merchant Trading to the American Colonies', *Business History Review*, 39.2 (Summer 1965), p. 152.

47 General Notes, *Wharton Family Papers*, Collection 708A, Historical Society of Pennsylvania (HSP), Philadelphia.

join his brother Theophylact in his dry goods and marine insurance firm.[48] After two years he relocated to Philadelphia to open his own dry goods business. Bache married Sarah Franklin, Benjamin's only daughter, just a year after arriving in Philadelphia. He continued as a Philadelphia dry goods merchant until he succeeded his eminent father-in-law as postmaster general in 1776. Bache would certainly have been familiar with his father-in-law's views regarding how to become a successful member of society. Benjamin Franklin recognized the need to become a gentleman in order to be a man of influence in Philadelphia.[49] He himself had worked his way up from an 'ordinary Mechanick' to an esteemed gentleman, and he wrote numerous tracts both about portraying oneself as a gentleman and about the need to actually become one.[50]

Another member, Levi Hollingsworth, on several occasions prior to and after joining the GFHC rode to hounds with Colonel James Coultas, setting off from Whitby Hall, Coultas's renovated English stone mansion near Darby, just south-west of Philadelphia. Coultas would have been familiar with the many fox hunts that took place in the vicinity of his English birthplace of Whitby in north Yorkshire in the late 1600s and early 1700s, including those at Bilsdale and Ainthorpe.[51] Hollingsworth was born in Elkton, Maryland, in 1739, one of 20 children of a disavowed Quaker and successful flour producer. At the age of 18 he took over the transportation end of his father's Maryland flour milling business, operating a shallop, a kind of coastal vessel, between Elkton and Philadelphia. Hollingsworth moved to Philadelphia in 1758 and settled into the flour-brokering business first with George Adams and then, in 1761, with Zebulon Rudolph. The Hollingsworth and Rudolph firm operated for over a decade, shipping grain, whiskey and flour between colonial and European, especially English, ports, and making huge profits as commission agents.[52] Hollingsworth began his family at a stone mansion on Dock Street, just around the corner from his business on Front Street, where many of Philadelphia's merchants, including fellow GFHC founders David Rhea, Joseph Wood and Isaac Wikoff, were located.[53]

The early adult life of Benjamin Chew, one of the founders of the GFHC, provides perhaps the classic case study of this process of Anglicization. Born

48   Eugenia W. Herbert, 'A Note on Richard Bache (1737–1811)', *Pennsylvania Magazine of History and Biography*, 100.1 (January 1976), pp. 97–103.
49   Wood, *Americanization*, p. 56.
50   Benjamin Franklin, 'Blackamore, on Mulatto Gentlemen', *Pennsylvania Gazette* (Philadelphia), 30 August 1733.
51   Bilsdale was established by George Villiers as a hunt for the nobility in the middle to late 1600s.
52   General Notes, *Hollingsworth Family Papers*, Collection 289, HSP, Philadelphia.
53   Wood, *Americanization*, p. 57; John Fanning Watson, *Annals of Philadelphia and Pennsylvania in the Olden Time: Or, Memoirs, Anecdotes, and Incidents of Philadelphia and its Inhabitants from the Days of the Founders* (Philadelphia: J. M. Stoddart & Company, 1879), I, p. 393.

into the family of a Quaker doctor in 1722, Chew grew up in Maryland.[54] When he was 14 he was sent to apprentice in the law office of Andrew Hamilton in Philadelphia.[55] Chew worked hard for four years learning the law and legal procedure, returning home, which was now in Dover, in the 'Lower' Kent County, south of the city, after the death of Hamilton in 1741.[56] Chew stayed and worked in Dover for a little less than two years before he was sent to Middle Temple in London at the age of 19. He observed London society while at this prestigious law school, but this alone would not have provided the social education needed for Anglicization. Fortunately, Chew kept a journal of his time in England, and it is in the pages of his journal that one can see the English cultural transformation at work on a malleable young mind.[57]

During his first few weeks in London Chew went to classes and spent all his free time in his lodgings feeling homesick, but he made a few friends, and he began venturing out with them. He attended the Drury Lane and Covent Garden theatres, seeing at least one performance a week. He saw Shakespeare and contemporary plays as well, such as George Farquhar's *The Constant Couple*.[58] Chew was also introduced to the less refined side of society by his fellow Middle Templars, including a boxing match at the Bear Garden, cockfights in Holborn and a visit to the 'tall Swede', quite a curiosity since the man was '8 Foott 2 Inches' tall.[59] Chew also began to read more. Besides his required reading, which included *Coke on Littleton*, he purchased many books at auction, including *Don Quixote* and the *Adventures of Joseph Andrews*.[60] Like any visitor to a foreign land, he visited the well-known tourist destinations, including St Paul's Cathedral and Windsor Castle.[61] He spent some time in the summer travelling around southern England, with a short stay at Colchester, touring castles, visiting the families and friends of fellow Middle Templars and riding in the countryside.[62]

---

54   Burton Alva Konkle, *Benjamin Chew, 1722–1810, Head of the Pennsylvania Judiciary System under the Colony and Commonwealth* (Philadelphia: University of Pennsylvania Press, 1932), p. 10.

55   Ibid., p. 25.

56   Ibid., p. 30. The Lower Counties on the Delaware comprised New Castle, Kent and Sussex counties, the present-day state of Delaware.

57   Benjamin Chew, *Journal 1743–1744*, Chew Family Papers, Collection 2050, Box 18, Folder 7, HSP, Philadelphia.

58   Ibid.

59   Ibid.

60   Ibid., 2 January 1744. 'Coke on Littleton' was the abbreviated title for Sir Edward Coke's *First Part of the Institutes of the Lawes of England: Or A Commentary Upon Littleton, Not the Name of the Author Only, But of the Law It Selfe*.

61   Chew described Windsor Castle in his journal, writing 'the Grandeur of the Rooms, the Richness of the Furniture & the beauty of the Paintings being far superior to any thing I had ever seen before fill's me with the most agreeable Surprise'. Chew, *Journal*, 4 June 1744.

62   Chew, *Journal*, numerous diary entries, specifically those on 3 and 4 June 1744, and between 28 June and 4 July 1744; S. Reeves to Benjamin Chew, letter, Chew Family Papers, Collection 2050, Series 2, Box 11, Folder 31, HSP, Philadelphia.

This was not Chew's first time in the saddle in England. In May he had gone riding in the country with Silvanus Grove, who had been a friend of Chew's since shortly after he arrived at Middle Temple.[63] It was during his time with Grove that he experienced English fox hunting. In mid-December 1743, while spending a few days with Grove at the country home of Jonathan Scarth in Essex, Chew 'went a hunting very early [...] and had pretty good Sport', although he 'return'd back to Ilford very much fatigued'.[64]

Chew learned of the death of his father in July 1744, but he did not return home immediately; he was still in England in October.[65] After his return home, Benjamin Chew established his law practice and was elected as a representative to the legislature of the Lower Counties. In 1754 Chew was appointed recorder of Philadelphia and Pennsylvania attorney general, but he was still not entitled to enter elite Philadelphia society. He did not socialize with the Norrises or Carpenters or any of the other prominent Quaker families of Philadelphia; in fact, he remained a resident of Dover until 1754, at which time he purchased a house on Front Street in Philadelphia for his family.[66] By 1757 Chew was heavily involved in Pennsylvania politics, but the traditional elite Quaker family dominance in the colony made Chew's position very uncomfortable. He cut his ties with the Quakers permanently the following year when he baptized his newborn son by his second wife, Elizabeth, at Philadelphia's Christ Church. Chew was now fully Anglican and permanently outside his native Quaker society.[67] It was at this time that he started private practice, and he became successful as a commercial lawyer and investor. During the early to mid-1760s, Chew continued to work at his private law practice, moved his growing family permanently to his country estate, Cliveden, in Germantown, and co-founded the GFHC.[68] Fox hunting was another way for him to establish himself as an English gentleman, different from the colonial Quaker definition of refinement and status.

---

63 Silvanus Grove (b. about 1711), a prominent London-Chesapeake merchant and English Quaker, was a friend and companion to Chew during his stay in England. In a letter written some forty years later, Chew refers to Grove as the 'dearest companion' of his youth. Benjamin Chew to Silvanus Grove, letter, Chew Family Papers, Collection 2050, Box 9, Folder 52, HSP, Philadelphia.

64 Chew, *Journal*, 11 December 1743; Jonathan Scarth was a Quaker merchant in London and Virginia, with several properties in Maryland. United States Reports, *Decisions of the United States Supreme Court*, Volume 9, *February 1809–February 1810*, 9 U.S. 344, Owings v. Norwood's Lessee, http://ftp.resource.org/courts.gov/c/US/9/9.US.344.html (last accessed 4 November 2010).

65 S. Reeve to B. Chew, letter, Chew Family Papers, Collection 2050, Box 11, Folder 31, HSP, Philadelphia.

66 Konkle, *Benjamin Chew*, p. 81.

67 The Chew family began its break with the Quakers in 1742. Dr Samuel Chew, Benjamin's father, was excommunicated by the Duck Creek Meeting for his November 1741 public profession in which he criticized the Quaker refusal to arm themselves, as he felt that military action for defence could be justified in Christian faith.

68 Konkle, *Benjamin Chew*, p. 96.

Benjamin Chew had clearly followed the path to success that had been blazed by the English merchants in England, but he was still not given full access to Philadelphia society. Chew himself understood that success alone would not secure him or his family passage. He was well aware that one had to acquire refinement, and he believed that this was possible when one followed English and not Philadelphia customs. This sentiment was expressed by Chew himself in October 1772 in a letter to his future son-in-law, who was attending Middle Temple in London. Chew informed him that learning the law was not the only goal while attending university in England: 'What you see and hear in such a place as London will not only enlarge your ideas but furnish you with a fund for conversation to the end of your days. You are to qualify yourself for the gentleman and lawyer.'[69] Chew offered another sentiment of advice: 'Mingle the dulce with the utile, and let your time be divided between the Law, History, Belles Lettres, society, and exercise, and learn to profit by the vices and foibles of others, and by copying the virtues and manners of those worthy of imitation.'[70] In other words, he was not in England just to learn an honourable profession, but also to become cultured in the English way – by listening, watching and replicating the life of the English gentleman, he who was most worthy of imitation. Replicating English fox hunting was a key element in this process.

Conclusion

Philadelphia professionals such as Benjamin Chew could not live the leisured existence of the elite and therefore acquired or adapted the trappings of wealth and status that would have been consistent with those of the English merchant gentlemen. They separated their homes from their workplaces, built country estates, consumed English goods, read books on varied subjects and displayed genteel behaviours.[71] They also modelled many of their social relationships on the English gentlemen, including meeting together in societies and clubs, and taking part in 'gentlemanly sports and pastimes'.[72] At the time of the founding of the GFHC, fox hunting was a sport of English gentlemen and those Englishmen who aspired to gentility. By creating the first subscription pack in America, the founders of the GFHC transplanted the most English of English

---

69 Benjamin Chew to Ned Tilghman, letter, Chew Family Papers, Collection 2050, Box 9, Folder 74, HSP, Philadelphia.
70 Ibid.
71 Indeed, Eliza Lucas Pinckney wrote in May 1740 that the people of Charleston, South Carolina, 'live very Gentile and very much in the English taste', suggesting that gentility and English culture were inseparable to colonists. Elise Pinckney (ed.), *The Letterbook of Eliza Lucas Pinckney, 1739–1762* (Columbia, SC: University of South Carolina Press, 1997), p. 7.
72 Bowen, *Elites*, p. 135.

sports, and with the hounds, foxes, rules and costumes came an element of English culture new to the colonies. This examination of the GFHC would seem to indicate that these 27 men wanted to be as closely associated with the life of an English country gentleman as possible, and that by employing Anglicization, with fox hunting perhaps the most characteristically English element, as a boundary for behaviour and a badge of identity, they were able to effect their transformation. Through the GFHC, they were in their own way making America more English, turning it from a colonial society into a provincial one, one which would be an equal partner in the British Empire. Many of these 'English' fox hunters would be disappointed when the political tensions of the 1770s revealed to them that no matter how much they admired England and copied its customs, such as chasing foxes around the country-side, they were still, in many English eyes, mere colonials. Of the 23 members who lived through the American Revolution whose stance in the conflict can be ascertained, 16 (70 per cent) chose the 'Patriot' side.[73] Ironically, it seems the Gloucester fox hunters' attempt to become English through fox hunting may ultimately have made them more American than they knew.

---

73 Francis B. Heitman, *Historical Register of Officers of the Continental Army During the War of the Revolution* (Washington DC: Rare Book Shop Publishing Company, 1914); Francis B. Lee (ed.), *Documents Relating to the Revolutionary History of the State of New Jersey*, Vol. II, *1778* (Trenton, NJ: John L. Murphy Publishing, 1903); Members of the State of Schuylkill, *A History of the Schuylkill Fishing Company of the State of Schuylkill, 1732–1888* (Philadelphia: The Members of the State of Schuylkill, 1889), pp. 348–404; G.B. Warden, 'The Proprietary Group in Pennsylvania, 1754–1764', *William and Mary Quarterly*, 3rd series, 21.3 (July 1964), p. 368; Allan Johnson and Dumas Malone (eds), *Dictionary of American Biography* (New York: Charles Scribner's Sons, 1930), p. 300; Robert Francis Oaks, 'Philadelphia Merchants and the American Revolution, 1765–1776', unpublished PhD thesis, University of Southern California, 1970.

Chapter 4

The Hidden English Diaspora in Nineteenth-Century America

William E. Van Vugt

'The American is only the continuation of the English genius into new conditions.' So wrote Ralph Waldo Emerson in 1856.[1] He was not alone in that assessment. Some twenty years earlier, Alexis de Tocqueville had defined Americans as 'the portion of the *English* people charged with exploiting the forests of the new world'.[2] Of course, things have changed since then. But for much of the long nineteenth century, what Emerson, Tocqueville and many others said had much truth to it. Early observers took the English foundations of American culture for granted – and for good reason. Because of the long, virtually uninterrupted migration of English (and other British) people to America – and Britain's long rule of the American colonies – English culture ran deep in America. In some ways it still does.

Despite the often bitter war for independence, the tight Anglo-American cultural ties remained, and even grew in some ways. According to the 1790 census, people of English origin or ancestry were by far the largest group, comprising about 60 per cent of the white population, or about half of the population if we include Africans. Meanwhile there was growing American 'Anglicization' as whites in search of their identity standardized their culture. Most white Americans, then, had a largely English understanding of their heritage. There were essential differences, of course, but the basic cultural patterns remained. Furthermore, almost immediately after the war, trade and migration resumed and Anglo-American economic ties developed. In

---

1   Ralph Waldo Emerson, *English Traits* (Boston: Phillips, Sampson, and Company, 1856), p. 42.
2   Alexis de Tocqueville, *Democracy in America*, trans. Arthur Goldhammer (New York: Library of America, 2004), II, p. 517.

fact, American independence transformed the Anglophone people from a single polity into an intercontinental world, and together, Britain and the United States formed an 'Atlantic economy' based on the free flow of capital and people.[3] Britain's economic and cultural ties with the United States were now actually closer and more mutually beneficial than those Britain shared with her remaining colonies. The two were the most intertwined sovereign nations in the world – and the 'Hidden English Diaspora' was at the centre of this world-shaping development. From 1815 to 1930 at least 12 million Britons permanently settled in North America, Australasia and South Africa (other estimates point to a total of 18.7 million not counting returns). For the English alone in the long nineteenth century, the numbers are close to 10 million – most of them settling in the United States.

During this same period the number of English speakers throughout the world grew from about 12 million to 200 million – a sixteen-fold increase.[4] The expanding use of the English language, which accompanied the English Diaspora, shaped the world profoundly. Otto von Bismarck was perhaps right when he allegedly declared that the decisive factor in modern history was that the people of North America speak English.[5] Even today, the impact of English on perceptions and world affairs should not be overlooked. Can it be mere coincidence that the three nations that invaded Saddam's Iraq were all Anglophone: the United States, the United Kingdom and Australia?[6]

The English Diaspora and the Modern World

Scholars are finding new ways of understanding how the English Diaspora shaped and continues to shape the modern world. Eric Richards points out that the Diaspora 'enhanced the reproductive capacity' of English and other British people. It had a 'primitive biological aspect' that 'entailed the

3   Already in the late 1780s four-fifths of Philadelphia's and virtually all of New York's imports were British. By 1790 about half of America's exports went to Britain, while 80 per cent of America's imports came from Britain. The Atlantic economy is explored most thoroughly in Brinley Thomas, *Migration and Economic Growth* (Cambridge: Cambridge University Press, 1954).
4   Richards points to Dudley Baines's estimates of a total of 18,700,000 emigrants, not counting returns. See Eric Richards, *Britannia's Children: Emigration from England, Scotland, and Wales since 1600* (London: Hambledon, 2004), p. 6; also James Belich, *Replenishing the Earth: The Settler Revolution and the Rise of the Angloworld, 1783–1939* (New York: Oxford University Press, 2009), p. 4. The 'modern British dispersion' is estimated at about 200 million British emigrants and their descendants – those who can claim descent from British and Irish emigrants. About 25 million in total came from the British Isles; see Richards, *Britannia's Children*, p. 4.
5   This was claimed by Winston Churchill; see Kathleen Burk, *Old World, New World: Great Britain and America from the Beginning* (New York: Atlantic Monthly Press, 2007), p. 380.
6   Robert J.C. Young also speculates on this question in *The Idea of English Ethnicity* (Oxford: Blackwell, 2008), p. 235.

disproportionate transfer of genes from the British Isles to the rest of the world'.[7] Niall Ferguson observes that it was the English Diaspora that 'turned whole continents white'.[8] And Robert Young sees the nineteenth-century English Diaspora as a key force in the 'formation of Englishness' and the very 'idea of English ethnicity'. The Diaspora translated Englishness (again, in Young's words) from a 'national identity of the English living in England into a diasporic identity beyond any geographical boundaries'.[9] The extensive Englishness of American culture, then, tended to obscure or hide the continuing Diaspora heading there.

The most recent interpreter of the Anglophone world, James Belich, sees Britain and America so closely tied together in culture and economics through migration that together they comprised an 'organic unity' that shaped the world through 'Anglo-Booms' of economic development. It was the hidden English Diaspora that made this possible, and that explains 'the gargantuan growth of Anglophone societies'. For Britain and America in particular, their relationship was unique because more than any other nations they had a 'shared culture as well as complementary economics, and the two reinforced each other'.[10] The English Diaspora, then, has special significance for America. As Richards concludes, 'the single most important fact' about the English Diaspora was 'its orientation to the American Republic'.[11]

Invisible Immigrants?

The notion that the common language and cultural base 'hid' the English Diaspora in America goes back a long time. Historian Charlotte Erickson called the English 'invisible immigrants' because the language and culture they shared with most Americans allowed them a comparatively rapid assimilation such that sometimes they were not even seen as true foreigners. But Erickson also cautioned against taking this notion too far, and pointed out that English immigrants still behaved 'ethnically' in some ways. Indeed, because of the similarities, some English faced unique challenges in their assimilation, stemming from unrealistic expectations of not having to adjust to American life, and being surprised by the differences. The 'invisibility' of English immigrants is a relative concept, subject to many exceptions, but still useful for understanding American immigration and identity.[12]

---

7   Richards, *Britannia's Children*, p. 255.
8   Niall Ferguson, *Empire: The Rise and Demise of the British World Order and the Lessons for Global Power* (New York: Basic Books, 2002), p. 60.
9   Young, *English Ethnicity*, pp. 22, 179, 231.
10 Belich, *Replenishing the Earth*, pp. 51, 86, 208.
11 Richards, *Britannia's Children*, p. 119.
12 Charlotte J. Erickson, *Invisible Immigrants: The Adaptation of English and Scottish Immigrants to the United States* (Leicester: Leicester University Press, 1972).

Sometimes the English Diaspora in America was very visible indeed. In the years during and after the Revolution, some English immigrants were 'ethnically profiled' for their questionable loyalties. The same was true during the War of 1812 and again when the two nations nearly went to war in the 1840s over unresolved boundaries. Furthermore, in spite of their relative 'invisibility', some English immigrants attempted to live apart in their own enclaves, as did many other immigrants. Notable attempts were made by Morris Birkbeck and George Flower in Edwards County, Illinois, in 1817; by John Ingle and Saunders Hornbrook the following year in Vanderburgh County, Indiana; and by George Courtauld in Athens County, Ohio, in 1820. These communities were doomed by the harsh American frontier environment, but more importantly by the lack of demand for them. Their common culture, language and religious institutions enabled the English to mingle more easily with Americans than other immigrant groups and filter into existing communities.[13]

Though English immigrants could be visible and had their own challenges with assimilation, their common language and culture gave them distinct advantages. English immigrants and culture have been considered so foundational for American identity that many Americans – including those from non-English backgrounds – often saw the English as the 'true' Americans, or the 'most American' of all peoples.[14] Some historians in effect promote this notion, consciously or subconsciously. Oscar Handlin's Pulitzer Prize-winning book on American immigration, *The Uprooted*, does not even mention the English, as if they were not true immigrants. John Bodnar's famous rejoinder, *The Transplanted*, hardly mentions them at all.[15] The same is true for other surveys of immigration. Why is this so? Apparently, in some minds the English did not fit into the American immigration experience: they were 'already' Americans. And though the concept of assimilation means the blending of cultures, it has often consisted of what amounts to 'Anglo-conformity'. Other immigrant groups have been measured against the English and the Anglicized native-born Americans in terms of their language and behaviour in the United States. Such Anglo-conformity has long been part of a 'bargain' to be accepted in American society: accept Anglo-cultural behaviour patterns and the immigrant will in turn be more accepted. Only in more recent times has this idea been seriously challenged – and not by all

13   William E. Van Vugt, *British Buckeyes: The English, Scots and Welsh in Ohio 1700–1900* (Kent, OH: Kent State University Press, 2006), ch. 3. The letters of Ingle and Hornbrook are published in William E. Van Vugt (ed.), *British Immigration to the United States: 1776–1914*, 4 vols (London: Pickering & Chatto, 2009), I.

14   Paul Spickard, *Almost All Aliens: Immigration, Race, and Colonialism in American History and Identity* (New York: Routledge, 2007), pp. 35–37.

15   Oscar Handlin, *The Uprooted: The Epic Story of the Great Migrations that Made the American People* (Boston: Little, Brown, 1973); also John Bodnar, *The Transplanted: A History of Immigrants in Urban America* (Bloomington, IN: Indiana University Press, 1985).

Americans. Some see the Anglo-world as normative. No wonder the English Diaspora in America often seems 'hidden'.[16]

The nineteenth-century English Diaspora was hidden by various things, not the least of which was a new economic and social context of migration. The Diaspora in America was propelled and energized by what Belich and others call 'settlerism', a powerful, revolutionary ideology that emerged in about 1815.[17] Settlerism marked a significant change in the attitudes of people, especially the English, towards migration. Migration within the Anglophone world, particularly to America, was no longer perceived as a desperate act that lowered one's status, as was common in the colonial period. Rather it was a hopeful act, a more positive move than simply escaping hardship, which raised one's status.

Occupations of English Immigrants

Research into the immigrant passenger lists and the British census bears this interpretation out, suggesting that opportunity was more important than adversity for most English immigrants. This is essential for understanding why theirs was a 'hidden' Diaspora, because the English did not have a unified theme of adversity to explain their arrival in America – as did virtually all others, the Africans and Irish being the most obvious examples. Generally speaking – and with many exceptions – most of the English who came to America in the nineteenth century seem to have been making essentially positive moves. Those threatened by technological displacement, unemployment and poverty were not as common as those whose occupations were still in demand in England and who still had a livelihood there. Even during the depression of 1840–42, and the famine-marked late 1840s, the most distressed were apparently not swelling the ranks of English immigrants: the handloom weavers and foundry workers, who were suffering technological displacement or unemployment at the time, were *not* leaving in significant numbers. Rather, it was the engineers, mechanics, skilled machinists, miners and others who were generally not facing unemployment in England who left in proportionately higher numbers.[18] Their letters back to England convey an enthusiasm for earning higher wages, gaining independence, securing a brighter future for their children and sometimes living in a land with more political and social equality and lower taxes. Much less often do we see indications of desperation.

Furthermore, letters and biographies reveal that even those who *were* facing unemployment or other hardships were often motivated primarily by

---

16   Milton Gordon, *Assimilation in American Life* (New York: Oxford University Press, 1964); Spickard, *Almost All Aliens*.

17   This is explored further in Belich, *Replenishing the Earth*, pp. 153–64.

18   William E. Van Vugt, *Britain to America: Mid-Nineteenth-Century Immigrants to the United States* (Champaign, IL: University of Illinois Press, 1999), p. 77.

American opportunity. Of all immigrants, the English – including those with jobs threatened by modernization such as handloom weavers – had the highest representation among those who could afford multiple tickets and travel with family members. They had some resources. And, most important, a large portion of the English immigrants were ultimately coming to America for land. They might work for years in their trade to accumulate sufficient capital, or combine craft work with farming. But surprisingly large proportions of immigrants – from an astonishing array of occupations – eventually took up farming in America. Many had a long-term goal all along to do so. Lawyers, doctors, soldiers, tradesmen of all kinds, even ballet dancers left England and became American farmers – some as late as the early twentieth century. Miners were especially likely to abandon the pick for the hoe. The shift from British industry to American farming is not that surprising because many of these people had some farm experience in England, took up non-agricultural work, and then made their long-delayed return to the soil in America.

English Farmers

As for English emigrant farmers themselves, one might expect to see a large, desperate movement following the repeal of the Corn Laws in 1846, which removed protection for English farmers, lowered prices and threatened their livelihoods. Repeal did have an impact: it forced many grain farmers to improve their land and methods in England to increase their production or perhaps raise more livestock to compensate for the falling grain prices. Yet some found it impossible to adjust because they lacked the capital necessary to increase their yields, or they farmed heavy clay lands that were hard to improve. Many of these farmers turned their eyes to America. Altogether, at mid-century farmers formed less than 9 per cent of the adult male labour force in England but nearly 20 per cent of the adult male emigrants. Young tenant grain farmers with some capital, but without the ability to adjust, seem to have predominated during this time of transition. And yet it is hard to characterize even this movement as an escape. Most could afford to emigrate as families. And though farmers unable to adjust did emigrate, it is also true that the opening up of new American lands inspired and enabled them to come to the United States. This was an especially viable option after repeal because the Erie Canal (financed largely by British investors) allowed English farmers to go west and exploit the new grain market opening up in their mother country. England and America were indeed an 'organic unity' creating an Anglo-boom of economic development.[19]

We also know from letters and other recently published sources that relatively prosperous farmers were also coming to the United States. Surprising

---

19 Ibid., ch. 3.

numbers were able to purchase land, even improved land, soon after or even upon their arrival – this in a time of falling prices in post-repeal England. They had much to gain from buying newly opened land in Illinois, Wisconsin and other parts of America's 'Old Northwest', where one could purchase land for the price of renting it for a few years in England. One might say that the 'pull' of American land was stronger than the 'push' of the repeal. Difficulties such as repeal for farmers or economic slumps for skilled workers were more the occasion than the cause of migration for people with long-term plans.[20]

Some English immigrant farmers stood out for raising agricultural standards, even though most ultimately had to assimilate to American agrarian conditions. Many were experienced in what was commonly called 'scientific farming', or, tellingly, 'English methods'. These methods, which had been developed in England in the eighteenth century, blended livestock farming with mixed crops, used manure extensively to preserve and improve the soil, and required much labour. English methods made economic sense in England, where labour was plentiful but land was scarce, but not so much in America, where land was plentiful, even free, but labour was scarce. So generally, the labour and land market forced English immigrant farmers to adopt American methods, which meant exploiting the land in order to maximize production. Nevertheless, English farmers still raised standards and made improvements that persisted in America. They imported many breeds of English livestock and helped open up the prairies by discarding the old notion that these soils were infertile and being among the first to settle on them. And because they had a long tradition of draining and farming wet soils in places such as Lincolnshire and Cambridgeshire, they could bring these techniques to the Old Northwest and other states with wetlands available for farming. Thus English farmers in America were remembered for both enhancing and adopting American agricultural methods.[21]

More 'Pull' than 'Push'?

Among non-agrarian immigrants we also see positive motives at play. Certainly there were poor English immigrants, but poverty does not explain the peaks of English migration that occurred in the early 1830s, the late 1840s to early 1850s, the late 1860s to early 1870s, and then the 1880s. For example, it was during the so-called 'Mid-Victorian Boom' of the early 1850s, when employment, wages and prospects were rising, that we see one of the most impressive spikes in English migration to America. And again, craftsmen, miners, farmers and skilled industrial workers were leading the surge, at a time of general improvement in England. Some miners and iron workers

---

20 Van Vugt (ed.), *British Immigration to the United States*.
21 Van Vugt, *Britain to America*, ch. 3; Van Vugt, *British Buckeyes*, ch. 4.

were leaving because of mine and mill owners' attempts to maximize their control and profits and lower wages, and because of the labour unrest that resulted (though this was more true in South Wales and Scotland than in England). And unskilled labourers, who were always common among the emigrants, were closer to the edge of subsistence. But for others, rising wages made migration more affordable and seem to have 'whetted their appetites' for more prosperity – for themselves and especially for their children. At the same time, America's lands and greater prospects for rewards – and the solid 'chains' of information and encouragement through letters from friends and family already in America – encouraged the English Diaspora.[22]

The relative prosperity (or perhaps more accurately the relative lack of desperation) of English immigrants is also suggested by the fact that they had higher proportions of elites – merchants, various professionals and those described as 'gentlemen'. In 1851 an estimated 400 male clerks, 700 merchants and 400 professionals (including lawyers, doctors, clerks and teachers) came directly from Britain. Others arrived via Canada. These people had always been relatively prominent among the immigrants because of the close economic ties between the two countries, and England's advanced, industrial economy required higher numbers of professionals, many of whom eventually turned to America. Additionally there were significant numbers of English women who had experience in medicine and teaching and contributed notably to American society, whether on the frontier or in the towns and cities.[23]

There is a danger of exaggerating this positive interpretation of the English Diaspora, its 'hidden' character, and of overdrawing the distinctions between English and other migrants. Recent research shows, for example, that, especially later in the century, St George's societies were more active than we had previously thought, giving aid to English immigrants and providing them with a familiar culture to help in their adjustment, much like other immigrant groups.[24] One can find examples of the English struggling with adjustment, and a recent scholar of immigrant letters concludes that the English 'certainly possessed a good deal of ethnicity'.[25] But still, the 'organic unity' of Anglo-American peoples and economies distinguished the English among other immigrants, provided them with opportunities to engage quickly and fully in the American economy and society, and helped hide the Diaspora.

---

22   Van Vugt, *Britain to America*, pp. 76–77, 154–55.
23   Ibid., pp. 111–12, 127–28.
24   Tanja Bueltmann and Donald M. MacRaild, 'Globalising St George: English Associations in the Anglo-World to the 1930s', *Journal of Global History*, 7.1 (2012), pp. 79–105.
25   David Gerber, *Authors of their Lives: The Personal Correspondence of British Immigrants to North America in the Nineteenth Century* (New York: New York University Press, 2006), p. 14.

The Economic and Religious Relationship

The special economic relationship of Britain and America was a boon for English immigrants. From the beginning, American industries were heavily if not totally dependent on English innovation and the immigrants who brought it. This applied to coal, iron, steel (including fine crucible steel), hard-rock mining and quarrying, cutlery, fine tools, pottery, the tin-plate industry and virtually all sectors of the textiles industries, including cotton, woollens and silk[26] (both spinning and weaving), calico printing and machine making. In some of these cases industries were directly transplanted to the United States by English and other British immigrants, complete with all the necessary skills, experience and sometimes even the machines. The English Diaspora produced a 'transatlantic industrial revolution' allowing the United States to become the world's second industrial nation.[27]

Like English immigrants, English investment was crucial to the American economy. British capital funded the Louisiana Purchase, the Erie Canal, railroads and industries. Meanwhile, London was underwriting the development of the American South's cotton lands: by 1838 about half of their bonds were held in England. Thus the growth of the American economy drew strength from the growth and vitality of the British economy, a fact that was also noted in the British press. And the enduring connection with Britain helped make the United States a major power. This was the economic context of the English Diaspora to America.[28]

Religion, another force brought by the English, also facilitated their assimilation and 'hid' their Diaspora. In colonial times the English transplanted the major Protestant religious denominations to America: the Congregationalists, Baptists, Quakers and Shakers, Presbyterians (who were mostly Scots or Scots-Irish), Anglicans/Episcopalians and most notably the Methodists. Though these denominations did take on American characteristics, especially on the frontier, they remained essentially English in their foundations and a place where new English immigrants could fit in. English newcomers did not have

---

26 See Richard D. Margrave, *The Emigration of Silk Workers from England to the United States of America in the Nineteenth Century* (New York: Garland Publishers, 1986); N. Tiratso, 'Coventry's Ribbon Trade in the Mid-Victorian Period: Some Social and Economic Responses to Industrial Development and Decay', unpublished PhD thesis, University of London, 1980.

27 David Jeremy, *Transatlantic Industrial Revolution: The Diffusion of Textile Technologies between Britain and America, 1790–1830s* (Oxford: Blackwell, 1981). Jeremy rightly cautions against exaggerating Britain's role in American industrialization but neither should it be underestimated. For many examples of English immigrants bringing skills and technology to American industry throughout the nineteenth century, see Van Vugt, *British Buckeyes*, ch. 5.

28 Frank Thistlethwaite, *The Anglo-American Connection in the Early Nineteenth Century* (Philadelphia, PA: University of Pennsylvania Press, 1959), pp. 10–12; Belich, *Replenishing the Earth*, pp. 180, 421–79.

to bring along their churches and form their own religious society, as did other immigrant groups. Their churches were already there, a place where they could hear familiar sermons and hymns and blend in with Americans.[29]

One particularly insightful example of how religion hid the English Diaspora is that of The Church of Jesus Christ of Latter Day Saints, or Mormons. This distinctly American movement resonated deeply with the English because they had the same evangelical roots. Already in 1837, only seven years after Joseph Smith published the *Book of Mormon*, Mormon missionaries arrived from America and targeted England's unemployed textile workers and others facing a bleak future. In 1840 the first English converts arrived in Nauvoo, moving on to Utah in 1848. Soon more than 5,000 other English converts arrived, and between 1853 and 1856 about 16,000 more followed. Many were recruited by the Church for their skills and were offered passage assistance in exchange for helping to build the settlement, and they were relatively invisible immigrants among their Mormon brethren. By 1870 nearly 38,000 English-born people were in Utah, forming nearly 20 per cent of the recorded population.[30]

Other English institutions that served to hide the English Diaspora in America include the English-modelled colleges, Masonic lodges and other fraternal organizations, which provided contacts between English and American members and served as convenient conduits for many skilled English immigrants.[31] American political institutions, despite their profound differences, were based enough on England's political tradition that the English could readily participate and assume positions of authority. No other immigrants were as quick to become governors, congressmen or judges. The essential commonality is more striking than the differences. As Gordon Wood sums it up, 'The most important fact about the [American] Founders may not have been the creativity of their imaginations but their Englishness.'[32]

The English Diaspora could also be hidden by the various reform movements, which were inherently transatlantic in nature and flourished in both England and the United States because of their shared religious culture. The temperance, abolition and other reform movements were linked by English immigrants and the extensive to-and-fro travel from both sides of the ocean by activists – abolitionism especially. In addition to the permanent immigrants, English abolitionists toured America and provided inspiration and assistance, particularly after 1833, when Britain abolished slavery throughout its empire. They financed William Lloyd Garrison's *The Liberator*, as well as Frederick Douglass's paper *The North Star*. The fact that in its first year of publication (1852) *Uncle Tom's Cabin* sold seven times more copies in Britain

29   Van Vugt, *British Buckeyes*, pp. 180–83, 189.
30   Van Vugt, *Britain to America*, ch. 9; Van Vugt, *British Buckeyes*, ch. 6.
31   Roger Burt, 'Freemasonry and Business Networking During the Victorian Period', *Economic History Review*, 56 (November 2003), pp. 657–88.
32   Gordon Wood on Bernard Bailyn, *New York Review of Books*, 13 February 2003, p. 53

than in the United States is a good indicator of the special attention that the English paid to American slavery. The vast majority of English immigrants hated slavery for all kinds of reasons, especially its inhumanity and violation of America's ideals of liberty and equality. And locally they were prominent in abolitionist movements. In this way the Anglo-American reform culture made some English immigrants part of the mainstream, and less visible.[33]

English immigrants' commonality with Americans was also reflected in their voting behaviour. Most other immigrants supported the Democrats, who generally welcomed immigrants and were opposed to social reform movements, especially temperance and abolitionism. But English immigrants overwhelmingly supported the Whigs and later the Republicans, many of whom were quite wary of immigrants, especially Catholics, and promoted government action in temperance, abolitionism and other reforms. The English voted as though they were already American.[34]

The Civil War and its Aftermath

In the American Civil War we see both the relative invisibility of English immigrants and their continued assimilation. At least 54,000 English fought for the Union, in greater proportions than any other immigrants. Letters and biographies reveal that many volunteered soon after their arrival – some virtually upon it. They had various motives, usually the right ones of hating slavery, wanting to purge America of its 'great stain' and preserving the Union. Some volunteered in order to squelch lingering doubts about their loyalty. Rather few were doing it for the pay without much regard for slavery, and still others fought for the Confederacy. But the English behaved uniquely because they signed up in American regiments, not even bothering to form their own, as all other immigrants did. They blended in with ordinary American regiments, as they did with society at large, and fought beside native-born Americans. English immigrants were to be found in nearly every situation and role in the Civil War, and in every major battle. Later in life, English immigrants looked back on the American Civil War as the most important event that made them full Americans.[35]

After the Civil War the new steamships took over immigration traffic: already by 1867 over 90 per cent of the passengers leaving English ports for America were on steamships. They were larger, faster, safer, better equipped

---

33 Van Vugt, *Britain to America*, ch. 9; Van Vugt, *British Buckeyes*, ch. 6; Van Vugt, *British Immigration to the United States*.

34 Paul Kleppner, *The Third Electoral System, 1853–1892: Parties, Voters, and Political Culture* (Chapel Hill, NC: University of North Carolina Press, 1979), pp. 61, 64, 147–48, 163–65; Van Vugt, *British Buckeyes*, p. 219.

35 Van Vugt, *Britain to America*, ch. 9; Van Vugt, *British Buckeyes*, ch. 6; Van Vugt, *British Immigration to the United States*.

and more closely regulated, though the voyage could still be miserable. Steamships encouraged migration among those who never would have sailed, and if America failed to satisfy they made a return to England easier. Steamships therefore facilitated the seasonal migration of temporary immigrants. Between 1860 and 1914 about 40 per cent of England's emigrants to America returned – a total of about 2 million returnees – the highest rate for northern Europeans, and roughly double the return rate of the Irish.[36] This high rate among the English is attributable to the seasonal immigrants, but also to the fact that, as was observed before, the English left less desperate circumstances than other immigrants and were thus more likely to find America wanting and reverse their migration decision.

After the war the English also continued their leadership in American labour movements. With their long tradition of Chartism, unionism and action for better and safer conditions in industries, English immigrants were natural labour leaders. Samuel Gompers, who was born in London to Dutch-Jewish parents, immigrated in 1863 and eventually became president of the American Federation of Labour, symbolizes this English leadership. English immigrants entering American labour fitted well into a culture that had derived much of its skills and labour movement from their former country.[37]

Settlement Patterns

English immigrants' settlement patterns reveal an ability to fit in just about anywhere as individuals or families in pursuit of opportunities. Aside from the few failed attempts at establishing their own colonies, the English generally filtered into existing society and were the least likely to form noticeable ethnic enclaves or neighbourhoods. At the state level they also showed an ability to settle in many places, reflecting their wide variety of occupational backgrounds and tendency to blend in. Certain states were especially attractive, especially in the Old Northwest, during much of the century. The greatest concentration of English immigrants in any state in 1850 was in Wisconsin: 6.2 per cent of its recorded population was born in England. In the following decade Illinois had the greatest net gain of English immigrants, followed by New York, Michigan, Wisconsin and Pennsylvania.[38]

After the Civil War, English miners headed west in such numbers that some of the highest concentrations of English immigrants, up to nearly a

---

36 Dudley Baines, *Migration in a Mature Economy: Emigration and Internal Migration in England and Wales, 1861–1900* (New York: Cambridge University Press, 1985), p. 140.

37 William E. Van Vugt, 'The British: English, Scots, Welsh, Scots Irish, 1870–1940', in Elliott Robert Barkan (ed.), *An Encyclopedia of United States Immigration History* (ABC–Clio Books, forthcoming 2012).

38 Charlotte Erickson, *Leaving England: Essays on British Emigration in the Nineteenth Century* (Ithaca, NY: Cornell University Press, 1994), pp. 60–64.

quarter of the population, could be found in the small silver-mining towns that sprang up in the mountains of Colorado, California and Montana, though their percentages fell as the mines became exhausted and the boom ended. But the copper, iron and lead mining communities that the English and Cornish established in the 1840s and 1850s continued to have fairly high concentrations. In 1880 about 12 per cent of the population of Houghton and Marquette counties, in upper Michigan, was recorded as English-born. And in 1880 Salt Lake County, Utah, recorded 22 per cent of its 31,977 people as English-born – a legacy of the earlier huge influx of English Mormon converts. In these specific places the English were relatively numerous, were often leaders in business and their communities, and were often remembered fondly as valued citizens. They blended in well, and yet were not necessarily 'hidden' but valued as people who reinforced the dominant white culture and helped build their communities.[39]

As the nineteenth century progressed, the interconnectedness of the British and American economies and the role of the English Diaspora reached new levels – often with astonishing results. For example, by 1890 Britain was getting 70 per cent of its grain imports from the American West. Britain was in effect 'outsourcing' its food supplies and in a sense 'recolonizing' America. Between the Civil War and 1900, over 500 joint-stock companies were formed in Britain to invest in the gold, silver and copper mines of the American West (of these, only 59 ever paid any dividends, the United States benefiting enormously from this investment). And London now had more American banks than did New York City.[40]

The growing linkage between the people and money of the two nations is perhaps most fittingly symbolized by the many marriages between English and American elites. As England suffered agricultural depression in the 1870s and landowners' incomes fell, some aristocrats facing the possibility of having to sell their lands found a solution in rich American women. The English had aristocratic titles but little cash, while America's richest businessmen had the opposite problem: more cash than they knew what to do with, but without the old-world prestige that could only come from the English aristocracy. By matching the rich daughters to cash-strapped lords, the English got the cash necessary to preserve their estates, the Americans the prestige and titles they craved. By 1903 more than 70 rich American women had married titled English men; more than 130 had done so by the First World War. Among the most famous Englishmen with American wives were Joseph Chamberlain, Rudyard Kipling, Lord Randolph Churchill and the Duke of Marlborough.[41]

---

39 Van Vugt, *Britain to America*; Van Vugt, 'The British'.
40 Belich, *Replenishing the Earth*, p. 480.
41 Ruth Brandon, *The Dollar Invasion: The American Incursion of the European Aristocracy, 1870–1914* (London: Weidenfeld and Nicolson, 1980); Burk, *Old World, New World*, ch. 7. During the entire, 'long' nineteenth century, 319 Americans married titled Britons.

This period also saw a decline in Americans' lingering Anglophobia, and even a budding Anglophilia among some. Americans were more likely to express a respect for the Queen, and the wealthy especially were commonly adopting English styles and tastes. The growing Anglo-American affinity was noticeable in England in 1877, when former President Grant toured England, met enthusiastic receptions and heard and delivered speeches hailing the common roots of English and American culture. And after President Garfield's assassination in 1881, the English exhibited such widespread expressions of grief and sympathy that commentators on both sides of the Atlantic sensed a growing Anglo-American friendship, purpose and commonality. English immigrants of this period could hardly have escaped such sentiments. The growing fascination and appreciation in England of American culture was symbolized in 1887 when Queen Victoria and many thousands of her subjects attended Buffalo Bill's Wild West Show at Earl's Court.[42]

The nostalgia and romance of the American West appealed to many English. The West was widely promoted in England as a place of opportunity for miners, ranchers and settlers of every sort. In 1860 there were over 55,000 English-born people living west of the Mississippi River. By 1900 there were nearly 145,000. Surprising numbers of elite English bought large tracts of western lands to create, or recreate, an aristocratic lifestyle that had eluded them in England. Some were children of landowners or lesser nobility who had no land or title to inherit, or they were members of the rising middle class, going west to have their own estates and a life of leisure, including fox hunting in equestrian gear. The first such settlement was established in Fairmont, Martin County, Minnesota, in 1856. Others were established after the war in Decorah and Le Mars, Iowa, and in Kansas. Unsurprisingly, all of these failed because of lack of experience, unrealistic expectations and harsh conditions. But the eccentricity of these peculiar English immigrants made them very visible indeed until they eventually went to American cities or returned to England.[43]

'New Immigrants' and Alienation

One aspect of the growing Anglo-American affinity was a conviction that the two Anglo-Saxon nations had a mission and destiny to spread their culture and enlighten the world. Social Darwinism, racial theory and the success of Anglo institutions and economy throughout the world convinced many that England and America had a right and duty to expand and dominate. Cecil Rhodes even envisioned a time when the two would re-unite politically in that global mission. More realistic people championed both British and American imperialism as the means of spreading Anglo-American culture and institutions. Rudyard

---

42 Van Vugt, 'The British'.
43 Van Vugt, *Britain to America*, pp. 118–21.

Kipling articulated this most famously in 'The White Man's Burden', which he wrote to encourage the Americans to keep and administer new territories acquired in the Spanish-American War. The perceived commonality of English and American culture and the 'invisibility' of English immigrants were also growing as the source of America's immigrants shifted more to southern and eastern Europe. This change was supposedly altering America's Anglo-Saxon identity from one largely derived from Britain and north-western Europe to one more diverse and multicultural, and less predominantly Protestant. These so-called 'new immigrants' provided a contrast that made the English seem even more similar to Americans of Anglo stock, and thus 'hidden'.[44]

To deal with growing urbanization, immigration and diversification the Progressive movement took shape, and English immigrants were involved with that too. The Salvation Army, founded in London in 1865, was brought to the United States in 1880 by English immigrants, and in 1904 Evangeline Booth arrived to take command. But the changing nature of America's immigrant labour force, the stresses of a rapidly urbanizing and industrializing society and the labour movement made some English immigrants feel more ethnic and alienated from American culture. From the late nineteenth century to the 1920s, for example, textile workers came from Bradford to Greystone, Rhode Island, and dominated the industry there for years, and like previous English immigrants they brought skills and experience and rose to important positions. But unlike previous English immigrants, they found assimilation slow and difficult in a society that was increasingly dominated by other immigrants and Americans who seemed different from the English. American culture was changing. These English newcomers did what they could to preserve their Englishness because it seemed under threat in industrial Rhode Island in the early twentieth century.[45]

Some of the English active in more radical labour movements gained reputations as socialists, even anarchists. One prominent example is John Turner, who was invited by the anarchist Emma Goldman to lecture in New York and was imprisoned at Ellis Island. Though Clarence Darrow took up his case and got him released, the Supreme Court ordered him to be deported in 1904. Hence an Englishman was the first alien ever deported from America for political beliefs. The association between the English and radicalism continued in the century, as many were blamed for the Seattle general strike of 1919, which was suppressed by federal troops, and were deported.[46]

Other English immigrants found themselves alienated from American life, in spite of their cultural closeness – some perhaps even because of it, as their similarities with America magnified the growing differences. With

---

44 Van Vugt, 'The British'.
45 Mary H. Blewett, *The Yankee Yorkshireman: Migration Lived and Imagined* (Urbana, IL: University of Illinois Press, 2009).
46 Vincent J. Cannato, *American Passage: The History of Ellis Island* (New York: Harper, 2009).

their common language and culture the English were often surprised and annoyed by Americans' strident nationalism and the pressure to praise their new country and condemn their old one. This problem went back to the Revolution, and was recorded by Charles Dickens and most other English travellers throughout the century. But in the twentieth century, many English immigrants seemed to be more culturally conservative. Those who were ideologically inflexible or who expected Americans to be more English in their traits and institutions found it hard to fit in fully. There were also some who had been pulled by unrealistic labour prospects and were physically or psychologically unfit for hard work. Some found the vastness of the land bewildering in comparison with the comparatively small island they had left.[47]

But it would be misleading to over-emphasize those examples where the English were so visible, resisted assimilation and saw only differences in American culture. These were a minority, and even those who continued to 'behave ethnically' in America eventually assimilated more quickly and completely than those of different languages and cultures. The 1920 census reveals that the English had the highest rate of intermarriage with Americans and were actually distinguished by their quick amalgamation with the native-born.[48]

Conclusion: Into the Twentieth Century

In the early twentieth century the English Diaspora headed increasingly to the Commonwealth. Already in 1905 Canada alone took in more English immigrants than did the United States, while the rest of the Commonwealth gradually increased its share. But this had less to do with frustrations over changing American culture than with a relative decline of American opportunity. Most industrial jobs were now going to unskilled immigrants. Meanwhile the British Empire Settlement Act of 1922 offered new incentives for the English to choose the Dominions over the United States, something which had long been a goal of British officials worried about their people going to competitor nations. Now the Empire could offer cheap or free land and assisted passages, as well as developing economies with plenty of opportunity for both skilled and unskilled workers, female domestic servants and those who wanted to farm or ranch. And the English could preserve their culture more fully in Canada, Australia or New Zealand than they could in the United States. By the First World War a mere 18 per cent of all English and Welsh emigrants were choosing the United States.[49]

47 This is explored further in Van Vugt, 'The British'.
48 E.P. Hutchinson, *Immigrants and their Children, 1850–1950* (New York: John Wiley and Sons, 1956).
49 Van Vugt, 'The British'; Kenneth Lines, *British and Canadian Immigration to the United States since 1920* (San Francisco: R&E Research Associates, 1978); N.H. Carrier

After the First World War the return rate of English immigrants fluctuated, but was always high, as it had been in the last half of the nineteenth century. In 1921 about 33,000 English immigrants arrived in the United States, but nearly 8,000 returned to England, for a return ratio of about 1 to 4. In 1928 only about 7,300 English arrived, but about 6,000 returned – an unprecedented ratio of 1 to 1.2. Other British immigrants of these years, particularly the Scots and Welsh, had much lower return ratios.[50] And again, this seems to indicate that, as in the previous century, the English were more likely to leave better circumstances in England and were thus more likely to be disappointed in America and return. They lacked the extensive adversity that pushed and defined other diasporas and made them so visible.

The common language and relative ease of assimilation of the English facilitated their migration and encouraged many to try America out, or to become seasonal migrants, in the knowledge that a return to England was always very possible. Moving from one place to the other, and maybe back again, was not as shocking as it was for other immigrant groups. The essential commonality of English and American culture, in spite of some deep differences, both stimulated the English Diaspora and caused high rates of return. And as English immigration to the United States slowed to a trickle, the English Diaspora in America remained relatively hidden but an essential foundation of the culture and economy of the United States.[51]

      and J.R. Jeffery, *External Migration: A Study of the Available Statistics, 1815–1950* (London: HM Stationery Office, 1953).

50   Van Vugt, 'The British'.

51   Ibid.

Chapter 5

An English Institution? The Colonial Church of England in the First Half of the Nineteenth Century

Joe Hardwick

Including the Church of England in a discussion of the formation of an 'English Diaspora' in the eighteenth and nineteenth centuries might, at first glance, seem highly problematic. Most of the literature on nineteenth-century Anglicanism has, after all, argued that the Church became less English as the century wore on. Classic Anglican theory held that 'Englishness' and 'Anglicanism' were coterminous: to be a citizen of the English state was to be Anglican. While a contemporary in 1800 might reasonably have coupled English and Anglican, from the 1830s onwards two developments challenged this relationship. First, constitutional reform in the late 1820s[1] confirmed that one could be both a citizen of the United Kingdom and a Roman Catholic or a nonconformist. Secondly, the worldwide spread of the Church – facilitated by missionaries from the seventeenth century onwards – resulted in a global and diverse Anglican faith characterized by multicultural and multi-ethnic churches that were not colonial facsimiles of the English Church 'back home'.[2] The Church of England had, by the time of the Lambeth Conferences of the later nineteenth century, become the global 'Anglican Communion'. Consequently, one might argue that a multicultural and global institution

---

1 The 1828 Sacramental Test Act, which allowed nonconformists to serve on municipal corporations, and the 1829 Catholic Relief Act, which allowed Roman Catholics to sit as Members of Parliament.

2 For the notion that expansion meant mutation and transformation, see W.L. Sachs, *The Transformation of Anglicanism: From State Church to Global Communion* (Cambridge: Cambridge University Press, 1993), and Brian Stanley, 'Afterword: The C.M.S. and the Separation of Anglicanism from "Englishness"', in Kevin Ward et al. (eds), *The Church Mission Society and World Christianity, 1799–1999* (Cambridge: Eerdmans, 2000), pp. 344–52.

such as the Church has little relevance for discussions about a putative English 'world' or 'diaspora'.

There is, however, another story to tell about the nineteenth-century Anglican Church, one that allows us to make the case for its inclusion in discussions about a 'hidden English Diaspora'. This story argues, contrary to the account given above, that the nineteenth century was a period when the Church attached itself more firmly to ideas of Englishness. The constitutional reforms of the late 1820s did not mean that the Anglican Church suddenly renounced its historic claim to be the Church of the 'English people'.[3] Although surprisingly little has been written about the relationship between the modern Church and Englishness,[4] a recent article by Arthur Burns points out that the various challenges confronting the Church after 1832 – the threat from dissent, the loss of its constitutional privileges, a 'free market' in religion in which denominations fought for adherents – stimulated the Church to make a renewed bid to be a national and English institution. In the late nineteenth and early twentieth centuries the Church consciously positioned itself at the forefront of national ceremonies, including coronations, commemorations and state funerals.[5]

So if the Church at home was trying to find new ways of underpinning its national credentials and its special relationship to the English people, what happened when it expanded overseas? Are historians correct to argue that the Church became less English as it migrated overseas? Or did colonial churchmen, like their metropolitan counterparts, assume that the colonial branch of the Church was as much the Church of the English people as the 'mother Church' back home? In short, did the Church play a role in the emergence of an English diaspora? With these questions in mind, this chapter will demonstrate that there was a cadre of Anglicans in the early and mid-nineteenth century who believed that the Church was not only an English institution, but that it would be the vital agent in a new, and more effective, form of colonization and settlement that would result in colonies that were miniature versions of England. This vision was premised on a particular idea of England, one whose parochial foundations in the rural squire–parson relationship were in sharp contrast to the industrial England that was just emerging. Therefore, the

---

3   The period after 1832 saw various proposals for how the Church could reconnect to the English people, the most famous being Thomas Arnold's 'Broad Church' manifesto, *Principles of Church Reform* (London: Fellowes, 1833).

4   This is not the case with the relationship between Protestantism and Britishness, a topic that has received considerable attention since Linda Colley's *Britons: Forging the Nation, 1707–1837* (New Haven, CT: Yale University Press, 1992). For doubts about the links between Anglicanism and Englishness, see Brian Young, 'A History of Variations: The Identity of the Eighteenth-century Church of England', in Tony Claydon and Ian McBride (eds), *Protestantism and National Identity: Britain and Ireland, c. 1650–c.1850* (Cambridge: Cambridge University Press, 1998), pp. 105–28.

5   Arthur Burns, 'The Authority of the Church', in Peter Mandler (ed.), *Liberty and Authority in Victorian Britain* (Oxford: Oxford University Press, 2006), pp. 179–200.

desire to create overseas replicas of England, this chapter argues, shows that Anglican clergymen, laymen and politicians (primarily but not exclusively belonging to a group labelled by historians 'orthodox high church') who voiced these ideas may well have been among the first to 'locate' an English diaspora. 'Diaspora', though an anachronistic term, is an appropriate way of describing the kind of imagined community of churchgoers that churchmen hoped to build. As we shall see, for many churchmen this diaspora would be inclusive, incorporating more than just committed Anglicans.

Divided into two sections, the chapter first samples a range of sermons, charges, clerical correspondence and periodical literature to explore the emergence, in the early nineteenth century, of the idea that the Church would play an integral role in the creation of Anglicized colonies, focusing in particular on North America and Australia. Many Anglicans in the period before (and indeed after) 1850 held to the idea that the Church was an essential means of establishing an empire that was knitted together by both a common polity and culture. The institutional aspect of this project was central. Unlike missionaries, for whom spreading the gospel was key, high church Anglicans believed that Church extension and the formation of England overseas could not occur without the extension of the Church's full institutional machinery of parishes, clergymen, congregations and bishops. The idea that religion was not enough on its own raises important questions about the extent to which English identity was, first and foremost, understood as being connected with English institutions rather than an organic English culture, race or folk tradition.[6]

The high Anglican concern to establish facsimiles of England across the settler empire has been explored by Howard Le Couteur.[7] Building on his work, the second section of this chapter shows how hopes of establishing replicas of the English Church overseas were frustrated: colonial churches were never replicas of the mother Church, nor can they be described as 'English' institutions or as transmitters of English values. But while the high Anglican vision of an English empire or diaspora with the Church at its heart was never likely to be realized – the settler colonies were too diverse, both ethnically and religiously – the persistence of the idea that the Church should be the necessary component of a kind of colonial Englishness is striking. Equally enduring was the more ambitious idea that Anglicanism could provide a common imperial faith that would bind together not only an English diaspora but also a 'Greater Britain'.[8]

---

6   The idea that institutions figured prominently in conceptions of English national identity in this period is touched on by Boyd Hilton in his *A Mad, Bad, and Dangerous People? England, 1783–1846* (Oxford: Oxford University Press, 2005), p. 715.

7   Howard Le Couteur, 'Anglican High Churchmen and the Expansion of Empire', *Journal of Religious History*, 32.2 (2008), pp. 193–215.

8   The increasing interest that churchmen of all denominations took in 'Greater Britain' as a mission field has been recently examined by Hilary Carey in her *God's Empire: Religion and Colonialism in the British World, c. 1800–1908* (Cambridge: Cambridge

The Transplantation of the National Church Overseas

The period between the loss of the American colonies in 1783 and the advent of representative government in the colonies of European settlement in the early 1850s was a period of dramatic expansion for the Church of England, just as it was for the other Protestant denominations and for Roman Catholicism. Of course the Church had an overseas presence before 1783: Anglican clergymen, churches and congregations existed throughout North America, while the East India Company maintained a handful of chaplains in its presidencies. But there were key differences in Church expansion after 1780. First, it had become a global affair, and secondly, it sought to establish the full institutional Church. The lack of bishops in eighteenth-century North America was seen by nineteenth-century Anglicans as the chief failing of previous Church extension, and was offered as an explanation for why Britain lost the colonies.[9]

The period after 1783, therefore, saw a more conscious effort to provide British settlers with the full Church machinery, the first Anglican bishoprics being established at Nova Scotia (1787), Quebec (1791) and Calcutta (1813). The British government did establish bishoprics in the West Indies in the 1820s and India and Australia in the 1830s, but from the 1830s onwards the imperial authorities were increasingly aware that such a policy was likely to alienate rather than integrate the empire; hence there was a move away from privileging any single denomination. For example, in the early 1830s the new Whig government phased out the annual grants that were made to the Society for the Propagation of the Gospel in the Canadas. Expansion of the Church and episcopate thereafter was left to voluntary effort. Moreover, 1841 saw the creation of the Colonial Bishoprics' Fund, a voluntary organization formed by prominent Anglican churchmen and laymen that went on to raise funds for eleven bishoprics between 1841 and 1850.[10] It should be remembered that the expansion of the *institutional* Church – primarily, though not exclusively, to serve European settlers – remained related but distinct from the expansion of *missionary* church activity with a conversion agenda.

By the 1830s and 1840s the global expansion of the Church came to be much more widely publicized within Britain. Alongside the missionary propaganda that focused on the conversion and civilization of the various 'dark' parts

---

University Press, 2010). Carey's book appeared after this chapter had been submitted for publication, so only limited use has been made of this valuable work. While this chapter broadly develops a similar argument to Carey – that Anglicans (mostly high church ones) did not renounce claims to represent the nation overseas – it pays more attention to the fault-lines in the Anglocentric basis of this vision.

9 For the debates surrounding attempts to establish colonial bishoprics in eighteenth-century North America, see Peter Marshall, *The Making and Unmaking of Empires: Britain, India, and America c. 1750–1783* (Oxford: Oxford University Press, 2005), pp. 41–42, 171.

10 Rowan Strong, *Anglicanism and the British Empire, c. 1700–1850* (Oxford: Oxford University Press, 2007), ch. 4.

of the earth, there appeared material that called for the expansion of the institutional Church, primarily for the growing number of English settlers who, as one clergyman put it in 1840, now seemed to be 'everywhere'.[11] Calls for the spread of the colonial episcopate and institutional Church were made by the East India Company chaplain, Claudius Buchanan, in a series of publications in the first decades of the nineteenth century,[12] and the annual reports of the SPG – the Church's primary outreach association – featured sermons justifying the expansion of the Church. The later 1830s and 1840s was a period when those responsible for the expansion of the Church made a determined effort to broadcast Anglican expansion to the public, with periodicals, bishop's journals, colonial Church histories and Church atlases all becoming available.[13] While Church histories gave celebratory accounts of the onward march of Anglicanism, Church atlases gave Anglicans the sense that they were members of a wider community of believers.

Within this wider context, what reasons did eighteenth- and nineteenth-century churchmen put forward in favour of overseas expansion? One reason, particularly prominent during the imperial crises of the 'age of revolution' period, was that the overseas Church was needed to raise the loyalty of recalcitrant colonial populations – whether these were slave, European or indigenous. An advocate of a bishopric in Calcutta in the late 1780s argued that the 'purifying, restraining and elevating influence' of a bishop would stamp out ominous signs of subversive political sentiment among Calcutta's European population.[14] There was also the theological argument that expansion was in accordance with the catholicity and universal truth of Anglicanism. Accompanying this was the providential notion that God had given Britain a vast empire in order to bring the gospel to the dark places of the earth. Rowan Strong's work shows that this kind of appeal to providence emerged in the early eighteenth century.[15] But there was also an argument that touched on ideas about national identity: the idea that the colonists should enjoy the blessings of the national English Church, just as they apparently enjoyed the blessings of other English institutions such as trial by jury and elected assemblies. As Charles Blomfield, bishop of London, wrote in 1840: 'Let every band of settlers, which goes forth from Christian England, with authority to

---

11   Benjamin Harrison to Edward Pusey, 13 February 1840, Liddon Bound Volumes, Pusey House Library, Oxford, vol. 47: Harrison to Pusey 1831–82, f. 42.
12   See Claudius Buchanan, *Colonial Ecclesiastical Establishment* (London: Cadell & Davies, 1813).
13   *The Colonial Church Atlas* (London: Society for the Propagation of the Gospel, 1842).
14   William Johnson, *A Circular Letter to the Most Reverend the Archbishops and Bishops of the Church of England* (London, 1788). Such arguments perhaps fed upon the negative stereotypes about emigrants common in the late eighteenth century; cf. James Belich, *Replenishing the Earth: The Settler Revolution and the Rise of the Angloworld* (Oxford: Oxford University Press, 2009), ch. 5.
15   Strong, *Anglicanism and the British Empire*, pp. 61–62.

occupy a distinct territory, and to form a separate community, take with it not only its civil ruler and functionaries, but its bishop and clergy.'[16]

Accompanying the idea that colonists should take with them customary institutions and rights was a second and more ambitious one: that the national English Church should provide a common institutional religion binding together Britain's colonies. A pan-imperial institution such as the Church, it was hoped, would be regarded as a symbol of imperial unity. After the loss of the American colonies in the 1780s a line of argument held that the continued unity of the empire demanded that colonies should replicate the institutions, values and civilization of England. The English Church was one such institution (the others being the monarchy and 'imperial' parliament) which would unify what was left of the British Empire. In 1805 Claudius Buchanan observed that 'English religion' was necessary to 'consolidate our widely extended dominions',[17] ideas that fed into the creation of the Calcutta bishopric.

English Church and British Empire in the 1840s

Although the notion that the *English* Church would serve as a unifying agent in a *British* Empire was pregnant with contradictions, it emerged with particular force during the emigration surges of the 1830s and 1840s. The expansion of the settler dominion in these decades prompted a renewed effort by churchmen to ensure that settlers were supplied with churches; the SPG, for instance, instituted a widespread fund-raising tour in England in the summer of 1839. The Tory Robert Inglis said in the Commons in 1843 that no colony deserved 'the name of a colony of Great Britain' that was not 'a miniature representation of England'. There was 'no surer bond of union', Inglis went on, 'than the bond of religious community', hence the need for an overseas English Church.[18] Similarly, at an SPG meeting in 1846, the Revd Henry Manning, the Tractarian who would later convert to Roman Catholicism, called for a stronger overseas Church on the basis of 'the law of nature' that stated 'that organized life shall reproduce the germ of its own organization'. For Manning it was the Church that was the 'basis of the perpetuity' of the British Empire. Despite the fact that churchmen were themselves struggling to build meaningful links between the different branches of the Church of England (the SPG's 1851 jubilee was the first time colonial, Irish, American and

---

16 Charles Blomfield, *A Letter to His Grace the Lord Archbishop of Canterbury, upon the Formation of a Fund for Endowing Additional Bishoprics in the Colonies* (London: Fellowes, 1840), pp. 8–9.

17 Claudius Buchanan, *Memoir of the Expediency of an Ecclesiastical Establishment for British India* (London: Cadell & Davies, 1805), p. 13.

18 *Hansard's Parliamentary Debates*, 3rd series, lxviii, cols. 577–78.

British churchmen met together), Manning and others remained wedded to the idea that the Church would provide the national religion that would bind together the empire.[19] The idea that both the *religious* content and *institutional* structure of the Church of England were necessary in the establishment of English colonies and a unified empire was crucial.

These contemporary comments are striking for two reasons. First, they reveal that many Anglicans had a remarkably narrow appreciation of the religious and ethnic composition of the colonies. Britain's colonies were, after all, British rather than English, and populated by more than just Anglicans. This would have been obvious to anyone who glanced at the 'blue books' on the religious composition of the colonies that colonial governors sent back annually to the Colonial Office from the early 1820s onwards. Intended as chronicles of the expansion of the colonial Church, such returns showed instead that Anglicans were rarely a majority in colonial populations. Despite such evidence, Anglican churchmen held that the colonies were English property, and – rather unconvincingly – asserted that multiple established churches were unnecessary because the colonists themselves regarded the Anglican Church as the Church of the British nation overseas. In 1816 Thomas Middleton, first bishop of Calcutta, explained that 'nothing could be more needless or more mischievous' than an established Presbyterian Church in India, because 'the English and the Scotch in India had hitherto been as one church and one nation'.[20] William Grant Broughton, bishop of Australia, called the Scots in New South Wales 'sour and wrongheaded' for asking for their own establishment.[21] In Upper Canada, John Strachan, archdeacon of York, Ontario, believed settlers would gravitate to the Church, and he confidently informed the lieutenant governor in 1820 that if Anglican clergy were more numerous, 'those who have not yet joined any denomination will attach themselves to the Established Church', a claim that was of course strongly resisted by non-Anglicans.[22] All this raises an important point: Strachan and others appear to have regarded the Church of England as the Church of much more than just the Anglican community. For Strachan, himself a Scot and a

---

19   *Proceedings at a Meeting Held in the Egyptian Hall, Mansion House, on Tuesday, March 17, 1846, to Increase the Means of Religious Instruction for the Emigrants and Settlers in the British Colonies, through the SPG* (London: Clay, 1846), pp. 26–27.

20   Thomas Middleton to William Wilberforce, 21 June 1816, printed in Robert I. Wilberforce and Samuel Wilberforce (eds), *The Correspondence of William Wilberforce* (London, 1840), II, p. 347.

21   William Grant Broughton to Edward Coleridge, 14 October 1839, Broughton Papers, Moore Theological Library, Sydney, 1/7.

22   George W. Spragge (ed.), *The John Strachan Letter Book: 1812–1834* (Toronto: Ontario Historical Society, 1946), p. 200. An 1830 public meeting petitioned against the Anglican Church's monopoly over one-seventh of the land in the colony, arguing that 'there is not any peculiar tendency to that Church among the people': *Upper Canada. A Copy of a Petition to the Imperial Parliament Respecting the Clergy Reserved Lands* (London: Traveller, 1831), p. 22.

convert from Presbyterianism, it was the Church of not only the English, but also the British overseas.[23]

The second striking feature is that such arguments were articulated with particular vigour *after* the imperial authorities started to abandon the traditional policy of creating colonial versions of the English church–state constitution. As stated above, from the early 1830s the British government cut back on Anglican privileges. Legislation such as the 1836 New South Wales Church Act, which ended exclusive endowments to the Church and granted state aid to each of the four main Christian denominations, suggested that the colonies would develop as multi-denominational, multi-ethnic spaces. But rather than dampen Anglican hopes, shifts in imperial policy only seem to have strengthened Anglican attachments to an English national identity. Interestingly, there are signs that Anglican churchmen were trying in this period to present themselves as spokespersons for the English community overseas. It was, for instance, Anglican churchmen who gave the sermons at St George's Society meetings in British North America.[24] The 1830s also did little to dissuade Anglicans from the belief that the Church would play a key role in spreading the English nation overseas. Indeed, William Broughton, bishop of Australia from 1836 to 1853, appears to have found a revived confidence in the competitive environment of the mid-1830s. In a letter to a friend in England in November 1837, Broughton explained that his aim was 'to make the Colonies so like England that they may form together [in] one body'. He had written in a similar vein a month earlier: 'it is not enough that the Church of England be secured in England [...] its principles must be carried out to the most distant quarters of the English <u>empire</u>. Wherever our language is, there our Church <u>should</u> be.'[25] The aims of men such as Broughton were far removed from the modest goals of colonial churchmen in the previous century. As Jeremy Gregory has shown, clergy in eighteenth-century New England sought only to 'refashion' colonies so that the Church of England stood equal with dissent.[26] But in the nineteenth-century empire, just as much as in metropolitan Britain, the weakening of the bonds between church and state perhaps stimulated the Church to both reassert its ties with the English people and to find ways of recasting itself as an 'established' and 'national' institution.

---

23 For Anglican cultivation of a 'British' identity in the Canadian context, see Michael Gauvreau, 'The Dividends of Empire: Church Establishments and Contested British Identities in the Canadas and the Maritimes, 1780–1850', in Nancy Christie (ed.), *Transatlantic Subjects: Ideas, Institutions, and Social Experience in Post-Revolutionary British North America* (Montreal: McGill-Queen's University Press, 2008).

24 One example of these sermons is G.J. Mountain, *Responsibilities of the Englishmen in the Colonies of the British Empire* (Quebec: J.C. Fisher, 1847).

25 Broughton to Joshua Watson, 9 November 1837, Broughton Papers Misc.; Broughton to Coleridge, 19 October 1837, BP 1/3.

26 Jeremy Gregory, 'Refashioning Puritan New England: the Church of England in British North America, c. 1680–c.1770', *Transactions of the Royal Historical Society*, 20 (2010), p. 93.

The comments of Broughton and others show that Anglican laymen and churchmen in the first half of the nineteenth century held to the idea that the Church would play a central role both in unifying the empire and in establishing miniature versions of England overseas, creating, as one clergyman put it at the opening of a college in Upper Canada in 1842, colonies that were 'noble suburban precinct[s] to metropolitan England'.[27] But who was articulating these ideas? The quotations above suggest that they could appeal to evangelicals (such as Claudius Buchanan) just as much as high churchmen (like Broughton). One might speculate that Anglo-Catholic Tractarians would have been less interested in national issues given the emphasis they placed on the catholicity of the Church of England, but it is suggestive that bishop John Medley of Fredericton – sometimes called the 'first Tractarian bishop' – said, in 1845, that 'building a Cathedral in this Province may in some sense be called a national work'.[28] What is clear is that particularly strong support for English Church colonization came from Oxford-educated high Anglicans in the 'Peelite' circle surrounding William Gladstone; as Gladstone would famously say, in 1855, the aim of colonization was the 'reproduction of the image and likeness of England'.[29] It was this group that would lend support to the most remarkable example of Anglican colonization: the venture to establish the Canterbury colony in New Zealand in the late 1840s.[30] What can be said is that it was primarily the Anglican elite who held to the notion of an Anglican-directed English colonization.

The creation of England overseas rested on two pillars. The first was that the Church ensured it monopolized the education of colonial youth. Archdeacon Strachan in Upper Canada noted in the early 1810s that 'the attachment of the inhabitants [of Upper Canada] must be founded on early habits & opinions & these can only be produced and cherished by a proper system of religious & moral instruction'.[31] The second pillar was the establishment of colonial churches institutionally identical to the home Church – whether in terms of structure, government, personnel or architecture. Middleton in Calcutta told his clergy that he wanted them to be 'in all respects placed upon the footing of parochial incumbents', and 'that each of them was to have his parish church, to which he was to be assisted in the superintendence of his

---

27 Henry Scadding, *The Eastern Oriel Opened* (Toronto: Rogers, Thompson, 1842), p. 8.
28 John Medley, 'Address' (1845), in Alan Hayes, *Anglicans in Canada: Controversies and Identities* (Urbana, IL: University of Illinois Press, 2004), p. 261.
29 W.E. Gladstone, 'Our Colonies' (1855), reprinted in Barbara Harlow and Mia Carter (eds), *Imperialism and Orientalism: A Documentary Sourcebook* (Malden, MA: Blackwell, 1999), p. 369
30 J.E. Cookson, 'Canterbury Association (*act.* 1848–52)', *Oxford Dictionary of National Biography*, http://www.oxforddnb.com/view/theme/93787 (accessed 19 November 2010).
31 Spragge (ed.), *Strachan Letter Book*, p. 81.

flock by churchwardens and overseers, as the parochial clergy in England'.[32] Similarly, Broughton, on taking up the Australian bishopric in 1836, stated that he sought to use 'all means to strengthen the Church of England in this quarter', a task that could only be done by 'enabling her to expand, wherever she goes, her proper system of polity: her orders of Bishops, priest and deacon'. Elsewhere he said his aim was to introduce in his colony 'under another name, the English parochial system of parson of the parish'.[33]

By the 1840s, however, criticisms were being voiced that not enough had been done to extend the episcopate. That decade therefore witnessed demands for a more effective kind of Church extension, one characterized by centralized ecclesiastical authority, doctrinal unity and more cohesive and hierarchical church structures. In an 1840 letter to the archbishop of Canterbury, Bishop Blomfield of London argued that 'it is not enough that we send out with [settlers] [...] a certain number of missionaries'. Blomfield called instead for a more ordered colonial Church: 'Each colony must have, not only its parochial, or district pastors, but its chief pastor, to watch over, and guide, and direct the whole.' 'An Episcopal Church without a bishop', he added, 'is a contradiction in terms.'[34] Blomfield's letter was a prompt for the Bishoprics' Fund in 1841, which in turn resulted in the creation of a global network of colonial bishoprics, a surge in the number of colonial clergy and the creation of new parishes and rectories across the Empire.

Perhaps the apogee of the idea that the institutional Church of England was the key to English colonization came in the late 1840s, with the creation of the Canterbury settlement in New Zealand. This project was led by a group of Anglicans who were influenced by Edward Gibbon Wakefield's ideas about a new form of 'systematic colonization' that would replicate overseas the institutions and structure of what was taken to be English society. The colony was to receive only English and Anglican settlers, and it was to have a class system and an established Anglican Church just like England's.[35] Canterbury, we might speculate, gives us an approximation of what an ideal society looked like for a group of mid-century high churchmen. Hopes that Canterbury would stand as a model Anglican and English colony were soon dashed: the colony could not attract an exclusive flow of English settlers, nor could its founders prevent inter-denominational marriages. The 1881 census showed that less than half of the colony's population professed allegiance to the Church of England.[36]

---

32 Henry Bonney, *Sermons and Charges, by the Right Reverend Father in God, Thomas Fanshaw Middleton* (London: Longman & Co., 1824), pp. 191, 201.
33 Broughton to Coleridge, 3 April 1840, BP 1/9; Broughton to Watson, 31 July 1837, BP Misc.
34 Blomfield, *A Letter to His Grace*, p. 5.
35 For further details on the settlement, see the chapter by Patterson in this volume.
36 K.A. Pickens, 'Denomination, Nationality and Class in a Nineteenth-Century British Colony: Canterbury, New Zealand', *Journal of Religious History*, 15.1 (1988), pp. 128–40.

An English Institution?
Shortcomings of the High Church Project

Canterbury's failure mirrored the wider failure of the Anglican aim of establishing colonial Englands. The major problem was that it proved impossible to create colonial churches that were institutionally identical to the one at home. But there were other problems as well. Ideas about replicating colonial Englands rested on a narrow reading of the ethnic and religious composition of the British Empire, and were founded on the increasingly problematic understanding that the English Church was coterminous with the English nation. Therefore, the fact that men such as Broughton continued to believe that transplanting England overseas could not happen without the institutional Church seems strange. But it perhaps speaks to the enduring power of an institutional definition of English national identity, namely the idea that institutions were central to English self-conceptions, and that their recreation was necessary for maintaining a connection with the mother country. Indeed, it may be that the notion that English identity was based primarily on institutional attachments explains why Anglican churchmen believed the Church could and should serve more than just those of English descent. The Anglicans studied here seem to have believed that non-English people could become members of an English colony – if not become Englishmen and women – if they attended and identified with the English Church.[37]

The second major problem with the Anglican project revolved around the idea expressed by Manning, Inglis and others that the institutional Church would not only help to create miniature Englands overseas, but would also provide a common imperial faith that would unite the English overseas, as well as – and this bold step was made – the inhabitants of the British Empire more generally. This ignored the fact that for populations of Scottish Presbyterians, nonconformist Welsh and Roman Catholic Irish, to say nothing of Hindus and Muslims, an imperial Anglican Church was likely to be more a source of disunion than union. This was also an idea that sought to claim for the Anglican Church a more privileged role than it in fact enjoyed abroad. Anglicans seemed slow to adapt to the changes in imperial religious policy implemented by both Whig and Tory after the mid-1830s: they still referred to the national Church that would unify what one of the Whig architects of this new imperial religious policy, Lord John Russell, called the 'English people' overseas.[38]

---

37 Significantly, in Upper Canada in 1813 John Strachan was desirous of welcoming into the Anglican fold a 'respectable congregation of German settlers on the river St. Lawrence'; he also believed that an Anglican college with French and English students would 'melt our population into one' and lead to Upper Canada becoming 'what alone can render it really valuable to the Crown[:] an English Colony'. Spragge (ed.), *Strachan Letter Book*, pp. 43, 59.

38 *Proceedings at a Meeting Held in the Egyptian Hall*, p. 15.

But the most striking problem with the high church vision of empire was that it failed to achieve its most basic task: establishing replicas of English institutions overseas. The English Church mutated in the course of transplantation. This was clearly the case when Anglicanism was introduced among non-European indigenous communities, but a similar process of modification and adaptation occurred in settler churches too. Some things of course remained the same – church architecture was largely modelled on English forms.[39] Moreover, settlers tried to replicate the norms of the English Church in their colonies, but the colonial environment, coupled with logistical problems, meant that colonial churches quickly developed unique institutional characteristics, complicating the claim that the Anglican Church overseas was an 'English institution'.[40] Two ways in which colonial churches differed from their metropolitan counterpart stand out.

The first was the unique diversity of the colonial clerical workforce. In some parts of the colonial Church there was a sizeable number of non-English clergy. For example, roughly one-third of the Anglican clergy in Upper Canada either had Irish backgrounds or had been educated at Irish higher education institutions, and there was a similarly important Scottish component around Bishop Strachan.[41] This conflicted with the aims of many colonial bishops who hoped for English clergymen. Bishop Perry of Melbourne wanted 'sound sensible sober-minded Englishm[e]n', while Broughton's early correspondence reveals his desire for the same kind of learned and scholarly men from the ancient universities who filled incumbencies back home: men who could transmit the right kind of gentlemanly and English values to the Australian bush.[42] But those responsible for recruitment had a hard time finding suitable candidates. Difficulties in tempting men overseas meant that colonial dioceses became home to a variety of clergy from non-university, Irish and evangelical backgrounds; not exactly the men Broughton and Perry had in mind. Indeed in 1850 Broughton explicitly told the SPG to stop sending him 'too large a proportion of Irish graduates'.[43]

The second feature that distinguished the colonial and metropolitan Church was the space available for lay involvement in colonial Church structures. Historians of the metropolitan Church have argued that as a result of the great Church reforms of the post-1832 period, the lay voice in Church affairs in England became increasingly marginalized, with bodies such as

---

39 E.J. Kerr, 'Designing a Colonial Church: Church Building in New South Wales, 1788–1888', unpublished DPhil thesis, University of York, 1977.
40 Le Couteur, 'Anglican High Churchmen', p. 215.
41 The important contribution made by the Church of Ireland to the Church in Upper Canada is addressed in Donald H. Akenson, *The Irish in Ontario: A Study in Rural History* (Montreal: McGill-Queen's, 1984), pp. 263–68.
42 Charles Perry to Broughton, 7 June 1850, BP Misc; Broughton to Coleridge, 19 October 1837, BP 1/3.
43 Broughton to Coleridge, 13 July 1850, BP 1/88.

churchwardens and vestries giving up responsibility for local church affairs to new centralized ecclesiastical structures such as the Church Commissioners.[44] The reverse seems to have been the case in the colonies, particularly those that did not have a bishop until later in the century. Here the task of financing and organizing the building of colonial churches fell on the laity, with the result that those who provided the funds claimed full control over church affairs – a situation that often led to bitter disputes once a bishop did show up.[45] While bishops did want episcopal control over church property and lay organizations, such as vestries, the tradition of lay involvement in the colonies continued into the later nineteenth century with the synods that most colonial dioceses established after the 1850s. Lay involvement in these synods did not come without a struggle. Bishop Broughton fought a losing battle in his diocese to try to prevent laymen from voting on doctrinal issues in his synod. At various flashpoints throughout the century, this empowered laity threatened to undermine the hierarchical structure that was central to the identity of the Anglican institution Broughton and others hoped to build.

One might question how seriously these features threatened what we have been calling the high Anglican vision of empire. For example, one might argue that there was space for Irish Protestants such as Church of Ireland clergy within an imperial Britishness if not an imperial Englishness; indeed a strand in recent historiography has emphasized that Irish Catholics and Protestants were more attached to the empire than they were to the Union.[46] But from another perspective these differences between home and colonial churches did pose a serious challenge to an Anglican imperial project that rested on transplanting the institutional Church intact. Church of Ireland clergymen and laymen were at the forefront of the campaigns for more lay-focused church synods. Broughton moaned about 'the prevalence of a levelling puritanical turn of thought among the laity' in his diocese, 'too much encouraged', he claimed, 'by certain Irish clergy'.[47] Irish churchmen also spearheaded attacks on the religious teaching at colonial Anglican colleges. In the late 1840s Broughton refused to ordain two Irish clergymen to the priesthood when they criticized the education provided at his St James' College in Sydney. Benjamin Cronyn, the Irish bishop of Huron, sparked a row with the aged Bishop John Strachan over Trinity College, Toronto, in 1860 – an institution that Cronyn regarded as 'dangerous to the young men

44 Frances Knight, *The Nineteenth-Century Church and English Society* (Cambridge: Cambridge University Press, 1994), ch. 5.

45 For discussion of a Calcutta example, see Joseph Hardwick, 'Vestry Politics and the Emergence of a Reform "Public" in Calcutta, c. 1813–1836', *Historical Research*, 84.223 (2011), pp. 87–108.

46 Jennifer Ridden, 'Britishness as an Imperial and Diasporic Identity: Irish Elite Perspectives c. 1820–1870s', in Peter Gray (ed.), *Victoria's Ireland? Irishness and Britishness 1837–1901* (Dublin: Four Courts, 2004), pp. 88–105.

47 Broughton to Watson, 9 February 1852, BP Misc.

educated there' owing to the 'unsound and unProtestant' education on offer.[48] These examples suggest that Irish churchmen could stand as serious critics of the kind of Church that high churchmen were building overseas.

So by mid-century colonial churches were developing distinct features and were emerging as self-governing institutions. While this did not necessarily mean that colonial churchmen developed unique colonial identities – Anglicans across the empire continued to look to Canterbury and England for spiritual guidance – there is evidence that even colonial churchmen began to see their dioceses as distinct spaces. For example, most colonial bishops began to favour the employment of clergymen who were sourced locally rather than from England. Bishop Strachan made a particularly early call, in 1815, for Canadian clergy who were suited to the colonial environment,[49] and even Broughton, in the 1840s, called for local clerical training colleges, partly because he realized that Oxford and Cambridge graduates were not best suited to the rigours of colonial work. Broughton and other bishops established their own theological colleges where they could provide a specialist colonial clerical training, while, in 1848, St Augustine's College opened in Canterbury, England, specifically for the training of colonial clergy.

Despite the increasing autonomy and growing sense of unique identity among colonial dioceses, the idea that Britain's colonies could be tied to the mother country by the bonds of Anglicanism was an enduring one, albeit increasingly articulated by only a minority. It reappeared in the later nineteenth century with the rise of 'Greater Britain', a term for the British settler dominion first used by Charles Dilke in 1868.[50] It is suggestive that, from 1876, the organ of the Commonwealth and Continental Church Society, which supplied settlers with clergy, was entitled *The Greater Britain Messenger*.[51] That Anglicans continued to believe the Church would occupy a privileged position in this Greater Britain can be seen in the ideas of the secretary of the SPG, Henry Montgomery, the former bishop of Tasmania. In his role at the SPG in the 1890s and 1900s, Montgomery sought to both unify the Anglican Church and to awaken it to its position as the church of a widely scattered 'Anglo Saxon race'. Styling himself 'archbishop of Greater Britain', Montgomery saw the Church, which he rebranded as an imperial church, as the unifying agent in a federated British Empire. His ideas were echoed by an American Episcopalian in 1900 who said that 'Greater Britain had been hardly a possibility save for the

---

48 J.J. Talman, 'Cronyn, Benjamin', *Dictionary of Canadian Biography Online*, vol. 10, http://www.biographi.ca (accessed 19 November 2010).
49 Because, he said, the English clergyman's 'manners & habits will not easily accommodate themselves to those of his parishioners': Spragge (ed.), *Strachan Letter Book*, p. 74.
50 The Church's claim to be the national Church of Greater Britain is studied in detail in Carey, *God's Empire*.
51 *The Greater Britain Messenger* (London, 1876–97).

development of the Missionary spirit in the Church of England.'[52] This vision mirrored that of Anglicans in the first half of the nineteenth century, and was one that rested on the same Anglocentric and narrow understandings of the religious and ethnic makeup of the British Empire.[53]

Conclusion: The National Church of a British Empire or an English Diaspora?

This chapter has argued that a discussion of the 'English diaspora' cannot overlook the role that Anglican churchmen played in locating its existence. The key reason for this Anglican interest was that many churchmen remained closely attached to notions of Englishness, despite the fact that colonial churches can hardly be described as 'English' institutions. While it is true that some Anglicans believed that the Church should concentrate on serving committed Anglicans overseas,[54] the sample of churchmen studied here suggests that some believed that the Church should restate its claim to national and established status, and that it should persist as the Church of an English people who were now spread globally. Although by the second half of the nineteenth century this was very much a minority position,[55] there continued to be the expectation among churchmen that, as Strachan put it in 1840, 'we are the Established Church of the Colonies as well as England'.[56] Though easy to dismiss as an obsolete relic, it is the persistence of these Anglican claims to establishment and nationality, both at home and overseas, that is striking. But as we have seen in the Anglican use of the concept of 'Greater Britain', churchmen's ambitions went beyond the English and the 'English diaspora'. Indeed, while Anglican churchmen did talk about 'the English' and the 'English empire', their interest in a 'Greater Britain' and their claim to be

---

52   C.F. Pascoe, *Two Hundred Years of the S.P.G.* (London: SPG, 1901), p. x.

53   This paragraph is based on Steven Maughan, 'Imperial Christianity? Bishop Montgomery and the Foreign Missions of the Church of England, 1895–1915', in Andrew Porter (ed.), *The Imperial Horizons of British Protestant Missions, 1880–1914* (Cambridge: Eerdmans, 2003), pp. 32–57.

54   When Lord John Manners – a member of the Canterbury Association – gave a speech in which he referred to the 'unprecedented force' of recent emigration, he acknowledged that the English settler was not always Anglican. Admitting that a considerable portion of 'vast crowd' of emigrants belonged to other communions, he still held that 'the great mass of English peasantry and artificers' were Anglicans. See Manners, *The Church of England in the Colonies. A Lecture Delivered before the Members of the Colchester Literary Institution* (London: W.H. Smith, 1851), p. 6.

55   As Hilary Carey points out, by the second half of the nineteenth century most would have argued that the lack of establishment in the empire, rather than its presence, was the basis for imperial unity: Carey, *God's Empire*, p. 13.

56   Strachan to the bishop of Exeter, 22 May 1840, Letter Books of John Strachan, Archives of Ontario, Toronto, MS 35 reel 11, Letterbook 1839–1843, p. 58.

the national Church of the British Empire does raise doubts about whether an 'English diaspora' is really the best way of conceptualizing the space or population that Anglican churchmen were seeking to reach out to.

A key outstanding question is whether membership of the Anglican Church did confer on individuals a claim to an English identity. The hostility that high churchmen such as Broughton showed towards Irish churchmen, and the fact that English bishops labelled them 'Irish' at moments of particular tension, suggests that membership of the Anglican Church, itself a very diverse institution, was no guarantee of Englishness. Another key issue is the extent to which non-Anglican denominations sought to present themselves as English when they migrated overseas. To take one example, recent work has shown that nineteenth-century patriotic English Benedictines sought to create an 'imperial English Catholicism' to challenge the Irishness of the British Catholic diaspora.[57]

Perhaps the most important question that this chapter has not addressed is what churchmen meant by 'England' and the 'English'. The evidence presented here suggests that throughout this period contemporaries confused 'England' with 'Britain', and assumed that the colonies were extensions of the former rather than the latter. The idea of England held by Bishop Broughton and other high churchmen seems to have been the hierarchical and paternal world of the squire–parson relationship. This vision was challenged by others in the colonies – for instance the Anglican laymen who challenged Broughton over the structure of colonial synods fixed upon a less hierarchical definition of England. For them the separation of powers that they were trying to achieve in the Church was in line with what they understood to be traditional English liberty and freedom of speech. Explaining who high churchmen were referring to by 'the English' is more difficult. They seem to have used the word in an expanded and inclusive sense, to include much more than just those who were of English descent: the Church, which they held was central to English identity, would encompass the Scots, Welsh and Irish, groups that would all be incorporated in an English empire, an English diaspora, a Greater Britain or a British Empire. Of course this rather ignored the small problem that these groups were unlikely to see the Church as a source of unity.

---

57 Aidan Bellenger, 'The English Benedictines and the British Empire', in Sheridan Gilley (ed.), *Victorian Churches and Churchmen: Essays presented to Vincent Alan McClelland* (Woodbridge: Boydell, 2005), pp. 94–109.

Chapter 6

The Importance of Being English: English Ethnic Culture in Montreal, c.1800–1864

Gillian I. Leitch

'The British Bow'
by C. Swain

Hurray! The bow, the British bow
The gallant fine old English bow!
Never flashed sword upon the foe,
Like arrow from the good yew bow!
What knight a solider weapon wields?
Thou victor of a thousand fields;
Are lances, carbines, thy compeers?
No, vouch it, Creedy and Poitiers!
With hearts of oak and bows of yew,
And shafts that like the lightning low,
Old England wore her proudest crown,
Nor bolt nor brand might strike it down!
Hurrah![1]

Published in 1835, this poem presented, for its Montreal readership, both an English identity and a British one, using the two interchangeably. The imagery is clear: the oak, the yew and the battles are all English, iconic signifiers of a sense of Englishness; but they are also British. In this conflation lies the problem that historians of the English face: how do we define English identity as distinct from British identity? In the Canadian context, but particularly in the province of Quebec, English identity is further problematized because English serves not only as an ethnic identity but also as the language of

---

1   *Montreal Courier*, 3 September 1835.

the conqueror. The division of language between French and English was an important one as it differentiated the old population from the new, the conquered from the conqueror, and complicated intergroup communication. English was not, as in the United States, a language of integration but a group identifier, dividing one group from the other.[2] The division between language groups – French and English – has long since marked tensions in Quebec, not least because English ethnic identity began to disappear in a blend of Britannia and language laws. As Bruce Elliot observed:

> In earlier generations it was quite fashionable to view Canada, a former British colony, as essentially an English country, or to consider the English and the French as the two 'founding peoples' or 'charter groups.' Though sensibilities towards the First Nations and immigrant peoples have changed, the result has not been a rush to study or define clearly the English experience in Canada. Unlike the Scots and the Irish, both of whom have attracted much scholarly interest, the English continue to be virtually ignored.[3]

According to Pauline Greenhill, the Canadian English 'have not been considered an ethnic group – in the sense that they are seen as lacking carnivalesque traditions – they are usually located solely in the domain of power'.[4] As the dominant group, and being seemingly less demonstrative than Irish and Scottish Canadians, the English became invisible; Charlotte Erickson gave similar reasons for their lack of presence in the United States.[5]

In seeking to recover the English as a distinct migrant group from the margins of history, this chapter examines English ethnic culture in Montreal, focusing not only on commemorations and ethnic festivals but also on sporting activities that helped bring immigrants together. Far from being invisible, these activities demonstrate that Montreal's English actively sought to identify as a group, often channelling their activities through voluntary associations. In so doing, they proclaimed their English identity and fostered a sense of community among themselves, while navigating in wider Montreal society. With this in mind, particular attention will be given to how the emerging expressions of Englishness served to cement community ties in a city with a large proportion of French-speaking Canadians.

While the institutions formed by the English in the nineteenth century, save for the Anglican Church, have folded, and their archives have disappeared, a

---

2   Paul-André Linteau, *Histoire de Montréal depuis la Confédération* (Montreal: Boréal, 1992), p. 47.
3   Bruce S. Elliot, 'English', *Encyclopedia of Canada's Peoples* (Toronto: University of Toronto Press, 1999), p. 462.
4   Pauline Greenhill, *Ethnicity in the Mainstream: Three Studies of English Canadian Culture in Ontario* (Montreal and Kingston: McGill-Queen's University Press, 1994), p. 4.
5   Charlotte Erickson, *Invisible Immigrants: The Adaptation of English and Scottish Immigrants in Nineteenth-Century America* (Miami, FL: University of Miami Press, 1972), p. 256.

range of other sources have been utilized for this study. Newspapers proved a particularly rich source for information on the activities of the English as a group, as well as associational activities. Colourful accounts of St George's Day celebrations, speeches and information on those in attendance, for instance, provide in-depth information not only on the nature of the celebrations but also their function and evolution over time. A number of English-language Montreal newspapers have been utilized, notably the *Montreal Gazette*, which was published throughout the period under study. Church records and personal papers supplemented the newspaper evidence.

The English in Montreal

The first half of the nineteenth century was a pivotal time for Montreal's English-speaking population: it was during this period that the English began to develop a sense of group identity in Montreal, establishing institutions and traditions that would support the community into the twentieth century. Before exploring the activities that members of Montreal's English immigrant community pursued collectively, however, it is first necessary to place that community within the city's wider immigrant circle.

Montreal, in the first half of the nineteenth century, experienced dramatic growth. While in 1809 the city's population stood at 12,000, that number increased significantly through steady immigration from Great Britain, as well as migration from rural Quebec, with a population of 90,232 being recorded in the 1861 census.[6] This growth was accommodated by a transformation in the city's economy, which changed from pre-industrial to industrial; capitalist industrialization and the growth in banking and insurance marked the diversity of the city's economy. Absolute numbers aside, the ethnic composition of Montreal throughout this period also underwent important changes. At the beginning of the nineteenth century, Montreal was a French-Canadian city. Although it had been under British rule since 1759, the expected rush of Protestant, English-speaking settlers had not occurred by 1800, with only a small number of Americans and Britons settling in the city. This was a population of merchants and civil servants, with many serving the colonial administration and the fur trade. The ethnic composition of the city's population changed at the end of the Napoleonic Wars. This was due to the post-war economic downturn, together with the influx of returning soldiers, which contributed to increased levels of migration to Canada, and to Montreal in particular. Most importantly, it was because of this post-war migration that Montreal's English-speaking population overtook that of the French Canadians. From

---

6   Jean-Claude Robert, 'Montréal, 1821–1871: Aspects de l'urbanisation', unpublished PhD thesis, École Haute des Études en Sciences Sociales, Université de Paris I, 1977, p. 167.

1832 until the late 1860s, the British English-speaking population maintained a majority status in Montreal. It was only after 1867, through renewed rural in-migration, that Montreal returned to having a French-Canadian majority.[7]

Montreal's position as a colonial port city provided it with a steady stream of transient immigrants, but many chose to stay. Most of the arrivals were British. Montreal, like many New World settlements, was a place of encounter, with English meeting Scottish, Welsh and Irish in ways not common within the British Isles. As Keith Robbins has argued, a sense of Britishness perhaps emerged more strongly in the colonies, where the ethnic composition facilitated contact between national groups from within the British Isles.[8] What is more, most of the arrivals from Britain would not have encountered French Canadians before. The divisions, then, of nationalities were clear and ever present given this unfamiliar 'other' in the new home. Yet Montreal was not a city of ethnic enclaves in the first half of the nineteenth century. Day-to-day living would necessitate seeing the 'other', be they English, Irish or French Canadian. Different groups could and did choose to come together to meet or worship: the constant exposure to the 'other' did not solely emphasize the differences between ethnic groups, it also allowed them to feel a part of a larger community, based on shared values and economic interests.[9] This was often expressed as a British identity, and one rooted in the colonial context.

Montreal's ethnic composition is difficult to measure in terms of official statistics, particularly when it comes to those born in Lower Canada: those collecting census data did not seek to capture their national origins. Instead, people were identified as British-Canadian or French-Canadian, with national identifiers being assigned only to those born outside Canada. This presents complications in terms of ascertaining the relative importance of each national group in relation to the city, particularly after the 1840s, when the Canadian-born British population increased.

In terms of percentages, Montreal's English-born were not a large group, never amounting to more than 7 per cent of the population throughout the period under study. The Scots-born were similarly weighted, also comprising 7 per cent of the population, dipping down to 3 per cent towards the end of the period under study. The Irish-born were the largest group among the British-born in Montreal, composing between 16 and 20 per cent of the population.[10]

In addition to ethnic background, but at times tied in with it, religion was another important boundary line in Montreal society. The city was home to a number of different religious groups: Anglican, Roman Catholic, Methodist,

---

7   Jean-Claude Robert, *Atlas historique de Montréal* (Montreal: Éditions Libre Expression, 1994), pp. 79, 93.
8   Keith Robbins, *Great Britain: Identity, Institutions and the Idea of Britishness* (London and New York: Longman, 1998), pp. 213–14.
9   Philip Buckner and Carl Bridge, 'Reinventing the British World', *The Round Table*, 368 (2003), p. 80.
10   Robert, 'Montreal, 1821–1871', p. 106.

Table 1: Percentage of Montreal's population by place of birth[a]

	French Canadians	British Canadians	England & Wales	Scotland	Ireland	USA	Other
1825	54	13	6	6	16	3	2
1842	42	19	7	7	22	1	1
1850	44	22	6	5	21	1	2
1861	48	25	5	4	16	2	1
1871	53	24	5	3	10	2	1

[a] Jean-Claude Robert, 'Montréal, 1821–1871: Aspects de l'urbanisation', unpublished PhD thesis, École Haute des Études en Sciences Sociales, Université de Paris I, 1977, p. 106.

Baptist, Unitarian and Jewish. This was not unusual for a colonial city of its size. The Church of England represented, to a degree, English identity in Montreal and, after 1835 in particular, the Anglican Church would assume an important role in the celebration of that identity with annual religious services. The Church of England was the most important Protestant denomination in the city in the early nineteenth century, having the largest congregation.[11] It could claim among its congregation some of the most prominent and powerful of Montreal's elite, including colonial administrators and military commanders. But in terms of the population ratio previously shown, with only 7 per cent of Montreal's population being English-born, the bulk of the Anglican worshippers could not have come from England. As John Irwin Cooper suggests, the vast majority of the Anglican congregation were in fact Irish.[12] The Church also counted among its adherents a significant number of Germans – remnants of the mercenaries hired by the British for the conquest and the American Revolution.[13] Despite this, its association with England was clear in the minds of Montrealers: the Anglican Church was the 'English' Church.[14]

St George's Day

Having situated the English within Montreal society, let us now explore the diverse public expressions of English ethnic culture. The first public celebration of a specific national identity in Montreal was organized by the English in

11 LAC, Recensement de la cite de Montréal, 1831, RG 17, Serie A 723, Vol. 13, 101; Janice Harvey, 'Upper Class Reaction to Poverty in Mid-Nineteenth Century Montreal: A Protestant Example', unpublished MA thesis, McGill University, 1978, pp. 19, 320.
12 John Irwin Cooper, *The Blessed Communion: The Origins and the History of the Diocese of Montreal, 1760–1960* (Montreal: Archives Committee of the Diocese of Montreal, 1960), p. 45.
13 Ibid., p. 16.
14 For example, *Montreal Gazette*, 5 October 1801.

1808. That it was the English who first acted in this defined way is surprising: the Irish and Scots were more associated with the celebration of their identity overseas.[15] It is not clear why the English chose to act at this particular moment in time, but they chose their patron saint, St George, as the vehicle.[16] The event held in his honour was important not only because it was the 'first', but because of the extravagant nature of the celebration itself, which was not to be repeated. The *Montreal Gazette* devoted a significant portion of its second page to lavish descriptions of the event, stressing its uniqueness. Celebrations began early in the morning with a flag-raising ceremony in front of the Montreal Hotel.[17] The men present then went indoors to drink cherry bounce,[18] before proceeding to another room where they were served a sumptuous feast with copious amounts of wine. The long day ended, at 10 p.m., with the lowering of the flag and the dispersal of the participants. The event was, at its heart, much like the many other male-only dinners that were popular among Montreal's elite, and fitted into the tradition of the supper club, which had, in Britain as in Montreal, marked some of the earliest incarnations of associational life.[19] The Beaver Club, established in Montreal in 1785, was a prime example of such male sociability, holding elaborate dinners governed by rules and filled with rituals.[20] Other male-only dinners were held in the city in honour of visiting dignitaries or events of local significance, such as the elections or appointments to posts in the government, the army or the church. They were small, exclusive gatherings that centred on food and drink. Alcohol was especially important in this type of event as 'it relaxes the people and lowers their inhibitions [...] helping the individuals to soften the edges and meld better into a group'.[21] The absence of women, and therefore of the social strictures that dictated behaviour in their presence, enabled the male participants to behave in a more relaxed manner.

---

15 Most particularly the Scots who, according to Johnson, changed nothing but their abode. Marjory Harper, 'Transplanted Identities: Remembering and Reinventing Scotland Across the Diaspora', in Tanja Bueltmann, Andrew Hinson and Graeme Morton (eds), *Ties of Bluid, Kin and Countrie: Scottish Associational Culture in the Diaspora* (Guelph: Centre for Scottish Studies, 2009), p. 29.

16 St George's Day was not regularly celebrated in England. Steve Roud, *The English Year: A Month-by-Month Guide to the Nation's Customs and Festivals, from May Day to Mischief Night* (Harmondsworth: Penguin, 2006), p. 196.

17 *Montreal Gazette*, 28 April 1808.

18 I am assuming that cherry bounce is an alcoholic beverage.

19 Robert Morris, 'Clubs, Societies, and Associations', in F.M.L. Thompson (ed.), *The Cambridge Social History of Britain 1750–1950, vol. 3: Social Agencies and Institutions* (Cambridge: Cambridge University Press, 1990), p. 396; Peter Clark, *British Clubs and Societies c. 1580–1800: The Origins of an Associational World* (Oxford: Oxford University Press, 2000), p. 70.

20 Lawrence J. Burpee, 'The Beaver Club', *Canadian Historical Association Report* (1924), p. 80.

21 Margaret Visser, *The Rituals of Dinner* (Toronto: Harper Perennial Canada, 1991), p. 274.

Montreal's St George's Day dinner of 1808 neatly fitted into the typical elite Montreal dinner. However, it had some distinct features. First, the event was filled with symbolism – symbols overtly connected to a sense of Englishness. With 30 men present, each, while not named, was made a representative of an English county. The whole day was framed by the theme of 'Yeongland' and its participants were 'Ancient Yeomen'; the venue was decorated like a medieval banqueting hall. The floor was 'strewed with green branches, and surrounded with common board benches such as have been in use long before the luxury of either carpets or chairs were known'. Guests ate off wooden trenchers, wearing medieval costumes, including 'Windsor Uniform, shoes tied with leather thongs and white worsted hose rolled over the knee'.[22] The herald who announced the dinner was 'dressed in the Tabard of England, three lions, or passant in a Field Gules, and wearing appropriate cap ornamented with a plume of white feathers'.[23] The image presented was that of England in the imagined days of chivalry.

The food served was equally symbolic. A meal of roast beef was served on a wooden trencher, which had been decorated with the flag of St George. The plum pudding arrived in similar style, and dessert was served on a white pedestal with St George on horseback killing the dragon, a figure of Britannia on either side. The gilt moulding had inscriptions in Latin praising St George, the king and the Prince Regent.[24] In fact, every surface imaginable was covered with some kind of symbolic image of England. Together with the choice of foodstuffs, these symbols of the old homeland were 'legacies of continuity',[25] linking the English community of Montreal with England. The toasts at the end of the evening reinforced the theme of the day, expressing strong attachment to England, the king, Alfred the Great, the Magna Charta, the battles of Poitiers, Cressy and Agincourt, Queen Elizabeth I and the constitution and other symbols of the English state and England.

St George's Day continued to be celebrated by Montreal's English population after 1808. It was, however, not an annual event, and was never held in the same elaborate style or as publicly as in its first incarnation. In fact, it disappeared from the newspapers until 1820, when the celebration of the day changed significantly as a result of George IV's adoption of St George's Day as his official birthday – a deliberate choice by the king to make him appear more English and less German.[26] This quasi-hijacking of the day by the state had a strong impact on how it was marked in Montreal, as its observance now

---

22   *Montreal Gazette*, 28 April 1808.
23   Ibid.
24   Ibid.
25   Hasia R. Diner, *A Hungering for America: Italian, Irish and Jewish Foodways in the Age of Migration* (Cambridge, MA: Harvard University Press, 2001), p. xvi.
26   Much as Charles II did in 1660 when he held his coronation on St George's Day. Carolyn Edie, 'The Public Face of Royal Ritual: Sermons, Medals and Civic Ceremony in Later Stuart Coronations', *Huntingdon Library Quarterly*, 53.4 (1990), p. 313.

became a regular annual fixture: St George's Day was celebrated in public without fail in each year of George IV's ten-year reign.

A subsequent effect was that the nature of the celebration changed from being an English day to a British day, celebrating the monarch at the head of the ever-expanding British Empire. In Montreal, the events were held outdoors and organized by the military. The day usually began in the late morning with a military parade and a review at the Champ de Mars, followed by the firing of guns and cannons from the Champ de Mars, the military headquarters, and the ships in the harbour.[27] In 1825

> The Champs de Mars was crowded to witness the parade of troops in Garrison. The 70th Regiment had a martial appearance and performed their exercises with great precision. The firing was admirable, and proved that great pains had been taken with the discipline of this excellent corps [...] Part of the 'Montreal Royal Cavalry' under Major Gregory, turned out, and went through some manoeuvres on the common near the wind-mills; they then returned through McGill and Notre Dame streets.[28]

The evening saw a ball or a dinner (all-male as was usual in the period), also often organized by the military.

Newspaper accounts of celebrations in this period, while often stating that 23 April was St George's Day, downplayed this aspect of its significance in preference to the fact of its marking the king's birthday. For instance, in 1821 the celebrations for the day were described thus:

> Monday last, being the day consecrated to the tutelary Saint of Old England and (what bestows it nearly as great as a distinction) being that appointed for the celebration of our Most Gracious Sovereign's Nativity, a royal salute was, at one o'clock, fired on the Champ de Mars by the troops in the garrison, and a holiday was celebrated at both the banks. In the evening, several respectable tradesmen and others [...] dined at the Neptune Inn [...] in the expression of the loyal sentiments stamped in the bosom of every Briton, in toasts to the prosperity of the British Empire, and to the happiness of the illustrious family at the head.[29]

It might have been St George's Day, but the events of the day honoured the king. All the descriptors are British, and there are no mentions of England or things English in connection with the actual festivities: the day had been transformed into a state/royal holiday.

---

27 For example: *Montreal Gazette*, 26 April 1820; *Herald*, 24 April 1822; *Canadian Courant*, 23 April 1825.
28 *Canadian Courant*, 27 April 1825.
29 *Herald*, 25 April 1821.

Cricket: 'as eminent in Canada, as [in] the Mother Country'?

With expressions of Englishness sidelined in St George's Day celebrations during the 1820s, other suitable forums emerged. Sport in particular was an important means of maintaining ethnic culture and identity among the English. Sport, as Gillian Poulter has demonstrated in her examination of sport and Canadian identity, was both a practice and a product of specific identities.[30] While the Scots pursued curling and shinty in Montreal during this period,[31] the English adopted cricket as their sporting flagship, with the Montreal Cricket Club being organized in 1822. In his history of sport in nineteenth-century Canada, Allan Elton Cox described Montreal's early cricket as 'an officer's privilege'.[32] Yet, while the military were indeed participants in the sport, it was presented in the city's newspapers as a civilian endeavour – and as a very English sport. Accounts of the events, and commentary about the Cricket Club, centred on the themes of Englishness, manliness, health and respectability. This was in keeping with what Philip Dodd identifies as descriptors of English identity (in England): it was 'vigorous' and 'manly',[33] and sport provided a ready outlet for this physical and gendered identity.

What is known of cricket in this early period comes entirely from the newspapers. The Montreal *Herald* in particular was an early promoter of the sport. In 1822, soon after the Montreal Cricket Club was organized, the newspaper published a series of letters and reports supporting the club and praising the benefits of the sport. It expressed the 'hope to hear that manly and healthy amusement will receive the support' of more interested men.[34] 'A Bystander' wrote:

> The game of cricket is conductive to health and peculiarly adapted to youth, especially those leading a sedentary life, as it expands the chest [...] and puts the whole muscular frame in motion, unattended with the least violence. It also adds much manly vigour and firm step so remarkable in an Englishman.[35]

'A Middlesex Man', in another letter, stated that 'with the projected union of the provinces, English customs and habits will get more generally introduced

---

30 Gillian Poulter, 'Becoming Native in a Foreign Land: Visual Culture, Sport and Spectacle in the Construction of National Identity in Montreal, 1840–1885', unpublished PhD thesis, York University, 1999, p. 10.

31 The Montreal Curling Club was an exclusively Scottish association founded in 1807. Shinty was promoted as a Scottish sport in Montreal in 1822. See Gerald Redmond, *The Sporting Scots of Nineteenth Century Canada* (London and Toronto: Associated University Presses, 1982), pp. 109, 118; *Canadian Courant*, 28 December 1822.

32 Allan Elton Cox, 'A History of Sports in Canada, 1868–1900', unpublished PhD thesis, University of Alberta, 1969, p. 10.

33 Philip Dodd, 'Englishness and the National Culture', in Robert Colls and Philip Dodd (eds), *Englishness: Politics and Culture, 1880–1920* (London: Croom Helm, 1986), p. 6.

34 *Herald*, 22 May 1822.

35 *Herald*, 29 May 1822.

so that in a few years the noble game of cricket will stand as eminent in Canada, as [in] the Mother Country'.[36] Cricket was more than just a game: it had transformative powers. This was important to underpin the emerging sense of Englishness, one envisioned by the cricket enthusiasts as a demonstration to others of the perceived moral, political and physical superiority of the English. With cricket being played regularly throughout the summer months, there were ample opportunities for other Montrealers to witness the game, if not necessarily to absorb the moral values that its supporters sought to promote.

By the 1830s, then, portions of Montreal's English population had established mechanisms for expressing their English culture through celebrations and activities such as cricket. Importantly, these were an integral part of a culture of national celebrations that marked the public life of those of British origin more generally. Along with St George's Day, St Andrew's Day and St Patrick's Day had become established and were celebrated fairly regularly. Even St David's Day was occasionally part of the annual calendar of events, for instance in 1816, when 'a number of the native sons of St. David, and several honorary sons's [sic] gave a ball and an elegant supper'.[37] The numbers attending such events were modest, ranging from about fifty to seventy, which highlights the events' exclusive nature. St Patrick's Day was the most regularly celebrated of the saints' days, becoming an annual occurrence from 1821. The addition of a mass in 1822[38] and a parade in 1824[39] made the commemoration of St Patrick's Day an all-day event. It was a day that, unlike the exclusive dinners, gave a large number of citizens an opportunity to participate in the expression of identity. It also gave the greater public a chance to be part of the celebrations as spectators. What is important is that the Irish celebrations would serve as a model for all saints' celebrations in the 1830s.

The Montreal St George's Society

The 1830s were difficult years in Montreal. Its English-speaking population was, by and large, conservative in its politics, so the changing political scene, marked by agitation from the Parti Patriote, left a sense of unease. The Patriotes sought political reform, which among other things would guarantee them power and privileges in the Assembly and extend democratic rights

---

36 *Herald*, 31 July 1822.
37 *Herald*, 9 March 1816.
38 ASSS, 14 March 1822, 'Recit de la congregation des rites qui permet celebrer solonnelle-ment la fete de Saint-Patrice dans l'eglise Notre-Dame', T95, 96, 97, Section 27, Dossier 3, 36.
39 Gillian I. Leitch, 'The Importance of Being *English*? Identity and Social Organisation in British Montreal, 1800–1850', unpublished PhD thesis, Université de Montréal, 2007, p. 149.

to more of the French-Canadian people.[40] Even before the actual violence of the rebellions of 1837–38, when troops were called out to quell agitation in St Charles, St Denis and St Eustache, political and social tensions were running high, and manifested themselves in Montreal's annual festive calendar and associational culture, which developed in organized forms in the early 1830s. There was, it seems, an intrinsic connection between a developing sense of French-Canadian identity and the formalization of ethnic culture in the British immigrant community.

Over the course of a year from 1834, the city of Montreal saw the creation of five national societies. This flurry of associational activity began after St Patrick's Day, when a group of Irishmen objected strenuously to a dinner given by Reformers (Parti Patriote): the Reformers had linked Irish identity to political ideas that were contrary to their own vision of Irishness. The more conservative Irish immediately formed the St Patrick's Society to reclaim their identity.[41] The Reformers then met together on 24 June in honour of St John the Baptist, also celebrating him with a dinner, and subsequently establishing a suitable associational home with the Société St Jean Baptiste. The society featured all the prominent patriots of Montreal, including a number of Irishmen and Scots.

Following a summer of elections accompanied by riots, and a cholera epidemic, the Scots decided after an eight-year break to celebrate St Andrew's Day. The elections that autumn, which had been violent and divisive, meant the loss of control over the government by the British Party, which represented a large proportion of Montreal's English-speaking population.[42] The Patriotes were becoming more radicalized, alarming many and agitating 'extremists within the English community of Montreal'.[43] Consequently, national saints served to reinforce identities as loyal and British. Those present at the St Andrew's Day dinner were described as representatives of all the national groups, who called upon the community to organize a St Andrew's Society.[44] Despite this call on Scots to organize, it was the English who took the initiative first, setting up a St George's Society. As the *Montreal Gazette* triumphantly announced on 24 January 1835, 'with much satisfaction', a St George's Society had been formed.[45] And while the formation of the society in honour of England's patron saint may be considered an explicit expression of English identity, the account of its intended membership points to something much

---

40 Allan Greer, *The Patriots and the People: The Rebellion of 1837 in Rural Lower Canada* (Toronto: University of Toronto Press, 1993), pp. 121–22.
41 This account of the formation of the Society comes from later histories. The Society only appears in the newspapers in 1835, already established and organizing the St Patrick's Day celebrations. Contemporary accounts do not exist.
42 Greer, *The Patriots and the People*, p. 164.
43 Ibid., pp. 138–39.
44 *Montreal Gazette*, 4 December 1834.
45 *Montreal Gazette*, 15 January 1835.

larger. The men who met together to form the society decided that, while they were honouring English identity, 'persons born in this Province – their parents being from any of the three kingdoms – are eligible to become members'.[46] The English, though organizing a specific national society, were also trying to provide other British groups in the city with an organization that would represent them. There existed, at this time, only a St Patrick's Society, and so there were no institutional places for the other British groups to go. Against the French-Canadian 'other', English and British conflated yet again in a way not evident elsewhere. By signalling that English identity could include other Britons, the English were willing to act as an umbrella. Moreover, this openness to other groups of British origin was clearly aimed at the Scots, who had not yet formed a society – though the *Gazette* urged the Scots in the city to do so.[47] And so they did, two days later.[48] The Scots were clearly not willing to share their identity under the banner of St George.

Once these British societies had been formed, it was time to celebrate the identities that they honoured. The St George's Society celebrations in 1835 followed the pattern set by the St Patrick's Society. The day began, at 11 a.m., with a procession formed at Rasco's Hotel, and ended at Christ Church, the Anglican cathedral.[49] The members of the St George's Society were joined by members of the St Patrick's and St Andrew's societies, marching together in an order agreed upon before St Patrick's Day.[50] The band of the 24th Regiment joined them. At Christ Church, Revd Bethune preached 'a most impressive sermon from Psalm 137, 5, 6', which carried the title 'Longing for Zion in Foreign Land'.[51]

While this was a religious service, specifically an Anglican one, it cannot be viewed only in its religious context: those in attendance were not only Anglicans. With members of the St George's Society and the other national societies present, a diversity of denominations were represented. In fact, one prominent member of the St George's Society, Abraham Joseph, an observant Jew, had no moral difficulty attending the Anglican service at Christ Church in 1847.[52] The new unity, in the face of the French Canadians, outweighed religious allegiances. Each national society attended the days of the other societies at their official churches – Anglican, Presbyterian and Catholic.[53] The church services acted as a public blessing upon the act of unity that the

---

46 Ibid.
47 Ibid.
48 *A Summary of the First Fifty Years, Transactions of the St Andrew's Society of Montreal* (Montreal: McQueen and Corneil, 1886), p. 6.
49 *Montreal Gazette*, 25 April 1835.
50 Hugh Allan, *Narrative of the Proceedings of the St Andrew's Society of Montreal from its formation on the 9th March 1835 until 1st January 1844, to which is appended lists of officers and the Constitution of the Society* (Montreal: J.C. Becket, 1855), pp. 8–9.
51 *Montreal Gazette*, 25 April 1835.
52 LAC, MG 24 I 61, Joseph, Abraham, Diary no X, 23 April 1847, pp. 215–16.
53 Leitch, 'The Importance of Being *English*?', p. 189.

procession and gathering in the church represented, as well as the recognition of the specific identity being commemorated. In so doing, the church services celebrated both their national differences and their common interests.

Yet religious services appear to have served primarily an inward function, providing an outlet for society members. The event that received the most attention in the press was the dinner held in the evening. In 1835 the account of the evening was preceded, in the *Montreal Gazette*, by this poem:

England Great and Free

Old England's praise thro' all the world,
Shall Fame this day resound;
St. George's banner floats unfurl'd,
O'er Britons gather'd round.
And may her King fore'er command
Our gratitude and praise;
Our distant friends and native land
Excite our warmest lays.
Then let this pray'r to Heav'n ascend,
That Britons long may be
To ev'ry nation, foe or friend,
The great and envied free!

And, oh, may charity abound
At this our festive board;
Nor let amongst us e'er be found,
The direful fiend – discord.
May friendship, love and harmony
Inspire our hearts to sing.
To great St. George, our patron saint,
Our country and our King!
Then let this pray'r to Heav'n ascend.
For England's great and free!
That Britain's sons in ev'ry land,
May e'er united be.[54]

An estimated seventy to eighty men were present at the dinner held at Rasco's,[55] with the whole celebration, from the poem in England's honour to the decoration of the room, being geared to underscore the Englishness of the occasion. The room was decorated with evergreens and had transparencies of the king's arms, St George and the dragon, the king in his coronation robes and the Duke of Wellington dressed as the Field Marshall of England.[56] The lavishness was continued with the food served – a baron of beef weighing

---

54   *Montreal Gazette*, 25 April 1835.
55   Estimate based on other dinners held at the same venue (where numbers were stated).
56   *Montreal Gazette*, 25 April 1835.

250 lbs was brought in on a charger borne by four Grenadiers. At the conclusion of the meal the song 'England Great and Free' (above) was sung, followed by 15 toasts. These included toasts to the day, the king, the royal family, the armed forces and other English and British institutions.

In the 1830s, then, the events held in honour of St George's Day combined elements of Britain and England, and were put forward to those present as elements of unity. For the organizers, being English meant loyalty, love of king and country, and common cause with those who shared the British institutions of state and Crown. By participating in other national days, and having the other national groups participate in their events, the St George's Society was fostering this unity, but still left space to reinforce their own sense of Englishness. Moreover, the associational form provided them with 'a measure of social solidarity and status recognition for members'.[57]

After the Rebellions

Once the rebellions had passed, Montreal began to enjoy a relative peace. That is not to say that there was no social unrest, but it was not on the same scale. This allowed the development of different types of associations geared to a wider variety of interests. The 1840s were marked by growth, change in politics and an expanding industrial economy. The St George's Society (and its sister societies) had been a direct product of the uncertainty felt by the English during the 1830s, yet while the initial reasons for the society's creation had passed, the benefits of the society for its members persisted. The continued attraction of a national society lay in its activities, notably the celebrations around St George's Day, but also the regular meetings and the raising of money for charitable works destined for their fellow Englishmen. This included the provision of financial aid to new arrivals[58] and eventually the establishment of the St George's Home which provided similar assistance to English immigrants.[59] These activities held great interest for the society's members, even if they were not always capable of keeping their financial commitments.

Importantly, the 1840s saw a distinct shift in the nature of national celebrations from the norms established in the 1830s: with the Patriote 'threat' gone, the saints' days now belonged solely to the individual society and group. In

---

57   Clark, *British Clubs and Societies*, p. 449.
58   The published annual reports of the St George's Society featured the distribution of funds to English in need, including money for food, firewood or passage to Upper Canada/Ontario or England.
59   The St George's Home was built in 1865 to provide lodging and care for English immigrants: *Montreal Gazette*, 24 April 1866; William Henry Atherton, *Montreal 1535–1914 under British Rule Vol II* (Montreal: S.J. Clarke Publishing Co., 1914), p. 493. The St Andrew's Society had opened its home around ten years earlier.

terms of the celebrations themselves, this meant that the society celebrating neither marched along in the parades nor was joined by its sister societies in the church for the annual service. It was only at the dinners that some members of the other societies' executives attended, but as representatives only, and consequently in smaller numbers. The societies remained symbolically linked but operated far more independently.

The St George's Society continued to be responsible for the organization of the main events of St George's Day: the parade, church service and dinner. Descriptions of their events monopolized newspaper coverage, but there were other events, described as private parties by the press, which also honoured St George. These were run on the periphery, neither advertised before the event nor described in great detail afterwards. However, the St George's Society did not monopolize English associational life. Associationalism generally boomed in Montreal during this period,[60] and several new cricket clubs formed that served to confirm the importance of sport as an associational anchor in Montreal's English immigrant community. The Aurora and Burnside clubs, for example, both started in 1847, continuing the tradition of cricket and offering more opportunities for play. An analysis of the names of the members published in relation to these clubs demonstrates the continued English nature of the sport. Of those whose origins are known, only three were not English.[61]

The Shakespeare Club was another association that formed in this period, in 1843. This represented a new angle of interest in expressing English identity. It was a literary society, created to promote the '[c]ultivation of elegant literature by the reading of essays, and debating upon subjects of general interest in view of the dramatic poets; and the concentration of such amateur dramatic ability, as may exist among its members'.[62] The club could not be said to be an 'English' one, as it attracted such members as the Scots John Young and Allan McNabb, and the Dutch artist Cornelius Kreighoff, who immortalized the club on canvas in 1847. Shakespeare, however, was a symbol of English identity and had been utilized occasionally in the celebrations of St George's Day as the subject of a toast. The fact that Shakespeare's birthday fell on St George's Day tied it closely to English expressions of identity. It also meant that the annual dinners of the St George's Society and the Shakespeare Club were held on the same day. Although there is no direct evidence of competition between the two groups for the presence of the English elite at their respective dinners, there clearly was an impact on how the day was celebrated at this time. In 1845 the St George's Society tried to incorporate Shakespeare's birthday into their festivities by sponsoring a theatrical production in honour of the bard the day before their dinner.[63] It does not seem to have been a popular event, however,

60   Leitch, 'The Importance of Being *English?*', p. 210.
61   Ibid., p. 212.
62   *Montreal Gazette*, 8 September 1843.
63   *Montreal Courier*, 21 April 1845.

judging by the reaction to it in the press. It was not repeated, and the fact that the performance was not a production of one of Shakespeare's works seems to have factored in its lack of success.

Another reason may have been that the St George's Society suffered from financial difficulties in the late 1840s. In 1848 the society's charitable committee, charged with providing over £190 of assistance that year, stated that the society's financial woes were the fault of 'the very small attendance of members of the Society, at quarterly meetings. The society made a specific appeal to its members to attend the quarterly meetings and pay their dues (25s annually and a 15s entrance fee).'[64] That year only 77 of the 158 members had done so, leaving the society £177 in arrears.[65] As a result, the society organized a charity ball to raise money, which was advertised in the papers. It was scheduled to begin after the traditional male-only dinner, thus keeping the components of the day as it had been celebrated in the years before. The event, designed to 'replenish the, at present, impoverished coffers of the Society', cost 10s for men, 5s for women and 25s for families; in addition, the dinner cost 15s.[66] The event was considered sufficiently important for the Shakespeare Club to leave their dinner at 9 p.m. to attend the ball.[67]

What contributed further complications was that the society experienced the loss of some of its founding members. George Moffat, the society's first president, retired from active service in the society, although not from Montreal public life, after 1840.[68] His death, in 1865, was greatly lamented by the society, but he had by then become more a symbol of the ideal Englishman than a member of the society. Likewise, John Molson Jr, another early executive member, reduced his involvement to lesser posts in the society.[69] The society still attracted the English-born, and its executive came from the business class, but the retirement of the old guard, while leaving the field open for new blood, did not result in similarly charismatic figures as the first generation of society leadership.

Despite these difficulties, the celebration of St George's Day continued under the aegis of the St George's Society, and competition for the day's dinner ended when the Shakespeare Club disappeared after 1850.[70] Even with the advent of the English Workingmen's Benefit Society in 1864, a national society that was geared to the city's non-elite English population,[71] the St George's Society was able to maintain its control of the day as the undisputed official

64 *Montreal Gazette*, 5 February 1849.
65 *Montreal Courier*, 13 January 1848.
66 *Montreal Courier*, 22 April 1850; *Montreal Courier*, 15 April 1850.
67 *Montreal Gazette*, 28 April 1850.
68 Leitch, 'The Importance of Being *English*?' database.
69 Ibid.
70 Conrad Graham, 'Cornelius Kreighoff and the Shakespeare Club', *Journal of Canadian Art History*, 24 (2003), p. 30.
71 The newspapers are silent as to the activities, membership or attitude of the English Workingmen's Benefit Society.

organizer. The St George's Society magnanimously invited the English Workingmen's Benefit Society to march in procession with them in the year of their foundation; 54 joined the society.

Although the St George's Society would continue on into the twentieth century, its heyday was in the nineteenth. This chapter finishes in 1864, an important year as 23 April marked not only St George's Day but the tercentenary of William Shakespeare's birth. The English (and others) in the city undertook to organize a series of commemorations. While these were not St George's Society events, members such as Moffat and the then President, J.J. Day, were heavily involved. The tercentenary was honoured with a gold medal for presentation at McGill for excellence in the study of English literature, a soirée-concert, a production of *Richard III*[72] and a promenade concert at the Crystal Palace.[73] The St George's Society had a more modest commemoration for Shakespeare. Joined by the English Workingmen's Benefit Society, the society, after their annual service at Christ Church, stepped into the grounds and planted an oak tree.[74] As the band of the Victoria Rifles played 'Brave Old Oak', the president, Mr Day, addressed the crowd and the English Workingmen's Benefit Society,

> [c]ongratulating them on their large turn out. He accepted it as a sign that the St. George's Society was not dying out, when in such weather such a number joined the procession. Englishmen were said to be cosmopolitan in their nature but he did not wish them to forget their love and allegiance to Old England.[75]

Conclusion

Like other migrant groups, Montreal's English population were quick to utilize public events to display their Englishness for the purpose of expressing shared roots. As elsewhere, associations played an important role in maintaining these roots, but these only emerged in the face of the radicalization of the French 'other' in Montreal: the organized St George's tradition was a direct response to the ethnic composition of Montreal, drawn upon by English migrants in the face of an increasingly vocal French population. Sport, especially cricket, was also of great significance, being held up to the public as a civilizing activity. Cricket served as an example of English identity and its positive characteristics, such as health, vigour and manliness.

Competition for control of national identity from other societies, such as the Shakespeare Club or the English Workingmen's Benefit Society, was a real concern for the St George's Society from the mid-nineteenth century

72   *Montreal Gazette*, 16 April 1864.
73   *Herald*, 21 April 1864.
74   *Montreal Gazette*, 25 April 1864.
75   *Herald*, 25 April 1864.

onwards. However, its recognized control of St George's Day meant that the St George's Society remained responsible for the principal festival of English identity in Montreal throughout the period studied and beyond.

St George and his day were the symbols most frequently used by the English elite as a means to publicly commemorate their identity and to bond with others in the city who shared their origins. The celebration of the national saint's day fitted into Montreal society as other British groups also utilized their patron saints and symbols and institutions of the British state to centre their communities. The identity that the English societies expressed through their activities was both English and British, each identifier serving the same group.

Chapter 7

Anglo-Saxonism and the Racialization of the English Diaspora

Tanja Bueltmann

[Anglo-Saxons] are apt to fly apart. […] They quarrel easily and do not easily forget. Their pride perpetuates their estrangement. In their spleen and factiousness they take the part of outsiders against each other. It is thus that the race is in danger of losing its crown. It is thus that it is in danger of forfeiting the leadership of civilization to inferior but more gregarious races, to the detriment of civilization as well as to its own disparagement. The most signal and disastrous instance of this weakness is the schism in the race caused by the American Revolution with the long estrangement that followed.[1]

Outpourings such as these by Goldwin Smith, historian, writer and journalist, found national and international audiences among the periodical- and book-reading public in the late nineteenth and early twentieth centuries. They also had quite focused potential audiences with the many associations connected to expressions of Englishness, Canadianness and Anglo-Saxonism in North America. Smith delivered his words, in fact, at the Canadian Club of New York in 1887, and would make similar statements amid much controversy at the St George's Society of Toronto a few years later. Smith's views reflect what Bell describes as 'a lost opportunity': after the American Revolution and subsequent schism, 'the two main branches of the Anglo-Saxon world had followed radically different trajectories, and the chance to act in unison had been forfeited'.[2] A supporter of continental union with the United States,

---

1   Goldwin Smith, *The Schism in the Anglo-Saxon Race: An Address Delivered Before the Canadian Club of New York* (New York: American News Company, 1887), p. 6.
2   Duncan Bell, *The Idea of Greater Britain: Empire and the Future of World Order, 1860–1900* (Princeton, NJ: Princeton University Press, 2007), p. 254.

Smith sought to overcome the schism, drawing on Anglo-Saxonism as 'a common lexicon [...] of [...] kinship and Anglo-Canadian affinity'.[3]

Anglo-Saxonism has its roots in the sixteenth century, making its way to North America with English migrants 'as part of their historical and religious heritage'.[4] In the eighteenth century Anglo-Saxon myths primarily served an internal function, for instance against royal absolutism in England. Anglo-Saxonism transformed, however, in the early 1800s when it was increasingly defined in terms of 'the innate characteristics of the race'.[5] This shift facilitated the use of Anglo-Saxonism for an external purpose, establishing boundaries between Anglo-Saxons and other races.[6] Importantly, it was also this shift, and the subsequent framing of Anglo-Saxons as a superior race, that ideologically underpinned expansionism in America by 1850.[7] Yet, as Kramer shows, 'Anglo-Saxonism would [only] reach the height of its explanatory power' in the late nineteenth century,[8] offering 'the alloy of superior but distinct racial elements'[9] to the English-speaking peoples. Contemporary celebratory songs and poems highlighted this superiority. Lilian Durban's 'Greater Anglo-Saxony' celebrated the realm of English-speaking people as one that 'shall the world command',[10] while for G.B. Adams the Anglo-Saxon race simply held 'the foremost place in the world [...] [not only because] of its domination as the largest [...] [but] because it stands for the best yet reached in ideas and institutions, the highest type of civilization'.[11] Goldwin Smith, then, was by no means alone in drawing on an Anglo-Saxon rhetoric of unity and superiority: his writings formed part of a substantial body of work on the subject.[12]

---

3 Edward Kohn, *This Kindred People: Canadian-American Relations and the Anglo-Saxon Idea, 1895–1903* (Montreal and Kingston: McGill-Queen's University Press, 2004), p. 8.
4 Reginald Horsman, *Race and Manifest Destiny: The Origins of American Racial Anglo-Saxonism* (Cambridge, MA: Harvard University Press, 1981), p. 9; also J.R. Hall, 'Mid-Nineteenth-Century American Anglo-Saxonism: The Question of Language', in Allen J. Frantzen and John D. Niles (eds), *Anglo-Saxonism and the Construction of Social Identity* (Gainesville, FL: University of Florida Press, 1997).
5 Horsman, *Race and Manifest Destiny*, p. 62.
6 For the wider role of race in American society, see David Blight, *Race and Reunion: The Civil War in American Memory* (Cambridge, MA: Harvard University Press, 2002); Edward J. Blum, *Re-forging the White Republic: Race Religion and American Nationalism, 1865–1898* (Baton Rouge, LO: Louisiana State University Press, 2007); Winthrop D. Jordan, *White over Black: American Attitudes Towards the Negro, 1550–1812* (Chapel Hill, NC: University of North Carolina Press, 2nd edn, 2011).
7 Horsman, *Race and Manifest Destiny*, discusses expansionism in particular in relation to the Mexican War and the wider 'world mission' of American superiority.
8 Paul A. Kramer, 'Empires, Exceptions, and Anglo-Saxons: Race and Rule between the British and United States Empires, 1880–1910', *Journal of American History*, 88.4 (2002), p. 1320.
9 Ibid., p. 1322.
10 Lilian Durban, *Anglo-American Magazine*, VI.6 (1901), p. 446.
11 G.B. Adams, 'The United States and the Anglo-Saxon Future', *Atlantic Monthly*, 78.465 (1896), p. 36.
12 For instance John L. Brandt, *Anglo-Saxon Supremacy or Race Contributions to Civilization* (Boston and Toronto: Badger and Copp Clark Co., 1915); J.R. Dos Passos,

In view of this wider context, the purpose of this chapter is twofold. First, it investigates the type of Anglo-Saxonism that Smith promoted, scrutinizing in particular how his ideas on Anglo-Saxon superiority and race related to discourses of imperial federation and continental union. Smith's writings and the debates they engendered offer important insights into how Canada's political position within the North American and British imperial contexts was framed by means of divergent appropriations of Anglo-Saxonism. Secondly, the chapter explores the nature of Canadian and American identity more broadly, probing Anglo-Saxonism's role as a trope of English ethnicity, particularly when used by English associations, to shed light on what can suitably be described as the racialization of the English Diaspora at the turn of the century.

Goldwin Smith and Anglo-Saxonism

Born in Reading, England, in 1823, Goldwin Smith was educated at Eton and Oxford, becoming Regius Professor of Modern History at Oxford in 1858. He only held that position for eight years, however, resigning in the late 1860s to look after his father, who had fallen ill. His father's subsequent suicide contributed to Smith's decision to leave Britain for the United States – a move motivated by an offer of a professorship of English and Constitutional History that Smith had received from Andrew Dickson White, president of newly established Cornell University. The non-sectarian principles on which Cornell was founded appealed to Smith, but 'he had no sympathy for its commitment to coeducation',[13] this being perhaps the main reason for his early departure from Cornell in 1871. Smith relocated to Toronto after leaving Cornell and was to stay there for the rest of his life, frequently embarking on extended trips to Britain,[14] as well as lecturing tours in the US.

It was in Toronto that Smith composed his most controversial articles for periodicals that included the *Canadian Monthly*, the first monthly to seek status as an independent national journal in light of 'a strong sense of nationalism in the new Dominion',[15] and his own *Bystander*. A prolific writer,

---

The Anglo-Saxon Century and the Unification of the English-Speaking People (New York and London: The Knickerbocker Press, 1903); W.T. Stead, *The Americanization of the World: Or the Trend of the Twentieth Century* (New York and London: Horace Markley, 1902); Josiah Strong, *Our Country: Its Possible Future and its Present Crisis* (New York: The American Home Missionary Society, 1885).

13 Ramsay Cook, 'Goldwin Smith', *Dictionary of Canadian Biography Online*, http://www.biographi.ca/009004-119.01-e.php?&id_nbr=7075 (accessed 22 March 2011).

14 Patricia Ashman, 'Smith, Goldwin', in James S. Olson and Robert Shadle (eds), *Historical Dictionary of the British Empire* (Westport, CT: Greenwood Press, 1996), II, p. 1027.

15 Marilyn G. Flitton, 'The Canadian Monthly, 1878–82', unpublished MA thesis, Simon Fraser University, 1973, p. iii; also pp. 18–32 for details on Goldwin Smith's involvement.

Smith had long since been a committed journalist, penning numerous articles and pamphlets on wide-ranging social and political themes. In fact, he was known less for his historical scholarship (which was in any case characterized by the absence of original research and a lack of 'objectivity')[16] than for the many controversies he was engaged in during his lifetime. At a time when the subject of history became increasingly scientific and source-based,[17] Smith's contention that history 'without moral philosophy' is 'a mere string of facts' fell short of winning much academic acclaim.[18]

One question that Smith was particularly concerned with was that of the relationship between Britain and its colonies – an issue he first began to think about when still at Oxford, publishing a series of letters on the subject of colonial emancipation in the *Daily News* between 1862 and 1863.[19] For Smith, the empire was a burden for England, and one 'serving only class interests'.[20] Asking whether the 'narrow escape we have had of a war in defence of Canada [ought not] to lead the nation to think seriously not only of the reduction of Colonial expenditure, but [also] of Colonial Emancipation', Smith argued that independence for the colonies would 'retrench our Empire, in order to add to our security and greatness'.[21] Underlying his argument was the idea that ties with the colonies were part of England's greatness, but that a formalized political empire was not necessary to maintain these ties: based on 'blood, sympathy, and ideas', Smith observed, ties would 'not be affected by political separation. And when our Colonies are nations, something in the nature of a great Anglo-Saxon federation may, in substance if not in form, spontaneously arise out of affinity and mutual affection.'[22] Consequently, there was no problem with including America in this conception, particularly as Smith was convinced that political dependence between 'an Anglo-Saxon colony and its mother country'[23] was unsound from the beginning; it was only the bond of the heart that could be renewed.[24] While Britain's military ensured that 'Anglo-Saxon, not French, should be the polity and the laws of the New World',

> it was impossible that the Anglo-Saxon realm in both hemispheres should remain forever under one government, when the hour of political maturity for

---

16   Cook, 'Goldwin Smith'.
17   Especially influential was Leopold von Ranke; see *The Theory and Practice of History*, ed. Georg G. Iggers (Abingdon: Routledge, 2011).
18   Goldwin Smith, *Lectures on Modern History, Delivered in Oxford, 1859–61* (Oxford and London: John Henry and James Parker, 1861), p. 90.
19   These later appeared in print in Goldwin Smith, *The Empire: A Series of Letters Published in The Daily News, 1862, 1863* (Oxford and London: John Henry and James Parker, 1863).
20   Bell, *The Idea of Greater Britain*, p. 121.
21   Smith, *The Empire*, pp. 1 and 11.
22   Ibid., p. 6.
23   Smith, *The Schism*, p. 7.
24   Ibid., p. 41.

the colonies had arrived, especially as there was a certain difference of political character between the Anglo-Saxon of the old country and the Colonist which prevented the same policy from being equally suitable to both.[25]

Here emerged Smith's principal belief: that although imperial federation was not a suitable form of government, close connections between Britain and the colonies were still crucial. In the first instance, Smith placed responsibility for the maintenance of connections in the hands of politicians, hoping that statesmen would step in to prevent further detachment between Britain and her colonies.

The spirit of revolution in America, and the subsequent independence of the American colonies, had complicated the situation in political terms, but not for Smith. Ties between the Anglo-Saxon branches were maintained through a shared culture and common heritage, making Anglo-Saxonism the central root for unity between all English-speaking peoples – official colony or not. As Smith had already observed in early 1865 when writing to the publisher of his *England and America*, his work was

> of one who does not regard America as a foreign nation, alien to our political concerns, but as the great colony of England, accidentally and temporarily estranged from the mother country [...] There are two lines of policy which may be pursued towards the great Anglo-Saxon community on the other side of the Atlantic. One is to treat it as a natural enemy, and do all in our power to break it up and destroy its greatness. The other is to treat it as our natural friend, to show on every proper occasion and in every way consistent with our honour [...] that we are sensible of the tie of blood which unites us to it, and to divest American greatness of danger to us by making it our own.[26]

Originally delivered as an address before the Boston Fraternity during the Civil War, and then published in the *Atlantic Monthly* in December 1864,[27] Smith uttered these words at a time when the relationship between the US and Britain was strained: in light of the sympathies with the South that many British officials and businessmen had expressed, Smith sought to represent the other side. Following Liberal ideals, his Anglo-Saxonism promoted 'a vision of the rapprochement of the English-speaking peoples' at a time of crisis.[28]

For immigrants from England more generally, the power of Anglo-Saxonism lay in its provision of a focus for unity. It was resolutely presented thus by contemporary writers, such as John Dos Passos in his *The Anglo-Saxon Century and the Unification of the English-Speaking People*, published

---

25   Ibid., pp. 8 and 23.
26   Goldwin Smith, *England and America* (Manchester: A. Ireland and Co., 1865), pp. iii–iv.
27   Goldwin Smith, 'England and America', *Atlantic Monthly*, 14.86 (1864), pp. 749–69.
28   Elisabeth Wallace, 'Goldwin Smith on England and America', *American Historical Review*, 59.4 (1954), p. 884.

in 1903.[29] Focusing on the 'inherent natural reasons or sympathetic causes which sustain a union', Dos Passos listed the factors that 'would render a national marriage between the United States and England justifiable, healthful, and prosperous':

> we find that we are of the same family; speak the same language; we have the same literature; we are governed substantially by the same political institutions; we possess similar laws, customs, and general modes of legal procedure; we follow the same tendency and methods of religious thought and practice; we have numerous inter-marriages and innumerable similarities in our sports, pastimes, drama, and habits of living – a natural community in everything important.[30]

Dos Passos envisioned the twentieth century as the Anglo-Saxon century,[31] and supported his ideas with 'much enthusiasm'.[32] Dos Passos and Smith thus utilized a rhetoric that drew upon the supposed shared racial qualities of the Anglo-Saxon, their language reflecting 'the growing general use of "Anglo-Saxon" as a synonym for "English"'.[33]

This growing general use was of special importance in the Canadian context. The continued Loyalism of Canadians had long accentuated differences between the Dominion of Canada and the American Republic, but the idea of common heritage began to supersede divisions between Canadians and Americans in the late nineteenth century. Two reasons explain this shift. First, America's rise as the key global powerhouse and the resulting Anglo-American rapprochement were crucial. As Kohn observes, by the end of the nineteenth century, 'the ideology of Anglo-Saxon superiority had become established as a reaction to a radically changing world, and its advocates applied it to both domestic and international problems'.[34] Anglo-Saxonism helped re-assert control on the political stage, cementing 'an Anglo-American accord'.[35] The second reason relates to the emergence of race as an important category of distinction between migrants of British stock and the mass of new arrivals into both Canada and the US in the late nineteenth century who hailed from other parts of the world, particularly southern and eastern Europe. Regardless of whatever divisions there may have been between Canadians and Americans, the latter suddenly emerged as welcome settlers, for instance in

---

29 Dos Passos, *The Anglo-Saxon Century*; Stead, *The Americanization of the World*; for the wider context, see Kohn, *This Kindred People*, pp. 196ff.

30 Dos Passos, *The Anglo-Saxon Century*, pp. 140–41.

31 This was a vision later picked up by his son, John Dos Passos Jr; cf. Michael Denning, *The Cultural Front: The Labouring of American Culture in the Twentieth Century* (London and New York: Verso, 1998), p. 197; also Virginia Spencer Carr, *Dos Passos: A Life* (Evanston, IL: Northwestern University Press, 2004), pp. 338ff.

32 *Yale Review*, 12 (1904), p. 445.

33 Joanne Parker, *'England's Darling': The Victorian Cult of Alfred the Great* (Manchester: Manchester University Press, 2007), p. 41.

34 Kohn, *This Kindred People*, p. 6.

35 Kramer, 'Empires, Exceptions, and Anglo-Saxons', p. 1320.

the Canadian west. As a contemporary observed, 'not only will such settlers make successful citizens, but they will help to give an Anglo-Saxon character to the social, economic and political development of the west'.[36] Americans concerned about the arrival of French Canadians in New England expressed similar views, with anti-Jewish and anti-Irish sentiments also playing an important role.[37]

For Smith, the arrival of non-British immigrants in increasing numbers into late nineteenth- and early twentieth-century Canada was certainly a concern, especially as this influx tied in with another issue: the further expansion of the British Empire and the subsequent dispersal of Anglo-Saxons from the motherland to places such as Australia. 'Deprived of a re-inforcement [*sic*]', argued Smith, the loss of new migrants from Britain to Canada 'is felt when that element has to grapple with a vast influx of foreign emigration'.[38] In this context, and although Smith had spoken of uniting all English-speaking peoples, the Irish were a problem. In fact, observed Smith, 'the political feud between the two branches of the [Anglo-Saxon] race [the US and Britain/ Canada] would now [...] be nearly at an end, if it were not for the Irish'.[39] He saw the Irish as clannish Celts, superstitious and thriftless, who were halting the progress of the industrious Anglo-Saxons.[40] Smith believed in the lasting character of races, and the Irish were not redeemable. As he wrote to his friend Lord Farrer in 1883, 'a better thing still would be if the Irish could be sent to Jamaica or some other Crown Colony, where they might undergo an industrial training and be a little civilized'. If that was not achieved, they would threaten 'with subversion every Anglo-Saxon polity on the globe'.[41] Therefore,

---

36   *Queen's Quarterly*, 9.4 (1901), p. 321.

37   Smith also wrote unfavourably of Canada's indigenous population, describing Indians as 'a race without a history and without a future'; cf. Goldwin Smith, *Canada and the Canadian Question* (Toronto: Hunter, Rose and Co., 1891), p. 63. Smith most clearly expressed his ethnocentrism in relation to the Jews; see Isaac Besht Bendavid, 'Goldwin Smith and the Jews', *North American Review*, 418 (1891), pp. 258–71.

38   Smith, *The Schism*, p. 25.

39   Ibid., p. 28. This point Smith emphasized in a letter to his friend Mrs Winkworth on 22 November 1887, cited in Arnold Haultain (ed.), *A Selection from Goldwin Smith's Correspondence: Comprising Letters Chiefly to and from his English Friends, Written Between the Years 1846 and 1910* (New York: Duffield & Company, 1913), p. 208.

40   Cromwell's actions in Ireland hence deserved praise as he had intended to end the clannishness of the Irish by introducing 'the order, legality, and settled industry of the Anglo-Saxon in its place'; Smith, *The Schism*, p. 29.

41   Goldwin Smith to Lord Farrer, Toronto, 14 January 1883, cited in Haultain (ed.), *A Selection from Goldwin Smith's Correspondence*, pp. 144–45. Smith's anti-Irishness had developed much earlier than this, however; see, for instance, P.J. Nowland, *An Irish Premier for English Statesmen: Being a Reply to a Letter of Mr Goldwin Smith* (Dublin: W.B. Kelly, 1867); this was a response to what was later published as Goldwin Smith, *The Irish Question: Three Letters to the Editor of the Daily News* (London: William Ridgway, 1868). Moreover, it was also picked up as far afield as New Zealand, for instance by the *New Zealand Tablet*, an organ for Catholic interests in New Zealand, which reprinted an article from the *Brooklyn Catholic Review* that was highly critical of Smith; cf. *New Zealand Tablet*, 2 March 1888.

it was perhaps for want of the strengthening of Anglo-Saxon superiority that Anglo-Saxonism was not automatically defined as exclusively English. While, for Goldwin Smith, the Irish were certainly excluded, Anglo-Saxonism could be used more inclusively, at times embracing Welsh and (Lowland) Scots. Edward E. Cornwall, in a study on whether Americans are an Anglo-Saxon people published in the *New York Times* in 1900, grouped Anglo-Saxons in this more inclusive sense, distinguishing them from 'Continental Teutonic' and 'Celtic'.[42]

While such inclusivity was possible, however, Smith was by no means alone in employing Anglo-Saxonism in a more exclusionary way. The *Anglo-Saxon*, a monthly periodical published in Ottawa between 1887 and 1900, for instance, constructed an English identity on the basis of an exclusive Anglo-Saxonism specifically against French-Canadian culture. The journal's editors and contributors focused on the ideological and political connections that existed with the homeland, 'advocating the international confederation of the Anglo-Saxon race', and its superiority.[43] Hence, while 'a common language is in itself a most important bond of union',[44] race offered an even more potent connector in political discourses, particularly in the late nineteenth century.[45] In light of these developments, and as a contemporary noted in *Scribner's Magazine*, the British would welcome the strengthening of Anglo-American ties or even an alliance 'in defence of the ideals of the Anglo-Saxon race'.[46] These examples document the use of tropes of English ethnicity that specifically included Anglo-Saxon rhetoric by a wide group of people – being increasingly drawn upon for the purpose of defining group boundaries within the English Diaspora on the basis of racial superiority. The examples also highlight that Anglo-Saxonism can tell us much about American and Canadian identity more broadly: located within the overarching narrative of Anglo-Saxonism in North America was an issue of much wider relevance, namely the Canadian question.

---

42 *New York Times*, 14 January 1900.
43 Paula Hastings, "'Our Glorious Anglo-Saxon Race Shall Ever Fill the Earth's Highest Place": The Anglo Saxon and the Construction of Identity in Late-Nineteenth-Century Canada', in Phillip Buckner and R. Douglas Francis (eds), *Canada and the British World: Culture, Migration and Identity* (Vancouver and Toronto: UBC Press), pp. 92 and 106.
44 Goldwin Smith, 'Anglo-Saxon Union: A Response to Mr. Carnegie', *The North American Review*, 157.441 (1893), p. 170.
45 At that time, in the US, Anglo-Saxonism underwent a further shift, becoming a 'glorification of the Anglo-Saxon "race"'. See Anna Maria Martellone, 'In the Name of Anglo-Saxondom, For Empire and For Democracy: The Anglo-American Discourse, 1880–1920', in David K. Adams and Cornelis A. Van Minnen (eds), *Reflections on American Exceptionalism* (Keele: Ryburn Publishing/Keele University Press, 1994), p. 84; also J.E. Chamberlain, 'A Dream of Anglo-Saxondom', *The Galaxy*, 24.6 (1877), p. 790.
46 *Scribner's Magazine*, December 1898, cited in Dos Passos, *The Anglo-Saxon Century*, p. 213.

The Canadian Question: Anglo-Saxonism, Imperial Federation and Continental Union

In Canada, Dominion status provided an effective backdrop to the expression of ethnic pride and loyalty to the Crown for English migrants, intellectuals and political thinkers alike – the latter two including those involved in the increasing number of groups debating Canada's political status. However, while there was agreement among them on shared Anglo-Saxonism, radically different agendas developed around it. One group comprised the promoters of imperial federation, for whom cross-cultural unity with Britain was the key to Canadian security and strength. Men such as John Castell Hopkins of Toronto, who was involved in founding the Ontario branch of the Imperial Federation League,[47] sought to promote the maintenance of close ties with Britain, thereby advancing Canada as the most reliable pillar of the wider British imperial world. For Canada itself, Hopkins believed, a close relationship with the motherland was the key for continued progress. In his philosophy, which was followed by other promoters of imperial federation, including prominent politicians such as George Denison, church minister George Monro Grant and educator George Robert Parkin, the 'free Republic' of the United States posed a threat – especially if Canada was to become independent. Independence would result not only in 'the most complete isola-tion from British power, protection or influence' but also, Castell Hopkins went on, 'complete dependence upon the will of the United States of America'. This, in turn, would require Canada to put protective mechanisms in place that would be costly, with the inevitable result that Canada would enter 'into the American union under the most humiliating conditions'.[48]

Such concerns were not shared by the second group, which saw continental union with the United States, rather than imperial federation, as the most promising political framework for North America. Among the promoters of continental union was Goldwin Smith, for whom Canada's future lay clearly in that union: it was 'the manifest political destiny of Canada'.[49] While Smith shared the goal of establishing a union of the English-speaking peoples with those advocating imperial federation, there was no further common ground. For George Denison and others, Smith, therefore, was the ultimate anti-imperialist, as his ideas of continental union were premised on the annexation of Canada to the United States, his rhetoric, observed Parkin,

47 Jeffrey A. Keshen, 'John Castell Hopkins', *Dictionary of Canadian Biography Online*, http://www.biographi.ca/009004-119.01-e.php?&id_nbr=8196&interval=25&&PHPSESSID=asl9m807j3efv24ktemudiphq6 (accessed 6 June 2010).
48 This and the previous quote are from John Castell Hopkins, *Canada and the Empire: A Study of Imperial Federation* (Toronto: C. Blackett Robinson, 1890), p. 16.
49 *Boston Evening Transcript*, 3 February 1891.

being 'intoxicated by [...] free trade'.[50] Imperial federalists sought to preserve Loyalist traditions and 'saw no inconsistency between promoting on the one hand Canadian nationhood and on the other the nation's membership of a larger British Empire'.[51] This was one of Smith's main concerns: those promoting imperial federation were, he was convinced, 'finally severing Canada from this continent [the US] and incorporating her in a federation, the centre of which is to be a European power'; 'American statesmen', he went on to urge, 'cannot blink the issue.'[52] For Smith, imperial federation meant further dependency and was thus a step backward from the colonial emancipation he had already envisaged in the early 1860s.[53]

A continental union between the US and Canada, on the other hand, would be less a union, but rather a reunion of those branches of the Anglo-Saxon race who naturally belonged together. 'Before their unhappy schism', Smith argued, '[Canadians and Americans] were one people. Nothing but the historical accident of a civil war ending in secession, instead of amnesty, has made them two.'[54] Smith continued in an 1887 speech before the New York Canadian Club:

> You and I, gentlemen of the Canadian Club of New York; you, natives of Canada, and some of you perhaps descendants of United Empire Loyalists domiciled in the United States; I, an Englishman, holding a professorship of History in an American University – represent the Anglo-Saxon race as it was before the schism, as it will be when the schism is at an end. We remind the race of the time when its magnificent realm in both hemispheres was one, and teach it to look for the time when that realm will be united again, not by political bond, which from the beginning was unnatural and undesirable, but by the bond of heart. While the cannon of the Fourth of July are being fired, and the speeches are being made in honor of American Independence, we, though we rejoice in the birth of the American Republic, must toll the bell of mourning for the schism in the Anglo-Saxon race.[55]

Smith reminded them that they, as

> heirs not of the feuds of our race, but of its glorious history, its high traditions, its famous names, can look with equal pride on all that it has done [...] and

---

50 George R. Parkin, 'The Reorganization of the British Empire', *The Century: A Popular Quarterly*, 37.2 (1888), p. 188.

51 J.M. Bumsted, *The Peoples of Canada: A Post-Confederation History* (Don Mills: Oxford University Press, 2008), p. 161.

52 Smith, 'Anglo-Saxon Union', p. 172.

53 It is worth noting that Smith's ideas of emancipation for the colonies specifically excluded Ireland. As previously noted, he saw the Celtic race as inferior and was hence opposed to Irish Home Rule, joining the Unionists in their opposition to it (though he generally considered himself a Liberal). See, for instance, Alan O'Day, *Irish Home Rule, 1867–1921* (Manchester: Manchester University Press, 1998), p. 128.

54 Smith, *Canada*, p. 267.

55 Smith, *The Schism*, pp. 6–7.

rejoice in the thought that though the roll of England's drum may no longer go with morning around the world, and though the sun may set on England's military empire, morning in its course round the world will forever be greeted in the Anglo-Saxon tongue and the sun will never set on Anglo-Saxon greatness.[56]

The central objective for Smith, therefore, was to ensure the healing of the schism, one that had been exacerbated by the 'evil memories' of the War of 1812.[57] For Smith, healing was an achievable goal because 'the Anglo-Saxons of Canada and the United States have the memory [...] only of [that] one war'. With this limited memory of dissent, and their common heritage, a unification similar to that between England and Scotland in 1707 would give Canadians and Americans 'as complete a security for peace [...] as is likely to be attained'. For Canadians, benefits would include an increase in prosperity, while for Americans commercial gains would be the key incentive.[58] Hence while the American Revolution had been the great failure of Anglo-Saxondom, Smith made a case for 'the Anglo-Saxons on this continent [...] [to] set aside the consequences of the schism and revert to the footing of common inheritance, instituting free-trade among themselves, allowing the life-blood of commerce to circulate freely through the whole body of their continent'.[59] Free trade between the US and Canada was the most logical step forward in that it offered a practical incentive for union:

> A grand idea may be at the same time practical. The idea of a United Continent of North America, securing free trade and intercourse over a vast area, with external safety and internal peace, is no less practical than it is grand. The benefits of such a union would be always present to the mind of the least instructed citizen. [...] Imperial Federation, to the mass of the people comprised in it, would be a mere name conveying with it no definite sense of benefit, on which anything could be built.[60]

Further to the 'practical' argument advanced, continental union was the most logical and feasible federation because it was also a moral one.[61] This was a point to which Dos Passos would give his blessing twenty years later: expressing regret that Goldwin Smith's idea of continental union was not met with 'widespread, overwhelming feeling in its favour', Dos Passos was in no doubt, in 1903, that 'annexation will come'. Hoping that it would 'not come by force', Dos Passos picked up some of the ideas Smith had developed in the 1880s and 1890s, promoting the 'true and loving marriage, with full volition on each side' among the two great Anglo-Saxon nations.[62]

56 Ibid., p. 39.
57 Smith, *Canada*, p. 108.
58 This and the previous two quotations are from ibid., p. 268.
59 Smith, *The Schism*, p. 42.
60 Smith, *Canada*, p. 261.
61 Ibid., p. 205.
62 Dos Passos, *The Anglo-Saxon Century*, p. 177.

However, while Smith found a late ally in Dos Passos two decades after the publication of *Canada and the Canadian Question*, he constantly collided with his contemporaries. Thus Robert Collyer, an English-born American Unitarian clergyman, argued that Smith was wrong to assume that the American hated England: it 'is the mother-land [for return visitors]. They go there to visit the sacred shrines of the old strong race from which they sprung [...] And so silken threads are spun which [...] will be twisted into strands and cables in time to bind us closer together, as we should be bound.'[63] For the imperial federalist Parkin, Smith was simply unfit to 'interpret the political history and actual position of Canada', while Grant accused Smith of having monopolized 'the journalistic exchanges between Britain and Canada in desiring to be the sole interpreter of Canadian affairs to British readers'.[64] Neither was criticism of Smith confined to North America, as he was condemned 'by the *Times* and attacked by Benjamin Disraeli as one of the "prigs and pedants" who should make way for statesmen'.[65]

Anglo-Saxonism, Race and English Ethnic Associationalism

Further to these attacks, Smith suddenly also found himself entangled in a fierce debate over his political convictions in the early 1890s in connection with his membership of the Toronto St George's Society. The debate that ensued provides a suitable prism to explore the use of the Anglo-Saxonism trope in English associations, offering a perspective on how the English Diaspora became increasingly racialized in the late nineteenth century. While those opposed to Smith usually expressed their dissent in their writings, through pamphlets or letters to newspapers, the most significant clash over Smith's defence of continental union took place in Toronto's St George's Society in 1893 – since both Smith and the imperial federalist John Castell Hopkins were members. Smith's presidency of the Continental Union Association of Toronto triggered the dispute.[66] For Castell Hopkins, the active promotion of union between Canada and the US constituted an act of treason on Smith's part 'to his sovereign, to England, and to Canada'. Castell Hopkins thus brought forward a resolution at a St George's Society meeting that requested Smith to tender his resignation as life member of the society, though it was not carried. A subsequent motion was more successful, stating that the society

---

63 Robert Collyer, 'Do Americans Hate England?', *North American Review* 150.403 (1890), p. 771.
64 Paul T. Phillips, *The Controversialist: An Intellectual Life of Goldwin Smith* (Westport, CT: Praeger Publishers, 2002), p. 114.
65 Cook, 'Goldwin Smith'.
66 See for instance Smith, 'Anglo-Saxon Union', pp. 170–85.

desires emphatically to place on record its strong disapprobation [...] and hereby expresses its extreme regret that the Society should contain in its ranks a member who is striving for an object which would cause an irreparable injury to this dominion, would entail a loss to the mother land of a most important part of her empire, and would deprive Canadians of their birth-right as British subjects.[67]

The motion 'was adopted without division' among the society's membership. While the motion no longer included the specific aim of expelling Smith, he was not pleased to have come under attack in this way, retiring from membership himself a few months later. Smith was disappointed that a society without an express political agenda would agree that his activities were politically motivated.[68]

This episode, though partly a result of personal animosity if Smith is to be believed, reflects on the nature of Englishness in North America more broadly – not least because it resulted in a flurry of newspaper coverage in both Canada and the US, as well as receiving attention in Britain.[69] Political undercurrents were picked up, with proponents of imperial federation clashing with the rhetoric of republicanism they saw inherent to a continental union, which sat uneasily with many English in Canada. Anglo-Saxonism and the unity it propagated could not trump imperial connections: there were clear limits to its use as a trope of English ethnicity, despite its power of appropriation for divergent interest groups. While much of the reportage was negative, describing Smith's annexation 'propaganda',[70] the Toronto *Globe* issued a defence, noting that 'Prof. Smith is an Englishman, with an Englishman's courage and an Englishman's honor',[71] and that he should not have been lampooned in the way he was by a society with the designated purpose of presenting English interests.

The role of the St George's Society in Smith's case is useful in understanding the wider function that ethnic associations played in the English Diaspora. Even if Anglo-Saxonism did not create widespread support for a US-Canada confederation, English associations offered a reference point for expatriates to establish transnational unity around annual festivals such as St George, barons of beef and tankards of ale. At the same time as they appealed to shared origins, associations also provided a forum for an amalgamated Anglo-American culture, at times echoing contemporary intellectual debates about the possibilities of stronger transatlantic union between the US and Britain, as well as stronger bonds between the US and Canada. While

---

67 *The St George's Society and Mr Goldwin Smith* (1893?), p. 7, National Library of Australia, CIHM/ICMH microfiche series, no. 38738.

68 *New York Times*, 4 March 1893; also Phillips, *The Controversialist*.

69 For example *Free Press* (Easton, PA), 29 March 1893; *New York Times*, 10 May 1893; *The Times*, 14 February 1893.

70 *Brandon Mail*, 26 October 1893.

71 Cited in the *New York Times*, 8 February 1893.

expressions of loyalty to the Crown were common in the US, the toast to the queen being drunk 'with all the enthusiasm that loyalty and gallantry could inspire in the breasts of Englishmen', they were made alongside those to the US president, showing warm loyalty to both.[72] English ethnic associations thus developed a standardized ritual form, especially around St George's Day, that appealed to dual loyalties and identities, linking to England and North America as a whole. Celebratory events, repeated on an annual basis, were of chief importance for the active promotion and maintenance of diasporic ties. These ties were increasingly framed in terms of race as the English in North America were joined by a common fraternal bond on the saint's day that interlocked with Anglo-Saxonism. In a telegram from the St George's Society of Hamilton, Ontario, to the New York Society, for example, the members stated:

> And if to-day, there is a closer bond of fraternal sympathy and race union among the scattered children of the inviolate isle, let us all right heartily render thanks to the Giver of all Good for that. For an intimate union of Anglo-Saxondom would be the hope of the world, forming an alliance not needing or desiring to assail any other power, and too strong to be assailed.[73]

Reflecting the 'superiority' of the Anglo-Saxon race, this was a point that would have appealed to Smith: while 'a common language is in itself a most important bond of union',[74] race offered an even more potent common denominator. As Charles Dilke had already noted, the 'true moral of America is the vigour of the English race'.[75] Goldwin Smith, no doubt, would have applauded this assessment. If Canadians believed in the democratic ideal, they would have to accept annexation of Canada by the American republic. This, in turn, would secure the superiority of Anglo-Saxondom in North America, particularly in light of the significant influx of non-British immigrants in the late 1890s. Yet while Smith's framing of Anglo-Saxonism in this way generated heated debate, the narrative of race that surrounded the Anglo-Saxon culture promoted by English associations was nonetheless celebrated.

One aspect of English associational activity that drew particularly strongly on Anglo-Saxonism was the annual church service held as part of St George's Day celebrations in many North American towns. In the first instance, these provided a 'safe' platform for the expression of racial discourses, there being a strong sense of religiosity in the Englishness promoted through St George. Reverend Dr Herridge, one of the chaplains of the St George's Society of Ottawa, which hosted the 1899 anniversary service, was certainly of this opinion. 'Your presence here this evening', he stated, was 'evidence that you recognise in

---

72 *New York Times*, 25 April 1853.
73 St George's Society of New York Annual Report for 1898, p. 11, New York Public Library, *ZAN-8373.
74 Smith, 'Anglo-Saxon Union', p. 170.
75 Charles W. Dilke, *Greater Britain: A Record of Travel in the English-speaking Countries during 1866 and 1867* (London: Macmillan and Co., 1868), I, p. 308.

religion a factor of national greatness.' England's greatness manifested itself
in the England of commerce; the England of literature; and the England of fire
and sword. The greatest England of all, however, was 'the England of the men
who fear God', one that promoted a sense of 'Christian patriotism'. Though
throbbing 'with the dear love of Fatherland', this patriotism recognized that
they were Canadians, upholding harmony, Christian faith and purity. The key
was that the Anglo-Saxon had always 'proved himself fit for transmigration,
and well qualified to display under far-off skies the characteristics which
he has been taught at home'.[76] Similar words had already been issued by
Revd T. W. Winfield a few years earlier:

> the English race and the English language have penetrated every continent
> and sailed every sea. They have preserved their national characteristics always
> and conserved all that was best and dearest to their hearts. Dispersed in every
> climate they are yet one in their love for the land that gave them birth and
> birthright, and whether Imperial Federation ever becomes a fact, politically or
> not – there is a federation that we trust nothing will ever destroy[77].

In other instances, the religiousness of Englishness shone through in a
sense of duty to aid deserving immigrants from England in the New World.
'And how must the stranger's heart be lifted up within him', noted Revd
Kendall in a St George's Day sermon before the Toronto St George's Society,
'if the poor needy English emigrant is met with the hearty response of the St
George's Society, "You are not a stranger; you are among English hearts."'[78]
For Revd Kendall, the love of England was 'scarcely less holy' than the love
of Christ. Importantly, this religiosity also promoted a much wider sense
of brotherhood, tying the ethnic activities of different English associations
together by drawing upon shared Anglo-Saxon racial qualities. This is particularly evident in the early part of the twentieth century. Following the First
World War, for example, church services in Ottawa were often joint affairs,
being held as the United Annual Service of the St George's Society, the Sons of
England Benefit Society and the Daughters and Maids of England.[79]

---

76 Quotes from '"England's Greatness": Anniversary Sermon Delivered to the Members
    of St George's Society of Ottawa and the Sons of England', 23 April 1899, pp. 1, 3–5,
    Library and Archives Canada, Mic.F. CC-4 no. 05558.
77 T.W. Winfield, *A Sermon Preached before the St George's Society, Emmanuel Church*,
    Ottawa, 26 April 1891 (no publisher, 1891) talks about the 'inherent qualities of the
    race', p. 2.
78 E.K. Kendall, *Christ Seen in the Stranger: A Sermon, Preached in the Cathedral Church
    of St. James, Toronto, Canada West, on the evening of St George's Day, 1860, on behalf
    of the St George's Society* (Toronto: Rowsell & Ellis Printers, 1860), p. 15.
79 For instance, St George's Society of Ottawa fonds, Minute Book 1924, Library and
    Archives Canada (Ottawa), MG28-V3. Such efforts also tie in with the links that were
    promoted through shared racial roots for the purpose of co-operation in time of war;
    see, for example, G.L. Beer, *The English-Speaking Peoples: Their Future Relations and
    Joint International Obligations* (New York: Macmillan, 1917).

At the heart of this Anglo-Saxonism lay Protestantism:[80] the religiosity of Anglo-Saxonism helped promote a sense of civic duty and commitment to the wider community. In New York, annual Thanksgiving services by the city's most prominent associations developed. These services grew continuously, attracting nearly 1,500 people in 1938, the societies and their members 'holding aloft the blessed torch of democracy' through Anglo-Saxon values when the threat of war was looming.[81] In conjunction with Christian ideals, which Dos Passos had described as 'one of the most potent influences towards the unification of the Anglo-Saxon people',[82] war served to re-affirm Anglo-Saxon unity. Associations played a crucial part in this, effectively connecting Anglo-Saxonism and Protestantism, sharing 'its virtues'.[83] Yet by framing events and activities around Anglo-Saxonism, English associations, like many contemporary writers, enshrined a sense of racial superiority, thereby contributing directly to the increased racialization of the English Diaspora.

Conclusion

Anglo-Saxonism had crossed to North America like other aspects of English identity and culture with the arrival of the first English migrants. Independently, there was also a rediscovery and reinvention of the importance of mytho-historical figures, such as King Alfred, whose remembrance in the Victorian period amounted to a cult movement that linked into the Anglo-Saxon idea in Britain.[84] The subsequent blending of cultural traditions within the wider Anglo-Saxon world was driven by ideas of a shared racial heritage and superiority, both of which became increasingly prominent from the late nineteenth century.

In Canada, discourses around Anglo-Saxonism and race pervaded debates on both imperial federation and continental union, revealing the degree to which Anglo-Saxonism could be used for divergent political purposes. It was an equally usable reference point for English associations in North America, reflecting the wider appeal of Anglo-Saxonism as a cultural symbol and trope of English ethnicity. What this highlights is that Anglo-Saxonism was more than a myth that lost its relevance 'as a historical explanation'.[85] It was a central belief system, framed around the idea of racial superiority, shared roots and familiar historical narratives. Importantly, it was a system that

---

80 Bell, *The Idea of Greater Britain*, p. 195.
81 *New York Times*, 21 November 1938.
82 Dos Passos, *The Anglo-Saxon Century*, p. 138.
83 Kramer, 'Empires, Exceptions, and Anglo-Saxons', p. 1321.
84 Parker, *England's Darling*.
85 James Belich, *Replenishing the Earth: The Settler Revolution and the Rise of the Anglo-World, 1783–1939* (Oxford: Oxford University Press, 2009), p. 5.

could be adopted for divergent, at times diametrically opposed, purposes.[86] Herein lay the strength of Anglo-Saxon rhetoric, and one that was also recognized by writers from abroad. Identifying the racial unity between Britain and America, German journalist Maximilian Harden observed, in *Die Zukunft* (*The Future*) in 1911, that 'Great Britain and North America tend to form a community of interests. On the two oceans, the Anglo-Saxons of the two continents group themselves together in unity of will. The hegemony of the white race will be theirs.'[87]

However, the situation was not as straightforward as Harden assumed: it was complicated by the geopolitical implications of Anglo-Saxonism and the tensions that at times existed between the US and both Britain and Canada, regardless of the idea of shared racial heritage. The debates that ensued in relation to Goldwin Smith's writings, as well as the controversy around his membership of the Toronto St George's Society, document these bigger tensions in miniature. What they also highlight, however, is that improving transatlantic relations should not be confused with a meaningful pan-Anglo-Saxonism. At the same time as W.T. Stead called for the 'merging of the British Empire in the English-speaking United States of the World', the United States was turning away from Anglo-Saxonism to Americanism.[88] American realities forced a rethink at the turn of the century. As Kohn argues, 'Anglo-Saxonism was out; Anglo-conformism was in.'[89] Among the English, though it slipped into gradual, arcane irrelevance, the term 'Anglo-Saxon' nevertheless continued to colour popular parlance in speeches and toasts that found audiences among the English Diaspora throughout North America and the wider Anglo-world.

---

86 Cf. Ramsay Cook, 'Canada: A Post-Nationalist Nation?', in Sima Godfrey and Frank Unger (eds), *The Shifting Foundations of Modern Nation-States* (Toronto: University of Toronto Press, 2004), p. 21.
87 Quoted in Beer, *The English-Speaking Peoples*, p. 98
88 Stead, *The Americanization of the World*.
89 Kohn, *This Kindred People*, p. 202.

Chapter 8

'The Englishmen here are much disliked': Hostility towards English Immigrants in Early Twentieth-Century Toronto

Amy J. Lloyd

> The Englishmen here are much disliked, and of the Canadians in this town it can only be said that they have "manners none and customs beastly." [...] [Their] ignorance of England is astounding, and the people are always asking you if you don't think Toronto is more up-to-date? They have a lot to learn yet, I can tell you; in all the refinements of life they are years behind us. I am simply longing to be home again, and never more to see this hateful place.

These words, written by an Englishwoman 'who recently went out to Toronto to be married', were published in the 14 February 1907 issue of the popular British penny-weekly magazine, *Pearson's Weekly*. Chosen for publication as her 'views on the country [...] are so different from what one generally hears from Canada', the editor asked, 'What have my other Toronto readers to say?'[1] They had, as it turns out, much to say in response to the Englishwoman's letter. As was explained by the editor in the 7 March issue, the letter had 'created a great deal of interest. Many letters from *P.W.*-ites who have been to Toronto have reached me.'[2] Over the next two months, extracts from 11 readers' letters were published in the magazine.

Importantly, discussion of the Englishwoman's letter was not limited to the pages of *Pearson's Weekly*. In the 18 April issue, the editor commented:

> A considerable amount of interest has been aroused, not only in England, but in the whole of Canada [...] This week's mail has brought me some scores of letters from residents in Toronto, many of which inclose [*sic*] cuttings from the

---

1   'Some of the Editor's Valentines', *Pearson's Weekly*, 14 February 1907.
2   'Pencil-Cases All', *Pearson's Weekly*, 7 March 1907.

TORONTO GLOBE containing columns of opinions from their readers on the statements made in *Pearson's Weekly*.[3]

Indeed, the letters in *Pearson's Weekly* had caught the attention of the *Globe*, a prominent Toronto newspaper. It printed some of the letters – including the original – in its 19 March issue, and asked its readers whether 'these extracts from Pearson's Weekly fairly represent the views of recent English immigrants as to Toronto and Canada generally'. Over the next few days, the newspaper was inundated with responses, leading the editor[4] to comment in the 23 March issue that the 'volume of letters from recent immigrants on their trials, disappointments and successes is quite too great for publication';[5] a few days later 'hundreds of letters' had been received.[6] Such was the volume of letters that the following notice was published in the back pages of the 29 March issue:

> Very many letters are still coming in from readers of The Globe who have not seen the notice that no further letters would be published. This is by way of acknowledgment as well as an explanation of the failure to print them. It would take more room than The Globe will be able to give to correspondence for months to publish the letters received on the question.[7]

Overall, the *Globe* published 36 letters in four separate instalments between 21 and 25 March 1907.

Thus, the publication in a popular British penny-weekly magazine of a letter by a disgruntled English immigrant living in Toronto resulted in a transatlantic explosion of dialogue and debate. This chapter analyses the letters published in the *Globe* and the reaction to them in the rest of the Toronto press, focusing particularly on the issue that generated the most controversy and discussion: why did many English immigrants face hostility in Canada? While this hostility has been identified by a number of historians, no detailed research has been carried out.[8] This chapter fills a gap in the

---

3   'Cases Stated', *Pearson's Weekly*, 18 April 1907.
4   The newspaper does not specify whether it was the editor or another writer on the *Globe*'s staff who introduced and commented on the letters that were published. For simplicity's sake, it has been assumed in this essay that it was the editor.
5   'As Others See Us', *Globe*, 23 March 1907.
6   Ibid., 25 March 1907.
7   'Has Served its Purpose', *Globe*, 29 March 1907.
8   Instead, in discussing this matter, most historians have relied on a small number of books and articles that were published in England and Canada during the early twentieth century. For example, P. Berton, *The Promised Land: Settling the West 1896–1914* (Toronto: McClelland and Stewart, 1984), pp. 138–45; P.A. Dunae, *Gentlemen Emigrants: From the British Public Schools to the Canadian Frontier* (Vancouver: Douglas & McIntyre, 1981), pp. 123–46; D. Hoerder, *Creating Societies: Immigrant Lives in Canada* (Montreal: McGill-Queen's University Press, 1999), pp. 111–13; N. Kelley and M. Trebilcock, *The Making of the Mosaic: A History of Canadian Immigration Policy* (Toronto: University of Toronto Press, 1998), p. 123; R.G. Moyles and D. Owram, *Imperial Dreams and Colonial Realities: British Views of Canada, 1880–1914* (Toronto:

existing scholarship, providing much-needed insight into the factors that contributed to the emergence of hostility against English immigrants in early twentieth-century Canada.

What makes this issue especially interesting is the fact that the British Isles were one of the preferred sources of immigrants during this period. Between 1896 and 1914, Canada experienced rapid economic growth and development, and immigration played an important role in the boom, with Canada receiving around three million immigrants during these years. Approximately one-third of the new arrivals were from Britain.[9] As in earlier periods, the British Isles were one of the preferred migrant sources: many Canadians saw themselves as British and regarded Canada as a British nation; hence it was thought that British immigrants would have fewer adjustment problems than immigrants from other countries and would be more likely to make a lasting contribution to their new home. The preference for British migrants was even more keenly felt during the economic boom years of the early twentieth century, when it was increasingly feared that, without significant immigration from Britain, Canada's population needs would be filled by immigrants of 'inferior classes'.[10] Yet despite their preferred status, English immigrants – who constituted a distinct ethnic group in Canada,[11] and formed around 80 per cent of all British migrants entering the country during the early twentieth century[12] – faced hostility. Why, then, were English immigrants seemingly both welcomed and detested?

Much of the analysis in this chapter is based on the letters published in the *Globe*, a daily newspaper published in Toronto that had one of the largest circulations in Canada.[13] The vast majority of the letters seem to have been written by recently arrived English immigrants: the editor was particularly interested in garnering their responses.[14] As far as can be established, the letter writers were from a broad section of society, although, given the wider

---

University of Toronto Press, 1988), pp. 134–37; H. Palmer, *Patterns of Prejudice: A History of Nativism in Alberta* (Toronto: McClelland and Stewart, 1982), pp. 24–25.

9   I. Ferenczi and W. Willcox, *International Migrations* (New York: National Bureau of Economic Research, 1929), pp. 364–65.

10 D.J. Hall, *Clifford Sifton* (Vancouver: University of British Columbia Press, 1985), pp. 259–60; Kelley and Trebilcock, *The Making of the Mosaic*, pp. 122–23.

11 This has been argued by A. Ross McCormack in 'Cloth Caps and Jobs: The Ethnicity of English Immigrants in Canada 1900-1914', in Rorgen Dahlie and Tissa Fernando (eds), *Ethnicity, Power and Politics in Canada* (Toronto: Metheun, 1981), p. 40.

12 Ferenczi and Willcox, *International Migrations*, pp. 364–65.

13 The *Globe* was also the leading national Liberal organ. It seems unlikely, however, that the *Globe*'s support of the Liberal party affected its coverage of this issue; both Conservatives and Liberals were in favour of English immigration. See P. Rutherford, *A Victorian Authority: The Daily Press in Late Nineteenth-Century Canada* (Toronto: University of Toronto Press, 1982), pp. 77, 238; M. Sotiron, *From Politics to Profit: The Commercialization of Canadian Daily Newspapers, 1890-1920* (Montreal: McGill-Queen's University Press, 1997), pp. 19, 71, 112–13, 121–22.

14 32 of the 36 letters were written by English immigrants, most of whom had recently settled in Canada. Cf. 'As Others See Us', *Globe*, 23 March 1907.

readership of the *Globe*, perhaps with a slight middle-class bias;[15] most seem to have been men.[16] Letters to the editor are not without problems as a source in historical analysis: some of the writers used nicknames, other names may have been pseudonyms. However, while it is certainly possible that a handful of letters were fabricated, the vast majority of letters and the views they contain seem to reflect the genuine concerns of a significant number of readers. Confidence is inspired by the fact that the letters present a variety of perspectives on the issue – no one viewpoint is pushed;[17] the existence of several of the correspondents who provided full names could be verified using census and passenger list data;[18] other competing newspapers in Toronto – including the *Star*, the *World* and the *News* – published articles and letters on the subject that confirmed the views being expressed in the *Globe*;[19] and the letters resulted in the founding of a widely supported organization, the British Welcome League, to address the issues that had been brought to light.[20]

Reaction in the *Globe*

Toronto was inundated with English immigrants during the early twentieth century. The Canadian-born decreased from 75 per cent of its population in 1901 to just 63 per cent by 1911. Most of this decrease was due to the settlement

---

15 Only one of the letter writers mentions his/her occupation, namely 'Cockney', who states that he is a mechanic. With some of the letter writers providing full names, it has been possible to trace four of the *Globe*'s letter writers in the Canadian and English censuses, and in Canadian and American passenger lists using www.ancestry.com. One of them was probably working class: William Hogg worked as a bill poster in England and Toronto. The other three were probably middle class: W.H. Adeney was a shipping and correspondence clerk in England and worked as a bookkeeper in a factory in Brant, Ontario; Albert Chamberlain worked as a bricklayer in England and as a city inspector in Toronto; and Sydney H. Wiggins was a salesman.
16 Only two of the letters appear to have been written by women, namely 'A Reader of the Globe' and 'C.E.F.' See 'As Others See Us', *Globe*, 22 and 25 March 1907.
17 Indeed, the *Globe*'s editor seems to have wanted to investigate the issue fully, seeking to present all sides of the subject, and it appears that this was accomplished. He particularly wished to know whether the Englishwoman's criticisms were accurate, and what could be done to improve the situation. Cf. 'As Others See Us', *Globe*, 21, 22, 23 and 25 March 1907.
18 See footnote 15.
19 See, for example: 'New-Comers and Native-Born', *Star*, 22 March 1907; 'Is there Too Much Immigration?', *Star*, 23 March 1907; 'Welcome Urged for Newcomers', *World*, 25 March 1907; 'Editorial Notes', *Mail and Empire*, 26 March 1907; 'Englishmen in Canada', *News*, 30 March 1907.
20 Had not many of the views expressed in the *Globe* been a genuine concern, particularly with regard to the disappointments and hostility faced by English immigrants, it seems unlikely that there would have been such a vigorous, substantial and sustained response. The founding of the British Welcome League will be addressed later in the chapter. See also 'To Welcome Britishers', *Globe*, 28 March 1907; 'Immigrants Given Aid', *Globe*, 19 April 1907.

in Toronto of immigrants from England, with the English-born rising from 12 per cent of the population to 19 per cent over the same period.[21] The English thus entered Toronto in large numbers during the early twentieth century, forming by far the largest group of foreign-born, and their settlement in the city did not go unnoticed. Indeed, the letters and articles published in the *Globe* and several other Toronto newspapers reveal that English immigrants were not always greeted warmly. Reacting to the Englishwoman's assertion in *Pearson's Weekly* that 'The Englishmen here are much disliked', it was almost universally acknowledged in the Toronto press that English immigrants often did face hostility in Toronto and southern Ontario more generally. Nineteen letters published in the *Globe* agreed with the Englishwoman, while only five expressed a contrary view; four other newspapers published articles and letters that were in agreement, while only one newspaper disagreed.

Those letter writers who did not agree with the Englishwoman in *Pearson's Weekly* – all of whom were recent English immigrants – claimed that Canadians and English immigrants generally got along well; they had found Canadians to be welcoming and always willing to lend a helping hand. 'G.E.', an Englishman who had moved to Ontario four years earlier, observed:

> When I came here I did not expect to be received with open arms. I was just an Englishman looking for means to earn a living [...] and to say that I was surprised at the way I was made welcome everywhere would not in the least express my words. I find, in my experience with Canadians, that they are a fine lot to get along with. I could mention cases where English families have been destitute, either through sickness or accidents, and have had their board and rents paid for them by Canadians.[22]

The one dissenting newspaper, the *Mail and Empire*, made a very similar point, observing in the 'Editorial Notes' section in the 26 March issue that:

> All immigrants from the Motherland are welcome in Canada, and there is not the slightest feeling against them. Canadians recognize that their own ancestors had to cross the ocean, and they see in the newcomers a repetition of the movement which made them the directors of the destinies of this marvellous country. To the English, the Irish, the Scotch, the Welsh, the right hand of fellowship is extended, and the hope is entertained that they will all do well in the new Dominion.[23]

---

21 By comparison, the Irish decreased from 6% to 4% of Toronto's population between 1901 and 1911, the Scottish increased from 3% to 5%, Americans remained at 3%, and Russians increased from 1% to 3%. Cf. *Fifth Census of Canada 1911* (Ottawa: Printed by C.H. Parmelee, 1913), II, pp. 426, 440; *Fourth Census of Canada 1901* (Ottawa: Printed by S.E. Dawson, 1902), I, pp. 2, 4, 417, 434–35.
22 'As Others See Us', *Globe*, 25 March 1907.
23 'Editorial Notes', *Mail and Empire*, 26 March 1907.

However, these were minority views.[24] Most letter writers in the *Globe*, and most of the articles and letters published in the four other Toronto newspapers, asserted that English immigrants often faced hostility in Toronto – from both the Canadian-born and from older cohorts of immigrants (all hereafter referred to as 'Canadians').[25] Many of the letters by English immigrants that were published in the *Globe* mentioned the hostility they had faced in Canada. 'X-Rays', an Englishman who had arrived in Canada in 1904, regretted to say, for instance, 'that there is strong prejudice against "the Englishman" in this country, and in some cases it reaches to a positive hatred'.[26] In a similar vein, 'J. Miller', a more recent arrival, stated that 'to be truthful, I found a lot of real antagonism against Englishmen and everything English'.[27] 'A Two Years' Resident of Ottawa' recalled how surprised he was upon arriving in Canada at

> the manner in which Englishmen appear to be detested. I have been to Australia, the Cape and various other parts of the empire, but have never seen Englishmen treated in the fashion I have noticed here. I have often wondered why the Canadian Government makes such strenuous efforts to induce the English to come over, considering the chilling reception waiting for them when they arrive.[28]

Further to revealing that hostility existed, the letters published also document how it manifested itself. A number of the *Globe*'s letter writers complained, for example, about being called 'cockneys', 'bronchos' and 'sparrows'.[29] 'A Reader of the Globe' gave a detailed example:

> I may say your correspondent only voices the cry of hundreds of our country-men, for Canadians as a people are extremely opposed to us English, as is proved

24 The *Mail and Empire*'s stance was likely coloured by the fact that it was the *Globe*'s main rival in Toronto – both in political terms (the latter being Liberal and the former Conservative) and circulation-wise (they were the two top-selling newspapers in Toronto during this period). Cf. Rutherford, *A Victorian Authority*, pp. 76–77, 217, 238–39.

25 See also 'Welcome Urged for Newcomers', *World*, 25 March 1907; 'Canadians and Englishmen', *Star*, 30 March 1907; 'Coatsworth Treasurer British Welcome League', *World*, 1 April 1907; 'For British Immigrants', *Telegram*, 28 March 1907; 'Welcome League for Englishmen', *News*, 28 March 1907; 'To Welcome Britishers', *Globe*, 28 March 1907.

26 'As Others See Us', *Globe*, 21 March 1907.

27 Ibid., 23 March 1907.

28 Ibid., 22 March 1907.

29 According to the *Oxford English Dictionary*, a 'sparrow' can mean a 'chirpy, quick-witted person', often used specifically with regard to Londoners (i.e. cockney sparrow). English immigrants probably objected to being branded 'cockneys' and 'sparrows' if they were not actually from the east end of London and if the term was used in derision. Cf. 'Sparrow', in *The Oxford English Dictionary: OED Online* http://dictionary.oed.com.ezproxy.webfeat.lib.ed.ac.uk/cgi/entry/50232314?single=1&query_type=word&queryword=sparrow&first=1&max_to_show=10 (accessed 13 February 2011). See also 'Englishmen in Canada', *News*, 30 March 1907.

by their rudeness when they chance to meet any. I was passing along King Street, Cobourg, the other night [...] when some young ladies came along. They could not pass without one of them hurling the epithet of "Sparrows" at us.[30]

'Nil Desperandum', an Englishman who had been living in Toronto for two years, commented that the letters in the *Globe* had shown 'a deep unrest on the part of Englishmen in the way they are treated by their hosts'. He added, 'Believe me, the unrest is real, and can you expect anything else than that the Englishman will kick when he is goaded by snubs and sneers and termed broncho, sparrows, cockneys.'[31]

Along with the calling of names came the ridiculing of English immigrants. As was succinctly summarized by the *Globe's* editor, 'the Englishman, proud of his race and of the fact that he is a subject of the greatest of empires, on coming out to Canada finds his accent and his method of working, his manner of dressing even, ridiculed. The evidence on this point is too strong to be pooh-poohed.' He also noted that this mockery was perhaps 'the most deep-seated grievance'.[32] As much was also picked up by the *Star* in its 23 March issue, where it said that it was

cruel to add to the pangs of homesickness the pain that is given by foolish mockery of peculiarities of manners and speech. Some may go to the extreme of copying the accent that is supposed to be of Oxford. Others may go to the extreme of mocking the accent that is supposed to be of lower social value. Let us do neither.[33]

The key question that remains, however, is why were some Canadians in Toronto and southern Ontario so openly hostile to English immigrants? Many letter writers in the *Globe* sought to provide explanations. With regard to Canadians, it was noted that some ridiculed English immigrants simply because they found them somewhat odd and different. As the editor of the *Globe* stressed, Canadians often found 'their mannerisms, their various accents, their airs, their ways of thinking, their ignorance of the commonplace things of our life [...] strange'.[34] Some letter writers attributed this to Canadian ignorance. 'Granby' – who had lived in Toronto for three years – claimed that he and his family 'soon felt the Canadian sneer and insult, but we soon understood it was pure ignorance as regards England and Englishmen'.[35] 'Traveller', who had also lived in Canada for three years, agreed: 'I have also

30 'As Others See Us', *Globe*, 22 March 1907.
31 Ibid., 25 March 1907.
32 Ibid., 22 March 1907.
33 'Is there Too Much Immigration?' *Star*, 23 March 1907.
34 'As Others See Us', *Globe*, 25 March 1907.
35 Ibid., 22 March 1907.

met Canadians who have kicks for the English, but generally he is speaking in this way from pure ignorance of England and the English.'[36]

What is interesting is that a majority of letter writers thought that the blame lay more at the feet of English immigrants themselves. Some argued that Canadian hostility partly stemmed from the fact that many English immigrants were not of the best quality; too many were poor workers – a fact that, over time, had soured Canadian impressions of English immigrants in general.[37] As much was emphasized by 'H.H. Holland', who had lived in Toronto since 1905. 'As a rule', he said, 'it is not the best class of my country-men that come to Canada for the purpose of earning a livelihood, and this probably explains their unpopularity.'[38] Albert Chamberlain, a bricklayer and later city inspector who had immigrated to Canada in 1881 from Glastonbury, England,[39] blamed immigration agents in England who

> are not particular enough about the class of people they send out here. I am told that they are paid so much per head, so that the more they send the more pay they receive, and for this ignoble reason persons are induced to come to Canada who are not good workers at home, and must, of necessity, prove undesirable when they arrive here.[40]

In general, there seems to have been an anxious feeling in Toronto that far too many immigrants from England were unsuited to Ontario's employment needs: the province desperately needed farm workers, and too many English immigrants were from cities, were unskilled and were unable or unwill-ing to undertake agricultural work. There was some unease that, while jobs could presently be found for such immigrants, if economic conditions were to worsen very serious problems would result.[41]

---

36 Ibid., 25 March 1907.
37 Dirk Hoerder argues that labour militancy among working-class English immigrants in Canada led to the popular image of slacking English workers during this period. Hoerder, *Creating Societies*, pp. 111–13.
38 'As Others See Us', *Globe*, 21 March 1907.
39 It has been possible to trace him using census and passenger list data.
40 'As Others See Us', *Globe*, 22 March 1907.
41 Historians have documented that many Canadians during this period feared that Britain was dumping its undesirables – particularly paupers from its slums – in Canada. As a result, there was deep suspicion of the work of charitable emigration societies. Moreover, Torontonians' fears regarding the long-term availability of jobs were realized in the economic recession that started in the winter of 1907, which led to a severe unemployment crisis in Toronto. See Berton, *The Promised Land*, pp. 138–45; McCormack, 'Cloth Caps and Jobs', pp. 40–41; M.J. Piva, *The Condition of the Working Class in Toronto, 1900–1921* (Ottawa: University of Ottawa Press, 1979), p. 72. In the newspapers, see 'The Flow of Immigration', *Star*, 13 May 1907; 'Englishmen in Canada', *News*, 30 March 1907; 'Is there Too Much Immigration?' *Star*, 23 March 1907; 'Welcome Urged for Newcomers', *World*, 25 March 1907; 'Welcome League for Englishmen', *News*, 28 March 1907; 'To Welcome Britishers', *Globe*, 28 March 1907; 'Why Immigrants Come to Toronto', *Globe*, 18 May 1907.

Another reason that was cited for the unpopularity of English immigrants was their tendency to grumble. Not unsurprisingly – given the arguments above – some letter writers noted that English immigrants often tended to complain in the workplace. For example, William Hogg, a bill poster from Berwick-upon-Tweed, England, who had immigrated to Canada in 1906,[42] stated that he had been working in Toronto for the past six months with 'three Scotchmen, five or six Canadians, two Germans and two Englishmen, and I am confident there were more complaints from these last two men than all the others put together. As a matter of fact, nobody grumbled but themselves. Prejudice against the Englishman, no doubt, arises from his own conduct.'[43] 'An Immigrant', who was most likely not English himself, provided even more compelling evidence, noting that 'A large employer of labor, himself of pure English stock, has stated in my hearing that he would not take an Englishman into his factory; that he had never employed an Englishman who did not turn out to be a grumbler and a kicker.'[44]

Fuelled by disappointment, however, English immigrants at times tended to grumble and complain about conditions in Canada in general. Some letter writers blamed the Canadian government and its immigration agents and propaganda.[45] Sydney H. Wiggins, a salesman from London who was then briefly living in Toronto,[46] criticized the dishonest advertisements and agents that 'lead the average Englishman by specious promises to expect far more than it is possible to realise'.[47] In summarizing the many letters received, the *Globe*'s editor also noted that

> many newcomers seem to be sorely disappointed with their position and wage-earning power. The people of Canada are not to blame for this, however, but the unscrupulous agents on the other side of the Atlantic who misrepresent conditions here and induce their dupes to believe that Canada is a species of latter-day Eldorado, whose cities are paved with gold.[48]

Along with grumbling and complaining, it seems that English immigrants were also prone to criticizing. This is certainly evident in the Englishwoman's letter and the many respondents in the *Globe* who agreed with her. For example, the Englishwoman proclaimed that Canadians 'have "manners none and customs beastly"'. Eleven of the *Globe*'s letter writers were in accord, with their letters cataloguing behaviours common among Canadians that they found particularly abhorrent. Among these, the chewing and spitting of tobacco by men in the street and the frequent use of foul language were the

---

42 It has been possible to trace him using census and passenger list data.
43 'As Others See Us', *Globe*, 25 March 1907.
44 Ibid., 22 March 1907.
45 See also 'Coatsworth Treasurer British Welcome League', *World*, 1 April 1907.
46 It has been possible to trace him using census and passenger list data.
47 'As Others See Us', *Globe*, 23 March 1907.
48 Ibid., 22 March 1907.

most frequently cited. 'Satisfied', an English immigrant who had lived in both Montreal and Toronto, summed up these complaints well:

> As regards manners, I'm afraid I agree with an English lady there, to a certain extent. I have in my mind men chewing tobacco on the cars and on the street, and not being at all particular about the spot they spit upon, the rough, jostling way they push along a crowded street, and the language they take such pains not to conceal.[49]

The Englishwoman also asserted in her letter that Canadians were ignorant of Britain and wrongly thought that Toronto was more 'up-to-date'. Seven of the *Globe*'s letter writers agreed with her. As 'J.G.S.C', a recent English immigrant, stressed, 'Torontonians are justly proud of their splendid city, but I, too, have noticed a singular want of knowledge of Great Britain and her commercial enterprises, and to compare Toronto with London in this respect is at least ludicrous.'[50] Similarly, 'Nil Desperandum' complained:

> The Englishman may be ignorant somewhat of Canada, but not nearly so much as the average Canadian is of England, or he would not [...] flaunt in their faces that England is behind, and we are ahead of England by a hundred years. You must remember the Englishman, if he is at all above the submerged tenth, has seen a great deal of England, and has seen very often more of Canada than the Canadian himself, and is better able to judge the two than the man who has never seen England and read little of it.[51]

This tendency to criticize, which often segued into correcting, was attributed by a number of letter writers to the fact that many English immigrants looked down on Canada and Canadians, seeing England and the English as superior. Moreover, such behaviour certainly did not ingratiate English immigrants to Canadians.[52] As 'C.C. Daines', a recent arrival who had only lived in Toronto for nine months, noted, 'the whole trouble with Englishmen amounts to this: that they will persist in praising everything English and ridiculing everything Canadian. Naturally enough the Canadian gets sick of hearing how things are done in England and of being shown how to do things in his own country.'[53] A Scottish immigrant remarked that 'Englishmen have the unfortunate faculty of thinking they know better than anyone else, and have nothing to learn, even in a new country, which does not tend to ingratiate them with Canadians, who are as independent and self-reliant as any people under the sun.'[54] An article in the *World* no doubt summed up a common

---

49 Ibid., 21 March 1907.
50 Ibid.
51 Ibid., 25 March 1907.
52 See also 'Englishmen in Canada', *News*, 30 March 1907.
53 'As Others See Us', *Globe*, 21 March 1907.
54 Ibid., 23 March 1907.

Canadian reaction: 'Don't try to tell us "How to do it." We may not know as much as they do at home, but we do know what is best here. Fit in.'[55]

In view of the accusations made, some contributors to the debate sought to improve relations between Canadians and English immigrants by providing advice to newly arrived immigrants on how to behave: avoid grumbling and criticizing, and adapt to Canadian conditions. 'Traveller' wrote:

> "When in Rome, do as the Romans do," is an old, but still very true saying. Consequently, I had to "get wise" quickly, and adapted myself to the conditions prevailing. I have met many "kickers" myself, and have always endeavored to give them good advice. [...] I am so much a Canadian now that if I meet a kicking Englishman I advise him to "shut up" or "get out". We don't want kickers.[56]

Similarly, 'A Four-Year Resident' advised:

> Let English emigrants to this country make up their minds to become Canadians, and they will find, as I have found, that in a short while they will find a host of friends worth having, and who, far from being ignorant, will show that they know how to appreciate any immigrants who think as much of their country as they do themselves, and who are not forever grumbling about nothing. The people of this country dislike a grumbling Englishman more than anything else, and an Englishman who is in a position where he hears a lot of it soon begins to dislike it himself.[57]

However, there was no general agreement on this advice,[58] and Albert Chamberlain certainly disagreed. He was amused 'to hear some of my countrymen tell the newly arrived settler that, if they want to get along in this country, they must forget the land of their birth and become full-fledged Canadians. Shame on any Englishman who would give such advice.' However, he added: 'No, sir, what we Englishmen want is not to forget our old home [...] but to remember that we are in a new country [...] and we must adapt ourselves to new methods by taking off our coats (leaving our old country methods behind when not applicable), and show the Canadian that we can hold our end up well.'[59]

---

55 'Welcome Urged for Newcomers', *World*, 25 March 1907.
56 'As Others See Us', *Globe*, 25 March 1907.
57 Ibid., 21 March 1907.
58 These divergent opinions stress the individual nature of ethnic identity: old world ties might be fully abandoned for the sake of complete assimilation suggests one, while an instrumentalist interpretation of identity could serve to reconcile old and new worlds.
59 'As Others See Us', *Globe*, 22 March 1907.

Sources of Strife

These examples certainly show that English immigrants constituted a distinct ethnic group in Toronto during this period: Canadians ascribed a separate identity to the English,[60] and English immigrants themselves asserted a group identity – a fact that accords with A. Ross McCormack's arguments concerning English ethnicity in early twentieth-century Canada.[61]

Furthermore, the examples traced here also highlight that there were many reasons why the English engendered hostility in early twentieth-century Toronto. First, the persuasive Canadian recruitment efforts in England that attracted many to settle in Canada[62] were blamed by some for fostering unrealistic expectations and for inducing many to come who were unsuited to Canadian employment needs. A lack of high wages and appropriate work led to disappointment among English immigrants in Toronto. The consequent complaints coming from recent English immigrants did not ingratiate them to Canadians. At the same time, the inundating of Toronto with immigrants who were perceived as unsuitable led to frustration among many residents.

What further complicated the relationship was that some English immigrants brought with them to Canada ideas, beliefs and assumptions that grated with many Canadians. Some English immigrants viewed Canada as being somewhat backward, primitive, underdeveloped and unsophisticated – inferior to its more advanced mother country, England. Tying in with this was the perception that Canadians themselves were ill-mannered, uncultured and ignorant. In view of their negative opinions of Canada and Canadians, some English immigrants evidently regarded themselves as ambassadors from the mother country, bringing with them English culture, customs and norms and entering Canada with little expectation that they would have to adapt – let alone become Canadian. Indeed, it seems that many were proud to be English – proud of their nation's accomplishments and position in the world.

Thus, it appears that many English immigrants viewed Canada through a patriotic and imperial lens. Many in England were patriotic during this period,[63] and it is not surprising that such sentiments were expressed by

---

60 This can particularly be seen in the stereotyping that occurred, which included name calling and the ridiculing of speech, clothing and behaviour: the English were ascribed specific ethnic qualifiers by others that classified them as a group for the purpose of singling them out.

61 McCormack, 'Cloth Caps and Jobs', pp. 38–40.

62 A.J. Lloyd, 'Popular Perceptions of Emigration in Britain, 1870–1914', unpublished PhD thesis, University of Cambridge, 2009, pp. 196–99, 250–56.

63 J. Benson, *The Working Class in Britain, 1850–1939* (London: Longman, 1989), pp. 148–51, 161–62; H. Cunningham, 'The Language of Patriotism, 1750–1914', *History Workshop*, 12 (1981), pp. 25–27; R. McKibbin, *The Ideologies of Class: Social Relations in Britain, 1880–1950* (Oxford: Clarendon Press, 1990), p. 24; S.M. Miller, 'In Support of the "Imperial Mission"? Volunteering for the South African War, 1899–1902', *Journal of*

English immigrants abroad. While imperialistic discourse was not used in the majority of the letters, Canada was part of the British Empire and most English immigrants would have been aware of this fact.[64] This no doubt influenced their behaviour in Canada: formerly British colonies and now a British Dominion, did this not then mean that Canada was inferior and subordinate to Great Britain; underdeveloped and in need of British guidance and assistance; and similar to Britain and desirous of replicating its ways, customs and culture?

As for Canadians, while many English-speaking Canadians regarded themselves as British and were proud that Canada was part of the British Empire, this did not necessarily mean that they embraced the Britain of the present or the people of Britain. Instead, the Britishness that Canadians espoused, as Kurt Korneski has suggested, 'reflected and spoke to geopolitics, spiritual qualities, politico-ethical principles, and visions of the future'. Britain itself was often seen as flawed, and Canada was held up as something of a 'better Britain', with greater economic potential, a less rigid class structure and a healthier population. Indeed, many Canadians had great pride in their country, sparked particularly by economic prosperity during this period.[65] As was noted by a 'Constant Reader' in a letter published in the *News*, '[w]e who have grown up with, and in this, our beautiful Canada, really believe we have as fine, if not, the best country under the sun'.[66] It was expected that the British Empire would eventually be transformed into an alliance of British nations, which would work together cooperatively and be equal in status.[67] Many Canadians thus did not appreciate English immigrants constantly referring to Canada's inferior status, criticizing and correcting Canadian ways and methods, and comparing Canada unfavourably to England. Moreover, despite common membership in the British Empire, English immigrants were not automatically embraced as compatriots. Instead, they were regarded as an 'other'; like other immigrants, they still needed to prove their worth and adapt

---

Military History, 69.3 (2005); J. Rose, *The Intellectual Life of the British Working Classes* (New Haven, CT: Yale University Press, 2001), p. 340.

64 Lloyd, 'Popular Perceptions of Emigration', p. 201.

65 C. Berger, *The Sense of Power: Studies in the Ideas of Canadian Imperialism : 1867–1914* (Toronto: University of Toronto Press, 1970), p. 260; P.A. Buckner, 'Introduction' and 'The Creation of the Dominion of Canada, 1860–1901', in Phillip A. Buckner (ed.), *Canada and the British Empire* (Oxford: Oxford University Press, 2008), pp. 6–8, 72–44; P. Hastings, 'Branding Canada: Consumer Culture and the Development of Popular Nationalism in the Early Twentieth Century', in Norman Hillmer and Adam Chapnick (eds), *Canadas of the Mind: The Making and Unmaking of Canadian Nationalisms in the Twentieth Century* (Montreal: McGill-Queen's University Press, 2007), pp. 151–52; K. Korneski, 'Britishness, Canadianness, Class, and Race: Winnipeg and the British World, 1880s–1910s', *Journal of Canadian Studies*, 41.2 (2007), pp. 167–68.

66 'Care of Immigrants', *News*, 3 April 1907. See also 'New-Comers and Native-Born', *Star*, 22 March 1907.

67 Buckner, 'The Creation of the Dominion of Canada', pp. 72–73.

to Canadian society and values – in other words, to become 'good and useful' Canadian citizens.[68]

However, it is significant that, unlike with other migrant groups, the hostility voiced in Toronto did not lead to much outright opposition to English immigration.[69] Instead, it was generally recognized that Canada needed immigrants, and immigrants from the British Isles were the most desirable group, since they were from the same stock as most of the present population. As the editor of the *Globe* stated, Canadians know 'that this vast wave of Anglo-Saxon immigration is of the very greatest advantage to the Dominion, and will, if continued, relieve the nation of many of the difficult problems that are inseparable from the mixing of many races in a new land'.[70] Consequently, despite their flaws, English immigrants had to be tolerated. After the publication of the letters in the *Globe*, some Torontonians, moreover, went a step further, arguing that they must not only be tolerated, but also welcomed and assisted: if this were to happen, they would be less likely to resort to behaviours that incurred hostility and would be more likely to become useful and productive citizens.[71] A direct consequence was the establishment of a British Welcome League – an organization whose purpose was to welcome recently arrived British immigrants to Toronto. The League was widely supported and eventually received funding from the Ontario government for its efforts.[72]

Conclusion

English immigrants did face some hostility in early twentieth-century Toronto. The factors that elicited this antagonism were undoubtedly not limited to Toronto, and, indeed, there is evidence that English immigrants faced hostility elsewhere in Canada.[73] It seems likely that this manifested

---

68 The phrase 'good and useful citizens' is used in a letter published in the *News*, 'Englishmen in Canada', *News*, 30 March 1907.
69 Immigration from other parts of the world, particularly from Asia and from central and eastern Europe, was often vigorously and widely opposed. Cf. Kelley and Trebilcock, *The Making of the Mosaic*, pp. 131–32, 134–35, 142–56.
70 'As Others See Us', *Globe*, 21 March 1907. See also 'Welcome Urged for Newcomers', *World*, 25 March 1907.
71 'As Others See Us', *Globe*, 25 March 1907; 'Not Only a Job but a Welcome is Needed', *World*, 23 March 1907.
72 'To Welcome Britishers', *Globe*, 28 March 1907; 'Immigrants Given Aid', *Globe*, 19 April 1907; 'British Welcome League', *News*, 18 April 1907; 'The British Welcome League', *World*, 18 April 1907.
73 That hostility existed in other parts of Canada is indicated in the letters in the *Globe*, as well as in the articles and books that have been investigated by other historians, many of which pertain to western Canada. These sources indicate that hostility in other parts of Canada probably differed slightly to that which existed in Toronto. For example, remittance men, who were, it seems, universally hated, appear to have

itself in areas – such as Toronto – where English immigrants were particularly numerous and thus conspicuous, and where they likewise overwhelmed local labour markets and competed for jobs with the Canadian-born and older cohorts of immigrants. More research needs to be done, however, to establish the exact nature of the hostility in other parts of Canada and how it varied over time (particularly in relation to economic conditions).[74]

Finally, what this study highlights is that, contrary to A. Ross McCormack's assertion, being English did not necessarily serve as a complete advantage in Canada in the early twentieth century.[75] English immigrants were not automatically viewed as compatriots. While many assimilated faster than immigrants from other countries,[76] it seems that this adjustment was not necessarily simple or straightforward. To be welcomed by Canadians meant having to adapt – to Canadian culture, methods, work opportunities – and the letters in the *Globe* reveal that not all English immigrants found doing so easy or even desirable. Moreover, it seems likely that the hostility that some met with during this process of adjustment probably ultimately served to slow their accommodation to Canadian society – consolidating, reinforcing and even heightening their sense of allegiance and affinity to their native land.

---

been more prominent in western Canada than they were in Toronto. Also, English immigrants' ineptness as farmhands seems to have been a source of more hostility in western Canada. See Berton, *The Promised Land*, pp. 138–45; Dunae, *Gentlemen Emigrants*, pp. 123–46.

74 Indeed, it seems that there were increased complaints about English immigrants during the recession that started later that year – that Canada was a dumping ground for failures and that English immigrants were providing unfair competition. See McCormack, 'Cloth Caps and Jobs', p. 41.

75 Green and MacKinnon have also found evidence of slow assimilation. A. Green and M. MacKinnon, 'The Slow Assimilation of British Immigrants in Canada: Evidence from Montreal and Toronto, 1901', *Explorations in Economic History*, 38.3 (2001); McCormack, 'Cloth Caps and Jobs', p. 48.

76 McCormack, 'Cloth Caps and Jobs', p. 51; E.W. Sager and C. Morier, 'Immigrants, Ethnicity, and Earnings in 1901: Revisiting Canada's Vertical Mosaic', *The Canadian Historical Review*, 83.2 (2002), pp. 18–21.

Chapter 9

Cousin Jacks, New Chums and Ten Pound Poms: Locating New Zealand's English Diaspora

Brad Patterson

Returning to New Zealand in 1926 following his only visit to 'the old Country', New Zealand journalist Alan Mulgan recorded his impressions of England in *Home: A New Zealander's Adventure*.[1] His first sight of land was 'a glimpse of heaven'. In London, Mulgan immersed himself in the city. From there he roamed widely, being particularly taken with 'the extent and loveliness' of the Home Counties, and entranced by the hedged fields and neat villages. The 'far stretching gracefulness' of Devon and Cornwall was not far behind, though he was less elated by the industrial Midlands and the harder, rougher North. He nevertheless acknowledged that they were a vital part of 'Home'. Wherever he went, expressing delight in the seemingly familiar, he responded to queries as to his actual place of birth with the intelligence that New Zealanders 'always speak of England as Home'.

Ironically, Alan Mulgan's origins, on his father's side, were not in England but in Ireland. Looking back on his life three decades later, Mulgan sought to explain, but certainly not deny, his Anglophilia.[2] While the Ulster counties may have held strong ties for his parents and grandparents, for subsequent generations English cultural influences had been omnipresent. The books read were English, English scenes hung on the walls and the news of the day came from the *Graphic* and the *Illustrated London News*. Indeed, London was much more vivid, more recognizable, than any New Zealand town save Auckland, in which Mulgan had grown up. Yet in 1958, nearing his eightieth year, he concluded that New Zealanders were not simply transplanted English.

---

1   Alan Mulgan, *Home: A New Zealander's Adventure* (London: Longmans, 1927).
2   Alan Mulgan, *The Making of a New Zealander* (Wellington: Reed, 1958).

In addition to establishing their own distinct identity, they had become part of an international family, the British; at their core these twin identities retained Englishness, English traditions and English values.

The Patterns of English Migration to New Zealand

That English culture was New Zealand's foundational culture is beyond question, a direct outcome of the English looming largest in migration inflows. From 1840 the English comprised the largest single group among New Zealand's overseas-born, consistently making up 50 per cent and sometimes over 60 per cent of those from the United Kingdom and Ireland (Table 1). Further, from the mid-1880s, when the native-born first exceeded the overseas-born, although they dropped sharply as a percentage of the total population, English-born New Zealand residents never fell below 100,000 in number, reaching nearly 150,000 by 1921, with even higher totals in the late twentieth century (Table 2). Yet until recently there has been little scholarly, or popular, interest in exploring the origins and characteristics of the ongoing post-1840 migration flows. Not until the past two decades have the Irish and Scots begun to attract serious attention,[3] while the New Zealand English still await their historian. Arguably deficiencies in reliable data have discouraged closer questioning, all individual census schedules prior to 1966 having been destroyed, and with debilitating breaks in the extant migration records. In a bid to at least partially fill the lacunae, in 1996 historians Jock Phillips and Terry Hearn launched the 'Peopling of New Zealand' project, the core being extended statistical analysis of New Zealand death registers from 1876.[4] While freely acknowledging the inherent deficiencies of information from this source, the researchers nevertheless present a convincing outline of the broad trends in migration to New Zealand from England, Ireland and Scotland to 1945 (Table 3).

As far as can be established, up to two-thirds of the few Europeans living in New Zealand prior to the commencement of systematic colonization in 1840 were English by birth.[5] That ratio was preserved in the founding decade, but there were important differences between the settlements established through the New Zealand Company and the government settlement of Auckland. Between 1840 and 1852 the New Zealand European population increased

---

3   Brad Patterson, 'Celtic Roots amidst the Fern: Irish-Scottish Studies in New Zealand', *Journal of New Zealand Studies*, 2–3 (2003–04), pp. 197–218.

4   Jock Phillips and Terry Hearn, *Settlers: New Zealand Immigrants from England, Ireland and Scotland, 1840–1945* (Auckland: Auckland University Press, 2008), pp. 15–20, 195–96. Their findings are more fully reported in 'Further Information – British and Irish Immigration', http://www.nzhistory.net.nz/node/370 (accessed 28 January 2011).

5   Phillips and Hearn, *Settlers*, pp. 27–30.

Table 1: Percentage distribution of United Kingdom and Ireland-born migrants, by country of origin, at census years 1851–1981

	England	Wales	Scotland	Ireland	Northern Ireland
1851	65.6	0.8	17.0	16.6	
1861	59.3	0.7	25.5	14.5	–
1871	49.7	1.0	27.3	22.0	–
1881	53.4	0.9	23.6	22.1	–
1891	53.5	1.0	23.7	21.8	–
1901	54.6	0.9	23.3	21.2	–
1911	58.5	1.0	22.6	17.9	–
1921	62.7	1.1	21.7	14.5	–
1936	62.7	1.7	24.1	11.5	–
1945	63.3	2.2	24.2	5.3	5.0
1951	65.7	2.3	23.0	4.7	4.5
1961	69.8	2.6	21.2	2.4	4.0
1971	72.3	2.8	19.0	2.4	3.5
1981	74.5	2.7	16.8	3.1	2.9

Source: New Zealand Census; 1851 figures estimated from New Ulster and New Munster Gazettes

Table 2: English-born and New Zealand-born as totals and percentages of the New Zealand European population, at census years 1851–1981

	Total English-born residents	English-born as % of New Zealand European population	Total New Zealand European population	New Zealand-born as % of New Zealand European population
1851	13,485	50.5	26,707	12.3
1861	36,128	36.5	99,021	27.9
1871	67,044	26.1	256,933	36.3
1881	119,224	24.3	489,933	45.6
1886	125,657	21.7	578,482	51.9
1891	117,070	18.5	634,058	57.8
1901	111,964	14.5	772,719	66.9
1911	133,811	13.3	1,006,761	69.8
1921	149,348	12.3	1,218,913	74.4
1936	140,422	9.4	1,491,484	80.3
1945	114,508	7.1	1,603,544	84.6
1951	125,957	6.9	1,823,796	91.7
1961	154,869	6.9	2,247,898	92.3
1971	180,513	6.8	2,633,299	92.8
1981	173,181	6.0	2,882,700	92.9

Source: New Zealand Census; 1851 figures estimated from New Ulster and New Munster Gazettes

Table 3: National composition of United Kingdom immigrants to New Zealand (percentages)

	England	Wales	Scotland	Ireland
1800–39	62.1	1.6	20.4	15.6
1840–52	64.3	1.1	20.6	13.5
Auckland	45.3	0.8	17.6	35.9
NZ Company	80.3	1.1	15.0	1.7
Discharged soldiers	42.8	0.2	2.6	54.4
1851 New Ulster Census	58.8	0.4	13.0	27.8
1853–70	46.6	1.1	30.2	21.4
Discharged soldiers	40.2	0.4	2.6	56.8
Auckland	52.9	0.4	17.8	27.8
Canterbury assisted	56.6	1.4	19.9	22.1
Otago miners	36.6	1.7	30.1	31.6
Westland miners	28.0	3.8	19.3	47.9
1871–90	54.6	0.8	21.5	21.7
Assisted	53.7 (incl Welsh)		18.4	27.9
1891–1915	65.0	1.1	22.2	10.9
1916–45	60.1	2.1	28.7	8.6

Source: Jock Phillips and Terry Hearn, Settlers: New Zealand Immigrants from England, Ireland and Scotland, 1840–1945 (Auckland: Auckland University Press, 2008), p. 52

by nearly 26,000. In the New Zealand Company's settlements – Wellington (1840), Wanganui (1840), Nelson (1842), together with offshoots New Plymouth (1841), the creation of the Plymouth Company, Otago (1848) and Canterbury (1850), the two latter formed through linked associations – the influx was overwhelmingly English, of the order of 80 per cent.[6] The emphasis was understandable: the company was an English enterprise, its London board a mix of city merchants and country gentry; its appointed agents were predominantly English, recruiting largely in English population centres; and most of its chartered vessels departed from English ports. The company-sponsored inflows peaked in 1842, dropped in the mid-1840s, and then moderately revived late in the decade. It was perhaps symbolic that the final settlement at Canterbury, launched under the aegis of the Church of England, should be envisaged as the most English of all. In the north of the North Island the settlement established around the colonial capital of Auckland provided a

6   Paul Hudson, 'English Emigration to New Zealand, 1839–1850: An Analysis of the Work of the New Zealand Company', unpublished PhD thesis, Lancaster University, 1997; J.S. Marais, *The Colonization of New Zealand* (London: Dawson, repr. 1968 [1927]).

clear counterpoint.[7] While even in Auckland the English (43%), many of them officials, comprised the single largest ethnic group, the influence was by no means total, and the Irish (35.9%) were in undisputed second place. The Auckland European population was augmented through the 1840s by independent arrivals from Australia and military personnel introduced after an outbreak of conflict with the northern Maori in 1844. Both Auckland and the company settlements took migrants from throughout England, but drew particularly from London and the Home Counties, especially Middlesex, the south-east, Cornwall, Devon and Somerset, the recruiters targeting districts, parishes and villages within counties, as has been shown in micro-studies of Kent and Cornwall.[8] In the case of the latter, streams coalesced, Cousin Jacks arriving directly in New Plymouth from Cornwall being augmented by substantial numbers arriving in Auckland via a stopover in South Australia.[9]

In the ensuing decade the New Zealand settler population near quadrupled, to almost 98,000 in 1861, then more than doubled again by 1871, net migration accounting for over 70 per cent of this increase. Yet, paradoxically, for the only time in New Zealand's history, the English comprised less than half (46.6%) of all arrivals. Migration from Scotland reached a percentage peak (30.2%) in these years, with the Irish component (21.4%) also high. This result was greatly influenced by the discovery of gold in payable quantities in the South Island and the renewal of armed conflict between North Island settlers and the Maori.[10] In contrast to the two major migration streams distinguishable prior to 1852, from the late 1850s there were three. Following the conferral of limited self-government in 1854, and the inauguration of a quasi-federal system, the new provinces were encouraged to seek migrants on their own initiative.[11] The activities of two, Auckland and Canterbury, stood out. At Auckland land grants were offered as an incentive to migrate (the 40-acre system) and special group settlements were promoted,[12] while the Canterbury design was more orthodox, assistance being primarily offered to working folk.[13] The schemes collectively attracted over 30,000 new settlers, the majority English and from the south, but with the Midlands emerging as a fourth source area. The second

---

7   John Horsman, *The Coming of the Pakeha to Auckland Province* (Wellington: Hicks Smith & Sons, 1971).

8   Paul Hudson, 'English Emigration to New Zealand, 1839–1850: Information Diffusion and Marketing a New World', *Economic History Review*, 54.4 (2001), pp. 680–98; Raewyn Dalziel, 'Emigration and Kinship: Migrants to New Plymouth, 1840–43', *New Zealand Journal of History*, 25.2 (1991), pp. 112–28.

9   Philip Payton, *The Cornish Overseas* (Fowey: Cornwall Editions, 2005), pp. 86–88, 199–200.

10 Michael King, *The Penguin History of New Zealand* (Auckland: Viking, 2003), pp. 207–09, 211–24.

11 W.D. Borrie, *Immigration to New Zealand 1854–1938* (Canberra: Demography Program ANU, 1991), pp. 13–18.

12 Horsman, *Coming of the Pakeha*, pp. 83–88.

13 R.H. Silcock, 'Immigration into Canterbury under the Provincial Government', unpublished MA thesis, University of Canterbury, 1963.

stream, drawn by gold, was a contrast in almost every respect. An Otago discovery in early 1861 sparked the first significant rush to New Zealand,[14] the population of the province more than doubling to 49,000 in three years. When the rushes spread to the South Island's west coast, an uninhabited wilderness acquired a population of 8,000 in just six months. Most were émigrés who had first tried their luck on the Australian goldfields. On the Otago fields the English, Scots and Irish were present in almost equal numbers, but on the west coast almost half the 1860s population (47.9%) was Irish, imposing a cultural character that was to endure.[15] In the case of the English, migrants from the south-west, principally Cornwall, were again noticeably over-represented. The third stream, that arising from the military operations in the North Island, is harder to quantify, the forces comprising both imperial regiments and local militia, but preliminary research suggests up to 40 per cent were English, with substantial numbers from the north of England and the south-west.[16] Alongside, military settlers with families were recruited to garrison disputed lands, with a comparable percentage of English origin.

The 1870s have been labelled New Zealand's 'great migration decade', the colony's population near doubling again and topping 500,000 for the first time in 1881. Stagnation then followed. Accelerated immigration was viewed as a partial palliative to economic difficulties in the late 1860s, the opening of new lands, closer settlement and the creation of infrastructure being stated objectives, the initiative driven by the colonial government through assisted passages, both free and subsidized, with a pledge of employment on arrival.[17] Though takers soon materialized, the inflows were far from regular, peaks in 1873–75 and 1878–79 being flanked by troughs, with the assisted passage schemes terminating in the early 1880s. English migrants totalled no more than 54 per cent of all migrants in the two decades, an indication perhaps that the English were less mobile than other groups from Great Britain and Ireland.[18] Previously migrants with agricultural backgrounds had been enticed, but with railways, ports and roads to be built and houses to be constructed, English cities received greater attention. A strong flow from the south-west continued, but future patterns were pre-figured by greater numbers from central England (Warwickshire, Oxfordshire, Lincolnshire) and from the north (Yorkshire, Lancashire). Agricultural distress and embryonic rural unionization inclined

---

14 Terry Hearn, 'Scots Miners on the Goldfields, 1861–1870', in Tom Brooking and Jennie Coleman (eds), *The Heather and the Fern: Scottish Migration and New Zealand Settlement* (Dunedin: University of Otago Press, 2005), pp. 67–85.
15 Lyndon Fraser, 'Irish Migration to the West Coast, 1864–1900', *New Zealand Journal of History*, 34.2 (2000), pp. 197–225.
16 Hugh and Lyn Hughes, *Discharged in New Zealand: Soldiers of the Imperial Foot Regiments Who Took Their Discharge in New Zealand 1840–1870* (Auckland: New Zealand Society of Genealogists, 1988); Borrie, *Immigration to New Zealand*, pp. 219–26
17 Borrie, *Immigration to New Zealand*, pp. 50–97.
18 John Morris, 'The Assisted Immigrants to New Zealand, 1871–79: A Statistical Study', unpublished MA thesis, University of Auckland, 1973.

villagers from middle and southern England to consider emigration.[19] Most made homes in the North Island bush settlements. Alongside them was a much smaller group drawn from throughout England, often scions of wealthier families, sent to New Zealand to make their way. Dismissed a little derisively by longer standing settlers and the local born as 'new chums', they frequently sought experience on larger pastoral properties or in developing local business.[20] Many succeeded, but a surprising number did not. The 1870s inflows from the Australian colonies almost totally dried up in the 1880s, with New Zealand falling into the deepest depression experienced in the colony to that time. Indeed, in some years there were net migration losses.

By the early 1890s the establishment of new export industries (frozen meat and dairy produce) had introduced a new period of prosperity, which with the exception of a brief recession between 1908 and 1910 continued until the outbreak of the First World War. Over the next quarter century the New Zealand European population near doubled again, to 1,095,000 by 1914, even if much of the augmentation was attributable to natural increase.[21] Rising commodity prices, full employment and high wages continued to act as magnets. Direct migration from Great Britain and Ireland remained at modest levels throughout the 1890s, but was offset by a steady stream from depression-hit Australia, a disproportionate number of whom were English.[22] After 1900 direct passages again picked up, with peaks of over 40,000 in 1908, 1912 and 1913. While the 1904 reintroduction of assisted passages delivered a boost, self-funding migrants bulked these flows. Overall, arrivals from England still dominated (65%), those from Scotland remaining constant and those from Ireland dropping away. With the increasing sophistication of the emerging dominion's economy bringing demands for new skills, Yorkshire, and especially Lancashire, now made significantly larger contributions. The south-east and the Midlands contributed smaller numbers, but the major change was the much reduced importance of the south-west.

The thirty years between 1914 and 1945 witnessed relatively slow population growth. The losses of war played a part (deaths, postponed marriages and low birth rates), but immigration was also much reduced. The 1945 New Zealand census reported that the New Zealand-born now made up 84.6 per cent of the population, with the English-born down to 7 per cent. Understandably, migration had drastically attenuated during the First World War, but it had appeared in the early 1920s that immigration would be vigorously promoted, a

19 Rollo Arnold, *The Farthest Promised Land: English Villagers, New Zealand Immigrants of the 1870s* (Wellington: Victoria University Press with Price Milburn, 1981).
20 H.W. Orsman (ed.), *Dictionary of New Zealand English* (Auckland: Oxford University Press, 1997), pp. 529–30.
21 *The New Zealand Official Year-Book, 1915* (Wellington: Government Printer, 1915), p. 114.
22 Rollo Arnold, 'The Dynamics and Quality of Trans-Tasman Migration, 1885–1910', *Australian Economic History Review*, 26.1 (1986), pp. 1–20.

British government proposal to settle demobilized ex-servicemen and women overseas introducing nearly 13,000 migrants between 1920 and 1923.[23] This morphed into a more permanent programme under the Empire Settlement Act of 1922, which delivered an estimated 6,000 British migrants per annum until 1927. These measures had the financial support of the British government, reflecting the dislocations of Great Britain in the 1920s. But New Zealand, too, was experiencing employment problems, a symptom of incipient resentment evidencing in frequent criticism of 'Homies', a pejorative term aimed mainly at the English migrants who made up more than 60 per cent of the post-1920 stream.[24] There was a certain incongruity in the reverence many New Zealanders still exhibited for 'Home' not translating into a warmer welcome for those from that distant place. Migrants from the north now accounted for over one-third of all English migrants. In addition to already initiated flows from the north-west, Lancashire, and to a lesser extent Yorkshire, the depressed mining areas of Durham and Northumberland assumed a new importance. While London and the Home Counties remained important recruitment areas, the south-west continued to dwindle in importance. Regardless of area, assisted immigration terminated with the Great Depression, the outbreak of the Second World War subsequently bringing migration to New Zealand to a complete halt.

In 1945 New Zealand found itself with a human resources shortage. After a gap of nearly twenty years assisted migration was once more viewed as the immediate palliative.[25] Between 1946 and 1976 New Zealand's population rose from 1.8 million to 3.2 million, including just over 416,000 British immigrants.[26] Although the range of European source countries widened, the desire to 'recruit British' remained. Ultimately, the New Zealand government underwrote the scheme, but as a gesture required the 76,000 successful applicants (mainly English) to make a £10 contribution towards their passages: thus the subsequent tag, the 'ten pound Poms'.[27] Four major peaks can be traced: 1952–53, 1957–58, 1961–66 and the largest of all, 1973–74. The attraction must have been considerable, for many times that number made their way to New Zealand independently. The end came abruptly. In April 1974 the New Zealand government introduced new immigration controls, the principal

23 Stephen Constantine, 'Immigration and the Making of New Zealand, 1918–1939', in Stephen Constantine (ed.), *Emigrants and Empire: British Settlement in the Dominions between the Wars* (Manchester: Manchester University Press, 1990), pp. 121–49.
24 Sinclair, *Destiny Apart*, pp. 104–07.
25 Megan Hutching, *Long Journey for Sevenpence: Assisted Immigration to New Zealand from the United Kingdom, 1947–1975* (Wellington: Victoria University Press, 1999).
26 Ruth S.J. Farmer, 'International Migration', in R.J. Warwick Neville and C.J. O'Neill (eds), *The Population of New Zealand: Interdisciplinary Perspectives* (Auckland: Longman Paul, 1979), pp. 31–59.
27 Orsman, *Dictionary of New Zealand English*, pp. 621–22; A. James Hammerton and Alistair Taylor, *Ten Pound Poms: Australia's Invisible Migrants* (Manchester: Manchester University Press, 2002).

object being to reduce the number of British migrants. This may have been in response to an unexpected escalation in arrivals in the previous year, but equally the new restrictions were almost certainly a reaction to the coincident British decision to enter the European Union. This constituted a major break with nearly 140 years of immigration tradition.

Canterbury: The Most English New Zealand Settlement?

Travellers' guides continue to expound the 'Englishness' of the South Island's former province of Canterbury, especially the city of Christchurch,[28] which is depicted as a classic Church of England cathedral city of stone buildings and tree-filled parks, the River Avon wending its way through the centre. Its university and an elite boys' school modelled on Eton are noted. Beyond the city transplanted English place names and monuments abound. The creation of the London-based Canterbury Association, an organization closely associated with the Church of England, its founders envisioned the settlement as an English utopia in the South Pacific.[29] When the first migrant ships arrived in December 1850, the intention was to create an orderly and tiered society akin to pre-industrial England, one almost exclusively English and Anglican. Canterbury thus offers a useful case-study for assessing the extent to which the ethnic characteristics brought with them by the first settlers were retained in subsequent decades.

It is now generally agreed that a class system, based on land ownership, did indeed develop, and that its upper tier came to dominate the political, economic and social life of Canterbury in the nineteenth century and beyond.[30] But it is equally clear that this was not primarily the outcome of a successful transplantation of English people, habits and traditions. The founding conception was of substantial mixed farms, similar to estates in southern England, colonial squires letting land to tenant farmers. What instead came to dominate were large-scale pastoral properties, and the holders were not necessarily drawn from the approved stock favoured by the Canterbury Association. Up to 1,000 Europeans, a number of them Scots Presbyterians, were already in residence in 1850. While legally the Canterbury Association had ownership rights to the settlement lands, these early settlers had to be accommodated. Further, there was an incursion by Australian-based

---

28   Laura Harper et al., *The Rough Guide to New Zealand* (New York/London: Rough Guides, 5th edn, 2006), pp. 604–05.
29   L.C. Webb, 'The Canterbury Association and its Settlement', in James Hight and C.R. Straubel (eds), *A History of Canterbury* (Christchurch: Whitcombe and Tombs, 1957), I, pp. 135–233.
30   Stevan Eldred-Grigg, *A Southern Gentry: New Zealanders Who Inherited the Earth* (Wellington: Reed, 1980); Jim McAloon, *No Idle Rich: The Wealthy in Canterbury and Otago, 1840–1914* (Dunedin: University of Otago Press, 2002).

graziers, some originally from Great Britain, others Australian-born, both groups of a very different stamp from the minor gentry among the direct arrivals. In subsequent decades it proved impossible to prevent non-English migrants from settling in Canterbury, much less to move on those already there. If it is accepted that membership of the Canterbury Provincial Council between 1853 and 1876 was restricted to the settlement's elite, no more than 53.5 per cent of the provincial councillors were of English birth.[31] That only 33.8 per cent of the English-born listed England as the country from which they had departed may explain the moderate 7 per cent giving Australia as birthplace. A further crude index of dilution is provided by the *Cyclopaedia of New Zealand*, a subscription directory published in 1903, which selectively listed the well-to-do and well connected.[32] While the proportion claiming English birth was highest (56%), the Scots (21.5%) and Irish (11.1%) made up substantial minorities.

If it proved impossible to keep the Canterbury elite select, the task with the rank and file was even more challenging. Between 1850 and 1881 the population of the province grew from less than 4,000 to over 100,000. Of the assisted migrants introduced, little more than half (54%) were from England, the Irish (16.4%) and the Scots (14.8%) bulking out the inflows.[33] The elite were seemingly pragmatic about recruitment, especially when the major calls were for labourers and domestic servants. High numbers of Irish arrived in the late 1850s and early 1860s, nearly half from Ulster. In the 1870s the Irish stream was sustained, earlier arrivals facilitating further migration through nominations. Among the English, there were deviations from the national pattern in terms of areas of origin.[34] Understandably, with the Canterbury Association taking the lead, there were strong clusters from London and Middlesex (17%) and the other London counties (11%). While the south-west still provided 18 per cent of the migrants, at Canterbury there was stronger representation from the northern counties, especially Lancashire and Yorkshire, from an earlier date. Intriguingly, over one-third of the English elite came from the north. What especially stands out, however, is that as early as 1871 the archetype New Zealand English settlement was no more English in composition than either Wellington or Marlborough, and considerably less so than Taranaki.[35] By 1900 it was Auckland, not Canterbury, that had become the favoured destination for English migrants, a trend strongly reinforced in the course of the twentieth century.

---

31   K.A. Pickens, 'The Origins of the Population of Nineteenth-Century Canterbury', *New Zealand Geographer*, 33.2 (1977), p. 73.
32   Ibid.
33   Ibid., p. 70.
34   Ibid., pp. 70–71.
35   K.A. Pickens, 'Denomination, Nationality and Class in a Nineteenth-Century British Colony: Canterbury, New Zealand', *Journal of Religious History*, 15.1 (1988), p. 128.

Equally, the bid to establish an exclusive New Zealand environment for Anglicanism was less than completely successful.[36] In 1851 Church of England adherents made up 85.4 per cent of those listing denominations, with Presbyterians on 4.4 per cent and other nonconformist religions and Catholics totalling around 4 per cent each. At that point Canterbury was more Anglican than England itself. Ten years later the province remained over-whelmingly Protestant in character, but the Church of England's share had dropped to 72.9 per cent, while the number of Presbyterians doubled, as did that of Catholics. Methodism now claimed over 10 per cent of churchgoers. By 1878 Anglicans scraped just 50.2 per cent of all adherents, Presbyterians registering a fourfold increase over 1851, and the Catholic share rising to 10.7 per cent. In subsequent decades Anglican numbers continued to erode. A large part of the explanation lies in the mid and late nineteenth-century pattern of migration. The English arrived early, but there were already Scots migrants on the ground and the Scottish settlement of Otago immediately to the south. Recruitment from Ireland in the late 1850s and early 1860s, then in the early 1870s, was augmented by population drift from the west coast goldfields. Yet there is strong evidence that the rural elite remained Anglican. In town Anglicans were rivalled in commerce and services by Presbyterians, while nonconformists were prominent in trades. In contrast, Catholics were heavily represented in more humble occupations, although they quickly exhibited occupational mobility. In a sense, Canterbury became a mixing bowl, ethnicities and denominations being thrown together.[37] Some barriers were hard to surmount, the Catholic/Protestant division remaining relatively firm, but even this weakened. Analysis of marriage registers indicates a steady increase in denominational, and also ethnic, crossovers, a number of those declaring themselves to be Anglicans in fact marrying in other churches.[38]

How English, then, was Canterbury after the first four founding decades? A convincing case has been made that much of the subsequent self-image has been more superficial appearance than reality. 'Englishness has mostly defined the city [...] [and province] [...] as a place,' writes historian John Cookson. This did not, and does not, mean it was, or is, 'the real thing'.[39] In the first four decades the settlers were compelled to compromise, to accom-modate the new environment. Between 1880 and 1914 the rise of the New Zealand-born led to greater emphasis on the contribution of the pioneer, regardless of origin or creed. This was the era in which a melded British-New Zealand identity emerged with some force. During the middle decades of the

---

36   Ibid., pp. 128–33.
37   Ibid., p. 137.
38   K.A. Pickens, 'Marriage Patterns in a Nineteenth-Century British Colonial Population', *Journal of Family History*, 5.2 (1980), pp. 188–90.
39   John Cookson, 'Pilgrims' Progress – Image, Identity and Myth in Christchurch', in John Cookson and Graeme Dunstall (eds), *Southern Capital, Christchurch: Towards a City Biography, 1850–2000* (Christchurch: Canterbury University Press, 2000), p. 13.

twentieth century, English Canterbury thrived as a romantic social memory, impetus being provided by centennials in 1940 and 1950. There was little linkage, however, to everyday concerns and, uncomfortably, on occasions sections of the community expressed hostility to new English migrants. Later in the twentieth century, as both New Zealand and Canterbury became more cosmopolitan, newcomers were received with relative indifference, Canterbury's Englishness surviving in the main as a tourist attraction, a commercial brand.

The British Empire, English Culture and New Zealand

As the Canterbury experience suggests, Alan Mulgan's equivocation in terms of identity was far from unique. The extent to which 'Englishness' and 'Britishness' came to be regarded as synonymous in the nineteenth-century Anglophone world has been central to vigorous recent debate,[40] and a drift between 'English' and 'British' was a common feature of evocations of identity in New Zealand. The hidden-ness of the English Diaspora owes as much to its synonymity with things 'British' as it does to any wilful exclusion by historians. For convenience, it is accepted that Britishness, as it came to be understood, was a utilitarian concept forged in the eighteenth century to encompass the peoples of England, Wales and Scotland. Its extension to the second overseas British Empire was of equal utility, providing cultural bonds holding the disparate parts together. Preoccupied with managing the United Kingdom and the empire, for most English there was little difference between Englishness and Britishness: Britain and the empire were first and foremost English creations.[41] While the Scots and Welsh, and subsequently the Irish, clung to their separate identities as a defence against English hegemony, until the late nineteenth century the English themselves saw little need to assert their distinctiveness.

Traditionally, New Zealand has been regarded as 'the most English' of the former Dominions. Yet the duality was evident from the beginning, the propaganda of the New Zealand Company in the 1840s laying stress on the creation of 'a little Britain across the seas'.[42] Small wonder, then, that as early as 1854 a returned settler could be 'persuaded that the New Zealander will retain more of the Briton than any other colonist [...] We have no other colony

---

40 John Hutchinson, Susan Reynolds, Anthony D. Smith, Robert Colls and Krishnan Kumar, 'Debate on Krishan Kumar's *The Making of English National Identity*', *Nations and Nationalism*, 13.2 (2007), pp. 179–203; Krishan Kumar, *The Making of English National Identity* (Cambridge: Cambridge University Press, 2003); Robert J.C. Young, *The Idea of English Ethnicity* (Oxford: Blackwell Publishing, 2008).

41 Kumar, *Making of English National Identity*, pp. 187ff.

42 Judith A. Johnston, 'Information and Emigration: The Image Making Process', *New Zealand Geographer*, 33.2 (1977), pp. 60–67.

which so much resembles England in climate, size and position.'[43] Even so, in the course of the nineteenth century the British persona took the stronger grip, with repetitive claims that New Zealand was indeed 'the Britain of the South'. In 1898 New Zealand historian William Pember Reeves could enthuse that New Zealanders were 'a British race in the sense in which the inhabitants of the British Isles scarcely are'.[44] In the early settlement decades migrants had clung to their individual national loyalties and traditions, these breaking down only as the overseas-born became a minority. Keith Sinclair has argued that, while embracing a British identity, New Zealand's native-born largely disregarded their particular ethnic roots;[45] Donald Harman Akenson offers a more cogent discussion of New Zealand Britishness.[46] Pointing out that significant Celtic ethnic identifiers were not so readily discarded, Akenson nevertheless concurs that melding led to the establishment of 'a new and syn-thetic "British" culture', a significant step towards the evolution of a distinct New Zealand identity. James Belich notes the long-held popularity of the slogan '98.5 per cent British', and that the most rabid exponents continued to assert that New Zealand was not just British but English, at least until the 1960s.[47] In New Zealand, he suggests, settlers from the British Isles, broadly defined, formed a new 'us', confronting a shared 'them', in this case Irish Catholics and the indigenous Maori. Yet by the early 1900s even the Maori, at least in some quarters, were being projected as 'brown Britons'.[48]

But what did being British in nineteenth- and twentieth-century New Zealand mean? And, more importantly in this context, where did the English fit in? Nearly sixty years ago J.C. Beaglehole offered a rather loose definition of Britishness: 'a system of mores, habits, of ways of thinking and assumptions and institutions that cover the whole of life'.[49] That the preponderance should be of English origin was considered axiomatic. More recently Robert Young has submitted that the most significant of those traits were less 'a set of cultural characteristics attached to a particular place' and rather more 'a transferable set of values that could be transplanted, translated and recreated anywhere in the globe'.[50] The most evident in New Zealand were incorporated in what

---

43   Thomas Cholmondeley, *Ultima Thule; Or Thoughts Suggested by a Residence in New Zealand* (London: John Chapman, 1854), pp. 324–25.

44   William Pember Reeves, *The Long White Cloud – Ao Tea Roa* (London: Horace Marshall & Son, 1898), pp. 399–400.

45   Keith Sinclair, *A Destiny Apart: New Zealand's Search for National Identity* (Wellington: Allen and Unwin, 1986), pp. 103–08.

46   Donald Harman Akenson, *Half the World from Home: Perspectives on the Irish in New Zealand 1860–1950* (Wellington: Victoria University Press, 1990), pp. 6–19.

47   James Belich, *Making Peoples: A History of the New Zealanders: From Polynesian Settlement to the End of the Nineteenth Century* (Auckland: Penguin Books, 1996), p. 315.

48   *Otago Witness*, 5 February 1902.

49   J.C. Beaglehole, 'Victorian Heritage', *Political Science*, 4.1 (1952), p. 29.

50   Young, *Idea of English Ethnicity*, p. 232.

elsewhere has been termed 'the standard British package': dynastic loyalism, Protestantism, cultural particularism and firm commitment to imperialism.[51]

An almost slavish devotion to the royal family was evidenced by the fact that by 1914 the most common statuary was of the 'Widow of Windsor', an 1899 editorialist observing that its proliferation was 'a symbol of our attachment to the British monarchy and our affection for the Motherland'.[52] Attachment to Protestantism, a key feature of Englishness, was little less strong.[53] From the outset it was intended that New Zealand be a Protestant country and migrant recruitment proceeded accordingly. Though never the established church, Anglicanism was at the forefront. By 1901 77.6 per cent of the European population claimed membership of five Protestant denominations, 54.7 per cent being distributed among those of English origin, with 40.7 per cent practising Anglicans.[54] A disproportionately large number of Maori were also members of the Church of England. The generic influence of English culture was inevitable, given that large numbers of the Scots and Irish who settled in New Zealand had already come under strong English influence prior to migrating. English influence dominated systems of government and the legal system, but was most pervasive in the almost universal use of the English language.[55] This fostered an overweening dependence on English literature and literary canons and a dependence on English popular culture, English fashions being faithfully followed. When public broadcasting came to New Zealand after the First World War, the model chosen was that of the BBC.[56]

What stood out was an unswerving sense of obligation to empire. New Zealand could be relied upon to respond to calls to arms, regardless of cost. At the outbreak of war with Germany in 1939, New Zealand's prime minister unequivocally reiterated the country's loyalty: 'Where [Britain] goes, we go; where she stands, we stand'.[57] The fealty was of long standing. At colonial conferences between 1897 and 1907, and at the first Imperial Conference in 1911, only the most distant colony consistently advocated closer union.[58] When dominion status was granted following the 1907 conference, New Zealand

---

51 Kumar, *Making of English National Identity*, p. 139.

52 Michael Dunn, *New Zealand Sculpture: A History* (Auckland: Auckland University Press, 2008), p. 25.

53 Hugh Jackson, 'Churchgoing in Nineteenth-Century New Zealand', *New Zealand Journal of History*, 17.1 (1983), pp. 43–59.

54 Terry Hearn, 'English', *Te Ara: The Online Encyclopaedia of New Zealand*, http://www.TeAra.govt.nz/en/english/11/2 (accessed 25 January 2011).

55 Peter Spiller et al., *A New Zealand Legal History* (Wellington: Brooker's, 1995); Elizabeth Gordon et al., *New Zealand English: Its Origins and Evolution* (Cambridge: Cambridge University Press, 2004).

56 Patrick Day, *The Radio Years: A History of Broadcasting in New Zealand* (Auckland: Auckland University Press, 1994), pp. 48–56.

57 Barry Gustafson, *From the Cradle to the Grave: A Biography of Michael Joseph Savage* (Auckland: Reed Methuen, 1986), p. 251.

58 Keith Sinclair, *Imperial Federation: A Study of New Zealand Policy and Opinion, 1880–1914* (London: Athlone Press, 1955), pp. 11, 21.

voted against acceptance. Moreover, as other of the traditional dominions sought to extend their independence, New Zealand stubbornly held back. Following the British Parliament's enactment of the Statute of Westminster in 1931, which established the legislative equality of the self-governing dominions and the United Kingdom, New Zealand was again reluctant to accept, sixteen years passing before the measure was ratified.[59] Not until the sense of betrayal engendered by Britain's decision in 1972 to abandon traditional relationships and join the European Community was the bond seriously threatened.

English Associations in New Zealand

In New Zealand, as throughout the empire, associations, clubs and societies were widely employed by the Scots and Irish as vehicles for preserving their cultures and identities, among other roles.[60] Yet, curiously, distinctively English associations are hard to find. Why English associationalism should have attracted limited interest is a question awaiting further research. That New Zealand came late in the colonizing sequence may have contributed, while the early numerical dominance of the English in the population may be pertinent. It has been suggested that in New Zealand the nineteenth-century settler population was too transient, atomized and individualistic to be much concerned with associational life, but recorded experiences indicate otherwise.[61] It is surely significant that in New Zealand the greatest interest in English associations appears to have been manifested just before and after the First World War, when, for most citizens, by that point second-, third- or even fourth-generation, the reality of England had become something remote, an idea rather than a memory. At the same time, for more recent New Zealand residents of English birth, especially post-First World War migrants, there was a recognition that they were no longer part of a majority but rather a shrinking minority.

Internationally, St George's societies, collectives of the better-off offering support to new migrants, constituted the most ubiquitous English associational

59 Angus Ross, 'New Zealand and the Statute of Westminster', in Norman Hillmer and Philip Wigley (eds), *The First British Commonwealth* (London: Frank Cass, 1980), pp. 136–58.
60 Tanja Bueltmann, *Scottish Ethnicity and the Making of New Zealand Society, 1850 to 1930* (Edinburgh: Edinburgh University Press, 2011); Gerard Horn, '"A loyal, united and happy people": Irish Protestant Migrants to Wellington Province 1840–1930: Aspects of Migration, Settlement and Community', unpublished PhD thesis, Victoria University of Wellington, 2010, pp. 203–32; Rory Sweetman, *Faith and Fraternalism: A History of the Hibernian Society in New Zealand, 1869–2000* (Wellington: Hibernian Society, 2002).
61 Miles Fairburn, *The Ideal Society and its Enemies: The Foundations of Modern New Zealand Society 1850–1900* (Auckland: Auckland University Press, 1989); for contrary arguments see the special issue of *New Zealand Journal of History*, 35.2 (1991).

grouping.[62] Side-by-side with Irish and Scottish ethnic associations, they widely proliferated by the mid-nineteenth century. Their dispersion throughout Australia was not, however, replicated in New Zealand. Scattered newspaper references to the 1859 formation of a St George's Society in Auckland apart, no further nineteenth-century records of these societies in New Zealand have been located.[63] The failure to take root may well have been linked to uncertainty as to purpose. In New Zealand there was inter-ethnic mixing to an unusual degree, the occasional St George's Day celebrations having to compete with already established gatherings on the colonial calendar. Further, the benevolent role crucial elsewhere had already been assumed by others. Following the formation in London of the Royal St George's Society in 1894, there were attempts to encourage groups in New Zealand, but responses were lukewarm, the only branch materializing being in Blenheim, population just over 3,000.[64] No enthusiasm was manifested in the major population centres. It was not until 1937 that a second New Zealand branch was born, and it had a mixed genesis. Set up in 1935 as a Buckingham Society, in the following year it became a Bucks, Berks and Oxford Society, less than twelve months later the English Home Counties Society, and finally the Royal St George Society (Wellington Branch).[65] There were close links with contemporary Wellington culture groups such as the English Folk, Dance and Song Society and the English Speaking Union.

To some extent the lack of a national association was offset by support for English county societies, these allegiances being arguably stronger. An attempt in 1889 to form a Wellington Society of Cornishmen met with little success, but more conspicuous and successful were Yorkshire societies, sometimes in combination with Lancashire societies.[66] While the lead was taken in Wellington (1895), Christchurch (1898) and Auckland (1901), in the years leading up to the First World War at least seven other societies formed in other parts of the dominion, all attracting respectable memberships. Significantly, these organizations spanned class and political divides, most leaders being from the elite, with the rank and file being middle class and white-collar or skilled tradesmen. With the focus social, the yearly round was marked by picnics, dances and formal dinners, and on those occasions the societies reached out to fellow societies, including those of the Celtic migrants. Yorkshire and Lancashire societies continued to flourish into the

---

62 Tanja Bueltmann and Donald M. MacRaild, 'Globalising St. George: English Associations in the Anglo-World to the 1930s', *Journal of Global History*, 7.1 (2012), pp. 79–105.
63 *Nelson Examiner and New Zealand Chronicle*, 7 May 1859; *Daily Southern Cross*, 17 April 1861, 23 April 1861.
64 *Marlborough Express*, 19 May 1905.
65 *Evening Post*, 25 November 1937, 26 April 1938.
66 See James Watson, '"Cooked in true Yorkshire fashion": The Failure of St George's Societies and the Success of Yorkshire Societies in New Zealand before the First World War', in present volume.

1930s, guests at the Wellington Yorkshire Society's 1937 Christmas celebration including representatives of the Men of Kent and the Kentish Men's Society, Society of Dorset Men of New Zealand, the Northumberland and Durham Society, and the newly formed Royal Society of St George.[67] The pity was that few of these societies were to survive long after the Second World War.

Ultimately more successful were the working-men's clubs that sprang up in New Zealand's towns and cities from the 1870s. Not to be confused with the mechanics' institutes and athenaeums of earlier years, whose primary purpose was self-improvement through education, these private clubs, though not completely eschewing educative and benevolent functions, were soon of a more social cast.[68] Their origins were in the industrial areas of the north of England. It was therefore understandable that, as the numbers of working men from these areas migrating to New Zealand increased, there should be a desire to replicate the facilities. The first to open were in the major centres – Wellington (1877), Dunedin (1877), Auckland (1878) and Christchurch (1880) – but in little more than a decade they had spread to most provincial towns and many smaller townships.[69] The extension of the movement to New Zealand was generally welcomed, colonial elites often assisting with the securing of suitable premises, it being believed that the clubs would 'encourage sobriety; promote that feeling of self-respect among members which is so valuable to the individual; encourage a spirit of camaraderie; and last, but far from least, be one important factor in solving the great class problems of the day'.[70] These expectations were arguably over-ambitious. Certainly camaraderie was encouraged, the memberships burgeoning. Within twelve months there were over 400 members in Dunedin, and by 1893 the Wellington membership totalled nearly 800.[71] Yet their very popularity proved a weakness if the clubs were to be vehicles for preserving English identity. While the ethnic bias is evident in early social programmes, by 1900 this had largely disappeared from the main centre clubs, the memberships being by then drawn from all sections of the colonial community. Moreover, far from being advocates of temperance, a crusading journal noted in 1906 that the '[Wellington] Working Men's Club undoubtedly does the heaviest bar trade in Wellington'.[72] Similar criticisms, not always fair, were expressed elsewhere. The positive parts the clubs played in promoting sport and general social activities were too often overlooked. Ironically, the working-men's clubs were to be the most enduring of the associations of English origin, not declining until the late twentieth century.

---

67   *Evening Post*, 16 December 1937.
68   Stevan Eldred-Grigg, *New Zealand Working People, 1890–1990* (Palmerston North: Dunmore Press, 1990), pp. 93–95.
69   Dates of establishment from centenary pamphlets in the collections of the National Library of New Zealand.
70   *Evening Post*, 27 August 1878.
71   *Otago Daily Times*, 26 September 1877; *Evening Post*, 10 August 1893.
72   *New Zealand Truth*, 8 September 1906.

As imperial fervour intensified in the 1890s and the early twentieth century, and the British-New Zealand identify took firmer form, a number of new societies were enthusiastically embraced. Their object was to foster patriotism and promote the imperial design.[73] They ranged from the narrowly focused Navy League, with its first branch in Auckland in 1896, to the League of Mothers, an immediate post-First World War creation. Typical was the Royal Victoria League, founded in London in 1901 'in memory of our late Gracious Queen', New Zealand branches soon following in Dunedin, Auckland, Wellington and Christchurch.[74] As an organization it stood for loyalty to the monarchy and the forging of links 'in the great chain of Empire friendship'. Further branches contributed to the war effort in the First World War, while in peacetime British immigration was supported and patriotic literature distributed. What set the Victoria League apart was that, while membership was open to both sexes, it was essentially a women's organization.[75] Of a different order was the Royal Overseas League, founded in London in 1910 as the Overseas Club.[76] In 1918 it amalgamated with the Patriotic League of Britons Overseas, and it was granted a Royal Charter in 1922. Its pledge was 'to maintain the heritage handed down by our fathers [...] binding together in closer friendship the peoples now living under the British flag'.[77] In 1913 its founder visited the dominion, successfully encouraging the setting up of New Zealand branches.

Of lengthier lineage, and with even more distinguished backers, was the Royal Colonial Institute, formed as the Colonial Society in 1868, subsequently becoming the Royal Empire Society in 1928.[78] Based in London, with the motto 'King and Empire', it was inward-looking, if influential, over its first four decades. When a 1909 decision to establish branches throughout the empire was followed by news of a mission to recruit new members, the decision was warmly welcomed.[79] The Institute's first New Zealand branch, indeed its first overseas branch, was formed in Christchurch in 1913, but in most parts of the dominion there were simply informal groups of 'Fellows', corresponding secretaries maintaining contact with London. In the years immediately after the First World War a second delegation travelled to New Zealand, but it was not until 1935 that a second branch was formed, this time

---

73 Sinclair, *Imperial Federation*, pp. 8–9.
74 Katie Pickles, 'A Link in "The Great Chain of Empire Friendship": The Victoria League in New Zealand', *Journal of Imperial and Commonwealth History*, 33.1 (2005), pp. 34–36.
75 Ibid.
76 Trevor R. Reese, *The History of the Royal Commonwealth Society 1868–1968* (London: Oxford University Press, 1968), pp. 148–52.
77 *Poverty Bay Herald*, 29 January 1913.
78 Reese, *History of the Royal Commonwealth Society*.
79 *Ashburton Guardian*, 9 February 1910; *Thames Star*, 4 July 1912.

in Auckland.[80] Organizations such as these proved more enduring than the strictly ethnic societies, continuing to function throughout the twentieth century and remaining today as cultural groups, if with different agendas.

Conclusion

Although New Zealand was the last of the traditional dominions to be settled, for much of the twentieth century European New Zealanders, certainly those whose ancestral origins were in Great Britain, exhibited a certain historical forgetfulness. So long as first-generation migrants comprised a majority of the population, they were well aware of, and clung to, their Englishness – for that matter Scottishness or Irishness. Equally, Geordies or Cousin Jacks knew they were different from Cockneys and Home Counties gentry. Yet within three generations, once the New Zealand-born were in the ascendancy, the regional and national differences blurred. There were exceptions – Irish Catholics for instance, bolstered by separate church and school, clung tenaciously to their identity and culture – but for the English the obscuring of distinctive identity was far-reaching. Most New Zealanders after 1900 evinced a relative lack of interest in their ethnic origins, settling instead for a hybrid 'British-New Zealand' identity. Alan Mulgan was a man of his time. Why this should have been so merits much deeper research. Sheer distance made maintaining contact with kin difficult, and until comparatively recently few, a small elite apart, had the ability, even the inclination, to make return journeys. This pattern was only broken in times of war. As importantly, most settlers were arguably more preoccupied with making lives in the new country than with clinging to the ways of the old. Further, as folk from throughout Great Britain and Ireland intermingled and intermarried, European New Zealanders became 'British' in a way that the inhabitants of the British Isles never could. The determination of Canterbury citizens to maintain an English façade, or the popularity of English folk dance in the late 1930s, might therefore be viewed as quaint aberrations. Recovering lost memories through historical inquiry is a process that has only just begun in New Zealand. While there were popular stirrings of interest in roots from the 1970s, scholarly response has been slower. Despite progress in delineating the patterns and processes of Irish migration to New Zealand, and in the past decade those of the New Zealand Scots, the English, by far New Zealand's single largest group, have still to attract in-depth research. The present chapter is an overview of how New Zealand's English Diaspora came into being. Its legacies await consideration.

---

80 *Poverty Bay Herald*, 8 October 1919; Reese, *History of the Royal Commonwealth Society*, pp. 208–09.

Chapter 10

'Cooked in true Yorkshire fashion': Regional Identity and English Associational Life in New Zealand before the First World War[1]

James Watson

There was no shortage of groups celebrating Scottish and Irish identity during the nineteenth century and early twentieth century in New Zealand: associational culture was a key aspect of the two migrant communities.[2] Caledonian societies were the Scots' most prolific association, with over 100 of them being formed up to 1930.[3] Gaelic and Scottish societies were also widespread.[4] There were Burns clubs, occasionally St Andrews societies, and even a Tattie and Herrin' Club in Dunedin.[5] On the Irish side, almost fifty branches of the Hibernian Society in New Zealand were founded between 1869 and 1900.[6] The St Patrick's Day sports organized by the Invercargill Irish Society were

---

1   A related version of this chapter first appeared as 'English Associationalism in the British Empire: Yorkshire Societies in New Zealand before the First World War', *Britain and the World: Historical Journal of The British Scholar Society*, 4.1 (2011), pp. 84–108. The author would like to thank the publishers for permission to include this related version here.

2   Tanja Bueltmann and Gerard Horn, 'Migration and Ethnic Associational Culture: A Comparative Study of New Zealand's Irish and Scottish Migrant Communities to 1905', in Vincent Comerford and Jennifer Kelly (eds), *Associational Culture in Ireland and Abroad* (Dublin: Irish Academic Press, 2010).

3   For details on the emergence of the first of the Caledonian societies, and their proliferation, see Tanja Bueltmann, *Scottish Ethnicity and the Making of New Zealand Society, 1850 to 1930* (Edinburgh: Edinburgh University Press, 2011).

4   Tanja Bueltmann, '"Brither Scots Shoulder tae Shoulder": Ethnic Identity, Culture and Associationism among the Scots in New Zealand to 1930', unpublished PhD thesis, Victoria University of Wellington, 2008, pp. 284–87, has a list of various local Scottish associations in New Zealand to 1930.

5   Bueltmann, '"Brither Scots"', p. 68.

6   Rory Sweetman, *Faith and Fraternalism: A History of the Hibernian Society in New Zealand, 1869–2000* (Wellington: Hibernian Society, 2002), pp. 210–16.

widely reported,[7] and in 1917 a Maoriland Irish Society was formed, '[o]pen to Irishmen of Irish Birth and Parentage'.[8] Similarly, during most of the nineteenth century the Orange Order operated as an organization for mostly Irish Protestants.[9] Even allowing for the Victorian enthusiasm for most things Scottish, and particularly things Highland, and for the fact that the Hibernians were a Catholic friendly society, there was clearly a tremendous enthusiasm among the Scots and the Irish to highlight their ethnic identity.

On the other hand, the English-born in New Zealand were little inclined to form associations to celebrate England or its patron saint. In 1905 the New Zealand governor, Lord Plunket, 'referred to the number of Scotch and Irish societies and the enthusiasm with which they celebrate Scotch or Irish Days or national occasions, as compared with the non-celebration of St. George's Day by English societies'.[10] And indeed, while a St George's Society existed in Auckland between 1859 and 1861, and held a public dinner to celebrate the saint's day,[11] it seems to have been focused on encouraging immigration from the British Isles, rather than just England. It produced 'an impartial account of the peculiar advantages which the Province of Auckland possesses as a field for emigration', and had it 'printed and extensively circulated throughout the United Kingdom'.[12] In 1888 the secretary of the London branch of the Society of St George sent circulars to New Zealand local bodies and newspapers, asking them to promote local branches of the society and celebration of St George's Day.[13] The circular appears to have occasioned little enthusiasm, one newspaper remarking that 'In many places in America the [latter] idea has been taken up, but it is doubtful if the colonists, who make merry on the Queen's and the Prince of Wales' Birthdays, will trouble about the matter.'[14] In 1903 the now Royal Society of St George again appealed through New Zealand newspapers for the formation of local branches. In Christchurch the *Star* noted that 'For some unexplained reason, St George's Day has never been observed in New Zealand, except as a bank holiday, and, judging from present appearances, it never will.'[15] In Nelson the *Colonist* merely found the society

7   *Grey River Argus*, 21 March 1902.
8   *New Zealand Truth*, 8 September 1917. See Sean G. Brosnahan, 'Shaming the Shoneens: The "Green Ray" and the "Maoriland Irish Society" in Dunedin, 1916–1922', in Lyndon Fraser (ed.), *A Distant Shore: Irish Emigration and New Zealand Settlement* (Dunedin: Otago University Press, 2000).
9   G.E. Horn, '"A loyal, united, and happy people": Irish Protestant Migrants to Wellington Province, 1840–1930: Aspects of Migration, Settlement and Community', unpublished PhD thesis, Victoria University of Wellington, 2010, pp. 202–30, 253–63.
10 *Evening Post*, 22 August 1905.
11 *Nelson Examiner and New Zealand Chronicle*, 7 May 1859; *Daily Southern Cross*, 17 April 1860, 23 April 1861.
12 *Daily Southern Cross*, 28 February 1860.
13 *Star*, 4 April 1888; *Bay of Plenty Times*, 6 April 1888; *Marlborough Express*, 23 April 1888; *Taranaki Herald*, 2 May 1888.
14 *Marlborough Express*, 23 April 1888.
15 *Star*, 24 April 1903.

itself 'worthy of respect'.[16] It appears to have been only in the small town of Blenheim, on the north-eastern corner of the South Island, that the appeal led to the creation of a society.

As the English constituted well over half of the settlers from the United Kingdom during the nineteenth century, and nearer two-thirds in areas outside strongly Scottish Otago and Southland, it is perhaps unsurprising that they saw little need to emphasize their distinct 'Englishness' by developing the equivalents of Caledonian, Scottish, Gaelic or Hibernian societies: their culture was predominant. Yet the English were disinclined to form ethnic societies even in Otago and Southland, where they were distinctly in a minority. It seems that the sense of a separate collective English identity in New Zealand was poorly developed.

In addition, there were some potential sensitivities, touched on by the editor of one provincial newspaper in 1900. He asked 'Why should the younger generation of English people not be taught to respect the memory of the good and brave St. George?', replying that, 'The answer is probably that we have our national holiday on the Queen's Birthday, and under the new Imperialism it is time to forget that we are Englanders and to count ourselves only as Britons.'[17] This divisive potential and the discomfort that it could provoke in New Zealand became evident in 1906, when the *Yearbook of the Royal Society of St George*, published in London, was condemned by the Wellington newspaper, the *New Zealand Times*.[18] The *Times* noted that the society expressed disappointment that in New Zealand only Blenheim had established a branch and the society speculated, wrongly, that a lack of correspondence from that branch indicated that it was defunct. However, the newspaper's editor considered that the lack of enthusiasm for the society in New Zealand was fully justified:

> To begin with, it is to be noted that membership of the society is 'restricted to English men and English women or their issue (wheresoever born), being British subjects.' The adjective 'English' is here used in the restricted sense as indicating people belonging to the 'dominant partner' in the United Kingdom; and the same narrow conception applies to all the patriotic objects of the society.

The editor was particularly incensed by an article in the *Yearbook* that criticized the English electorate for allowing a government to come to power in London that was led by a Scotsman (Campbell-Bannerman) and had no Englishmen in prominent ministries. The Liberal-supporting *Times* understandably detected 'the cloven hoof of political partisanship' in this criticism. The *Times* concluded:

---

16   *Colonist*, 24 April 1903.
17   *Poverty Bay Herald*, 21 April 1900.
18   *Marlborough Express*, 9 May 1906.

Bearing in mind the narrow aims of that organisation, we are proud of New Zealand's attitude towards it. We have here people from all parts of the Empire, engaged in building up a newer and brighter Britain, and we have no time for these old prejudices and rivalries. 'We do not at all despair of New Zealand,' says the report before us. Perhaps not; but New Zealand may well despair of the Royal Society of St. George.

English County Associations in New Zealand

In contrast to the few fleeting examples of English national societies, several English county associations were formed in New Zealand before the First World War. County societies could claim to have their origins in the county feasts and county clubs in London that had existed from at least the seventeenth century,[19] but no reference to this venerable heritage was made in New Zealand. To the extent that they claimed an exemplar, it appears to have been the Society of Yorkshiremen in London that was formed in 1891.[20]

Wellington's Yorkshiremen took the lead at the beginning of 1896.[21] Over the next few years Yorkshire societies were also formed in Timaru, Auckland, Masterton, Wanganui and possibly Hawke's Bay, while Lancashire and Yorkshire societies developed in Dunedin, Nelson and Gisborne.[22] Given the relatively small size of some of these centres and the fees the societies requested, they attracted a significant membership: in 1898 the Yorkshire Society in Wellington had 103 members, in 1899 that in Christchurch had 173 and, in 1901, that in Auckland had a hundred.[23] The annual dinner of the society in Wellington was typically attended by the prime minister and the leader of the opposition, and very frequently by the governor; local members of the House of Representatives and the mayor were almost always present. The annual picnic of the Christchurch society attracted around 350 members and friends in 1899, and 'over three hundred' attended a social gathering it held in the winter.[24] Furthermore, the Wellington society, which claimed the title of the Yorkshire Society of New Zealand, not only congratulated members on the prominence it had achieved locally but also declared that 'judging from the complimentary notices which have appeared in a number of London and

19   Peter Clark, *British Clubs and Societies 1580–1800: The Origins of an Associational World* (Oxford: Clarendon Press, 2000), ch. 8.
20   David Neave, 'The Identity of the East Riding of Yorkshire', in Edward Royle and John Duncan Marshall (eds), *Issues of Regional Identity* (Manchester: Manchester University Press, 1998), p. 185.
21   *Evening Post*, 6 November 1895; *Star*, 2 May 1898.
22   *Timaru Herald*, 20 August 1900; *Thames Star*, 8 August 1900; *Wanganui Herald*, 24 July 1907; *Evening Post*, 19 May 1910, 14 September 1911; *Otago Witness*, 30 January 1907; *Nelson Evening Mail*, 24 April 1908; *Poverty Bay Herald*, 20 January 1913.
23   *Evening Post*, 17 November 1898; *Star*, 19 April 1899; *Observer*, 28 September 1901.
24   *Star*, 27 January 1899, 27 July 1899.

provincial journals it would seem that the Yorkshire Society of New Zealand is almost as well known in England as in the Britain of the South'.[25]

The example of the Yorkshire societies appears to have led to the creation of other county societies: the Lancashire Society in Wellington was formed in 1898 and that in Christchurch the following year. A Cornish Society was formed in Wellington in anticipation of the visit of the Duke of Cornwall and York in 1901, and the spur appears to have been that the Yorkshire Society had decided to present the duke with an address and members of the Cornish community wanted to do likewise.[26] Their appeals for all Cornishmen in New Zealand to add their names to the address and for local branches of the society to be formed were widely publicized. Societies were also established in Timaru, Christchurch and Dunedin; the Wellington Cornish Society was still extant in 1906.[27] However, despite considerable fraternal support from the respective local Yorkshire societies, neither stand-alone Lancashire societies nor Cornish societies appear to have flourished in the way that the Yorkshire societies did.

The Success of New Zealand's Yorkshire Societies

The presence of large numbers of settlers from a particular county, a critical mass, was a major factor in the emergence of a county society. The Auckland Yorkshire Society was apparently founded by a Dr Walker, who 'in wending his way down Queen-street [*sic*], met one after the other a host of fellow-countrymen, and he considered that with so many "Yorkies" about it would be a good idea to start a club'.[28] Settlers in New Zealand from Yorkshire were certainly less well represented than those from south-east and south-west England in proportion to their areas' shares of the population of England and Wales.[29] However, given that the northern county was the third most populous in the Great Britain, even under-representation meant a large number of people – enough to form societies.[30] The same applied to Lancashire, the most populous of England's counties. Although Cornwall had a much smaller population than Lancashire or Yorkshire, it was very much a county of emigration and the massive over-representation of 'Cousin Jacks' among

25 *Evening Post*, 11 December 1900.
26 *Poverty Bay Herald*, 1 April 1901.
27 *Evening Post*, 20 October 1906.
28 *Observer*, 28 September 1901.
29 Jock Phillips and Terry Hearn, *Settlers: New Zealand Immigrants from England, Ireland and Scotland, 1800–1945* (Auckland: Auckland University Press, 2008), p. 70. Cumberland and Westmorland constituted the most over-represented mainland region between 1891 and 1915, but they provided less than 2 per cent of English migrants to New Zealand in that period.
30 A slightly over-represented Yorkshire provided 11.2 per cent of English migrants between 1891 and 1915. Ibid., p. 72.

immigrants to New Zealand meant that their numbers had rivalled those of each of the other two counties for most of the nineteenth century.

Moreover, a strong sense of a separate regional identity was key to the formation of a county society. While London and its neighbouring counties were vastly over-represented as the origins of English settlers in New Zealand, they do not seem to have given rise to a society in this period. Conversely, a considerable degree of county patriotism came with the settlers from Yorkshire, Lancashire and Cornwall. Not only was Yorkshire comparatively distant from London, but it also had a long tradition of presenting itself as a counterweight to the capital and things 'down south'. The slogan 'biggest, bonniest and best' that boomed out across halls in New Zealand came ready-made from home.[31] It is probably significant that the only English county or regional societies in New Zealand outside of Yorkshire or Lancashire during this time appear to have been Cornish: Cornwall, was, like Yorkshire, distant from London and had a strong tradition of independence and a distinctive local dialect, indeed a local language

This strong sense of regional identity in the three counties appears to have persisted. The British Social Attitudes Survey in 2001 revealed a comparatively weak regional identification in England as a whole, with only 45 per cent of respondents saying that they were 'very' or 'somewhat' proud at living in their region and 52 per cent stating that they 'didn't think of myself in that way'.[32] In contrast, 70 per cent of respondents in Yorkshire and Humberside took pride in belonging to that region, a level equal to that found in the north-east. The north-west was not far behind on 63 per cent. Respondents in the south-west registered a lower-than-average pride in their region, but it is very likely that those in Cornwall did not identify with that broader area.[33]

The existence of a network of Yorkshire societies internationally also appears to have encouraged their establishment in New Zealand. Addressing a meeting he had called to discuss the possible establishment of a Yorkshire Society in the comparatively small South Canterbury town of Timaru, H.B. Kirk declared that 'Yorkshire Societies were inaugurated, not only in New Zealand, but in the Australian colonies, Canada, and Scotland, and he [...] would not wonder whether they were in Ireland. Somehow or other, all the world over, they would find, like "Paddy" and the Scot, Yorkshiremen were

---

31   For a discussion of the size of the county as a matter of pride historically, see Neave, 'East Riding', p. 184. Other features of the Yorkshire identity are discussed in Tony Gore and Catherine Jones, 'Yorkshire and the Humber', in Irene Hardill, Paul Benneworth, Mark Baker and Leslie Budd (eds), *The Rise of the English Regions?* (London: Routledge, 2006), p. 137.

32   Quoted in Ross Bond and David McCrone, 'The Growth of English Regionalism? Institutions and Identity', *Regional and Federal Studies*, 14.1 (2004), p. 8.

33   Martin Jones and Gordon MacLeod, 'Regional Spaces, Spaces of Regionalism: Territory, Insurgent Politics and the English Question', *Transactions of the Institute of British Geographers*, 29.4 (2004), pp. 433–52.

planted.'[34] New Zealand newspapers reported such societies in Durban, Bournemouth (United Kingdom), Montreal and Sydney.[35]

It is also possible that the first formation of Yorkshire societies in New Zealand in the 1890s and early 1900s was linked to the fact that during that period immigrants arriving from Yorkshire were more strongly represented in terms of the county's population than before; indeed they seem to have been slightly over-represented.[36] The development of a woollen textile industry in New Zealand during the late nineteenth century seems to have brought a significant number of Yorkshire people to the country. The Wellington Woollen Company opened a mill in 1886 at Petone, a few miles from the capital, and employed around two hundred workers 'under the supervision of skilled experts, many of whom were specially brought to the Colony to assist in this growing concern'.[37] In 1897 members of the Yorkshire Society in Wellington announced their intention 'to pay a visit to Petone where a large number of Yorkshiremen reside'.[38] The following year 'the members of the Yorkshire Society and their lady friends' were invited to a 'social [...] by their brother "Yorkies" of Petone'.[39] In 1906 the committee 'drew attention to the large number of Yorkshiremen arriving in the colony, and impressed upon all members the desirability of inducing all new arrivals to become members of the society'.[40]

However, at least in the case of Wellington and Christchurch, the societies were not led by recent immigrants. Despite the enthusiasm of comparatively new arrivals for mixed socials, dances and picnics, the leadership and usual activities of the Yorkshire societies in those cities suggest that they were dominated by older men and their interests. An observer of the Wellington society noted that once the business of a meeting was transacted, members took to smoking their pipes.[41] The predominance of males, particularly older males, probably discouraged the regular involvement of many recent immigrants. It is perhaps significant that all the New Zealand Yorkshire societies, and apparently those in Australia, eschewed the title of 'Society of Yorkshiremen' favoured by the London body and used the gender-neutral title 'Yorkshire Society'. In 1893 New Zealand had led the world in extending the franchise

---

34 *Timaru Herald*, 13 August 1900.
35 *Grey River Argus*, 2 December 1902; *Evening Post*, 2 April 1898, 9 January 1908; *Poverty Bay Herald*, 24 February 1914.
36 This suggests that the rise in Yorkshire emigration to New Zealand occurred rather later than the peak of Yorkshire emigration overall, which was in the 1880s. Dudley Baines, *Migration in a Mature Economy: Emigration and Internal Migration in England and Wales, 1861–1900* (Cambridge: Cambridge University Press, 1985), pp. 244, 263.
37 *The Cyclopedia of New Zealand [Wellington Provincial District]* (Wellington: Cyclopedia Company, 1897), p. 829.
38 *Evening Post*, 10 June 1897.
39 *Evening Post*, 24 August 1898.
40 *Evening Post*, 13 December 1906.
41 *Evening Post*, 20 January 1898.

to women and Australia followed a decade later. Yet there were only limited moves to include women in the societies. Early in 1899 an advertisement for a monthly meeting of the Wellington society for the first time declared that 'A lady may accompany each member'.[42] This concession was apparently restricted to the kinswomen of members.[43] Not to be outdone, the annual meeting of the Christchurch society authorized its committee 'to take steps to alter the rules so as to admit ladies as members of the Society'.[44] Despite the reported enthusiasm for these changes, most monthly meetings and annual dinners, as opposed to socials and picnics, appear to have continued in the previous mature masculine mould, and it was noted in Wellington that 'the innovation of inviting members of the gentler sex to be present at some of the meetings did not meet with the response that was anticipated'.[45] In 1908 admitting women in imitation of the Yorkshire Society in Sydney was recommended as a means of reinvigorating the Wellington society.[46]

On the other hand, not all the societies catering for Yorkshire people were as conservative. The Lancashire and Yorkshire Society in Dunedin was organized differently, with monthly meetings being 'basket socials' and eight out of 15 of its Committee of Management in 1908 were women.[47] The Lancashire and Yorkshire Society in the comparatively isolated town of Gisborne, far up on the east coast of the North Island, appears to have operated around regular 'monthly meetings of a social character', particularly dances.[48] It initially had a 'ladies committee', but then introduced women onto the main committee and all meetings included women as well as men.[49] The Gisborne society was also relatively ecumenical, inviting not only people from Lancashire or Yorkshire, but anywhere in 'the North of England, and their friends' to its evenings.[50]

Rather than indicating the enthusiasm of a recent surge of immigrants, the timing of the establishment of most of the Yorkshire societies would seem to be more related to the fact that an earlier generation of emigrants from the county was now sufficiently established to have the time and money to support such organizations. Furthermore, they were reaching a time in life when reflecting back nostalgically on one's youthful experiences is not uncommon. One stalwart of the Yorkshire Society in Wellington, who donated fifty pounds to its funds, had arrived in the settlement in 1841.[51] A report on the first annual dinner of the Yorkshire Society in Auckland noted that 'Men who were well past the prime, and who had not seen Yorkshire since

---

42 *Evening Post*, 11 April 1899.
43 *Evening Post*, 13 April 1899.
44 *Star*, 19 April 1899.
45 *Evening Post*, 12 December 1899.
46 *Evening Post*, 10 December 1908.
47 *Otago Witness*, 5 August 1908.
48 *Poverty Bay Herald*, 27 March 1913.
49 *Poverty Bay Herald*, 24 January 1913, 22 February 1913, 11 December 1913.
50 *Poverty Bay Herald*, 8 April 1914.
51 *Evening Post*, 20 February 1913.

the days of boyhood, gave correct pictures of the county as it was in those days.'[52] One of the first presidents of the Lancashire and Yorkshire Society in Dunedin was Charles Bean Rainton, who was born at Scarborough in 1833 and arrived in Otago in 1861.[53] At the inaugural meeting of the Yorkshire Society in Wanganui in 1907, 'Famous scenes such as the Great Ripon Historical Pageant, the passing of the first Reform Bill demonstrations [1832], and the opening of Leeds Town Hall [1858] were described by eye witnesses.'[54] In 1898 the elderly William Rolleston declared to fellow Yorkshiremen in Wellington that 'What little ambition I have left in me is that some day at no distant date I may be able to revisit the county I left 40 years ago. Nevertheless, New Zealand is the finest country on this earth.'[55] Three years later Sir John Hall told a farewell meeting that 'There were family reasons for his visiting the Home Country, but there was one great reason, and that was that he wanted to see the Old Land and his old friends once more, and at his time of life, nigh four-score, if he wanted to do that, there was but little time to lose.'[56] Such farewells for visits 'home', or welcomes back, were not uncommon in accounts of activities of the Yorkshire societies.[57] They also featured in reports from the Wellington Cornish Society.[58]

The older age of the leading lights of the societies may well also have been reflected in the fact that the consumption of alcohol remained a feature of their annual dinners. They did not get caught up in the contemporary enthusiasm for abstention, indeed prohibition. In 1907 a Primitive Methodist minister and ardent prohibitionist, originally from Keighley, attended the annual dinner in Wellington:

> Finally, my brethren, he proposed the toast of his 'well-watered' country [sic], and he asked the guests to drink it in lemonade. Never since the sons of men took to liquor did lemonade assume such variegated colours. Some glasses might have contained beer, they looked so like it; other lemonades looked for all the world like claret; and not a few resembled good old Scotch![59]

Many settlers who flourished in New Zealand during the early years of European settlement did so through sheep farming, initially largely for the production of wool. Such farming was particularly successful in southern and eastern New Zealand, where most of the Yorkshire societies were located. Yorkshire was a great producer of wool as well as a great manufacturer of

---

52   *Observer,* 28 September 1901.
53   *Otago Witness,* 24 February 1909.
54   *Wanganui Herald,* 5 August 1907.
55   *Evening Post,* 4 November 1898.
56   *Poverty Bay Herald,* 19 March 1901.
57   See, for example, *Evening Post,* 5 April 1900, 9 June 1904, 12 October 1905, 9 November 1905, 12 December 1907, 12 March 1914; *Star,* 25 April 1900.
58   See, for example, *Evening Post,* 7 March 1906.
59   *New Zealand Free Lance,* 14 September 1907.

woollen goods and a significant number of those who had secured sheep-based fortunes in New Zealand were Yorkshiremen.

The choice of leadership for at least some of the Yorkshire societies seems to have reflected this and the presence of these wealthy and socially prominent individuals at the head of the societies in Wellington, Christchurch and Timaru may well have contributed to their success. While in each case businessmen made the first move to launch a society, individuals from sheep-owning backgrounds soon took over. Thus in Wellington T. Bedford took the lead, but a year later the Revd John Chapman Andrew, the owner of Ica Station in the Wairarapa, was the president.[60] In the case of Christchurch the meeting that inaugurated the society was called by a businessman, H.B. Kirk, owner of a brick and tile works.[61] It was held in the rooms of the Canterbury Industrial Association, which represented manufacturers and therefore protectionist interests, which in turn generally supported the Liberal government. Kirk indeed later described himself as 'a pronounced Liberal since the time the late Sir George Grey became Premier of New Zealand'.[62] Yet he expressed the hope that Sir John Hall and William Rolleston,[63] wealthy landowners and probably Canterbury's foremost free-trade and opposition politicians, would agree to be president and vice-president respectively '[t]hough he differed from both these gentlemen in politics'.[64] Sir John Hall had indeed displaced Kirk's hero Sir George Grey as premier in 1879. Both Hall and Rolleston accepted the posts the society offered and Sir John Hall in particular was to become something of a sponsor of it. Following Rolleston's death in 1903, Arthur Edgar Gravenor Rhodes, who was a New Zealand-born member of another elite landowning family and who had not previously served as an

---

60 Andrew was born at Whitby. Educated at Oxford University, he became an Anglican clergyman and emigrated to New Zealand in 1856. In 1882 the Ica Run consisted of 18,339 acres. Andrew was 74 at the time he became president of the Yorkshire Society. John Acheson, 'Andrew, John Chapman', in Claudia Orange (ed.), *The Dictionary of New Zealand Biography*, Volume II, *1870–1900* (Wellington: Auckland University Press/Department of Internal Affairs, 1993), pp. 6–7.

61 Kirk was around 56 when the Yorkshire Society in Christchurch was formed. He was born in the village of Thorner and began work as a miner at Farnley, near Leeds. He had arrived in New Zealand in 1863, working initially as a labourer. *The Cyclopedia of New Zealand [Canterbury Provincial District]* (Christchurch: Cyclopedia Company, 1903), p. 1023.

62 *Cyclopedia [Canterbury]*, p. 1024.

63 Hall was born in Hull and emigrated to New Zealand in 1852. In 1891 he owned Terrace Station in Canterbury, consisting of 29,763 acres and worth £94,264. Hall was 73 when the Yorkshire Society was formed in Christchurch. W.J. Gardner, 'Hall, John', in W.H. Oliver (ed.), *The Dictionary of New Zealand Biography*, Volume I, *1769–1869* (Wellington: Allen and Unwin/Department of Internal Affairs, 1990), pp. 172–74; Rolleston was born at Maltby Hall near Rotherham and came to New Zealand in 1858. He was 66 when the Yorkshire Society was formed in Christchurch. W.J. Gardner, 'Rolleston, William', in Oliver (ed.), *The Dictionary of New Zealand Biography*, Volume I, *1769–1869*, pp. 372–74.

64 *Star*, 2 May 1898.

officer of the society, replaced him as vice-president. Rhodes was a lawyer, a graduate of Cambridge University and a former mayor of Christchurch. When Kirk, having moved to Timaru, promoted the formation of a Yorkshire Society in South Canterbury in 1900, he appears to have been again in search of landowning prominente of Yorkshire origin to lead it. Again he succeeded, with George Heaton Rhodes of Claremont Station (4,000 acres), another New Zealand-born graduate of Cambridge University, agreeing to be president.

Other Yorkshire societies in New Zealand do not seem to have followed this pattern. In the case of Dunedin, the fact that the Lancashire and Yorkshire Society held its meetings in the Trades Hall suggests that it was unlikely to have looked for wealthy members of the sheep-farming elite to lead it. One of its early presidents was a builder and contractor, 'a well-known expert in the building of bakers' ovens and range setting'.[65] Moreover, the demand for elite leadership may well have been indicative of the fact that so many of the early non-sheep -farming activists had arrived in the mid-nineteenth century, when the land-holding elite was particularly prominent. No Yorkshire Society seems to have had a sheep-farming president in 1914.

Activities of the Yorkshire Societies

Despite the typical member not being a recent immigrant, it is still possible that the greater Yorkshire migration to New Zealand at the turn of the century may have indirectly encouraged the formation of the societies. Some of the older men involved seem to have been motivated in part by a desire 'to render friendly assistance and information to [the] Yorkshiremen' now arriving in greater numbers.[66] 'Wherever such a society exists, Yorkshiremen coming to the place would seek out the president or secretary and they could give him useful advice and if necessary the funds of the society might be able to afford him a few shillings to put in his pocket.'[67] Such assistance was likely to be across classes as well as generations. In Wellington and Christchurch, 'affording assistance and advice to such of their countrymen as might need help' was one of the objects of the society.[68] Indeed, in 1898 the annual meeting of the Wellington society was told that 'the chief object of the Society's existence was to assist unfortunate and needy county-men' and the subscription was doubled to two guineas to finance this.[69] The small amounts of assistance actually handed out, such as the £2 12s disbursed to 'distressed Yorkshiremen' in Wellington in 1908, probably reflected the generally healthy state of the

---

65 *Otago Witness*, 24 February 1909.
66 *Timaru Herald*, 20 August 1900.
67 *Timaru Herald*, 31 October 1900.
68 *Star*, 2 May 1898.
69 *Evening Post*, 17 November 1898.

New Zealand economy at the time.[70] In 1903 the president of the Wellington society claimed 'They assisted the needy where possible, and endeavoured to find employment for new arrivals.'[71] Four years later a member of the Wellington society's committee advised the newly formed Wanganui society to follow his society's lead:

> The Society's membership in Wellington included many influential business men with a very energetic President and secretary. They advertised their Society well so that any Yorkshireman arriving from the Old Country could readily find the Society's officials and they then made it their business to give every possible assistance. They had placed numbers of their countrymen in good billets, and he hoped the Wanganui Society would grow strong and be a powerful mutual help association.[72]

The annual meeting of the Lancashire and Yorkshire Society in Dunedin was told in 1908 that 'They had also been able to assist strangers from the Old Country and from other parts of the Dominion to find situations on arriving in Dunedin.'[73]

Aside from this philanthropic aspect, the business of the Yorkshire societies was social and cultural, celebrating together what members saw as the unique attributes of their county. The regional accent was given particular prominence. At the monthly evening meetings in Wellington and Christchurch recitations in 'dialect' were popular, while the menus for those societies' annual dinners were interspersed with remarks and mottoes for which outsiders would have required a translation. Similarly, the advertisement for the Wellington society's dinner in 1902 declared 'Cum, lads, an' yoh can smook, an' sing, an' jaw; we're bahn ta hev pyanner laikin an' lots o' summat more.'[74]

The dishes served at such annual dinners were presented as typically Yorkshire fare, 'cooked in true Yorkshire fashion'.[75] Besides beef with Yorkshire pudding, these could include York hams, tripe and onions, sheep's trotters, mince pies and apple pie with cheese.[76] Ox-tail, roast lamb and suckling pig could also feature.[77] Musical celebration of county culture was also frequent – even an example from the other side of the Pennines was welcome. Prime Minister Seddon demonstrated his talents to the Wellington Yorkshire Society 'by a vigorous rendering of the appropriate song "Hard Times Come Again No More", and a Lancashire *patois* ditty [that] brought

---

70   *Evening Post*, 10 December 1908.
71   *Evening Post*, 27 August 1903.
72   *Wanganui Herald*, 15 November 1907.
73   *Otago Witness*, 5 August 1908.
74   *Evening Post*, 23 August 1902.
75   *Marlborough Express*, 13 January 1896.
76   *Evening Post*, 16 January 1896.
77   *New Zealand Free Lance*, 30 August 1902.

down the house'.[78] A more elevated musical patriotism was not neglected, with the song 'Yorkshire, My Yorkshire' featuring at a Wellington meeting in 1910.[79]

A keynote of the county societies was the promotion of social unity in New Zealand. Their members were emphatically not the 'whingeing poms' of Antipodean contempt, fresh off the boat and already full of denunciations of the shortcomings of the new land.[80] They were eager to recognize and celebrate the opportunities that immigration to New Zealand had provided to them. Their annual dinners featured fulsome toasts to their adopted country and on a number of occasions in Wellington the president of the local New Zealand Natives Association, an organization of New Zealand-born men of European descent, was an honoured guest. The founder of two Yorkshire societies declared to members in Timaru that 'though Yorkshire was a grand piece of country, he must congratulate them on the change they had made in coming to New Zealand and to South Canterbury'.[81] At the Wellington Yorkshire Society's annual dinner in 1903, a newcomer and an old identity both sang the praises of their new land:

> In proposing the toast of 'The Land We Live In', Dr. Barraclough gave a 'new chum's' impressions of this colony in an eloquent speech brimming over with appreciation. Mr. H.D. Bedford, M[ember] H[ouse of] R[epresentatives], a native of Leeds, most of whose life has been spent in this colony, generally endorsed the proposer's commendation, and was daring enough to assert [...] that in nearly every point they liked to institute a comparison, their adopted country excelled the country of their birth.[82]

Friendly relations also seem to have prevailed between the county societies, and indeed between them and 'ethnic' societies. In Wellington the Yorkshire Society assisted its Lancashire counterpart to organize[83] while in 1899 the Christchurch Lancashire Society held social gatherings in the Caledonian Society Hall.[84]

The Yorkshire Societies and Imperialism

Likewise the county societies were deeply immersed in the imperial patriotism that was evident in the 1890s and fanned to new heights by the Boer War. From the beginning, speakers at the Yorkshire Society meetings drew

78 *Evening Post*, 14 January 1897.
79 *Evening Post*, 15 September 1910.
80 At the annual dinner of the Yorkshire Society in Wellington, the Revd W.H. Walton, originally from Halifax, declared 'that the worst colonials were the people who came from Home and ran New Zealand down'. *Evening Post*, 23 September 1913.
81 *Timaru Herald*, 31 October 1900.
82 *Evening Post*, 27 August 1903.
83 *Evening Post*, 4 November 1898.
84 *Star*, 3 May 1899.

attention to the role that Yorkshiremen had played in bringing New Zealand into the British Empire. Captain James Cook loomed understandably large in this pantheon of imperial heroes. As in Australia, the societies strongly supported moves to erect monuments to the great navigator, particularly one in Queen Charlotte Sound.[85] Having achieved this, with government assistance, the Wellington Yorkshire Society pushed for a memorial to Edward Gibbon Wakefield, who had been responsible for forming the New Zealand Company that sent colonists to Wellington, Nelson and New Plymouth.[86] Contemporary imperial figures, such as Sir Harry Rawson, the governor of New South Wales, Sir Wilmot Fawkes, admiral of the Australian fleet, and, on far from obvious grounds, the Irish-born and London-raised Lieutenant Ernest Shackleton, were all claimed to be 'Tykes'.[87]

British imperial power was the mainstay of the security of a remote New Zealand and most members of the societies were eager to support anything that strengthened that shield at a time when anxiety was being expressed that Britain and its empire were in decline. Coincidentally, the inauguration of the Yorkshire Society in Wellington at the beginning of 1896 took place during the crisis that followed the Jameson Raid, amid fears of war in South Africa and possibly with Germany.[88] Attending the inauguration, Prime Minister Seddon made reference to the situation and linked it to New Zealand's interests in the Pacific:

> New Zealanders were essentially Britishers, and he felt sure that they were in sympathy with the English Government in the firm stand that was being taken in regard to matters abroad. He hoped that the Government would have the support of everybody in the matter of foreign nations getting a footing on islands adjacent to New Zealand.

When the Boer War broke out in 1899, the Yorkshire Societies in Christchurch and Wellington took the lead in organizing patriotic concerts to raise funds to support the volunteers going to fight.[89] A few months later the Christchurch Yorkshire Society took great pride in the fact that New Zealand and Yorkshire units had fought alongside each other in battle at what became known as New Zealand Hill in South Africa.[90]

Celebratory references to the empire continued to mark Yorkshire Society gatherings after the war ended. The practice of singing the National Anthem at

---

85 *Evening Post*, 10 April 1913.
86 *Evening Post*, 23 September 1913.
87 *Evening Post*, 9 January 1908.
88 The announcement that moves were being made to form a Yorkshire Society was published in early November 1895, before the crisis broke. *Evening Post*, 2 November 1895.
89 *Star*, 16 December 1899; *Evening Post*, 24 January 1900.
90 *Star*, 25 April 1900.

the end of the Wellington society's annual dinner began in 1907.[91] At the 1909 annual dinner the prime minister, Sir Joseph Ward, declared that 'There was no country so British and so loyal in the Empire as New Zealand. Its onward course was assured, if all would co-operate to make it a greater dominion than to-day.'[92] As leader of the opposition, William Massey also looked to the future: 'He looked forward to the time when the Commonwealth of Australia, and the Dominions of New Zealand and Canada, would stand together to hold the Pacific.' The following year Ward referred to the recently formed Union of South Africa and declared that 'New Zealand, too, perhaps in a more humble way, would take part in the development of the Empire, with which they were one in sentiment, one in desire, and one in tradition. (Applause).'[93] Massey tapped into current imperial concerns: 'The British Empire was not decaying, and would not decay so long as there were these young vigorous nations within its bounds. (Applause). And of them New Zealand was last, perhaps, but not least. (Applause.)'

When the issue of compulsory military training arose in 1909, a debate on it at the Wellington society was followed by a vote of two to one in its favour.[94] At the society's annual dinner two years later, Sir James Carroll, a Maori MHR representing a European seat, who had twice been acting prime minister when Sir Joseph Ward was in Britain, strongly defended compulsory military training in the lead-up to the 1911 General Election. His speech was enthusiastically received by the 'Yorkies'.

> If they had any love for the country which was their home, any pride in the supremacy of the British nation, any ambition to keep in the foremost rank of the peoples of the world, let them look to the defence of their country, to the training in physical and military proficiency of the youth of New Zealand, and the future would be assured. (Loud applause).[95]

Conclusion

Organizations celebrating 'Englishness' had little success in New Zealand before the First World War. In the first place, there seems to have been only a weak sense of a collective 'English' identity among the English-born or English-descended majority, in contrast certainly to the Scottish and Irish settlers. Secondly, the assertion of a separate Englishness by the majority potentially threatened to divide a community that placed a strong premium

---

91 *Evening Post*, 3 September 1907. The newly formed Lancashire and Yorkshire Society in Gisborne adopted this practice for its social gatherings. *Poverty Bay Herald*, 27 March 1913.
92 *Evening Post*, 26 October 1909.
93 *Evening Post*, 20 September 1910.
94 *Evening Post*, 8 July 1909.
95 *Poverty Bay Herald*, 4 October 1911.

on social cohesion and working towards a 'British' and imperial destiny. New Zealand's security in particular depended on a strong United Kingdom, and its division into competing nationalities boded ill for the safety of a small settler society in the South Pacific. Moreover, as a strong majority in the colony, the English had less reason to feel their interests were threatened and to band together in self-defence. In contrast to the failure of St George's societies, Yorkshire societies flourished in several centres. They could draw upon myths about the county and its people that were widely held, not least among its own inhabitants, to celebrate a separate Yorkshire identity. Yet they were doing this as another minority, not as a potentially disturbing reminder that the English were ultimately dominant. So they could celebrate their identity without for a moment threatening imperial or national unity. Indeed, Yorkshire societies constantly reiterated pride in and loyalty to both the British Empire and New Zealand itself.

Why Yorkshire societies took the lead and were so much more successful than the Cornish and separate Lancashire societies during this period is unclear. The establishment of the Society of Yorkshiremen in London in 1891 may have been pivotal, though this raises the question as to why other counties did not follow suit or were less successful in doing so. In Wellington and Christchurch (and also Timaru), the Yorkshire societies were able to gain the patronage of wealthy individuals who were socially and politically prominent. One reason they could do this was that many such people in those areas of New Zealand had established their wealth and prominence through wool farming during the mid-nineteenth century and Yorkshire was a great county for the production of wool as well as woollen textiles. Flourishing Yorkshire societies in both the capital and 'the southern capital'[96] certainly provided encouragement and to some extent an example for the formation of similar societies elsewhere.

---

96 John Cookson and Graeme Dunstall (eds), *Southern Capital: Christchurch: Towards a City Biography, 1850–2000* (Christchurch: Canterbury University Press, 2000).

Chapter 11

Englishness and Cricket in South Africa during the Boer War

Dean Allen

The mid-to-late nineteenth century witnessed a tremendous growth in cricket's significance across the globe. Within Britain and the colonies, the game came to symbolize the very essence of English Victorian society and the promotion of white Anglo-Saxon values. 'It is difficult to underestimate the importance of cricket in Victorian life', explains Keith Sandiford. The game 'was a ritual as well as recreation, a spiritual as well as a sporting experience. Its values were used freely by politicians, philosophers, preachers and poets.'[1] It became the 'imperial game' and, above all else, it was an English creation.

Cricket spread to all societies across the Anglo-world where organized games were played: India, the Caribbean and Australia. Here it had been transformed from a simple, pastoral game into a powerful and symbolic force representing all that was deemed by the ruling classes to be worthy in the Anglo-Saxon character. 'In a fiercely nationalistic era Englishmen regarded cricket, an exclusively English creation unsullied by outside influence, as proof of their cultural supremacy.'[2] It was a time of complacency, security and opulent pride. Victoria had expanded her empire to South Africa and here too cricket came to symbolize 'Englishness' and the civilizing mission of the Englishman abroad.

Cricket's attraction to the English Diaspora, being the conscious community of expatriate English around the world, came in its exclusiveness, its codes of practice and an ethos that made it distinctly 'English'. Cricket was a product of England. Its customs and traditions had been shaped in the

---

1 K.A.P Sandiford, 'England', in B. Stoddart and K.A.P. Sandiford (eds), *The Imperial Game* (Manchester: Manchester University Press, 1998), p. 9.
2 Ibid.

mother country and, as such, it was seen to reflect the enlightened superiority of Anglo-Saxon culture. For the English in South Africa, cricket played a key role in how they imagined the world viewed them and saw the game as an expression of their moral worth. In 1877 Charles Box produced *The English Game of Cricket*, in which he explained to the 'outside world' how the 'manly and noble game' of cricket is 'a perfect physical discipline, an admirable moral training. It is food to the patriotic conviction, and fire to the patriotic soul [...] Even down to the minutest [*sic*] point it is in harmony with those conservative tendencies and habits which are as eminently English as the warm love of freedom is English.'[3] Indeed, by the time of the Boer War, cricket's ethos had been transferred to colonial South Africa.

Not only did Victorian cricket engender a deep sense of white, elite and distinctively masculine Englishness, it was also seen to be beyond the conception of those foreign to British tradition and culture. For Britons, cricket epitomized the spread of English influence throughout the world, while for the English Diaspora in colonial settings such as South Africa the game represented a tangible link with 'home'. This chapter begins by investigating the social construction of cricket during the Victorian era and its portrayal as the archetypal 'Englishman's game'. The renowned cricket writer Neville Cardus once reflected how 'cricket somehow holds up the mirror to the English nature'[4] while novelist E.W. Hornung, himself a product of the Victorian age, declared in *Kenyon's Innings*: 'My dear fellow, it was only a game – yet it was life.'[5] 'In the late Victorian period and for at least the first half of the twentieth century', explains Jack Williams, 'cricket was taken to encapsulate the essence of England and had a key role in how the English, particularly the economically privileged, imagined their national identity.'[6] Alongside an examination of cricket during the 1899–1902 war in South Africa, this study will consider cricket's link to Victorian society and explore the key agents and institutions responsible for instilling the sense of 'Englishness' upon the game both within South Africa and back in England during the Boer War era.

Cricket and Victorianism

Based on the rigid class system of Victorian society, cricket's social formation during this time mirrored the hierarchies that existed both within British and colonial society. Patrick Morrah captures the link between cricket, empire and identity:

---

3   C. Box, *The English Game of Cricket* (London: The Field Office, 1877), p. 12.
4   N. Cardus, *English Cricket* (London: Collins, 1945), p. 9.
5   Quoted in M. Tozer, 'Cricket, School and Empire: E.W. Hornung and His Young Guard', *International Journal of the History of Sport*, 6.2 (1989), p. 159.
6   J. Williams, *Cricket and Race* (Oxford: Berg, 2001), p. 1.

the fundamental causes of the blossoming of golden cricket lay deeper – in the character of the age itself. The Victorian era was one of solidarity, the building up of British prosperity and security after the desperate struggle of the Napoleonic wars. As the age progressed its paramount characteristic became self-confidence. Britain was the most prosperous nation in the world; wider still and wider were the bounds of empire set; the upper classes were entrenched in power, and nobody questioned their right to rule.[7]

During this period the game had become, as Holt explains, *the* English national sport via its spread from the eighteenth-century gentry to the growing Victorian middle classes and industrial workers of the cities.[8] While the winter sport of football remained divided from the outset into its 'associa-tion' and 'rugby' codes, cricket became *the* universal English summer game with great cricketers emerging as national figures in a way other sportsmen could never achieve.[9]

The English had transformed cricket into more than a game. For Keith Sandiford, the social centrality of Victorian cricket was fostered, nurtured and maintained by key institutions and agencies such as England's public schools and churches which regarded the game as a major cultural virtue and, therefore, worth promoting within society.[10] The moral, social and physical attributes of sport were extolled in Victorian times. England had become a true world power and behind its success, many believed, was the national passion for sport:

> Much less than any other nation do the English need to be taught the art of preserving health. They are admitted to be the strongest of races – proof enough that they are the healthiest [...] Racing, riding, rowing, skating, curling, and among field sports cricket, with the like hygienic agencies, must, and do in great measure, quicken Englishmen, and make them to a great extent what they physically and morally are.[11]

As Taylor has shown, public school athleticism shaped the ideal of manhood and character, differentiating gentlemen from the 'masses' and creating the amateur–professional distinction that dominated English and colonial sport for over a century. 'This high-minded moral guidance was rooted in notions of self-discipline and virtue and was indicative of the puritanical strain in nineteenth century British *bourgeois* philosophy.'[12] It found voice in *Athletic News* in 1876:

---

7   P. Morrah, *The Golden Age of Cricket* (London: Eyre and Spottiswoode, 1967), p. 148.
8   R. Holt, 'Cricket and Englishness: The Batsman as Hero', *International Journal of the History of Sport*, 13.1 (1996), p. 48.
9   Ibid.
10 Sandiford, 'England', p. 11.
11 Box, *The English Game of Cricket*, pp. 72–73.
12 H. Taylor, 'Play Up, But Don't Play the Game: English Amateur Athletic Elitism, 1863–1910', *The Sports Historian*, 22 (2002), p. 78 (italics in original).

Moralists may well give this subject a portion of their consideration. Excellence in athletics is only possible to those who cultivate habits of temperance, and it is the critical period between youth and manhood that habits and inclinations are formed which may influence a person's entire subsequent career. The young athlete is less likely to stray from the right path than those who have no such motive to control them, and hence a great social problem would be in a fair way to be solved.[13]

The 'right path' was to serve one's country and inevitably for many this meant a career in the military. At the time of the Boer War in South Africa, many speakers and preachers were visiting the public and preparatory schools to press home the imperial message. One such orator was cricketing enthusiast E.W. Hornung, author of the best-selling Raffles tales and brother-in-law of Sir Arthur Conan Doyle.[14] At Uppingham, Hornung's old school, a cadet corps was thriving. In February 1900 C.H. Jones, the commanding officer, left for active service in the Boer War, and his adventures in Africa were reported in the school magazine in vivid detail: 'We hear that Mr. Jones has killed five Boers single-handed. We congratulate him heartily on the exploit and hope that he will dispose of many more.'[15]

As well as the supposed virtues of the sport, part of cricket's appeal to the Victorians was its heritage and tradition. Historians were prone to emphasize the antiquity of the game and point to the fact that it pre-dated other team ball sports in the country. Early records of the game were fastidiously maintained and this helped create the rich heritage that was transferred to places such as South Africa. It was the early eighteenth century that saw cricket established in south-east England, its homelands being the villages of Kent, Surrey and Sussex. It was also well known in London.[16] A match with a team purportedly representing the best cricketers of a county had been played as early as 1709. The old written rules date from 1744, the year when interest in the game

---

13   *Athletic News*, 15 July 1876, p. 4, cited in Taylor, 'Play Up, But Don't Play the Game', p. 78.

14   In July 1914, less than a month before the start of the First World War, Hornung had characteristically chosen 'The Game of Life' as the title for one of his last school sermons: 'the way we played for our side, in the bad light, on the difficult pitch, the way we backed up and ran the other man's runs; our courage and unselfishness, not our skill or our success; our brave failures, our hidden disappointments, the will to bear our friend's infirmities, and the grit to fight our own: surely, surely, it is these things above all others that will count, when the innings is over, in the Pavilion of Heaven'. E.W. Hornung, quoted in M.A. Tozer, 'Sacred Trinity – Cricket, School, Empire: E.W. Hornung and his Young Guard', in J.A. Mangan (ed.), *The Cultural Bond: Sport, Empire, Society* (London: Frank Cass, 1992), p. 17. This was typical of the cricket–war rhetoric preached within Britain's public schools since the days of the Boer War.

15   From the *Uppingham School Magazine*, September 1900, p. 265. Cited in Tozer, 'Sacred Trinity', p. 18.

16   D. Brailsford, *British Sport. A Social History* (Cambridge: Lutterworth Press, 1992), p. 46.

had reached such a level that spectators paid for admission to a match at the Artillery Ground in London.[17] Around 1750 the famous Hambledon Club was founded under the captaincy of Richard Nyren and 'modern cricket, as we know it' began in earnest.[18]

Throughout the empire, assumptions about the English nature of cricket and of the morality of the game were linked with perceptions of cricket as essentially a sport of the English countryside.[19] True, the game had originated in the rural areas of the Sussex Weald and adjoining counties, but it was the Victorian cricket writers who were responsible for portraying village cricket as the epitome of English life. Charles Box, for one, wrote how 'all ranks and conditions of society, either theoretically or practically, participate to some extent in the game'.[20] However, while it was played, as Box suggests, within all levels of society, the upper classes and those in control chose not to dwell upon the game's essentially exclusive nature. As Williams explains, 'cricket was portrayed as a mirror of social cohesion, reflecting the assumption of many from the privileged classes that social relations in England were characterised by harmony and cooperation'.[21]

Of course, such cordiality was a façade. In reality, 'few other cultural institutions made so clear the inequalities of economic status and social background or demonstrated to individuals their place in the social hierarchy'.[22] Cricket's egalitarianism was thus an illusion both in Victoria's Britain and throughout South Africa because cricket enforced barriers of class, race and gender and did little to remove them.[23] The reality in fact lay in sustaining exclusivity because the Victorian elite, in England and the colonies, remained determined to protect both their status and their privileges. A conscious investment, both financially as well as morally, was thus launched

---

17 Monday 18 June 1744, Kent vs. All England; see P. Wynne-Thomas, *The History of Cricket: From the Weald to the World* (London: HMSO, 1997), pp. 14–15, 29.

18 *The Times, The M.C.C. 1787–1937* (London: The Times Publishing Co., 1937), p. 22. According to the National Book League, 'it is impossible to over-estimate the part played by this small Hampshire village in the subsequent development of the game. From its formation about 1750 by "Squire" Powlett until the M.C.C. came into being in 1787 the Hambledon Club was the supreme arbiter and included amongst its members all the principal patrons of the game'. National Book League, *Cricket. A Catalogue of an Exhibition of Books, Manuscripts and Pictorial Records Presented by the National Book League with the Co-operation of the Marylebone Cricket Club* (London: Cambridge University Press, 1950), p 24.

19 Williams, *Cricket and Race*, pp. 15–16.

20 Box, *The English Game of Cricket*, p. iii.

21 J. Williams, *Cricket and England. A Cultural and Social History of the Inter-War Years* (London: Frank Cass, 1999), p. 15.

22 Ibid., p. 114.

23 As David Frith explains of the Golden Age: 'Class distinctions held firm, in cricket as in real life, though it has long been a prime claim for English cricket that it has brought all breeds of men together in a pavilion. This it may have done, creating an additional mystique, but it could never bring about any real fusion of species.' D. Frith, *The Golden Age of Cricket 1890–1914* (Guildford: Lutterworth Press, 1978), p. 12.

by the bourgeoisie. Indeed, as Sandiford points out, 'the political economy of Victorian cricket underlines [the] class segmentation and the social directives which drove it. Millions of pounds were spent on cricket during the last thirty years of the nineteenth century when the game underwent explosive growth at village, league and county levels.'[24]

At the time of the first English cricket tours to South Africa the game had assumed an importance beyond that of the other major sports. 'The Victorians revered cricket as an institution because they believed that, like the Church and the Crown, it had a key role to play in English life. Their cultural and political leaders looked upon it as having specific and vital functions to perform.'[25] These functions included the spread of English culture abroad as well as the establishment of a 'privileged set' within the colonies themselves. As Merrett and Nauright explain, 'The ability to appropriate and dispense English culture as the measure of social acceptability gave English-speaking whites and those they chose to include a real sense of cultural and moral power and superiority.'[26]

South Africa and 'Cricket Imperialism'

Sport in South Africa developed at a time of British imperial expansion and by the outbreak of the Boer War in 1899, cricket had become intertwined with notions of empire and English cultural supremacy throughout the country.[27] As part of the cultural imperialism designed to cement ties between Britain and its dependants, sport's development in South Africa mirrored the progression of English influence throughout the territories.[28] Indeed, if we look at cricket as an example, it was not long before South Africa was accepted into England's exclusive 'club of empire'. As Williams explains:

> Test cricket was played only between England and colonies or former colonies. As cricket was believed to express a distinctively English morality and as apologists for the Empire stressed the moral obligation to extend the benefits

24 Sandiford, 'England', p. 24.
25 Ibid., p. 29.
26 C. Merrett and J. Nauright, 'South Africa', in B. Stoddart and K.A.P. Sandiford (eds), *The Imperial Game* (Manchester: Manchester University Press, 1998), p. 57.
27 See, for example, in the case of cricket, D. Allen, 'South African Cricket, Imperial Cricketers and Imperial Expansion, 1850–1910', *The International Journal for the History of Sport*, 25.4 (2008), pp. 443–71; and D. Allen, 'South African Cricket and the Expansion of Empire', in D. Malcolm, J. Gemmell, N. Mehta, J.A. Mangan, B. Majumdar, and M. Dyreson (eds), *Cricket: International and Interdisciplinary Perspectives* (London: Routledge, 2009).
28 For a useful examination of sport and cultural imperialism, see A. Guttmann, *Games and Empires: Modern Sports and Cultural Imperialism* (New York: Columbia University Press, 1994), pp. 171–88.

of British rule, the nature of cricket as an imperial game meant that cricket and imperialism became mutually supporting ideologies.[29]

Cricket was originally taken to the Cape by the British military in the period between 1795 and 1802, but the first clubs did not emerge until the 1840s, moving northwards in the 1850s and 1860s. As elsewhere, cricket's imperialists viewed the spread of the game as an indicator of a colony's cultural and social development. Throughout the colonies of southern Africa elite schools such as Bishops in Cape Town and Grey High School in Port Elizabeth were established along the lines of Eton, Harrow and Winchester to propagate this message and English games were naturally part of the curriculum. England batsman and future captain Pelham Warner for one associated South Africa's evolution with the spread of cricket throughout the region: 'Step by step we have forced our way up north, and the cricket-pavilions that have sprung up along our track may almost be called the milestones on the road of the nation's progress', he exclaimed in 1900.[30] Such 'progress' had been rapid as English sport was still in its infancy throughout South Africa going into the 1870s. Only a few clubs had been established in the larger centres such as Cape Town, Pietermaritzburg and Port Elizabeth, and with no regional or national associations having been formed there was little in the form of official competitions or leagues. South Africa was fertile ground for England's empire builders to exert their cultural imperialism through sport.

By now sport had become a constituent part of England's colonization process and the development of the various codes followed a recognizable pattern in their spread throughout the other colonies of southern Africa. The 1890s had witnessed the colonization of Rhodesia (now Zimbabwe) and with it the almost seamless introduction of English sport into the new territory. Even before the historic Pioneer Column of 1890 had reached Fort Salisbury Rhodesian settlers had, according to Winch, already played their first cricket match in the shadow of the hills that overlook the Providential Pass near Fort Victoria.[31] Administration of the game was needed and as early as 1898 the English-styled Rhodesian Cricket Union was formed.

It is clear, then, that cricket's development in southern Africa in the years preceding the Boer War followed closely the path of British imperial expansion. A difficult country to administer, the pioneer cricket officials in South Africa were successful in galvanizing the different centres into a sense of shared 'English' identity through the sport. Within its 'Articles of Constitution' the governing body of South African cricket (the South African Cricket Association) from 1898 divided the colony up into the following districts: Western Province, Eastern Province, Border, Natal (including

---

29 Williams, *Cricket and Race*, p. 1.
30 P.F. Warner, *Cricket in Many Climes* (London: William Heinemann, 1900), p. 176.
31 J. Winch, *Cricket's Rich Heritage: A History of Rhodesian and Zimbabwean Cricket 1890–1982* (Bulawayo: Books of Zimbabwe, 1983), p. i.

Zululand), Transvaal (including Swazieland), Orange Free State (including Basutoland), Griqualand West and Bechuanaland (including Rhodesia).[32]

Formed in the 'style of the MCC',[33] draft rules of the new association were passed at the inaugural congress of delegates, held at Kimberley on Tuesday 8 April 1890.[34] 'The object of the Association', it was stated, 'shall be to foster and develop cricket throughout South Africa' with the onus on promoting cricketing links with the mother country.[35] With its headquarters in Johannesburg, the association from the outset expressed its specific duty in 'the management of Currie Cup Tournaments, and the visits of English teams to South Africa, and South African teams to England'.[36]

As politicians divided South Africa into manageable districts, cricket reinforced English administration through its competition and organization. As it had done in places such as India, English sport would perform the important role in South Africa of imparting a sense of English imperial kinship across an otherwise fragmented and disparate region. Sport's volunteer administrators were pivotal to this process and represented, as Baker suggests, an ethos that made sport an ideal vehicle on which to promote abroad the ideals of Victorian English society.[37]

During this era cricket reinforced a white, colonial exclusivity throughout Southern Africa. The 1886–87 inter-colonial tournament had included a white team from British Bechuanaland (now Botswana) with Rhodesia becoming a member of the South African Cricket Association in the 1904–05 season.[38] The inclusion of these white colonial teams from outside South Africa took precedence over non-white teams from within the country, leading Nauright to argue that 'racial solidarity [became] more crucial [...] than national-based solidarities'.[39] Certainly cricket's colonial community preserved a privileged position within South African society. Surrounded by a large local population linguistically constructed as 'uncivilized', the ability to appropriate English

---

32 Cited in Transvaal Cricket Union. *Yearbook 1898–99* (Johannesburg: M.J. Wood, 1898), p. 5.
33 The view of contemporary cricket journalist Charles Finlason, writing in the *Daily Independent*, 23 November 1888, quoted in J. Winch, *England's Youngest Captain* (Windsor: Windsor Publishers, 2003), p. 185.
34 See J.T. Henderson (ed.), *South African Cricketer's Annual. Season 1889–90* (Durban: Robinson, Vause & Co, 1890), p. 140. The delegates met at Glover's Athletic Bar in Kimberley and voted William Hopley to the chair. He was a respected figure, being a Cape Town advocate with a strong cricket background. Cricket writer and administrator Harry Cadwallader was elected as Hon. Secretary of the new association.
35 See G.A. Parker, *South African Sports. An Official Handbook* (London: Sampson Low, Marston & Co., 1897), p. 47; Transvaal Cricket Union, *Yearbook 1898–99*, p. 5.
36 Parker, *South African Sports*, p. 47.
37 See N. Baker, 'Whose Hegemony? The Origins of the Amateur Ethos in Nineteenth Century English Society', *Sport in History*, 24.1 (2004), pp. 1–16.
38 See L. Duffus, *Play Abandoned* (Cape Town: Timmins, 1969).
39 J. Nauright, *Sport, Cultures and Identities in South Africa* (London: Leicester University Press, 1997), p. 26.

culture and pastimes provided this group with a certain sense of moral power and superiority.

However, while English-speaking whites looked to 'home' origins for their cultural lead, aspects of this culture were inadvertently transferred to the local population. Cricket, as Sandiford claims, may have been a vital element in Anglo-Saxon culture,[40] but it would be incongruous not to explore how the game affected the other sections of South African society. In 1900 Pelham Warner had claimed how 'the natives of whatever race show no anxiety to learn the game, nor do the Dutch, save only those who, from their education, or from their contact with our residents, have grown to be practically Englishmen themselves'.[41] Despite such rhetoric, there is ample evidence to suggest that cricket was being played by the non-English population in the years prior to the Boer War.

By the late nineteenth century distinct cultural groups had emerged within South Africa. Apart from the two white groups, there existed those of mixed race or 'Coloureds' predominantly found in the Cape, migrant workers brought to Natal from the Indian subcontinent as well as the indigenous African peoples present throughout the country. Although there is relatively little known or recorded about the history of black cricket in South Africa, research by Odendaal suggests that its origins date back to shortly after the inauguration of the white game in the country.[42] In the Western Cape the standard of cricket was such that a Malay team was awarded a little-known fixture against W.W. Read's English side of 1891[43] while in the Eastern Cape cricket was particularly well developed among the African population after the game was introduced by missionaries and the first English garrisons. Indeed there were reports of Africans playing cricket in Queenstown as early as 1862 while the first African cricket club was founded in Port Elizabeth in 1869.[44]

While non-white cricketers had proved their proficiency at the game, their involvement in first-class competition was never seriously considered. International fixtures especially remained the realm of the gentleman tourist

---

40 Sandiford argues that apart from dress and language, some observers in the nineteenth century termed cricket the most significant and most visible part of Anglo-Saxon culture. See K.A.P. Sandiford, 'Introduction', in B. Stoddart and K.A.P. Sandiford (eds), *The Imperial Game* (Manchester: Manchester University Press, 1998), p. 2.
41 Warner, *Cricket in Many Climes*, p. 176.
42 Key works by Odendaal on the subject include *Cricket in Isolation* (Cape Town: Don Nelson, 1977); 'South Africa's Black Victorians: Sport and Society in South Africa in the Nineteenth Century', in J.A. Mangan (ed.), *Pleasure, Profit, Proselytism. British Culture and Sport at Home and Abroad 1700–1914* (London: Frank Cass, 1988); and *The Story of an African Game* (Cape Town: David Philip, 2003).
43 The match was arranged as an 'additional' fixture on the itinerary of the tourists and remained the only match to be played in South Africa between a black side and a 'white' touring team until the African XI met Derrick Robins' side in 1973. See Odendaal, *Cricket in Isolation*, p. 325.
44 See R. Archer and A. Bouillon, *The South African Game: Sport and Racism* (London: Zed Books, 1982), p. 79.

whose 'breeding' and skin-colour were as fundamental as his cricketing ability.[45] Organizations such as the South African Coloured Cricket Board, the South African Bantu Cricket Board and South African Indian Cricket Union were initiated by the African, Malay, Indian and Coloured communities in South Africa in order to foster their own involvement in the game.[46] 'That they did so at all', suggests Sandiford, 'speaks volumes for the awesome power of cultural imperialism which, historically, has proved as capable of inspiring mimicry as enforcing obedience.'[47] Inevitably, non-white participation in middle-class sport dwindled as the realization descended that any aspirations of joining the white community as 'equals' would not be fulfilled in sport or in any other sphere of life.

Alongside the South African Cricket Association, cricket's development throughout the regions was aided by a number of wealthy colonial benefactors to the game. Scotsman James Logan, who made his home in the Cape Colony in the late 1870s, has been referred to as 'the second of the three great patrons of [South African] cricket'[48] and was instrumental in the organization of both of England's tours to the continent during the 1890s.[49] Along with Abe Bailey, Logan represented a new age of colonial 'tycoon' in southern Africa who recognized the power of the 'imperial game' in promoting English culture throughout South Africa at the turn of the twentieth century. Logan's support for South African cricket came primarily in the years preceding the Boer War, culminating with his own tour to Britain in 1901. Bailey then took over, following the end of the war, and from 1902 became the game's principal benefactor.[50]

Following his involvement in the foundation of the Imperial Cricket Conference in 1909, Abe Bailey went on to instigate the ill-fated Triangular

45 All internationals in South Africa's pre-1990s history were against white sides. See J. Gemmell, *The Politics of South African Cricket* (London: Taylor & Francis, 2004).
46 Odendaal, *The Story of an African Game*.
47 Sandiford, 'Introduction', pp. 3–4.
48 H.S. Altham and E.W. Swanton, *A History of Cricket* (London: George Allen & Unwin, 1948), p. 311. (The others were Sir Donald Currie and Sir Abe Bailey.)
49 For an analysis of the contribution of James Logan to the development of South African cricket, see D. Allen, 'James Logan and the Development of the Imperial Game', *Sporting Traditions*, 26.1 (2009), pp. 49–69; and D. Allen, '"Cricket's Laird": James Logan', in B. Murray and G. Vahed (eds), *Empire and Cricket: The South African Experience 1884–1914* (Pretoria: UNISA, 2009).
50 In 1907 J.T. Henderson, the editor of the *South African Cricketer's Annual*, detailed the contribution of Bailey to cricket in South Africa since 1902: 'It was mainly though his [Bailey's] instrumentality that the Wanderers Club [of Johannesburg] arranged the visit of the Australian Team of 1902. Two years later Mr. Bailey sent a team to England, which cost him over £2,000; in 1905 he materially assisted the Transvaal Cricket Union in the matter of their M.C.C. guarantee; and when the question arose of sending away the present South African Team, Mr. Bailey came forward with financial assistance. For two seasons past he has paid for a professional coach at the Johannesburg colleges and schools.' J.T. Henderson (ed.), *South African Cricketer's Annual: Season 1906–07* (Pietermaritzburg: Times Printing & Publishing Co., 1907), p. 174.

Tournament of 1912 – a competition between South Africa, England and Australia designed to cement South Africa's place in cricket's 'imperial club' of nations.[51] Prior to the tournament, Bailey proclaimed that 'the cricket result should be a secondary consideration to all lovers of Empire. That a spirit of true national comradeship will be produced must be the desire of every cricketer throughout the King's Dominions.' He added that he hoped that 'the strengthening of the bonds of Union within the Empire [will be] one of the many outcomes of the great Tournament'.[52] It was all part of the rhetoric that had begun decades earlier with the arrival of English imperialism and cricket to the shores of South Africa.

Cricket and Conflict

When the Boer War broke out in 1899 cricket was established in South Africa and its influence would impinge on both sides during the campaign. At the time of war whites constituted only one-fifth of the total population of South Africa, yet the cultural division that existed within this group was all too apparent. Most nineteenth-century Afrikaners were men of the country, their sporting activities confined largely to riding and shooting – skills that made them formidable enemies against the British. English-speaking South Africans, on the other hand, tended to organize themselves in clubs within the towns, a habit given impetus by the soldiers who came to fight Queen Victoria's wars in South Africa and the English-speaking public schools that flourished under British governance. Some of the clubs were formed for a single sport: cricket, rugby, soccer, tennis and cycling. Others, like the Wanderers in Johannesburg and Collegians in Pietermaritzburg, were multi-purpose, with vastly superior facilities.[53] In sport, as in other areas of life, these two diametrically opposed communities could not have been more different.

When war was declared in October 1899, it was generally believed both in England and throughout colonial South Africa that the ragged bands of untrained Boer soldiers could never mount a credible attack on the British army, and that the war would be over by Christmas. But, as history proved, the South African War was set to continue for the next three years. Crucially, within England itself, an era of imperial expansion and cheap military victories had militarized English society to a significant degree during this

---

51   See B. Murray and C. Merrett, *Caught Behind: Race and Politics in Springbok Cricket* (Johannesburg: Wits University Press, 2004), pp. 7–8.

52   A. Bailey, 'Cricket in South Africa', in P.F. Warner (ed.), *Imperial Cricket* (London: London & Counties Press Association, 1912), p. 324.

53   Reader's Digest, *South Africa's Yesterdays* (Cape Town: Reader's Digest Association, 1981), p. 233.

period.[54] Nationalistic and militaristic teaching in schools, cadet corps and boys' associations and involvement in the various organizations connected with the army, such as the volunteers and militia, were all elements that led to militarization during this era.[55] Popular masculinized figures of the time, cricketers included, served in the armed forces and the subject matter of the music halls also conveyed an influence that heightened the nation's awareness of military matters and the role of the army in expanding the empire.[56] Moreover, recruiting figures for the army, the militia, the volunteers and the yeomanry between 1881 and 1898 reveal that just over 22 per cent of the entire male population between the ages of 17 and 40 had some form of military experience just prior to the outbreak of the Boer War.[57] Certainly it would appear that powerful pre-war influences helped shape the popular response to the war itself.

Despite the rhetoric, however, the struggle for control of South Africa came at a time when the maintenance of a demanding empire was beginning to tax an already burdened Britain. The military, the schools and the Church became major tools in securing the foundations of hegemonic control in the colonies and were vital if English imperial influence was to be sustained.[58] The English were aware, according to Green,

> that if insurrection were to rear its ugly head at two or three outposts simultaneously, then their resources, already stretched to the limit, might snap altogether [...] The answer, they felt, lay in a combination of psychological warfare, discipline and decorum, good manners and plenty of churches, propaganda by polite pretext.[59]

In South Africa, cricket increasingly played its part in this process – with the number of cricket tours around the time of the Boer War providing an indication.[60] The relationship between cricket and the expanding empire was already well established by the time of the first English tour to South Africa in 1888–89, prompting the conservative *Blackwood's Magazine* to imperiously exclaim in 1892 how 'the Englishman carries his cricket bat with him as naturally as his gun-case and his India-rubber bath'.[61]

---

54 K.T. Surridge, *Managing the South African War, 1899–1902* (Woodbridge: Boydell Press, 1998), p. 62.

55 Ibid., p. 63.

56 Ibid., p. 63.

57 M.D. Blauch, 'British Society and the War', in P. Warwick and S.B. Spies (eds), *The South African War* (Harlow: Longman, 1980), p. 215.

58 For a useful examination of the relationship between religion, cricket and empire, see Sandiford, 'England', pp. 9–33.

59 B. Green, *A History of Cricket* (London: Guild Publishing, 1988), p. 197.

60 For a detailed account of South African cricket around this period, see D. Allen, *Logan of Matjiesfontein: Cricket, War and Empire in South Africa* (Cape Town: Penstock, forthcoming).

61 Cited in R. Holt, *Sport and the British* (Oxford: Oxford University Press, 1989), p. 6.

Sport continued to be played extensively by both the English and the Boers throughout the conflict. An investigation of military sport exposes its value to both sides during the campaign and highlights cases where sport even crossed the conventional boundaries of politics and warfare.[62] With English forms of sport already established within South Africa by the late 1800s, cricket and rugby in particular were popular among loyalists in the towns and cities when war broke out. Both games represented a discernible link to the British Empire and reinforced key elements of a middle-class, Anglophile culture shared by many within the colonial executive of South Africa.

Cricket remained *the* sport of the English during this era – a product not only of strict social divisions within South Africa but also a legacy of the pre-war tours. In 1888 the first English tour of South Africa took place. Under the management of Major R. Gardner Warton and captained by C.A. Smith, the team played and won two tests against a representative South African side at the Wanderers Club in Johannesburg.[63] For colonial relations the tour was significant in raising the profile of cricket in South Africa and marking the year when the Currie Cup was born. Sir Donald Currie, founder of the Castle Shipping Line, offered the cup as a floating trophy to the South African team that showed the best form against the English tourists. Kimberley were the first recipients in 1888. As with Australia some years earlier, South Africa had seemingly arrived as an accepted cricketing colony and in doing so had strengthened English colonial ties through sport.[64]

South Africa had visited England for the first time in 1894, and Lord Hawke led a troubled tour back to South Africa during the 1895–96 season. Coming at the time of the ill-fated Jameson Raid, Anglo-Boer tensions were at a peak and the tour was constantly shrouded by the political crisis in the country.[65] Three years later Hawke was persuaded by James Logan to bring out a second tour to South Africa. The country, however, had not regained its stability: 'The English had a considerably easier task before them in South Africa when armed with bats and balls than when provided with the more formidable equipment of bullets and bayonets.'[66] The railway line had been extended from Kimberley to Bulawayo in 1897 and two matches were to be played during

---

62 See D. Allen, 'A Far Greater Game: Sport and the Anglo-Boer War', unpublished Masters thesis, University of Stellenbosch, 2002.

63 It would have been common at this time for a team of England's status to have faced teams who batted more than 11 men. England's first game against Western Province, for example, saw them having to dismiss 22 opponents. See M. Lee and R.K. Stent (eds), *Southern Africa at Sport* (Cape Town: Cripple Care Association, 1960), p. 61.

64 For an insight into Australian cricket's colonial past, see W.F. Mandle, *Going it Alone: Australia's National Identity in the Twentieth Century* (Melbourne: Penguin, 1978).

65 For a first-hand account, see Lord Hawke, *Recollections and Reminiscences* (London: Williams and Norgate, 1924). Also see S.H. Pardon (ed.), *John Wisden's Cricketer's Almanack for 1897* (London: John Wisden & Co., 1897).

66 P.C. Standing, *Cricket of To-Day and Tomorrow* (London: Caxton Publishing, [1902]), p. 135.

this tour for the first time in Rhodesia. With players such as Jimmy Sinclair emerging, South African cricket had also shown a remarkable improvement since the previous tour.[67] However, the threat of unrest once again loomed menacingly over the country. Cecil Rhodes had resigned as prime minister of the Cape Colony as a result of the Jameson Raid but was again involved in Cape politics. Lord Milner, governor and high commissioner of the Cape Colony, was in London to discuss the Transvaal problem with the foreign minister, Joseph Chamberlain. The Boer War was imminent.

Bats and Bayonets

As South African sports writer E.J.L. Platnauer reflected in 1908: 'For the next two years there was no cricket [...] a more potent force was at work, making history in another and sterner fashion. Cricketers were transposed into soldiers and fought more serious battles elsewhere.'[68] The onset of hostilities in 1899 brought cricket to a halt in much of South Africa, although the game did not disappear entirely from the veldt. During the first phases of the war the British troops were too busy with the war effort to really indulge in their passion for cricket – but they seized the opportunity to play whenever they could. On Deel's Farm near Bloemfontein on Easter morning of 1900, Lumsden's Horse were 'inches deep in mud. When the rain ceased and sunshine appeared for an hour in the afternoon, they played cricket – reminding them of home no doubt, and of Easter Mondays as the day of all others appropriate to cricket.'[69]

During the guerrilla phase, however, they had the time. When the imperial forces reached Pretoria in June 1900 a cricket match was played on the racecourse to celebrate. The 14th Brigade Bearer Company defeated the 26th Company Royal Engineers by 17 runs.[70] In August 1900 Captain F.D. Price of the 1st Durham Royal Engineers witnessed a match between Major Robert Poore's XI and Pretoria.[71] Poore was the epitome of the English 'cricketing soldier' and had played for Hampshire just before the war. A prolific scorer, from 12 June to 12 August 1898 he had scored 1,399 runs for his county with an average of 116.58.[72] The match of 24 November, however, had to be abandoned as the 9th Company Royal Engineers received orders to proceed to Rustenburg. All play ceased as 'all hands set to work packing up'.[73]

67   R. Knowles, *South Africa versus England: A Test Cricket History* (Cape Town: Sable Media, 1995), p. 35.
68   E.J.L. Platnauer (ed.), *Sport and Pastime in the Transvaal* (Johannesburg: Geo Wunderlich, 1908), p. 20.
69   H.H.S. Pearse, *A History of Lumsden's Horse* (London: Longmans Green, 1903), p. 130.
70   *Pretoria Friend*, 5 July 1900.
71   F.D. Price, *The Great Boer War, 1899–1901. Letters* (York: Boer War Books, 1987), p. 132.
72   B. Green, *The Wisden Book of Obituaries* (London: Queen Ann Press, 1986), p. 716.
73   Price, *Great Boer War*, p. 143.

Figure 1: 'Cricket and War': British soldiers playing cricket while in the front line in South Africa during the Anglo-Boer War. (Source: Public Collection, Anglo-Boer War Museum, Bloemfontein, South Africa)

In support of this, the MCC's journal, *Cricket: A Weekly Record of the Game*, regularly carried features during the war of the game being played in the far reaches of conflict-torn South Africa. The January 1902 edition, for example, highlighted 'cricket at the Modder River', an account submitted by Lieutenant A.U. Udal, a supply officer with the Army Service Corps. Despite problems with boundaries and finding suitable opposition, the game of cricket was clearly important to Udal and the soldiers in his garrison:

> We take a great deal of trouble with our pitch, though it kicks a bit at times, but outside the pitch the ground is very, very broken, and full of thorns [...] and to stop a hard drive at cover or mid-off with a few thorns in the ball takes some doing.[74]

Earlier in the conflict, when Ladysmith was first besieged, the MCC's journal reported how cricket continued in the town and how a match was 'brought to a premature conclusion because the players attracted the shells of the Boers, who did not seem to be of a sporting turn of mind'.[75]

Evidence suggests that cricket was also enjoyed by members of the Republican forces. At the besieged town of Mafeking an extraordinary exchange took place. Towards the end of April 1900 an English patrol inspecting

---

74 A.U. Udal, *Cricket: A Weekly Record of the Game*, 30 January 1902, p. 2.
75 *Cricket: A Weekly Record of the Game*, 25 January 1900, p. 7.

railway lines to the south-west of the town found a letter addressed to Colonel Baden-Powell from Sarel Eloff, commandant of the Johannesburg Commando and one of Paul Kruger's 35 grandsons:

> Dear Sir,
>
> I see in *The Bulawayo Chronicle* that your men in Mafeking play cricket on Sundays, and give concerts and balls on Sunday evenings. In case you will allow my men to join in, it would be very agreeable to me, as here, outside Mafeking, there are seldom any of the fair sex, and there can be no merriment without them being present. In case you would allow this we could spend some of the Sundays, which we still have to get through round Mafeking, and of which there will probably be several, in friendship and unity. During the course of the week, you can let us know if you accept my proposition and I shall then, with my men, be on the cricket field, and at the ballroom at the time so appointed by you.
>
> I remain,
> Your obedient friend,
> Sarel Eloff,
> Commandant.[76]

Baden-Powell, his biographer records,[77] read the letter with a sardonic smile – a Sunday cricket match with the Boers – and sent his answer to the Boer lines under a white flag:

> Sir,
>
> I beg to thank you for your letter of yesterday, in which you propose that your men should come and play cricket with us. I should like nothing better – after the match in which we are at present engaged is over. But just now we are having our innings and have so far scored 200 days not out against the bowling of Cronje, Snyman, Botha and Eloff, and we are having a very enjoyable game.
>
> I remain,
> Yours truly,
> R.S.S. Baden-Powell[78]

That such an exchange might occur in modern warfare may seem unthinkable, yet this incident, although isolated, not only indicates a mutual appreciation for cricket but also the cultural impact of the game during this period.

Apart from sport played in the veldt, the war, it would appear, also had an unexpected effect on the evolution of 'colonial' games within South Africa.

76 Quoted in J. Winch, *Cricket in Southern Africa* (Rosettenville: Windsor, 1997), p. 44.
77 W. Hillcourt, *Baden-Powell, The Two Lives of a Hero* (Cape Town: Heinemann, 1964), p. 197.
78 Quoted in Winch, *Cricket in Southern Africa*, p. 44.

Highlighted through the work of Van der Merwe there is a suggestion that Afrikaners only took up sports such as cricket and rugby en masse after learning the intricacies of the games in British prisoner-of-war camps.[79] In total 27,000 Boers were captured during the war and 24,000 of them were sent to prisoner-of-war camps abroad in the British enclaves of St Helena, Ceylon, India and Bermuda. As Van der Merwe notes, sport came as a natural deliverance from the adversity of the camps and it was during this period that a large percentage of the Boer prisoners were introduced to cricket for the first time.[80] Dispirited and a long way from South African shores, it is not of course without irony that many Boers chose the quintessential game of their captors to see out their sentence.

Given their colonial heritage and the availability of resources, cricket became the favoured sport of the camps in both Ceylon and India, and while the 1901 South Africans were touring the cricket fields of England another contest was taking place. On 5 and 6 July 1901 a match took place between a team of Boer prisoners from Diyatalawa and the Colombo Colts in Ceylon.[81] The Boers, who were given parole for the match, had already established a cricket club at Diyatalawa with a healthy membership of over seventy.[82] 'The Boers can bowl and the Boers can field and they are by no means indifferent performers with the knife and fork but at batting, well one must defer final judgement upon this delicate point until the return match' was the *Ceylon Independent*'s condescending verdict on the Boer's performance.[83] According to the English press the match was 'an example of the influence of the great English game, which made the Briton and Boer forget the dark battlefields of South Africa and join together in cricket's manly toil'.[84]

It was easier of course for the English to be magnanimous at this stage. Resistance from the Boers was fading as the might of imperial power brought the war to its inevitable conclusion. Frequently the captive Boers had joined the English in sporting activities. Cricket it seems, in these distant outposts, had not only been introduced by the English as a means of cultural expression but was now achieving some success in establishing common ground between themselves and those they wished to assimilate.

---

79 F.J.G. Van der Merwe, 'Sport and Games in Boer Prisoner of War Camps during the Anglo-Boer War, 1899–1902', *International Journal of the History of Sport*, 9.3 (1992), pp. 439–55.
80 Ibid.
81 *Ceylon Independent*, 5 and 6 July 1901.
82 According to the *Ceylon Independent*, as a condition of this parole, the team had 'given their word that they would not enter in the discussion of any "controversial" subjects', the press included. *The Ceylon Independent*, 5 July 1901.
83 *The Ceylon Independent*, 6 July 1901.
84 Cited in E.M. Wessels, 'Tog Speelden wij Jolly Cricket!', *Knapsak*, 3.2 (1991), p. 19.

Conclusion

It was, however, not as simple as that. Effectively two models of government and two kinds of society were in competition for mastery of South Africa during the latter part of the nineteenth century. One was British, industrialist and capitalist, based upon profit and intent on unifying South Africa under its control; the other Boer, patriarchal and agrarian, more segregationist and determined to resist imperial pretensions and preserve its independence and traditional prerogatives. What resulted was the Anglo-Boer War of 1899–1902, a conflict that affected the whole future of South Africa, including sport.

For 'Englishness' to be sustained in South Africa during this period it was important that other elements of society be 'persuaded' to adhere to an English way of life. 'Sport was an integral part of this whole process of assimilation and mobilisation', explains Odendaal. 'British games, particularly cricket, which the Victorians regarded as embodying "a perfect system of ethics and morals", were taken almost as seriously as the Bible, the alphabet and the Magna Carta.'[85] And eventually, of course, these sports would supersede traditional, pre-colonial forms of recreation in popularity as England's cultural and political influence became cemented in South Africa during the final decades of the nineteenth century.

With the game a cultural bond of the white imperial fraternity, cricket, in the words of Birley, now became 'the cornerstone of Empire; the citadel of true sporting values'.[86] Providing a training ground for service to empire, the sport countered the insecurity of colonial society by elevating England as the source of all light while at the same time securing its place as a 'sociological and psychological "road map" permitting chosen inhabitants of empire to develop and maintain emotional ties within an ordered, secure environment'.[87] South Africa had seen the sport develop since its early introduction by the British military and by the end of the nineteenth century cricket had become an important social institution, promoting a sense of Englishness and fitting in with the structure and relations of the empire. As elsewhere, cricket in South Africa retained an air of English exclusivity, with Afrikaner reluctance to adopt the sport following the war a pertinent example of the tensions inherent in all hegemonic relationships.[88] The black population would, of course, be

---

85 Odendaal, 'South Africa's Black Victorians', p. 196.
86 Derek Birley, *Land of Sport and Glory. Sport and British Society, 1887–1910* (Manchester: Manchester University Press, 1995), p. 16.
87 J.A. Mangan, 'Britain's Chief Spiritual Export: Imperial Sport as Moral Metaphor, Political Symbol and Cultural Bond', in J.A. Mangan (ed.), *The Cultural Bond: Sport, Empire, Society* (London: Frank Cass, 1992), p. 6.
88 For a discussion on this, see D. Allen, 'Logan's Golden Age: Cricket, Politics and Empire, South Africa, 1888–1910', unpublished PhD thesis, University of Brighton, 2008.

discriminated against throughout all realms of society – a feature not only of South African society but of British colonization everywhere.

The spread of English sport and culture throughout South Africa was further galvanized by the sports tours around the time of the Boer War. Imperialists, empire builders and sports enthusiasts all argued that sport, and cricket in particular, fostered emotional loyalties between England and those who settled in the colonies, with *The Field* claiming in 1896 that:

> The value of international matches at various games between England and her colonies [...] will be found to be equal, if not surpass, as a factor in the manufacture of goodwill, any treaty, commercial or political, that ever was drawn up [...] Our interchange visits for carrying friendly war into another's country by means of bat and ball do eminent service in keeping alive the kindredship of blood.[89]

While English forms of sport were eventually adopted by the local population, for the indigenous elite these sports served an explicitly political function from the outset. Intent on using sport as an instrument of 'improvement' and assimilation, indigenous clubs frequently gave themselves imperial-sounding names. Indeed many middle-class Africans believed respectability could be gained by emulating the social role of practices such as cricket within the white community. 'Despite the obvious contradictions', suggests Odendaal, the African bourgeoisie 'glorified things "British" (the ideal) as against things "colonial" (the reality).'[90] Through sport they felt empowered to assert their own self-conscious class position while paying homage to the classic Victorian ideals of 'civilization', 'progress', 'Christianity' and 'Empire'. Despite such aspirations, the reality of English colonial life was, of course, somewhat different.

In the nineteenth century and for the first half of the twentieth century, the notion of the sports field as a place of equals did not exist. Only those of the same economic class, social status and race played together. The Boer War was fought at a time when South African sport had already evolved under the influence of the English public school system. Sports exemplified class and racial divisions – black and white as well as Boer and Briton – and this was an accepted part of South African society. The English game of cricket epitomized this.

When the war finally came to an end in May 1902, cricket had left its mark. With the game already popular in South Africa, its influence permeated both sides during the conflict, and this was set to continue in the years that followed. The dust of hostilities had barely settled when South Africa received the

---

89 *The Field*, 27 June 1896.
90 Odendaal, 'South Africa's Black Victorians', p. 200.

Australians on their way back from defeating England in the Ashes.[91] This was followed by a third South African tour of Britain in 1904. Colonial ties were being reinforced through cricket. Emergent post-war Afrikaner nationalism would also mean that cricket's association with the ideology of England and imperialism would deepen. The 'Englishman's game' had been established in South Africa and for the English Diaspora it would remain an important symbol of Englishness long after the last shots of the Boer War had been fired.

---

91   See W.H. Coleman, *South Africa versus England and Australia Test Cricket 1888–1928* (London: Old Royalty Book Publishers, 1928), p. 103.

Chapter 12

An Englishman in New York?
Celebrating Shakespeare in America,
1916

Monika Smialkowska

*Now through the Interlude gates, and from all sides, a jocund festival pours into
the illumined space [...]: the folk-festival of Elizabethan England. Simultaneously,
in different parts, as in a merry rural fair, various popular arts and pastimes
begin, and continue together: Morris dancers and pipers, balladists and play-
actors, folk dancers, fiddlers, clowns, and Punch-and-Judy performers romp,
rant, parade, and jingle amongst flower-girls and gay-garbed jesters spangling
by the bright venders' [sic] booths.*[1]

Though recreating a May fair in rural Elizabethan England, the actual re-
enactment of this scene did not occur in the English countryside. Instead, it
was presented in front of thousands of spectators at Lewisohn Stadium in New
York City. The year was 1916 and the occasion was the 300th anniversary of
William Shakespeare's death. As part of the festivities commemorating that
event, New Yorkers participated in Percy MacKaye's 'community masque',
Caliban by the Yellow Sands, which included a '[c]elebration of an Elizabethan
May Day Festival on the outskirts of an English town'.[2]

It may seem peculiar that the inhabitants of a modern American metropolis
should indulge in old-fashioned rural customs in honour of a long-departed
English poet, especially at a time when the United States was experiencing serious socio-political problems, including increased immigration from
eastern and southern Europe and uncertainty as to entering the First World

---

1   Percy MacKaye, *Caliban by the Yellow Sands* (Garden City and New York: Doubleday,
    Page & Co., 1916), p. 110.
2   MacKaye, *Caliban by the Yellow Sands*, title page and p. 196. 'Community masque' was
    a hybrid dramatic form, consisting of dialogue, *tableaux*, group dancing and singing,
    in which amateur performers, drawn from the local community, participated.

War. Even more strangely, *Caliban by the Yellow Sands* was not an isolated event that could be attributed to the eccentric tastes of a prominent individual or group. Across the US, wide sections of American society participated in hundreds of Shakespeare tercentenary tributes, many of which reconstructed the 'merry old England' of the Elizabethan period.[3] With this in mind, this chapter examines the issues of 'Englishness' that were repeatedly broached in American Shakespeare tercentenary celebrations. To what extent was Shakespeare seen as 'English' by their participants? What was their definition of 'Englishness' and why were they so fascinated with it? And, finally, what purposes did that version of 'Englishness' serve in 1916 and how was it adapted to fit the American context? To answer these questions, the idea of Elizabethan England promoted by the tercentenary entertainments will be explored, together with their representations of Shakespeare and Elizabeth I.

Adopting Shakespeare while Rejecting 'Englishness'

The adoption of Shakespeare into the American literary canon has not been unproblematic. As Michael Bristol suggests, 'Shakespeare's centrality in American culture may be construed as a kind of anomaly.'[4] This is due to Shakespeare's association with the 'old world' and its aristocratic and monarchical structures of authority, inimical to American democratic principles. Kim Sturgess connects this with a concept of 'Englishness' that Americans have repudiated since the War of Independence:

> [T]he American state was conceived in direct opposition to England and [...] throughout the following century, Americans created and celebrated an image of the 'English enemy' that helped to unite the population and, in the process, to define the American nation. Prior to the threats posed in the twentieth century by Communism and more recently 'terrorism', England, with her trade empire, was considered to be the primary danger to the continued success of the American 'revolution'.[5]

Consequently, had Americans 'followed the rhetoric of the original leaders of the Revolution', Sturgess argues, they 'might have been expected to reject Shakespeare as an unwanted English anachronism'.[6] Yet by the nineteenth century they had not only embraced Shakespeare, they had made his work

---

3   For an overview of the American Shakespeare tercentenary tributes, see Monika Smialkowska, '"A democratic art at a democratic price": American Celebrations of the Shakespeare Tercentenary, 1916', *Transatlantica*, 1 (2010), http://transatlantica.revues.org/4787 (accessed 3 March 2011).

4   Michael D. Bristol, *Shakespeare's America, America's Shakespeare* (London: Routledge, 1990), p. 2.

5   Kim C. Sturgess, *Shakespeare and the American Nation* (Cambridge: Cambridge University Press, 2004), p. 10.

6   Ibid., p. 3.

central to their own national identity, excepting him from their overall rejection of 'Englishness'.[7] This is exemplified in the way that American newspapers used a quote from *Henry VI Part One* to celebrate victory over the British army at the Battle of New Orleans in 1815. As Sturgess observes, the papers' anti-Englishness did not extend to Shakespeare: 'while the English were seen as defeated "wolves", the nationality of Shakespeare was ignored'.[8]

The Shakespeare Tercentenary in the US: Renegotiating 'Englishness'

Interestingly, however, American 1916 tercentenary celebrations often foregrounded Shakespeare's English roots rather than ignoring or obscuring them. This was frequently done through recreating popular English customs of Shakespeare's era. Probably the most large-scale reconstruction of such customs was the one included in the New York production of *Caliban by the Yellow Sands* mentioned at the beginning of this chapter. However, similar activities were organized for the Shakespeare tercentenary across the nation. In the months leading up to the celebrations, tercentenary activists recommended making performances of traditional English songs, dances and games an important part of the forthcoming festivities. A booklet of *Suggestions for Exercises in Elementary Schools*, prepared by the Committee for Supplementary Celebrations of the New York Shakespeare Tercentenary, advocates involving children in such pastimes. Among other suggested activities, the booklet includes 'Old English Singing Games', such as 'London Bridge' and 'The Jolly Miller'; 'Old English Games and Dances', such as 'Three Dukes' and 'Brighten Camp'; and 'Old English Dances', such as 'Gathering Peascods' and 'Maypole Dance'.[9] Similarly, a manual prepared by the Drama League of America for schools and colleges made 'a special plea for the type of Old English May Day Festival', explaining: 'It is in this way that the folk-spirit, school-spirit and community-spirit may best be introduced.'[10]

This promotion of Elizabethan folk customs and their community-building effects belonged to the vogue for mediaeval and Renaissance culture that, as David Glassberg demonstrates, developed in the US at the turn of the twentieth century. This trend was initiated by American intellectual elites, who were trying to improve the state of the nation's cultural and leisure

---

7 Ibid., p. 47.
8 Ibid., p. 35.
9 *New York City Shakespeare Tercentenary Celebration: Suggestions for Exercises in Elementary Schools* (New York: Department of Education, 1916), pp. 4–9, courtesy of Dartmouth College Library.
10 Drama League of America, *The Shakespeare Tercentenary: Suggestions for School and College Celebrations of the Tercentenary of Shakespeare's Death in 1916*, ed. Percival Chubb (Washington DC: National Capital Press, [n.d.]), p. 12.

pursuits, rescuing them from 'rowdyism and commercialism' and giving them a sense of beauty and moral integrity.[11] As Glassberg points out, Elizabethan England – 'the land of their ancestors' – was particularly attractive for these cultural reformers, offering 'artistic alternatives to the drabness of modern industrialism and the wanton revelry of commercial amusements, while reinforcing social order and the nation's Anglo-American identity'.[12] Recreating versions of Elizabethan England was a way of promoting the centrality and alleged superiority of a specific cultural strand: the Anglo-American heritage of the nation's established elites.

This can be seen as part of Americans' ongoing engagement with their English heritage in the process of defining their nationhood. As Sturgess points out, as a result of territorial expansion and the need to consolidate its increasing dominions and heterogeneous population, the nineteenth-century US sought a unifying identity that would help to justify its emerging imperial ambitions. This identity was found in the concept of 'Anglo-Saxonism', which came to denote the allegedly superior heritage of the early American settlers. Thus constructed, Anglo-Saxon identity was associated with such qualities as the love of freedom and democracy, as well as the dominance of the English language and cultural achievement.[13] Crucially, however, Sturgess argues that Anglo-Saxonism and Englishness were not identical: the first term denoted cultural and 'racial' heritage, and the second 'the political system of England', a distinction that helped Americans 'celebrate a cultural inheritance, while at the same time reject[ing] the political entity called England'.[14] It is important, however, to note that Sturgess classifies the 'differentiation between good – i.e. Anglo – and bad – i.e. English – cultural dominance' as 'subtle' and 'complex'.[15] In practice it seems difficult, if not impossible, to separate cultural heritage fully from the political system within which it developed, and the boundaries between the two may not always be clearly demarcated.

The figure of Elizabeth I is symptomatic in this respect: while she was associated with desirable elements of cultural heritage – the romanticized 'merry old England' and the 'golden age' of the Elizabethan Renaissance – she

---

11   David Glassberg, *American Historical Pageantry: The Uses of Tradition in the Early Twentieth Century* (Chapel Hill, NC: University of North Carolina Press, 1990), pp. 34–40 (p. 35).
12   Ibid., p. 37.
13   Sturgess, *Shakespeare and the American Nation*, pp. 99–121. See also Robert J. C. Young, *The Idea of English Ethnicity* (Malden, MA: Blackwell, 2008), esp. pp. 177–95. For applications of the ideas of Anglo-American identity building to the Shakespeare tercentenary, see Thomas Cartelli, *Repositioning Shakespeare: National Formations, Postcolonial Appropriations* (London: Routledge, 1999), pp. 63–83; and Coppélia Kahn, 'Caliban at the Stadium: Shakespeare and the Making of Americans', *Massachusetts Review*, 41.2 (2000), pp. 256–84.
14   Sturgess, *Shakespeare and the American Nation*, p. 108.
15   Ibid., p. 108.

was also undeniably part of the political system of aristocratic and monarchical privilege. Faced with such ambivalent situations, Americans constantly needed to negotiate what constituted suitable forms of Anglo-Saxon heritage and what came close to the unpalatable English power structures. *Shakespeare, the Playmaker* is a tercentenary tribute that illustrates these negotiations particularly well.[16] By focusing on the representations of Shakespeare, Elizabeth I and Elizabethan England in that text, this chapter traces the attempts to define an 'Englishness' acceptable to 1916 America.

Defining 'Englishness' in North Dakota: *Shakespeare, the Playmaker*

Shakespeare, the Playmaker was 'a communal masque designed and written by a group of twenty students at the University of North Dakota to commemorate the tercentenary of the death of William Shakespeare'.[17] It was performed on 12 and 13 June 1916 at the outdoor Bankside Theatre on campus. This entertainment is notable for its sustained engagement with Elizabethan and Jacobean England. Its two main parts (framed by a prologue, interlude and epilogue) are set in English locations during Shakespeare's lifetime, and introduce many historical figures from the period. The first part of the masque takes place in Greenwich on the Thames, in 1588, on *'the eve of the Armada'*.[18] It consists of a welcome offered by local inhabitants to Queen Elizabeth, who arrives with her court from London (see Figure 1). The simple folk greet her with a song and present her with a country dance and a badly botched performance of 'Pyramus and Thisbe', penned by the as-yet-unknown playwright, William Shakespeare. As the director of the entertainment, Frederick Koch, explains in his prefatory statement, 'this portion of the masque [was] designed to suggest a possible origin for the Players' Scenes from *A Midsummer Night's Dream*'.[19] The second part of *Shakespeare, the Playmaker*, presenting a May fair in Gravesend on the Thames, happens about twenty years after the first episode. During the fair Shakespeare – now an established playwright – encounters

---

16 Lyle M. Bittinger et al., *The Book of Shakespeare, The Playmaker, Written in Collaboration by Twenty Students of The University of North Dakota, Under the Direction of Professor Frederick H. Koch of the Department of English, Designed for the Shakespeare Tercentenary Commemoration by The Sock and Buskin Society, for Presentation at The Bankside Theatre on the Campus of The University of North Dakota* (Grand Forks, ND: University of North Dakota, 1916); repr. from *The Quarterly Journal of the University of North Dakota*, 6.4 (July, 1916), pp. 309–64.
17 Frederick H. Koch, 'Communal Play Making', in Bittinger et al., *Shakespeare, The Playmaker*, pp. 7–8 (p. 7).
18 Bittinger et al., *Shakespeare, The Playmaker*, p. 21.
19 Frederick H. Koch, 'Shakespeare, the Playmaker', in Bittinger et al., *Shakespeare, The Playmaker*, pp. 9–10 (p. 10).

Figure 1: Greeting Elizabeth I in *Shakespeare, the Playmaker* (Courtesy of the Department of Theatre Arts, University of North Dakota)

travellers returning from the New World. The stories and 'souvenirs' they bring from their voyages inspire him to conceive the idea of *The Tempest*.

Thus, against the background of Shakespeare's plays and imaginary episodes from his life, both parts of the masque retell significant moments of English history, focusing in particular on the averted Spanish invasion of 1588 and on the beginnings of colonial expansion. Through this quasi-historical reconstruction, the entertainment develops its interpretation of 'Englishness' and America's English heritage, producing ambiguities, contradictions and blind spots that provide an insight into the ideological manoeuvres required to mould Shakespeare and his England in ways that suited the needs of the US in 1916.

The masque clearly uses Shakespeare's work and historical period in such a way as to make them point directly to America. In his introductory notes, Koch spells this out explicitly in relation to the second part of the entertainment: 'The entire conception is designed to portray Shakespeare's interpretation of the New World.'[20] Moreover, in the masque's prologue, the visionary Astrologer credits Shakespeare with the power of presaging America's development up to the present day:

> [Shakespeare's] own prophetic gaze
> Looks out across the rolling deep, to this
> Fair continent, America, wherein
> A newborn race shall rise to praise his name
> After three centuries.[21]

---

20   Ibid., p. 10.
21   Bittinger et al., *Shakespeare, The Playmaker*, p. 20.

While Shakespeare becomes America's prophet, the masque itself envisages 'a new heaven and a new earth for Elizabethan England'.[22] This apocalyptic phrase can be taken to mean that Elizabethan England is not ideal and will only find its perfected version in the New World across the Atlantic. It also implies that the masque will engage in a project of 'renewing' or reconstructing Elizabethan England in such a way that it may provide an acceptable heritage from which can arise the 'newborn race' of the American nation.

In this respect, the masque's time-frame seems significant. With its first part taking place in 1588 and the second part about twenty years later, the entertainment encompasses two distinct historical periods, Elizabethan and Jacobean, even though Koch explicitly mentions only the former. However, the masque claims that it is the latter period that *represents the full fruition of English national life*.[23] This poses a number of questions. First, what is the difference between the two historical moments and why does the masque represent the later one as more fully developed in relation to the English national life? And, secondly, why is this allegedly more developed period subsumed into its predecessor's designation, rather than named accurately after the ruler who was then on the throne? A closer examination of the masque offers some answers to these questions.

The First Part: Elizabethan England

The entertainment's first part presents Elizabethan England at a moment of imminent crisis – a country under threat of invasion by the Spanish Armada. Nevertheless, its common citizens are full of simple joy, embodying the conventional image of 'merry old England'. At the beginning of the episode, '*A group of sailors, a jester, a number of tradesmen, and the village folk enter. The sailors join gayly [sic] with the villagers in a lively dance, while the merchants and their wives look gravely on with evident enjoyment*.'[24] This stage direction paints a picture of a happy community, uniting disparate groups in pursuit of wholesome rustic pleasures.

Moreover, the commoners in this episode are filled with patriotic devotion to their queen and country. They greet Elizabeth with a song containing the following words:

> God save Britannia's queen;
> God save her majesty. [...]
> Bless this her isle, her royal seat [...]
> This thronéd isle, this home of kings,
> This land where laughter ever rings [...]

---

22 Koch, 'Shakespeare, the Playmaker', p. 9.
23 Bittinger et al., *Shakespeare, The Playmaker*, p. 39.
24 Ibid., p. 21.

Let every loyal British son,
Support the right 'till life is done.[25]

It is worth noting that the masque anachronistically uses the terms 'Britannia' and 'British' instead of 'England' and 'English' here, despite the fact that this episode takes place before even the perfunctory unification of England and Scotland under James I in 1603. This appears even more striking when one considers the echoes between this song and John of Gaunt's famous speech from *Richard II*:

This royal throne of kings, this sceptred isle,
This earth of majesty, this seat of Mars [...]
This blessèd plot, this earth, this realm, this England [...][26]

The phrases 'throne of kings' and 'sceptred isle', which in John of Gaunt's speech refer to England, in the masque become 'home of kings' and 'thronèd isle' and are applied to Britain. This may be simply the result of a common slippage between the terms 'England' and 'Britain': overall, the masque is not consistent in applying these terms or the symbols associated with them. For example, Elizabeth arrives in a *'royal barge, displaying a banner which bears the red cross of St. George on a white ground',*[27] not the Union Jack. However, the use of the words 'Britannia' and 'British' here may be considered significant. The song, apart from *Richard II*, clearly echoes 'God save the King/ Queen', an anthem associated not so much with Elizabethan England as with the British Empire. In a similarly anachronistic manner, earlier on in the masque Elizabeth is called 'the Empire queen'.[28] These associations fit with the masque's concern with the exploration and colonization of the New World.

The interest in colonial enterprise, which comes to dominate the second part of the masque, is already strongly indicated in the first part. Surrounding Queen Elizabeth in the first episode are iconic sea adventurers of the period: Francis Drake, Walter Raleigh, Martin Frobisher and John Hawkins.[29] Moreover, the conflict with Spain is presented not only as the matter of a potential invasion of England, but also in the context of the competition for

---

25 Ibid., p. 27. It should be noted that this song, together with the entire Armada episode, can be read as expressing American solidarity with Britain in the First World War, which the US had not yet entered.
26 William Shakespeare, *The Life and Death of King Richard the Second*, in *William Shakespeare: Complete Works*, ed. Jonathan Bate and Eric Rasmussen (Houndmills: Macmillan, 2008), pp. 833–91, II.i.40–50.
27 Bittinger et al., *Shakespeare, The Playmaker*, p. 26.
28 Ibid., p. 19.
29 Young points out that these explorers were established in the Victorian period as 'the resourceful English of the incipiently Protestant Elizabethan age [...] exemplifying the greatest qualities of the English in the epic formation of the nation.' Young, *The Idea of English Ethnicity*, p. 217.

colonial supremacy. Francis Drake makes this clear when he says: 'Ah, what care we for Spanish strength? [...] England yet will win for herself a place upon the seas and in the New World.'[30] The masque presents England's predicted victory as due not to the superior strength of the English fleet or arms but to the fine qualities of Englishmen. Lord Howard sees Spanish sailors as inferior to English ones: 'all their fine men are not such as England's seamen',[31] later elaborating: 'Methinks our ships are not enough, or of a size to oppose such enemies. But England's spirit doth not wait for weapons.'[32]

The Interlude: Looking Forward to America

This belief in 'England's spirit' carries over to the interlude that bridges the first and second part of the masque. The Astrologer, who plays the choric role in the entertainment, proclaims England's victory over the Armada thus:

> From vale and hill the voice
> Of Freedom sounded: "Britons, strong and firm,
> Your children yet unborn cry out to you –
> Make good your answer!" [...]
> [England's] sons arose
> And met the foe in deadly combat – fought
> And won; for nature's elements combined
> To crush the enemy. The stars, which in
> Their courses fought against the Spanish might
> Rejoiced to see the land of England saved.[33]

This speech attributes the military triumph to the Britons' qualities of strength, firmness and love of freedom.[34] It also makes a claim that the English cause was favoured by nature and fate: 'nature's elements' and 'the stars'. These ideas are not dissimilar to those of the advocates of the concept of 'manifest destiny' in America.[35] Moreover, the masque makes a connection between the allegedly natural superiority of Elizabethan 'Britons' and the qualities of their American descendants. The 'children yet unborn' can be interpreted as those who will come to inhabit the 'New World' across the ocean. This interpretation is supported by the answer that the Chorus of Stars makes to the Astrologer's speech:

---

30 Bittinger et al., *Shakespeare, The Playmaker*, p. 26.
31 Ibid., p. 25.
32 Ibid., p. 35.
33 Ibid., p. 37.
34 This extract is also a good example of the way in which the masque often uses the terms 'Britain/British' and 'England/English' interchangeably.
35 See Sturgess, *Shakespeare and the American Nation*, pp. 101–02.

Yes, England's spirit won that day
And set the land forever free;
And that same spirit found its way
To waiting lands beyond the sea![36]

The Second Part: Jacobean England

Thus, the masque's first part and interlude establish some of the key characteristics of the 'English spirit' embodied in the Elizabethan period – merry disposition, loyalty, courage and love of freedom – and a connection between this spirit and America. What may be puzzling, however, is that the entertainment seems to suggest that this image of Elizabethan England is somehow imperfect and in need of further improvement. The second part of the masque promises to present this improved version:

> *The scene is Gravesend, a little Kentish village on the Thames, where ships from foreign lands discharge their cargoes, and where, in Elizabethan times, visitors from abroad were formally welcomed by the London Corporation. Some twenty years have elapsed since the coming of the Armada, and the scene represents the full fruition of English national life.*
>
> [...] *In another part of the village, a May fair is in progress and at intervals the shouts of the merry-makers break the stillness. [...] A group of townsmen bearing a Maypole enter.*[37]

Only now, some twenty years after the defeat of the Armada, does 'English national life' seem to have reached its 'full fruition'. What has changed in those twenty years to bring about this sense of completion, and what is the masque's definition of the fully formed 'English national life'? At first sight it seems that the changes have not been great: the rustic setting, the presence of the merry-makers and especially the Maypole suggest the familiar image of 'merry old England'. However, the indication is that this England is becoming much more business-orientated than its Elizabethan predecessor: the quay on the Thames has by now developed into a busy trade port, 'where ships from foreign lands discharge their cargoes'.

The imagery of thriving commercialism saturates the second part of the masque. It is telling that the rustic entertainments presented in the first episode were partly a spontaneous expression of merriment and partly an offering to the queen. In the second part, however, these entertainments belong to a May fair, represented not only as a communal festival but also as a bustling site of commercial activity.[38] Here, traditional folk characters and

---

36 Bittinger et al., *Shakespeare, The Playmaker*, p. 37.
37 Ibid., p. 39.
38 For an analysis of the ambiguities of the Early Modern marketplace as both a place of communal pastimes and of commercial exchanges, see Peter Stallybrass and Allon

popular pastimes appear against the backdrop of buying, selling, bargaining and vendors' hawking cries.[39] This fair is also a place of business competition: '*Peter Bloff, the peddler, incessantly crying his wares, tries to drown the voice of the monger, who is proclaiming his latest ballad.*'[40] When the action of the second part of the masque begins on the idyllic village green, a pastoral song 'It was a lover and his lass' from Shakespeare's *As You Like It* is heard.[41] However, when the May fair starts, the vocabulary soon becomes concerned with trade, as Bloff sings a pedlar's song from *The Winter's Tale*:

> Will you buy any tape,
> Or lace for your cape [...]?
> Come to the pedlar;
> Money's a meddler,
> That doth utter all men's ware'a![42]

The noise of commerce mixes with and competes with the folk pastimes. While Robin Hood and his troupe perform the Morris dance, '*the children swarm about the pastry cooks who have been crying their wares thruout [sic] the scene.*'[43] Vendors' cries of 'Come buy! Come buy!' provide a backdrop for the antics of the hobby horse.[44] Some of the carnival pastimes themselves have commercial underpinnings. When a puritan complains about a 'witch' chasing local children, the mayor replies: 'Fool! Know you not that yon witch is none but Widow Goodman *hired* to be our witch this day?'[45] Similarly, a puppet show is not an amateur offering but a paid performance at '[t]woppence apiece'.[46]

Interestingly, most of the quotations used in this scene come not from one of Shakespeare's 'festive' comedies but from Ben Jonson's city comedy, *Bartholomew Fair*.[47] Thus, the masque's representation of 'the full fruition

---

White, *The Politics and Poetics of Transgression* (Ithaca, NY: Cornell University Press, 1986), pp. 27–79.

39 Bittinger et al., *Shakespeare, The Playmaker*, pp. 39–43.
40 Ibid., p. 41.
41 Ibid., p. 39.
42 Ibid., p. 42.
43 Ibid., p. 45.
44 Ibid., p. 42.
45 Ibid., p. 46; the emphasis is mine.
46 Ibid., p. 44.
47 According to C.L. Barber, 'festive comedies', such as *A Midsummer Night's Dream*, *Twelfth Night* or *As You Like It*, lead to resolution of conflict through the inversion of normal social roles and communal merry-making. See C.L. Barber, *Shakespeare's Festive Comedy: A Study of Dramatic Form and Its Relation to Social Custom* (Princeton, NJ: Princeton University Press, repr. 1972 [1959]). City comedies, on the other hand, tend to be satirical and often expose social vices without remedying them. See Brian Gibbons, *Jacobean City Comedy: A Study of Satiric Plays by Jonson, Marston and Middleton* (London: Methuen, 2nd edn, 1980 [1968]).

of English national life' is based to a significant extent on a play in which the action is motivated by greed and amoral behaviour, and which teems with cheating, stealing and excess. At first sight, this may seem like an odd model for Americans to imitate. However, perhaps the city comedy's concern with the energy and opportunities, as well as the pitfalls, of the emerging seventeenth-century capitalism suited American needs better than the quaint, wholesome, yet feudal image afforded by an unmediated Elizabethan pastoral setting.

The representation of early capitalist enterprise is further developed and combined with colonial expansion in the last section of the masque, which deals with Shakespeare's encounter with the travellers returning from the New World. In this scene, based on motifs from *The Tempest*, the participants of the May fair – Shakespeare among them – are confronted with stories, an artefact and two native inhabitants brought over from America.[48] Strikingly, the masque's English characters see the exploration of the New World in terms of financial gain. One of the returning sailors, John Holdsworth, says explicitly that he and his companions 'set forward to discover gold'.[49] Moreover, he admits that he 'filched' a painting of an Indian god from the sleeping natives, and he proceeds to make money by displaying it as a curiosity: '*The entire crowd is now giving attention, and Holdsworth seizes the opportunity to take up a collection.*'[50] Similarly, John Oxenham talks about strange, monstrous inhabitants of the New World: 'men like fish, and fish like men. [...] A very hagseed, a race which none would own.' However, he immediately acknowledges that owning one of those hybrids would indeed be profitable: 'Had I one such in England, 'twould make my fortune on a holiday.'[51] This confirms the masque's representation of 'holidays', such as the May fair, as money-making opportunities rather than just as occasions for community building. Moreover, England at the beginning of the seventeenth century is pictured as an outward-looking country, seeking to make profit out of colonial expansion. Twenty years after the Armada, England no longer fears foreign invasion; instead, it is becoming a major player on the world stage.

The final important difference between the masque's representations of England in 1588 and twenty years later lies in the attitudes towards royalty and aristocratic privilege displayed in both scenes. The first part of the masque

48 In the performance they were played by two Chippewas from the local reservation.
49 Bittinger et al., *Shakespeare, The Playmaker*, p. 48.
50 Ibid., p. 49.
51 Ibid., p. 54. There are echoes of Shakespeare's *The Tempest* here (Prospero's description of Caliban as 'hag-seed' and Stephano's speculations of potential gain to be made by putting Caliban on show in England). See *The Tempest*, in *William Shakespeare: Complete Works*, ed. Bate and Rasmussen, pp. 6–51, I.ii.426 and II.ii.24–28. For an outline of the interpretations of Caliban in the context of American colonization, see Alden T. Vaughan and Virginia Mason Vaughan, *Shakespeare's Caliban: A Cultural History* (Cambridge: Cambridge University Press, 1991), pp. 118–43.

is firmly set within a monarchical system. Elizabeth I and her courtiers are among the key characters; the reason for the festival is to pay homage to the queen on her visit. Even before her arrival, the visual images that dominate the scene are a *'temporary throne'* prepared for Elizabeth and *'a partially decorated arch mark[ing] the landing place of the royal party'*.[52] Similarly, the song that is repeated throughout the episode, 'God save Britannia's queen', is full of regal imagery. The queen's landing at the quay is the epitome of pomp and majesty:

> When the barge stops at the landing, Lord Leicester and Sir Walter Raleigh very ceremoniously assist the Queen to the quay. The Usher of the Black Rod advances to meet her, pages carry a canopy above her, and the two ladies-in-waiting carry her train. The crowd cheers in wild enthusiasm.[53]

As the crowd's cheers demonstrate, the prevailing hierarchical system is not only deeply entrenched but also generally accepted.

The second part of the masque presents a very different picture, with royalty and aristocracy conspicuously absent. The highest representatives of power present in this scene are civic authorities: the mayor of the town and two constables. There are only two passing references to the king in this part of the masque, neither mentioning his name. One is almost an afterthought when a townsman raises a toast to the tapster: 'Good drawer of ale, here's to you and – the King – God save him!'[54] This is a far cry from the persistent repetition of 'God save Britannia's queen' in the first part of the entertainment. The other reference to the king is perhaps even more telling. It occurs when the mayor describes Shakespeare as 'the friend of common folk no less than a king's favorite'.[55] The tone here becomes egalitarian, with common folk valued 'no less' than a monarch.

Overall, the 'full fruition of English national life', which *Shakespeare, the Playmaker* locates at the beginning of the seventeenth century, is characterized by several distinctive features. It seems less bound by monarchical and aristocratic hierarchy than the preceding Elizabethan period. Indeed, hereditary privilege in the second part of the masque is obscured and replaced by more democratic, civic forms of power. Another characteristic of the 'fully developed' English life in the masque is the emphasis on business and trade. The scene teems with commercial energy, and business acumen seems to have become the dominant characteristic of the 'English spirit'. This strong focus on enterprise pertains both to the domestic setting and to the budding colonial venture, which now plays an important role in English national life.

---

52 Bittinger et al., *Shakespeare, The Playmaker*, p. 21.
53 Ibid., p. 26.
54 Ibid., p. 46.
55 Ibid., p. 43.

Problems with Constructing Acceptable 'Englishness' in America

Thus, a close analysis of *Shakespeare, the Playmaker* reveals a process of constructing a version of 'Englishness' that will constitute an acceptable heritage for the US at the beginning of the twentieth century. This 'Englishness' consists of the characteristics that can be easily applied to Americans: love of freedom and democratic institutions, commercial energy and enterprising spirit. Constructing this heritage, however, requires a considerable imaginative and conceptual effort, involving historical inaccuracies, contradictions and the overlooking of inconvenient facts.

In *Shakespeare, the Playmaker*, the crucial blind spot lies in incorporating the Jacobean period under the label of 'Elizabethan England' and almost entirely writing James I out of history, while simultaneously proposing that the time when he reigned was the epitome of 'English national life'. In fact, favouring Queen Elizabeth over James I was a common feature in American Shakespeare tercentenary tributes. Unlike James, Elizabeth appears as a character in several dramatic entertainments, including a pageant produced in Atlanta, a masque performed in Wellesley, Massachusetts, and another masque published in *The Drama* in 1915 as a template for organizing Shakespeare celebrations across the nation in the following year.[56] Similarly, the Drama League of America's suggestions for celebrating the tercentenary in schools include a 'processional' with 'a third-grade boy representing Shakespeare [...] or a third-grade girl representing Queen Elizabeth'.[57] Representing James I is not proposed. Later on, the same publication claims that Shakespeare 'appealed to the stirring, youthful age of Elizabeth' and associates him with 'Elizabethan vitality', while ignoring the fact that a significant part of his career belonged to the Jacobean period.[58]

The focus on Elizabeth and the marginalization of James seems to be a significant factor in American constructions of an acceptable 'English' heritage. A number of reasons for this phenomenon can be proposed, among them James I's Scottish, rather than English, origins, as well as his association with the increased absolutism under the Stuart dynasty, inimical to American republicanism. Another possibility is that Elizabeth may have been seen as a more malleable figure for Anglo-American heritage making because of her gender. It is plausible that, in order to make the image of monarchy less

---

56 Armond Carroll, *A Pageant and Masque for the Shakespeare Tercentenary* (Atlanta, GA: Atlanta Center, Drama League of America, 1916); Isabelle Fiske Conant, *Will o' the World: A Shakespearean Tercentenary Masque* (Wellesley, MA: Mangus Printing, 1916); Alice C.D. Riley, *The Lover's Garden: A Flower Masque, Arranged from Shakespeare for the Tercentenary*, in *The Drama*, 20 (November 1915), pp. 695–714.

57 Drama League of America, *The Shakespeare Tercentenary*, p. 5.

58 Ibid., p. 47.

threatening and more palatable to their anti-monarchical society, Americans chose to represent it under a feminized guise, as something that contributed to their heritage but was powerless to jeopardize their democratic ideals.

In this respect, it is significant that *Shakespeare, the Playmaker* foregrounds the queen's stereotypically 'feminine' characteristics. The stage direction that introduces her specifies that *'paint and powder, as well as the ravages of time, are visible on her face'*,[59] hinting at her vanity and concern with her appearance. Moreover, she is represented as capricious and unpredictable. When the threat of the Spanish Armada is being debated, she *'interrupts and prevents further discussion'*, saying: 'Such trifles well can wait. Let us a-hawking go.'[60] When Leicester tries to object, she silences him with: 'My Lord of Leicester, think you we know not our own minds? You are ever ready to suggest other than we.'[61] Subsequently, she *'rises slightly from her throne and strikes his ear with her fan'*.[62] The queen's behaviour, especially her use of the epitome of feminine paraphernalia, the fan, implies a gendered representation. Simultaneously, her petulant words and blithe disregard of the matters of state in favour of frivolous pleasures infantilize her. If she embodies an epoch, then, it is the 'stirring, youthful age of Elizabeth',[63] which perhaps can be indulgently accepted as America's distant childhood, which the nation has by now outgrown.

Moreover, Elizabeth I, under her familiar nickname of 'good Queen Bess',[64] becomes a romanticized figure of folklore, associated more closely with the semi-mythical 'merry old England' than with the sphere of real-life politics. As such, she can perhaps be fictionalized, manipulated and shaped into whatever suits American needs more easily than James I, for whom no such persona exists. Within the sphere of popular perceptions and folklore, it becomes possible to conflate features of different historical periods, selecting their most convenient aspects and obscuring those that do not fit into the acceptable image of Anglo-American heritage.

Shakespeare, the Playmaker describes this heritage as 'the realm of Shakespeare and of good Queen Bess'.[65] While this phrase uses royal vocabulary, it applies it to a popular playwright and to a queen who has been made to sound folksy and familiar. This implies that the masque's authors were interested in cultural heritage – literature and popular imagery – rather than in accurately reproducing the period's socio-political background. In terms of Sturgess's analysis, the masque pays tribute to 'a cultural inheritance' while

---

59 Bittinger et al., *Shakespeare, The Playmaker*, p. 26.
60 Ibid, p. 35.
61 Ibid.
62 Ibid., p. 36.
63 Drama League of America, *The Shakespeare Tercentenary*, p. 47.
64 Bittinger et al., *Shakespeare, The Playmaker*, pp. 37, 40.
65 Ibid., p. 37.

rejecting 'the political system of England'.[66] This, however, is only possible through painstaking manipulation of historical facts and figures, which often reveals its own fictionality.

Conclusion: A Fractured Anglo-American Identity

In effect, the American Shakespeare tercentenary activists were engaged in constructing an Anglo-American identity that could consolidate the US's disparate ethnic groups, while also justifying the nation's increasingly dominant position on the world arena.[67] The English language and culture, epitomized by Elizabethan England and its most famous son, Shakespeare, seemed to be the perfect tools for achieving these goals. Using them, however, was riddled with pitfalls: it could bring America too close for comfort to political structures inimical to its republican traditions. Hence, delicate negotiations were needed, and even those did not always manage to cover all the ideological contradictions that emerged when trying to adopt an 'Anglo-Saxon' heritage but reject the 'English' political system.

These contradictions are most clearly revealed in the tensions between democratic and hierarchical notions of culture, which surface in the literature of the tercentenary. American contributors often emphasize that their intention is to present Shakespeare as 'the playmaker and poet of the people'[68] and a 'democrat'.[69] However, the vocabulary of monarchy and empire tends to sneak into the ways in which Shakespeare and the English language are described by the American tercentenary tributes. For example, Albert Hatton Gilmer entitled his tercentenary masque *King Shakespeare*,[70] while Pauline Periwinkle followed Heine in calling Shakespeare 'the Emperor of Literature'.[71]

The paradoxical oscillation between democratic and hierarchical imagery in the American Shakespeare tercentenary celebrations is symptomatic of the ways in which their producers attempted to negotiate a version of 'Englishness' acceptable to the US in the early twentieth century. These negotiations were not entirely successful, since some aspects of the English political system that should be anathema to American republicanism persistently crept in to 'taint' the desirable Anglo-Saxon cultural heritage. The situation was complicated even further by the fact that the American Shakespeare tercentenary

---

66 Sturgess, *Shakespeare and the American Nation*, p. 108.
67 See Cartelli, *Repositioning Shakespeare*, p. 75.
68 Koch, 'Shakespeare, the Playmaker', p. 9.
69 R.L. Batts, 'Shakespeare, Purveyor to the Public', in *A Memorial Volume to Shakespeare and Harvey*, ed. by A.C. Judson, J.T. Patterson and J.F. Royster, *University of Texas Bulletin*, 1701 (1 January 1917) (Austin, TX: University of Texas, 1917), pp. 47–67.
70 Albert Hatton Gilmer, *King Shakespeare: A Masque of Praise for the Shakespeare Tercentenary* (Boston, MA: Ginn and Co., 1916).
71 Pauline Periwinkle, 'Tercentenary of Death of Shakespeare in April', *Dallas Morning News*, 3 April 1916, p. 13.

celebrations were not a centrally coordinated, top-down affair, but arose from the grassroots interest of disparate groups and individuals. As a result, they acquired a strong local focus, and hence could not easily promote a single, fit-for-all version of national identity. What may have been appropriate to the metropolitan elites of New York City did not necessarily fit Atlanta's needs, or even those of some minority groups within New York itself.[72]

Consequently, the image of 'Englishness' constructed by the Shakespeare tercentenary was somewhat unstable and self-contradictory. Cecil Sharp, an English folklorist who contributed to the creation of the Elizabethan interlude in *Caliban by the Yellow Sands*, delightedly commented about the feeling produced by the multi-ethnic cast engaging in 'traditional English pastimes':

> It was like a puff of fresh country air laden with the smell of the hedgerows coming in the midst of artificial, exotic surroundings. [...] No country in the world can be gay in the simple, fresh way that England can – it is our contribution to civilization. I felt more proud of being an Englishman than I have ever felt before. And the spirit of the tunes and dances was such that all participants became infected by it and for the moment they became English, every Jew, German, French, Italian, Slav of them.[73]

Despite Sharp's optimistic image of a natural spread of 'simple' Englishness, the situation in the US in 1916 was anything but simple. It was not only the surroundings, but also the American concept of 'Englishness' that was artificial, imperfectly defined and fraught with ideological pitfalls and contradictions. This may be the result of 'Englishness' being transformed from a diasporic identity, defined primarily in relation to the mother country, to the foundation of a dominant cultural identity of the new host country, such as the US. In such circumstances, the historical realities of the original culture can clash with the needs of the emerging nation, leading to cultural negotiations marked by compromise and ambivalence.

---

72 See Smialkowska, 'A democratic art', and Monika Smialkowska, 'Shakespeare and "Native Americans": Forging Identities through the 1916 Shakespeare Tercentenary', *Critical Survey*, 22.2 (2010), pp. 76–90.

73 Quoted in Maud Karpeles, *Cecil Sharp: His Life and Work* (London: Routledge and Kegan Paul, 1967), p. 133.

Chapter 13

The Disappearance of the English: Why is there no 'English Diaspora'?

Robert J.C. Young

According to Eric Richards in his definitive book on British emigration, *Britannia's Children* (2004), between 1500 and 1900 some 20 million people emigrated from the British Isles, one of the largest diasporas ever known.[1] Though many of them were Irish, Welsh or Scots, it is reasonable to assume that a substantial proportion of them were English. Yet there is little sense today of an English Diaspora. Unlike the Irish or the Scots, or even other ethnicities such as African, Armenian, Chinese, Indian, Greek, Gypsy, Korean, Lebanese, Palestinian or Vietnamese, no one discusses the English Diaspora. All those millions of Englishmen and women who emigrated over the centuries seem to have disappeared off the face of the earth. Where did they get to? What has become of them? Why did they not hold on to their identity in the same way as other groups? Why did they not create their own diasporic identity? Why, compared to other diasporas, has the English Diaspora been so little studied? Does this tell us something about the historical processes of the English Diaspora, or the implicit priorities of the contemporary academic construction of history? How important were factors such as the British Empire itself, or the nineteenth-century construction of ideas of race and ethnic identity, in the disappearance of the English? How do we reconcile the tendency for the English to be lost to sight once they had emigrated with the extensive writings on Englishness developed during the Victorian period? How is it, in short, that the English Diaspora has disappeared?

---

1 Eric Richards, *Britannia's Children: Emigration from England, Scotland, Wales and Ireland since 1600* (London: Hambledon 2004).

If you ask people about the English Diaspora, initially they typically assume that you are talking about 'ex-pats', groups of whom remain alive and well all over the world, holed up in bars along Hollywood Road in Hong Kong, or on the Victoria and Alfred waterfront in Cape Town watching the cricket or the rugby sevens.[2] It seems that the English maintain their English identity only when they are temporarily exiled from the homeland. Once they actually emigrate, unlike the Irish and everyone else, they lose it. Why is this? One fundamental answer must relate to the concept and practice of Diaspora itself, which essentially refers to emigrants who maintain their identity as part of a distinct minority culture within the larger culture to which they have emigrated. This 'minority' culture must not be too large or too small. Too large and it becomes the majority. Too small and it becomes the individual who must, perforce, assimilate, unattached to any other group that maintains its identifiable characteristics of origin. What was particular about the English was that, almost without exception, when they emigrated in substantial numbers they moved to places where the English were in the majority or were in control as colonial rulers. Instead of being minoritarian, as is the norm for all those diasporic groups mentioned above, the English Diaspora was majoritarian. In that situation it was by definition impossible for them to define themselves against the different majority culture.

Where the English were not in the majority but were nevertheless identified with colonial power, for example in Kenya, this allowed them a distinct form of life sustained by the authority of colonial rule, but at the same time one that could not be distinguished, or separated, from colonial rule itself. After decolonization, it was typical for settlers in this situation to emigrate elsewhere (for example South Africa or Rhodesia). Where there had been a minority English Diaspora settler population, as in East Africa, the fact that the minority effectively held control of power made its situation very different from that of a typical diasporic population such as the Ukrainians in the USA. Negotiations for independence were typically fraught, given that the white minority feared a handover of power to the black majority. In Kenya, attempts by the New Kenya Party, led by Michael Blundell, to negotiate a multi-racial settlement were rejected by many white settlers who, for the most part, left at independence.[3] The history of Rhodesia does not need to be rehearsed here, but offers a good example of a common perception among diasporic settler populations, namely that the 'home' government has in some sense betrayed them, which then encourages different forms of identification (white Rhodesians typically moved to South Africa or Australia rather than 'back' to Britain). Arguably, the only country in the world where one could locate an identifiable 'English Diaspora' would be South Africa, where independence

2   See Robert Bickers (ed.), *Settlers and Expatriates* (Oxford: Oxford University Press, 2010).
3   Keith Kyle, *The Politics of the Independence of Kenya* (Basingstoke: Palgrave, 1999).

from colonial rule came with dominion status in 1910, but the presence of large numbers of other immigrants who had arrived over the centuries – Dutch (Afrikaans), Jews, Indians – as well as the majority black population meant that those of English origin remained relatively distinct, and, after 1948, not in power as a group. Up to the abolition of apartheid, arguably the English Diaspora did maintain something of a separate identity, often in the form of liberal opposition to the regime; since majority rule, most have been keen to incorporate themselves as part of the 'new South Africa'.

The British African colonies offer the few examples of British settler colonies where the British or English emigrants remained in the minority. If we think of the other main emigrant destinations (the USA, Canada, Australia, New Zealand) the situation is very different. With the exception of the USA, whether willingly or unwillingly (Australia, Canada), these colonies were given independence with dominion status. The American War of Independence and the rise of colonial nationalism at the end of the nineteenth century meant that, however much the English in England may have wished otherwise, those in the settler colonies sought to establish their own distinctive identities. The only exceptions to this rule are those smaller English colonies that have sought to define themselves against a larger English neighbour that has developed its own independent identity, as in the cases of Canada and New Zealand, where a certain Englishness, of which the marker is the use of the adjective 'Royal', continues to be emphasized even while a national multicultural identity is encouraged at the same time.

However different and independent they may have become, it remains the case that these countries embody the form of the English Diaspora. What is distinctive about the English Diaspora is that its modality has taken the form of independent sovereign states, ones that include the minoritarian Diaspora of other peoples (e.g. Canada, USA). Despite their independence, these sovereign states maintain a certain form of profound relationality to England and the British Isles, not least in their language, together with their economic, political and legal systems. While fundamentally allied in political terms (aside from independence movements, and the British–American war of 1812–14, they have always fought wars on the same side), the diasporic 'English' around the world, embedded in sovereign states, in typical English fashion are more concerned to reflect upon their minor differences than to acknowledge commonality. The focus of attention, strongly encouraged by the national government, usually falls on the development of a distinctive national identity rather than on the lingering poetics of relations to England or Englishness.

The demands of nationalist history have meant that these processes of transformation, and the establishment of new identities, have received the lion's share of attention. Yet, as Leonard Tennenhouse has shown so effectively with respect to the American colonists, the framework of Diaspora in many ways offers a more appropriate way of conceptualizing how the early

American colonists thought of themselves, even after independence.[4] In the case of a sovereign state diaspora, as a nationalist consciousness developed (and was then enforced, retrospectively, with earlier history and cultural production reinterpreted) over an extended historical period, English identity was subjected to particular, local transformations rather than held on to through forms of fossilized cultural memory as a way of maintaining identity. How this process operates can be illustrated in terms of what happens to the English language: while on the one hand some expressions or words remain that fall out of use in Britain itself (for example, the American term 'yard' for garden, which is Chaucerian English), on the other hand new words and expressions are introduced that make the language locally distinctive. Accents are preserved and developed in the same way. With diasporic minorities, where numbers are smaller and the language is typically used more privately, languages tend to preserve older forms but not develop new ones. Analysis of the English Diaspora therefore has to take a different form from investigation of other diasporas, one that would have most in common with that for two other European colonial powers, the Spanish and the Portuguese.

This model of 'sovereign state Diaspora' comes closer to a version of colonial history than to the contemporary mode of Diaspora studies. Its characteristic mode is that of a dialectical tension between the view from the metropolitan centre, which sees the colonies as essentially dependent peripheries, and that from the colonies themselves where an independent form of living and set of national values are increasingly asserted. While the local population initially typically see themselves as essentially English and maintain English values, especially in their educational systems, over the centuries a counter-impulse develops to claim distinctive identities. The degree to which even that distinctive identity remains locked in a dialectic with the 'mother country' is aptly illustrated by an early volume arguing for the validity of Australian and other non-British literatures in English: *The Empire Writes Back* (1989).[5] Here, paradoxically, the very mode of the assertion of an independent 'postcolonial' literature from outside Britain acknowledges its continuing dependency on a mentality that maintains a colonial relationality: it declares its autonomy by 'writing back' to the former imperial centre. Despite the assertion of independence, the implicit audience remains the British reader – ironically assuming a certain kind of reader with an imperial consciousness who no longer exists.

---

4   Leonard Tennenhouse, *The Importance of Feeling English: American Literature and the British Diaspora, 1750–1850* (Princeton, NJ: Princeton University Press, 2007).

5   Bill Ashcroft, Gareth Griffiths and Helen Tiffin, *The Empire Writes Back: Theory and Practice in Post-Colonial Literatures* (London: Routledge, 1989).

The Englishman Abroad

This complex push-and-pull relation between Britain and its sovereign diasporas requires much more investigation within the context of Diaspora studies. At the same time, it has to be acknowledged that there is something curiously evanescent and spectral about English identity that also contributes to its invisibility. Many distinctive features of Englishness are internal rather than external. Let's take as an example the most famous alumnus of Northumbria University, in one of its earlier incarnations as Northern Counties College of Education, Gordon Sumner, otherwise known as Sting. Sting's famous song about an English Diaspora, 'An Englishman in New York', was originally written in 1987 about Quentin Crisp, the extraordinarily eccentric Englishman who had moved to New York six years earlier. In the video version, easily available on YouTube, the Englishman is doubled and generalized to include Sting himself as well as Crisp. Sting's long hair and Crisp's camp, hyper-effeminate sexuality invite us to recall the common perception on the part of macho foreigners that all Englishmen are gay, while countering it with the argument that it is in fact much more manly to suffer the ignorance of others in order to 'be yourself'. The Englishman is defined by being courageous enough to be himself.

What else does this contemporary video tell us about the English Diaspora? If we consider the lyrics, it is noticeable that it either does not take much to define an Englishman, or else that there's not much that defines him – just two things in fact. One is that the Englishman prefers tea to coffee, today perhaps a less fundamental marker between the English and the Americans than it used to be; this is followed by the approving invocation of the phrase 'Manners maketh man', as 'someone said'. That someone was William of Wykeham in the fourteenth century, and the expression has ever since been the motto of Winchester College and New College, Oxford. It is interesting that Sting blends his observations about the unorthodox Quentin Crisp with these very traditional typologies of Englishness – tea and a gentlemanly gentleness of manner, entities that, as he points out, are indeed alien in the United States. Nonetheless, gentlemanliness and tea-drinking are hardly enough to form the basis of a collective English ethnic identity, even setting aside the gender exclusion involved.

The Englishman being manly enough to dare to be himself rather than conform to the uniform demands of a collective identity (which asserts another traditional characteristic of Englishness, individualism and the toler-ance of eccentricity) is linked in the song to the repeated line about Green Card holders in the US, who are given the charming status of 'legal aliens' as opposed to the illegal aliens or 'illegals'. It is noticeable that the video shows the two men as not only individual but solitary, their separate walks down Fifth Avenue in the snow contrasting with the socialized warmth of the African-American band who are playing the music inside together. The modesty of being yourself, no matter what they say, even though it may leave you alienated from others gives us one clue to the question of English invisibility, namely the emphasis on individualism rather than collectivity. For a long time the English have prided themselves on their eccentric individuality and tolerance of the eccentric individuality of others, and this principle remains the basis of the political theory of the state that dates back to Hobbes, as well as the powerful ideology of economic liberalism derived from Adam Smith that has dominated English political life for centuries. As Samuel Smiles put it in what is perhaps the definitive nineteenth-century account of the English national character as individual diligence, his hugely popular *Self-Help* of 1859 (readers of that most English of writers, V.S. Naipaul, will recall that Samuel Smiles was ironically Mr Biswas's favourite reading) – 'Government [is] a reflex of the individualism of a nation.'[6] The English may see themselves as English but their individualism means that they do not easily then form collectivities, since by definition that would deny their Englishness.

The most graphic example of this remains the illustration in the work of the (himself eccentric) Scottish racial theorist Robert Knox in the 1850s. In his book *The Races of Men*, he defined the difference between the English (or Saxons in his case, since he wanted to include lowland Scots in the English) and the Celts in terms of a tendency to individuality versus collectivity, and illustrated the typical Saxon individual not by an image of a certain physical type of human being but by a large detached house 'standing always apart, if possible, from all others'.[7] The invisibility of the Saxon male is made more interesting by the presence in the illustration of two tiny figures to the right: close examination reveals them to be two ladies sitting talking to each other on a garden seat. This unexpected sociability is thus ascribed to women, just as it is to the 'feminine' Celtic race in general, while the male remains solitary and visible only via his property. As is also the case in the English legal system, it is, in some sense, property itself through which the Englishman has traditionally represented himself – whether it be house or empire.

Race

Knox's book suggests another answer to the question of why it is so difficult to find or define the English Diaspora, which is that historically it has always proven hard for racial theorists to define the English as a race, just as it is now counter-intuitive to define Englishness as an ethnicity. As I argued in my book, *The Idea of English Ethnicity* (2008), attempts to define the English in the terms of racial theory have always been stymied by the degree to which the

---

6   Samuel Smiles, *Self-Help: With Illustrations of Character and Conduct* (London: John Murray, 1859), p. vii.

7   Robert Knox, *The Races of Men: A Fragment* (London: Renshaw, 1850), p. 40.

historical record makes it very clear that the English are mixed, the product of successive invasions from all over Europe.[8] As Daniel Defoe put it in the Preface to his famous satire of 1701, 'The True-Born Englishman', 'speaking of *Englishmen ab Origine*, we are really all Foreigners our selves'.[9] While certain nineteenth-century historians and early 'Saxonist' racial theorists represented themselves, their culture and the English more generally as Saxon or Teuton – Samuel Smiles was still talking about the 'energy characteristic of the Teutonic race' in *Self-Help* in 1859[10] – when the new 'science' of racial theory actually analysed the population they pronounced them irrefutably mixed. Racial theory, unexpectedly, was in this case progressive, for it actually destroyed the argument that the English were a single homogeneous race. By the same token, the argument that they were ethnically heterogeneous made it harder to produce a single identity for them. I have argued that the fundamentally incorporative definition of Englishness offered by Matthew Arnold and others that developed from that time onwards has allowed the gradual, though certainly still conflictual, incorporation of others within a fundamentally multicultural framework within England. Since Arnold, being English has generally been defined according to an inclusive model rather than an exclusionary one. Openness to otherness and the ability to change while incorporating it involves the exact opposite of what is required to maintain any distinctive identity; it is precisely these qualities that mean that, in a diasporic situation, when faced with a different ethnic and cultural environment, the English will not live on as a group by means of a fixed identity that looks back to their past point of origin.

Ethnicity

Just as the English have never been defined as a race, neither have they, following the invention of the concept after the Second World War, been defined as an ethnicity. The English, of course, generally do not see themselves in those terms – a point of view emphatically affirmed in 1948 by that most 'English' of Englishmen, the American T.S. Eliot.[11] But nor do others – for example, in *Ethnicity, Inc.* (2008) John and Jean Comaroff comment that, in the United Kingdom,

> the sale of English and Celtic heritage are expanding apace [...] Inside its own borders, England, known historically for its indifference to difference – although it now seems simultaneously more *and* less tolerant – is also witnessing

---

8   Robert J.C. Young, *The Idea of English Ethnicity* (Oxford: Blackwell, 2008).
9   Daniel Defoe, 'Preface' to 'The True-Born Englishman', in J.T. Boulton (ed.), *Daniel Defoe* (London: Batsford, 1965 [1701]), p. 52.
10 Smiles, *Self-Help*, p. ix.
11 T.S. Eliot, *Notes Towards a Definition of Culture* (London: Faber and Faber, 1948), p. 53.

a rapid growth in the ethnic industry. Here too, ethno-marketing is imploding [*sic*]. Firms are popping up with names like Namaste-UK Ltd... Punjab Kitchen Ltd... Ethnic Interiors Ltd...[12]

Here the Comaroffs move from English and Celtic heritage to 'ethnic' industries that seem entirely devoted to British Asian goods without pausing to comment on the differences, namely that their 'English' version of Ethnicity Inc. is Asian. Ethnic England, for the Comaroffs as for others, means 'ethnic minority' England. As so often, 'English' means simply white, the absence of ethnicity. Ethnic identity, like diaspora identity, emerges most strongly when the term or the concept of minority can be attached to it. In the US, 'ethnic' has exactly the same marker, that is, non-white and usually non-English-speaking. The Comaroffs' casual claim that the English have historically been indifferent to difference is interesting. It is not clear whether the English are being criticized for being intolerant or for simply not noticing difference enough – though the idea that they have not noticed difference is hardly sustainable when one thinks of historical attitudes to the Irish, Jews or Catholics. But if not indifferent to difference, then they have perhaps been indifferent to their own sameness, given that, as I have suggested, they have always defined their own sameness as difference (individualism).

How do you construct a collectivity that is based on singularity and a principle of difference? This is a problem that philosophers such as Jean-Luc Nancy and Georgio Agamben have wrestled with, without choosing to examine the English example.[13] The English themselves are invisible, unmarked as an ethnicity where they are a majority, indifferent to difference, especially their own. One reason, it could be said, why the English Diaspora has disappeared is because they have always been indifferent to their own difference, always reluctant to characterize it as sameness, to corporatize their difference into an ethnic or even national brand. It is this indifference to their own difference and, especially, the fact that their own difference has become indifferent, a difference that is not a marker of difference to themselves or to anyone else, that constitutes a major reason for the invisibility of the English Diaspora. If we think of the way in which diasporas are defined or define themselves – primarily through ethnicity or national identities – we can see why the English are in trouble. Not only do they have no defined ethnicity, but when we look at the component parts of how transnational ethnicities themselves are constituted – through food, religion, language, nationalism – we can see that the English have no typical relation to any of these. None of them allows the English to claim their identity as difference.

---

12   John L. and Jean Comaroff, *Ethnicity, Inc.* (Chicago: Chicago University Press, 2009), p. 17.
13   Jean-Luc Nancy, *The Inoperative Community*, trans. Peter Connor et al. (Minneapolis, MN: University of Minnesota Press, 1991); Giorgio Agamben, *The Coming Community*, trans. Michael Hardt (Minneapolis, MN: Minnesota University Press, 1993).

Food

We encounter the same feature of invisibility with English food. No country is more famous for not having a specific cuisine, apart from meat eaten with lots of starch – potatoes, chips, pastry, pies. For other ethnicities, food is often identified with home. In the nineteenth century the English made great efforts to supply indentured labourers who had been sent from India to Trinidad, Mauritius or Fiji with their own food so that they would not become homesick. But in all the travel accounts of Englishmen or women wandering the globe, or settling in far-off parts, how often do we read of them being homesick for English food? Wherever they went, the food was better – and we can get a sense of this in Kipling's *Kim* where Kim recoils in horror when he is served English food, while frequently affirming by contrast a relish for Indian food – a relish that in the past fifty years has been adopted by the entire population of Britain. In fact this was entirely predictable. The very blandness of English food meant that the highest compliment that you could offer a dish was that it was 'tasty' – that is, that it actually had a taste. Hence the preference for conveniently portable sauces that added a strong taste: Bisto, Bovril, Branston Pickle, Daddies Sauce, English mustard, HP Sauce, Marmite, Oxo…

Religion

All over the world food has been a way of keeping ethnic identity and identification alive, and so too has religion – most notably in the Jewish Diaspora. For the English, there is a problem here too. Actually there are two interrelated problems. The English state, and to that extent English national identity, is bound to the Church of England, of which the monarch is the 'supreme governor'. The Church of England was extended around the world hand in hand with empire, so that, as John Wolffe remarks in *God and Greater Britain*, the two became altogether identified.[14] Today, however, the globalized Church of England has had to refashion itself in the post-imperial era, renaming itself as the Anglican Church, which is organized as thirty-nine independent provinces around the world (the Queen is only supreme governor of the Church of England), with the Archbishop of Canterbury not its head, but rather *primus inter pares* (first among equals). The historical globalization of the Church of England, and the subsequent independence of the globalized parts of the Anglican Church today, means that it is hard for the English to define themselves through it. This institutional fluidity, where identifiable English institutions have become so internationalized or globalized that they no longer seem specifically English, is at the heart of the problem with respect

---

14   John Wolffe, *God and Greater Britain: Religion and National Life in Britain and Ireland 1843–1945* (London: Routledge, 1994).

to many potential English ethnic identifications – in different ways much the same is true for other institutions such as cricket and football, English law, the English language or even Shakespeare.

In the case of religion, there is a further wrinkle which is that, since the eighteenth century at least, the Church of England has always been the church of the middle and upper classes, while the working classes tended to be what used to be referred to, somewhat contemptuously, as 'chapel people' – Methodists, Covenanters, Baptists, Quakers, Evangelicals etc.[15] While the Church of England was easily identified with the elite authority of imperial rule, the vast majority of English settlers came, of course, from the working classes – they were economic migrants for the most part looking for a better life than their impoverished existence in England. So the settlers and their descendants, starting with the Pilgrim Fathers, would be more likely than not *not* to identify with the official religion of their homeland. How different from the situation of the Catholic Irish who defined themselves, and were themselves defined, by their relation to the Catholic Church as opposed to the official established Anglican Church of Ireland.

Religion thus raises another fundamental issue, that of class. While it was the working classes who were forced by circumstance to emigrate, Englishness tends to be identified through the characteristics of the upper class, the class that governed the empire. The split between the cultural identities of the governing and emigrating classes has contributed profoundly to the disappearance of the English. Englishness is typically identified with upper-class rituals or institutions – cricket, Wimbledon, Ascot, traditional tailored men's clothes, going 'up' to Oxbridge, in a word, the life of the gentleman – rather than with the working class or those who the English in England in Jean Rhys's novels refer to as 'horrid colonials'. Being colonial English was itself a kind of lower-class marker, something to be sniffed at or mocked, as in Noel Coward's song on the British Raj, 'I wonder what happened to him'. Apart from Sting's cup of tea, English working-class culture, by contrast, is identified with football, beer, fish and chips, and other more international pleasures. Working-class people do not actually identify with much that is seen by foreigners to be quintessentially English, since it is often in practice defined against them as a class marker, which means that they are more likely to identify with other English cultures that have developed along more democratic working-class lines – such as American or Australian. This is the reason why the English have always found it easy to assimilate to the US, historically the destination of the majority of English emigrants, and then to vanish entirely into the individualist mentality of the popular culture of the former colony. Similarly, despite the changes since 1972 when white-only immigration was ended, Australian culture remains in many ways an English

---

15 A single literary example would be the character of Joseph in Emily Bronte's *Wuthering Heights* (1847).

working-class culture. It could be argued that diasporic English still identify with English working-class culture, except that today for historical reasons, being examples of sovereign diasporas, that culture is called American or Australian. This also helps to explain why the English middle and upper classes remain dismissive of American and Australian 'vulgarity' as they characterize it, which (since vulgar means the crowd, i.e. the masses, i.e. the working class) hits the spot exactly. The English Diaspora, you might say, was the wrong class for it ever to be able to be fully 'English'.

Language

After religion, a major factor binding ethnic communities together is their language. Speaking a non-mainstream language from a distant part of the globe, for example Gujarati in Queen's, New York, is the golden key through which you are immediately recognized as a *bona fide* part of the Diaspora. For this reason, today second- or third-generation immigrants to the US or Britain often seek to learn their parents' or grandparents' language, which they have 'lost'. This is also problematic for the English. In the nineteenth century attempts were made to found a core of Englishness on the English language, as an alternative to race. In an era when the international language was French and English was less ubiquitous, this seemed more possible, though it had to encounter one problem which was insoluble, namely that the people of what was by then already the largest country of English-speaking people, the United States, would never want to define themselves as English (indeed this was the very period when their language was being redefined as 'American'). Nevertheless, politico-linguistic institutions such as the English-Speaking Union were founded in this era to heal the rift between the two countries divided by a common language, as Bernard Shaw famously put it. One of the last examples of this impulse came from Winston Churchill who, as part of his invention of the so-called special relationship between Britain and the United States, wrote a four-volume *History of the English-Speaking Peoples*.[16] This particular configuration was made relatively meaningless as a result of the globalization of English after the Second World War through American economic, military and technological power. You can hardly look for the English Diaspora abroad by congregating with those who speak English.

---

16   Winston S. Churchill, *History of the English-Speaking Peoples*, 4 vols (London: Cassell, 1951–56).

Nationalism

England is perhaps unique, certainly among European countries, in that it never developed a serious nationalist movement; or perhaps, rather, in that what nationalism it developed – in the early modern period, often evoked by the Victorians as the Elizabethan 'Merrie England' – preceded the development of nationalism as a form of political identity and state organization. By the time nationalism in its modern form was maturing at the end of the eighteenth into the early nineteenth century, the England at the heart of the British Empire saw it as a potential political threat – either from their rivals in Europe, or as a potential discourse of liberation from empire, as in the Americas, north and south. For many years in the nineteenth century, it was often cited as a matter of pride that the English had not succumbed to the nationalism of the French or the Germans. The Englishman, *The Times* argued in 1852, was a 'born cosmopolite', free of the 'follies of nationality'.[17] The English saw themselves at the head of a larger empire, and that empire was always heterogeneous. Nationalism was dangerous because it was generally anti-imperial. At the centre of a heterogeneous empire, England was always on the back foot with respect to nationalism and could not encourage its own.

So despite the attempt by some to augment English nationalism by appropriating English folk culture at the end of the nineteenth century – Morris dancing, pageants and the like – the English never really went through the regular formations of nationalism or therefore produced its normative identifications.[18] It was much more typical for emigrants to identify themselves regionally – particularly those from Yorkshire, Lancashire or Cornwall – than nationally. Beyond the regions, England of course was also at the centre of a more local multinational empire, Britain or the United Kingdom. Nationalism in its nineteenth-century form in Ireland, Scotland and Wales certainly developed and largely dates from this period, for the most part in antithesis to England. In order to sustain the Union, the English establishment defined itself precisely by not being anchored to the individual nation of England, once again indifferent to its own difference. Symptomatic of this was the indifference to what the English were called, and here we come to the perennial English/British chestnut. The country of the English is called, variously, Great Britain or the United Kingdom, though people, especially abroad, still often, perhaps predominantly, refer to it as 'England'. Given current nationalist sensitivities, together with anti-racist sensitivities in which English means white, we are all now urged to describe ourselves as British (originally a term used for those from the empire rather than from England), even though Scots can still call themselves Scots, Welsh Welsh etc. Small wonder there is no

---

17 Cited in Young, *The Idea of English Ethnicity*, p. 233.
18 Krishan Kumar, *The Making of English National Identity* (Cambridge: Cambridge University Press, 2003).

English Diaspora when even the English in England are no longer allowed to call themselves English!

There is, however, a further problem with the use of the term English, which also relates to the invisibility of the English Diaspora. This is that the English Diaspora is not seen as a diaspora because diasporas are largely, though not exclusively, thought of as essentially forced, whereas the British Empire was constructed by force in the other direction. A diaspora that was the product of the power of the nation of the diaspora is not the way that we generally conceive of diasporas today, even though this would also be true of some other diasporas such as the original Greek Diaspora around the western and eastern Mediterranean. Of course, the majority of English emigrants were forced in a different way, economically or otherwise. While the English working class were dispersed or dispersed themselves around the world in search of a life free from hunger, in the second half of the nineteenth century ideologists of the British Empire attempted to appropriate Englishness as a way of holding the empire together by cultural rather than political affiliations. Charles Dilke, J.A. Froude and J.R. Seeley all conceptualized the empire as a set of 'other Englands'. The imperialists globalized Englishness, which meant that it became less and less attached to anything that could be located as specific to England itself. As I argued in my book on English ethnicity,

> the concept of Englishness in the nineteenth century was not so much developed as a self-definition of the English themselves, as a way of characterizing the essence of their national identity – after all, being English already, they hardly needed it. It was rather elaborated as a variety of what Benedict Anderson has called 'long-distance nationalism', though of a distinct kind.[19]

Rather than being the creation of the far-off diasporic community, as Anderson describes, Englishness was created *for* the Diaspora – an 'ethnic' identity designed for those who were precisely not English, but rather of English descent – the peoples of the English Diaspora moving around the world: Americans, Canadians, Australians, New Zealanders, South Africans. 'To us', Seeley wrote, 'England will be wherever English people are found.'[20] Englishness was constructed as a translatable identity that could be adopted or appropriated anywhere by anyone who cultivated the right language, looks and culture. It then offered a common identification with a homeland that had often never been seen. Englishness paradoxically became most itself when it was far off. As Kipling put it with characteristic succinctness – 'What do they know of England who only England know?'[21]

---

19 Young, *The Idea of English Ethnicity*, p. 1; Benedict Anderson, *The Spectre of Comparisons: Nationalism, Southeast Asia, and the World* (London: Verso, 1998).

20 John R. Seeley, *The Expansion of England: Two Courses of Lectures* (London: Macmillan, 1897), p. 141.

21 Rudyard Kipling, 'The English Flag', in *Rudyard Kipling's Verse. Definitive Edition* (London: Hodder and Stoughton, 1949), p. 221.

Although it is questionable to what extent the English around the world were persuaded by this imperial ideology of Englishness – its appeal was largely limited to those who aspired to upper-class status – we can see some literary examples of those who were seduced by its ideology in those far-off pilgrims who came to identify with it, from Henry James to T.S. Eliot, from Nirad Chaudhuri to V.S. Naipaul. The problem, however, was that once that imperial identity began to wane, Englishness itself was left as a relic identified with the old imperial ways, indifferent to difference in the modern sense when it should have been alert to it and all the identities of difference that have since emerged. All those English around the world celebrated by Dilke et al. no longer wanted to identify with the imperial centre, if they had ever wanted to in the first place. We could say that since 1776, with the dismantling of empire and the rise of independent states, the English Diaspora gradually disappeared and became invisible: at once a history of the establishment of separate sovereignties and of a shedding of origins, of disconnection rather than continuing transnational identification. While the informal alliance of 'le monde anglo-saxon' continues to operate at a fundamental level, the descendants of the English among its empowered populations do not sustain themselves in any typical diasporic formation.

Index

Printed and bound by CPI Group (UK) Ltd, Croydon, CR0 4YY

09/06/2025

14685950-0002